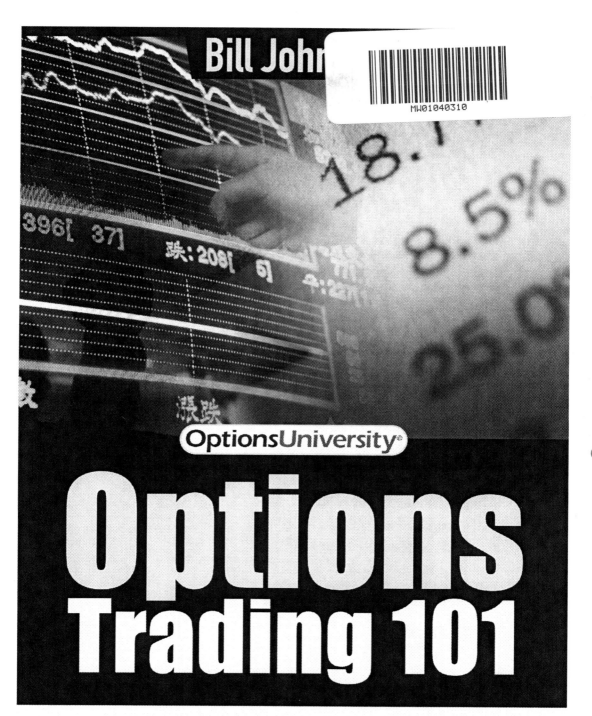

Bill John

OptionsUniversity®

Options
Trading 101

From Theory to Application

New York

Options Trading 101
From Theory to Application

by Bill Johnson
© 2007 Bill Johnson. All rights reserved.

ISBN   978-1-60037-237-7   (Paperback)
ISBN   978-1-60037-249-0   (Hardcover)

Published by:

MORGAN · JAMES
THE ENTREPRENEURIAL PUBLISHER ™
www.morganjamespublishing.com

Morgan James Publishing, LLC

1225 Franklin Ave. Ste 325

Garden City, NY 11530-1693

Toll Free 800-485-4943

www.MorganJamesPublishing.com

 Habitat
for Humanity®
Peninsula
Building Partner

Interior Design by:
Bonnie Bushman
bbushman@bresnan.net

Table of Contents

Table of Contents

Table of Contents

Table of Contents

Introduction

Chances are that you're reading this book because you're brand new to options. You've heard about them but can't really explain what they are to someone else. You'd like to start trading them but have lots of questions and nobody seems to have the answers you're looking for. This book is for you!

At Options University, we believe there is only one way to teach; you must start by learning the most fundamental concepts. While it is possible to provide a quick overview and send you on your way with a false sense of confidence we know that it will only be detrimental in the long run. This is the "ready, fire, aim" approach that often used by most books and instructors. Instead, we make sure you truly understand the essence of an option and what makes it different from stock. Once we cover these core competencies, we then introduce to some basic strategies that you'll be able to use immediately. But don't underestimate these strategies just because they're labeled as basic. On the contrary, it is the basic strategies that often pack the most punch and are most widely used – even by professional traders. Advanced strategies, even though they appear far more complex, are just moderate extensions of the basics. If you understand the concepts presented in this book, you will make a smooth transition into advanced strategies if you choose to continue further with options trading. Most importantly, you will have enough knowledge to confidently use the most powerful trading tool ever to hit the financial markets.

Before we get started, let's clear up the one unfair misconception that you have probably heard: Avoid options because they are too risky.

As you will find out, options were created to *manage* the risks and rewards of stock investing, which is certainly a good feature. However, if you talk to investors or traders about options you will find there are a myriad of opinions. To some investors, the word "options" suggests feelings of risk, gambling, speculation, and reckless investing. To others, options mean hedging your bet, insurance, and good money management. How can the same asset cause two opposing views? The reason is that both can be correct. *It depends on how you're using the options*. Credit cards are a good analogy. One person can use them to spend excessively and end up in bankruptcy while another uses them to pay for an emergency car repair after being stranded on a deserted road. Are credit cards good or bad? Just as with options, the answer depends on how they are used and managed. Be wary of people who tell you to not waste your time with options because they are too risky because we can show you strategies that completely *eliminate* risk. What's important is that you are able to separate which feature of an option is a benefit *for you* and which is a risk *for you*. A risk to someone else may be a benefit for you and the options market will let you earn money for assuming that risk.

After reading this book, you will know which strategies are right for you and which are too risky. It all depends on your goals and risk tolerances. We want to show you how options can be used to enhance and strengthen your current investment style.

Those who choose to not learn about options may be overlooking the most important and powerful investment tool available. It is our experience that the people most skeptical of options are the ones who often see the most benefits. We believe, by the end of this book, you will find at least one new strategy that appeals to you and that means you're a little bit better than you are at this point. And that's good investors eventually become great – by continually getting a little bit better. At least take the time to understand options; you can always decide to not use them. But our guess is that this book will only open the doors to a new and exciting investment world you never thought possible. So let's begin our journey and answer a frequently asked question; that is, why is there an options market?

Why is there an Options Market?

New traders and investors are often overwhelmed by the different financial products available. They are kept busy enough trying to understand and choose between stocks, preferred shares, bonds, mutual funds, closed-end funds, ETFs (Exchange Traded Funds), UITs (Unit Investment Trusts), REITs (Real Estate Investment Trusts), and CMOs (Collateralized Mortgage Obligations).

And now you want to add options?

You must understand that whenever a new product is created, there are always new variations designed to fill slightly different needs. For example, when the Model T was first invented, it solved the broad problem of transportation. People didn't really care what it looked like. In fact, it is rumored that Henry Ford once quipped, "Customers can have any color they want as long as it's black." The Model T was only meant to solve the broader issues of transportation. Namely, getting from Point A to Point B.

But once the Model T appeared, others soon came to market with modifications to solve different problems. Today we have many variations such as SUVs, vans, four-wheel drive trucks, extended cabs, crew cabs, compacts, hybrids, and convertibles. While they are all forms of transportation, they fill different needs.

The financial markets are no different from any other product. As problems arise, new financial products are developed to handle them. The stock market was created as a way for publicly traded companies to raise cash. For example, In March 1986, Microsoft had its IPO (Initial Public Offering) and sold 2.8 million shares for $21 per share. That amounted to an instant check for $58,800,000 for Microsoft. In a relatively short time and very efficiently, Microsoft created nearly 59 million dollars for them to grow.

The creation of the stock market solved a very important problem of raising capital but it also introduced a new problem. That problem is risk. If you buy shares of stock, you are buying a piece of the company and that purchase creates the potential for high rewards. Many investors who bought shares of Microsoft in 1986 are millionaires many times over today. But that potential for high reward comes with the potential for high loss. In early 2001, Enron was regarded as a market leader in the energy trading business and one of the largest corporations in the world. Later that year, it filed for what was to become the largest bankruptcy in United States history. Many investors lost their life savings by investing in Enron. So are stocks good or bad? Obviously, it depends on what happens to the stock's price – and that is something we cannot know beforehand. In other words, there is risk associated with stock investing. In order to make the financial markets run smoother, it would be nice to invent ways to *manage the risk* involved with stock investing. And that's exactly the problem that options solved.

Risk for Sale

 Believe it or not, the options market was designed to allow investors to either accept or transfer risk. The options market is technically a market for dealing in risk. You're probably wondering who would ever want to willingly accept risk. Odd as that may sound, we do it all the time. When you buy an auto insurance policy, you are paying a fee to the insurance company. In exchange for that fee, they are accepting the risks associated with you having an accident. The insurance company is *accepting* risk in exchange for cash. You are paying cash in exchange for *transferring* the unwanted risk. The agreement between you and the insurance company created an intangible market – the market for risk. So to answer the question of who would ever willingly accept risk, you must remember that someone is getting paid to accept that risk. If the fee is high enough, you can be sure that someone will step in and accept the risk.

This highlights why the options market is perceived to be so risky. After all, it is a market whose only product for sale is risk. As stated before, the riskiness of options depends on how you're using them but now we can state it a little more clearly: It depends on whether you are transferring or accepting risk. None of us would consider the car insurance market to be risky since we use it to transfer risk away from us. However, the insurance companies see it quite differently. It depends on which side of the agreement you're on.

The options market works on a simple principle in that, while many investors wish to reduce risk, there are some people who actively look for risk. These people are called *speculators*. Speculators are willing to gamble for big profits; they aren't afraid to take a long shot if there is potential for big money. People who patronize casinos and play state lotteries are acting as speculators. If there are speculators out there who are willing to accept risk in the stock market, wouldn't it make sense to be able to transfer it to them? Of course, in order to make it worth their while, we will have to pay them some money to accept that risk. So if there is a risk you wish to avoid, you can do so by purchasing an option. Conversely, if there is a risk you're willing to assume, you can get paid through the options market to accept the risk for someone else. So while one investor may be using options to avoid risk, it is possible that the person on the other side of the trade is a speculator willing to accept that risk. Investors who do not understand this interplay between investors and speculators hear both sides of the story and that's where the confusion comes in.

Unfortunately, this confusion often makes many investors avoid options altogether. This is a big mistake in today's marketplace. As our economies expand, our financial needs increase and that's why you see so many new financial products coming to market. Each product is different – sometimes only in small ways – but each provides the solution to a specific problem. Options allow you to selectively pick and choose the risks you want to take or avoid. *And that is something that cannot be done with any other financial asset.* Because you can select the individual risks to take, options can be used in very conservative as well as very speculative ways. It's all up to you. If you'd like to make the stock market a less risky place, options are your answer. If you'd like to increase the risk and speculate more efficiently for bigger profits, options are your answer too.

Let's get started and find out how you can improve your investments from this mysterious market.

Chapter One

Introduction to Options

What is an Option?

Options are simply legally binding agreements – contracts – between two people to buy and sell stock at a fixed price over a given time period.

There are two types of options: **calls** and **puts**. A call option gives the owner the right, not the obligation, to *buy* stock at a specific price over a given period of time. In other words, it gives you the right to "call" the stock away from another person. A put option, on the other hand, gives the owner the right, not the obligation, to *sell* stock at a specific price through an expiration date. It gives you the right to "put" the stock back to the owner. Option buyers have rights to either buy stock (with a call) or sell stock (with a put). That means it is the owner's choice, or *option*, to do so and that's where these assets get their name.

Now you're probably thinking that this is sounding complicated already. But options are used under different names everyday by different industries. For instance, we are willing to bet that you've used something very similar to a call option before. Take a look at the following coupon:

Pizza coupons and call options have a lot in common in the way they work. This pizza coupon gives the holder the *right* to buy one pizza. It is not an obligation.

If you are in possession of this coupon, you are not required to use it. It only represents a right to buy. There is also a *fixed price* of $10.00. No matter how high the price of pizzas may rise, your purchase price is locked at $10.00 if you should decide to use it. Last, there is a fixed time period, or *expiration date*, for which the coupon is good.

Now let's go back to our definition of a call option and recall that it represents:

1) **Right to <u>buy</u> stock**

2) **At a fixed price**

3) **Over a given time period**

You can see the similarities between a call option and pizza coupon. If you understand how a simple pizza coupon works, you can understand how call options work.

Now let's take a look at a put option from a different perspective. Put options can be thought of as an insurance policy. Think about your car insurance, for example. When you buy an auto insurance policy, you really hope that you will not wreck your car and that the policy will "expire worthless." However, if you should total your car, you can always "put" it back to the insurance company in exchange for cash. Put options allow the holder to "put" stock back (sell it) to someone else in exchange for cash. Remember, if you buy a put option, you have the:

1) **Right to <u>sell</u> stock**

2) **At a fixed price**

3) **Over a given time period**

As you will find out, the mechanics of calls and puts are exactly the same – just in the opposite direction. If you buy a call, you have the right to buy stock. If you buy a put, you have the right to sell stock.

Option Sellers

We know that buyers of options have rights to either buy or sell. What about sellers? *Option sellers have obligations.* If you sell an option, it is also called "writing" the option, which is much like insurance companies "write" policies.

Buyers have rights, sellers have obligations. Sellers have an obligation to fulfill the contract if the buyer decides to use their option. It may sound like option buyers get the better end of the deal since they are the ones who decide whether or not to use the contract. It's true that option buyers have a valuable right to choose whether to buy or sell – but they must pay for that right. So while sellers incur obligations, they do get paid for their responsibility since nobody will accept an obligation for nothing.

There are some traders who will tell you to always be the buyer of options while others will tell you that you're better off being the seller. Hopefully, you already see that neither statement can always be true because there are pros and cons to either side. Buyers get the benefit of "calling the shots" but the drawback is that they must pay for that benefit. Sellers get the benefit of collecting cash but they have a drawback in that there are potential obligations to meet. What are the sellers' obligations? That's easy to figure out once you understand the rights of the buyers. The seller's obligation is exactly the opposite of the buyer's rights. For example, if a call buyer has the *right to buy* stock, the call seller must have the *obligation to sell* stock. If a put buyer has the *right to sell* stock, the put seller has the *obligation to buy* stock.

These obligations are really *potential* obligations since the seller does not know whether or not the buyer will use their option. For example, if you sell a call option you *may* have to sell shares of stock, which is different from saying that you will definitely sell shares of stock. For call sellers, you will definitely have to sell shares of stock *if* the call buyer decides to use their call option and buy shares of stock. If you sell a put option, you *may* have to buy shares of stock. For put sellers, you definitely must buy shares of stock *if* the put buyer decides to use their put option and sell shares of stock.

It's important to understand that options only convey *rights* to buy or sell shares of stock. For example, if you own a call option, you do not get any of the benefits that come with stock ownership such as dividends or voting privileges. (Although you could acquire shares of stock by using your call option and thereby get dividends or voting privileges). But by themselves, options convey nothing other than an agreement between two people to buy and sell shares of stock.

Now that you have a basic understanding of call and put options, let's add some market terminology to our groundwork.

The Long and Short of It

The financial markets are filled with colorful terminology. And one of the biggest obstacles that new option investors face is interpreting the jargon. Two common terms used by brokers and traders are "long" and "short" and it's important to understand these terms as applied to options.

If you buy any financial asset, you are "long" the position. For example, if you buy 100 shares of IBM, using market terminology, you are long 100 shares of IBM. The term "long" just means you own it. Likewise, if you buy a call option, you are "long" the call option.

If "long" means you bought it then "short" means you sold it, right? Not quite. Some people will tell you that "short" just means you sold an asset but that is an incomplete definition. For example, if you are long 100 shares of IBM and then sell 100 shares you are not short shares of IBM even though you sold 100 shares. That's because you bought the shares first and then sold them, which means you have no shares left.

However, let's say you bought 100 shares of IBM and then, by accident, entered an order online to sell 150 shares of IBM. The computer will execute the order since it has no way of knowing how many shares you actually own (maybe you have shares in a safe deposit box or with another broker). But if you really only owned 100 shares then you would be "short" 50 shares of IBM. In other words, you sold 50 shares you don't own. And that's exactly what it means to be short shares of stock. It means you sold shares you do not own. However, when we short shares in the financial market, it's not meant to be by mistake – it is done intentionally. How can you intentionally sell shares you don't own? You must borrow them. In order to further understand what it means to be "short" and how that applies to options, let's take a quick detour to understand the basics of short selling.

Traders use short sales as a way to profit from falling stock prices. Assume IBM is trading for $70 and you think its price is going to fall. If you are correct, you could profit from this outlook by entering an order to "short" or "sell short" shares of IBM. Let's assume you decide to short 100 shares. Your broker will find 100 shares from another client and let you borrow these shares. Although this sounds like a lengthy, complicated transaction it takes only seconds to execute.

In terms of the mechanics, shorting shares is similar to making a purchase on your credit card. Your bank finds loanable funds from somebody else's account to let you borrow and you then have an obligation to return those funds at some time. How complicated is it to short shares of stock? About as complicated as it is to swipe a credit card at a cash register.

Let's assume you short 100 shares of IBM at $70. Once the order is executed, you have $7,000 cash sitting in your account (sold 100 shares at $70 per share) and your account shows that you are short 100 shares of IBM – you sold shares that you do not own. Do you get to just take the $7,000 cash, close the account and walk away? No, once you short the shares of stock, you incur an obligation to replace those 100 shares at some time in the future. In other words, you must buy 100 shares at some time and return them to the broker. Obviously, your goal is to purchase those 100 shares at a cheaper price.

Let's assume that the price of IBM later drops by $5 to $65 and you decide to buy back the shares. You could enter an order to buy 100 shares and spend $6,500 of the $7,000 cash you initially received from selling shares. Once you buy the 100 shares, your obligation to return the IBM shares is then satisfied and you are left with an extra $500 in your account. In other words, you profited from a falling stock price. This profit can also be found by multiplying the number of short shares by the drop in price, or 100 shares * $5 fall in price = $500 profit. If you have shorted 300 shares of IBM, you would have ended up with a 300 shares * $5 fall in price = $1,500 profit. Of course, if the price of IBM had risen at the time you purchased them back, then you'd be left with a loss since you must spend more than you received to return the shares. If short selling still sounds confusing, just realize that the short seller generates profits in the same way as a stock buyer but by entering transactions in the opposite order. For instance, when you buy stock, you want to buy low and sell high. When you short stock, you want to sell high and buy low. If you short a stock and then buy it back at a higher price, you're left with a loss because you really bought high and sold low.

Short selling works because traders are obligated to return a fixed number of shares and not a fixed dollar amount. In our example, you shorted 100 shares with a value of $7,000. Your obligation is to return 100 shares of IBM and not $7,000 worth of IBM. If you can purchase the shares for less money than you received, you will make a profit.

This is not meant to be a course in shorting stocks but rather a way to understand what the term "short" really means when applied to the stock or options market. *Shorting means you receive cash from selling an asset you don't own and then incur some type of obligation.* In the case of shorting stocks, your obligation is that you must buy back the shares at some time.

If you short an option, you have sold something you don't own. You get cash up front and then incur some type of obligation depending on whether you sold a call or put. If you short a call, you get cash up front and have the obligation to sell shares of stock. If you short a put, you get cash up front and have the obligation to buy shares of stock. The cash is credited to your account immediately and is yours to keep regardless of what happens to the option. That is your compensation for accepting an obligation much like the premiums you pay to an insurance company.

 When you sell (short) an option you will receive cash, which yours to keep regardless of what happens in the future.

The following table may help you to visualize the rights versus obligations relationships:

	LONG	SHORT
Call	Right to buy stock	Obligation to sell stock
Put	Right to sell stock	Obligation to buy stock

Notice that the long and short positions are taking opposite sides of the transaction. For instance the long call (call buyer) must be matched with a short call (call seller). The long call has a *right* while the short call has an *obligation*. Rights and obligations are opposites. In addition, the long call gets to *buy* while the short call is required to *sell*. Buying and selling are also opposites.

For put options, the long put (put buyer) must be matched with a short put (put seller). As with call options, it is the long position that has the *right* while the short position has the *obligation* (opposites). The long put, however, has the right to *sell* while the short put is required to *buy* (opposites).

This arrangement is required to make the options market work. Both parties (the buyer and seller) cannot have rights. Both cannot buy nor can they both sell. One side has the right to buy (or the right to sell) while the opposite side has the obligation to complete the transaction.

This arrangement is often a source of confusion for new traders. They wonder how the option market can work if everybody has a right to buy or sell. The answer is that it is only the *long* position that has the rights. The *short* position has an obligation. It is important to understand this relationship when going through this book, especially when you get to strategies.

> (*i*) Long options have rights. Short options have obligations.

Getting Out of a Contract

 We just learned that you can get into an option contract by either buying or selling a call or put. But once you're in the contract, is there a way to get out of it at a later time? The answer is yes. All you have to do is enter a *closing transaction* (also called a *reversing trade*). In other words, you can always "escape" your obligations by simply doing the reverse set of actions that got you into the contract in the first place.

For example, if you are short an option and decide at a later time you don't want the corresponding obligation you can get out of it by simply *buying* the options back. This is much like you do with shares of stock if you are short. However, just because you can get out of the contract doesn't mean that you can avoid any losses that may have accrued. The price you pay to get out of the contract may be higher and, in some cases, much higher than the price you originally received from selling it – just as when shorting shares of stock. But the point is that you can get out of a short option contract by simply buying it back.

If the idea of buying back a contract sounds confusing, think of the following analogy. You probably have a cell phone are locked into some type of agreement such as a one-year *contract*. Cell companies do this to prevent people from continually shopping around and jumping to the hot promotion of the month. However, your cell provider will also have some type of "buy back" clause in the contract. That is, if you wish to get out of the agreement, you must pay a fixed amount of money, perhaps $200, and you can escape your remaining obligations. If you pay this fee, the company cannot take you to court later and say that you didn't fulfill your obligations. The reason is that you bought the contract back – it no longer exists between you and the company. That's the fee they specified to end all obligations.

This is mathematically the same thing that happens when you buy back a contract in the options market. Although it is not a fee to end the contract, what you're really doing is going long and short the same contract thereby eliminating all profits or losses beyond that point. If you're long the contract and you're short the same contract then you've effectively ended all obligations.

Likewise, you can get out of long call option by simply doing the reverse; that is selling the same contract that you own. Because of this possibility, most option traders simply trade the contracts back and forth in the open market rather than using them to buy or sell shares of stock. As we will later see, trading option contracts is a big advantage because they cost a fraction of the stock price.

 You can always get out of an option contract at anytime by simply entering a reversing the trade.

Let's make sure you understand the concepts of long and short calls and puts by using our pizza coupon and car insurance analogies. If you are in possession of a pizza coupon, you are "long" the coupon and have the right, not the obligation, to buy one pizza for a fixed price over a given time period. In the real world, you do not buy pizza coupons; they are handed out for free. But that doesn't put an end to our analogy because the basic idea is still there. Since you are holding the coupon that means you are the one with the rights to use it and that's the role of the long position. The pizza store owner would be "short" the coupon and has an *obligation* to sell you the pizza if you choose to use your coupon. You have the right; he has the obligation.

If you buy an auto insurance policy you are "long" the policy and have the right to "put" your car back to the insurance company. The insurance company is "short" the policy; they receive money in exchange for the potential obligation of having to buy your car from you. Whether you make a claim or not, the insurance company keeps your premium just as you will when selling options. That's their compensation for accepting the risk.

In the real world of car insurance, you cannot just force the insurance company to buy it back for any reason. There are certain conditions that must be met such as that it was wrecked or stolen. You can't just put it back to the insurance company because you don't like it anymore or because it has depreciated. However, in the real world of put options, you can sell your stock at a fixed price for *any* reason while your put option is still in effect. There are no restrictions. Of course, you wouldn't want to do that if the fixed price you'd receive is less than the current market price. The main point is that if you are long a put option, you call the shots. You have the rights. You have the "option" to decide. You have the right to sell your stock for that fixed price at any time during the time your "policy" is in effect.

The Options Clearing Corporation (OCC)

Okay, this may sound good in theory but how do we know that the short positions will actually follow through with their obligations if you decide to use your call or put option?

The answer is that there is a clearing firm called the *Options Clearing Corporation*, or OCC. The OCC is a highly capitalized and regulated agency that acts as a middleman to all transactions. When you buy an option, you are really buying it from the OCC. And when you sell an option, you are really selling it to the OCC. The OCC acts as the buyer to every seller and the seller to every buyer. It is the OCC that guarantees the performance of all contracts. By performance we obviously do not mean profits but rather that if you decide to use your option, you are assured the transaction will go through. In fact, ever since the inception of the options market and the OCC in 1973, not a single case of unfair or partial performance has ever occurred. If you'd like to read more about the OCC, you can find their website at www.OptionsClearing.com.

Before reading further, make sure you understand the following key concepts:

||||||||||||||||||||||||||||||||||||||||||||||||||||||||||||||||||||||||||||||||

 Key Concepts

1) Long call options give the buyer the right to BUY stock, at a fixed price, over a given time period.

2) Short call options create the obligation to SELL stock at a fixed price, over a given time period.

3) Long put options give the buyer the right to SELL stock, at a fixed price, over a given time period.

4) Short put options create the obligation to BUY stock, at a fixed price, over a given time period.

5) Option sellers (calls or puts) keep the cash regardless of what happens in the future.

6) The OCC acts as a middleman to all transactions.

||||||||||||||||||||||||||||||||||||||||||||||||||||||||||||||||||||||||||||||||

More Option Terminology

We're almost ready to talk about real call and put options but we first must go over some other market terminology that you'll need to understand. We just covered the terms "long" and "short," which are critical for understanding who has the right and who has the obligation with any particular strategy. But we have a lot more ground to cover before talking about strategies. Next, we must venture into the remaining terms we will be using throughout the book.

Underlying Asset

In the pizza coupon example, we would say the *underlying asset* is a pizza. Notice that the coupon limited us to how many pizzas we can purchase; we cannot purchase all we want. In addition, the coupon is not good for any brand of pizza but only the one advertised on the coupon. Call and put options work in similar ways. The underlying asset for a call or put option is generally 100 shares of stock. There are exceptions (which we'll talk about later in Chapter Four) to this rule such as certain stock splits or mergers. But when options are first issued, they always represent 100 shares of the underlying stock.

The "brand" of shares we can buy is determined by the call or put option. For example, if we have a Microsoft call option, we have the right to buy 100 shares of Microsoft. In this case, Microsoft would be the *underlying stock*. The price of an option is tied to or *derived* by the underlying stock. Because of this, options are one of many types of *derivative* instruments. A derivative instrument is one whose value is derived by the value of another asset.

Strike Price (Exercise Price)

In our example, the pizza coupon states a specific purchase price of $10.00. No matter what the price of pizzas may be when you get to the store, you are locked in to the price of $10.00. If this were an option, we'd call this "lock in" price the *strike price*, which is really a slang term that comes from the fact that we have "struck" a deal at that price.

Another name for the strike price is the *exercise price*. The reason for this is that if you choose to use your option, you must submit *exercise instructions* to your broker, which is handled with a simple phone call. With a pizza coupon, you just "hand in" the coupon but in the world of options you must "exercise" the option through your broker.

If you exercise a call option, you must pay the strike price (since you're buying stock) and that's why the strike price is also called the exercise price. It's the price you will pay for exercising the option to purchase shares of stock. If you are short a call option, you'll receive the strike price (because you're selling stock). The exercise price is the price that will be paid by the long position and received by the short position.

The opposite is true for put options. If you exercise a put, you'll receive the strike price since you are selling shares of stock. The short put will pay the strike price since they are the required to buy the stock. The exercise price is the price that will be received by the long put and paid by the short put.

We'll talk more about exercising options later but, for now, just understand that the strike price and exercise price are two terms for the same thing. They both represent the fixed purchase or selling price.

Expiration Date

Notice that the pizza coupon also has an *expiration date*. You can use this coupon at any time up to and including the expiration date. Equity options (options on stock) always expire on the third Friday of the expiration month. Technically speaking, equity options expire on Saturday following the third Friday but that is really for clearing purposes. That extra day (Saturday) gives the OCC (Options Clearing Corporation) time to match buyers and sellers while the contract is still legally "alive." From a practical standpoint though, the last day to close or to exercise your option is the third Friday of the expiration month. After that, it's no longer valid. So just because you may read that options expire on Saturday, don't think you can get up Saturday morning and call your broker with exercise instructions – it's too late. The third Friday of the expiration month is your *last* day (not the only day) to close or exercise the option. (If Friday is a holiday, the last trading day will usually be the preceding Thursday.)

Although a pizza storeowner may allow you to turn in an expired coupon, there's no such thing with the options market. The second that option expires, it's gone for good. There are some index options, such as options covering the S&P 500 Index that expire on the third Thursday of the expiration month. However, we will only be discussing equity options in this book so whenever we talk about the expiration date, we will always be referring to the third Friday of the expiration month unless otherwise stated.

American versus European Styles

As stated before, most option contracts are simply bought and sold in the open market without a single share of stock ever changing hands. However, if you wish to physically trade shares of stock, you must exercise your option. When can you exercise your option? The answer to that depends on the *style* of option. There are two styles of options: *American* and *European*. The style of option has nothing to do with its origin as implied by the names "American" and "European." Instead, the style simply tells us when the option may be exercised. American style options can be exercised at *any* time through the third Friday of the expiration month. European style options, on the other hand, can *only* be exercised on the third Friday of the expiration month. You generally do not get to select which style of option you want. All equity options (that is, options on stock) are American style and can be exercised at any time. Most index options are European style. There are a few indices that offer both such as the OEX (S&P 100 Index), which is American style and the XEO which is the European version of the same index.

It may sound like the American style option has a big advantage over a European style. After all, for example, if a stock is really flying high it would be nice to exercise a call option and buy the shares at a cheaper price and immediately sell the shares to capture a profit. We're going to find out in Chapter Four that exercising a call option early for this reason is a big mistake. You will find out that most of the time you are better off just selling the call option in the open market rather than exercising it.

This book is written from the perspective of equity options so we will assume that all options discussed are American style unless otherwise stated. We only differentiate the terms "American" and "European" so you will know what it they mean if you hear them later while continuing to learn about options. The bottom line is that all equity options are American style, which means the long position can exercise them at any time during the life of the option even though it is rarely optimal to do so.

 The last day to buy, sell, or exercise your options is the third Friday of the expiration month.

Physical versus Cash Delivery

If you exercise an equity option, you will either buy or sell the actual (physical) shares of the underlying stock. This is called *physical delivery* or *physical settlement*.

On the other hand, most index options, such as SPX (S&P 500), are *cash settlement* rather than physical delivery. In other words, if the long position exercises an index option, he receives the cash value of the option rather than taking actual delivery of all the stocks in that index. Just realize that not all options settle in physical delivery. As you continue to learn more about options you will hear the terms "physical settlement" and "cash settlement" and it's important you understand what these terms mean.

Exercise versus Assign

We said earlier that it is the long positions that get to exercise their options. What do short positions get to do? Nothing. Remember, short positions have no rights. The short position may get a phone call from their broker stating that they have just purchased or sold shares of stock due to a call option they sold. If you are required to buy or sell shares of stock due to a short option, it is called an *assignment*.

If you get assigned on an option, your broker will notify you the next business day to inform you of the assignment. They may say something like, "I'm calling to inform you that you've been assigned on your short call options and have sold 100 shares for the strike price of $50."

The words exercise and assign should only be associated with long and short positions respectively. However, in the real world, if you are assigned on a short option, brokers may say things like "you got exercised" on an option even though it is technically incorrect. Long positions exercise. Short positions get assigned. In truth, it doesn't really matter in practice if an incorrect phrase is used such as "you got exercised" rather than "you got assigned" as long as you understand the message. However, if these terms are used, you do need to understand the difference. Most books and literature on options carefully choose between the words "exercise" and "assign" and you need to understand the actions they are referring to.

Let's run through some examples to be sure you understand. If you are long a call option, you have the right to exercise it and buy shares of stock. If you are short the call, you might get assigned and be required to sell shares. If you are long a put option, you have the right to exercise it and sell shares. If you are short the put option, you could get assigned and be required to buy shares. To continue further, if a long call holder uses his call to buy shares of stock he would say, "I exercised my call." The short call holder would say, "I got assigned on my call."

It is important to understand that once you submit exercise instructions to your broker and the shares and cash have exchanged hands it is an *irrevocable* transaction. Make sure you want to exercise before submitting instructions. Also, many firms have cutoff times after which exercise instructions cannot be changed (even though the shares or cash may not have yet been exchanged). Check with your broker as to what these times are before you submit exercise instructions.

Option Basics

You now have enough information to understand some hypothetical call and put options. These two assets – calls and puts – are the building blocks for every option strategy you will ever encounter. This is why it is crucial that you understand the rights and obligations that they convey. Most misunderstandings with option strategies stem from not understanding (or simply forgetting) who has the right and who has the obligation.

Because options are binding contracts, they are traded in units called *contracts.* Stocks are traded in shares; options are traded in contracts. An option contract, just like a pizza coupon, will always be designated by the underlying stock it controls along with the expiration month and strike price. For example, let's assume we are looking at a Microsoft June $30 call.

We'll show you shortly where you can look up actual option quotes and symbols for options but for now let's make sure we understand what this option represents.

Using your understanding of pizza coupons, what do you suppose the buyer of one contract is allowed to do? The buyer of this call has the right (not the obligation) to purchase 100 shares of the underlying stock – Microsoft – for $30 per share at any time through the third Friday in June. (Remember that the expiration date for stock options is always the third Friday of the expiration month.) The buyer of this coupon is "locked in" to the $30 price no matter how high Microsoft shares may be trading. Obviously, the higher Microsoft trades, the more valuable the call option becomes.

To understand this concept a little better, assume that you have found a piece of property valued at $300,000 and wish to buy it. But you'd first like spend a few days researching the area before buying it. If you do, you'll run the risk of losing it to another investor. What can you do? You can go to the broker and put down some money to hold the property for you. For instance, you may pay $500 for several days' worth of time. If you decide against the property, you lose the $500. These arrangements are done all the time in real estate and are called "options" on real estate. Assume that you pay the $500 for five days worth of time and are now locked into a binding agreement to buy the property for $300,000 over the next five days. Now suppose that some news is spreading that the area is about to be commercially zoned and some big businesses are interested in it. Property in the area goes up dramatically overnight. But even if you decide to not buy the property, don't you think that somebody else would love to be in possession of the contract that you have giving them the right to pay $300,000? Of course they would. And these people will start offering you large amounts of money for you to sign over the contract to them. You could just sell it to them and they could sell it to others. This is exactly what most traders do with the equity options market.

Now let's go back to our option example. How much will it cost you to use (exercise) your call option? Because you are buying 100 shares of stock, the strike price must be multiplied by 100 as well. If you were to exercise this Microsoft $30 call option, you would pay the $30 strike * 100 shares = $3,000 cash. This is called the *total contract value* or the *exercise value*. In exchange for that payment, you'd receive 100 shares of Microsoft. It works just like a pizza coupon. You pay a fixed amount of cash and receive some type of underlying asset. Most brokers charge a standard stock commission to exercise your options. If you exercised this call, your broker would probably charge you their regular commission for buying 100 shares of stock. After all, the long call option is simply a means for buying regular shares of stock.

To restate a previous point, it is important to understand that if you buy call or put options, you are not required to ever buy or sell shares of stock. Further, you do not ever need the shares of stock in your account at any time. Most option contracts are opened and closed in the open market without a single share of stock changing hands. Even though you're allowed to purchase or sell stock with your options, most traders never do. Instead, they just buy and sell the contracts in the open market amongst other traders.

Now let's assume we are looking at a Microsoft June $30 put option. Think about your auto insurance policy and try to figure out what this option allows you to do. If you buy this put option, you have the right to sell 100 shares of Microsoft for $30 per share at any time through the third Friday in June. Because you are locking in a selling price, put options become more valuable as the stock price falls. If you exercise this put option, you are selling 100 shares of Microsoft, which means you will have 100 shares of Microsoft taken from your account and delivered to someone else. In exchange, you will receive the $30 strike * 100 shares = $3,000 cash. If you exercise this put, your broker would probably charge the regular stock commission for selling 100 shares of stock since the put option is simply a means for selling regular shares of stock.

What if you only wish to buy or sell fewer than 100 shares of stock? You can do that but in a roundabout way. Using the call example above, let's say you only wanted to buy 60 shares of Microsoft for $30. You would still exercise the call option for 100 shares and then immediately submit an order to sell 40 shares (which would carry a separate commission). Each contract is good for 100 shares and you must buy and sell in that amount. But there's nothing from stopping you from immediately entering another order to customize those amounts to suit your needs. Likewise, if you exercised a put option but only wanted to sell 60 shares of stock, you would have to exercise the put and sell 100 shares and then immediately place an order to buy 40 shares.

Options are Standardized Contracts

The reason that options are inflexible as to the number of shares is because options are standardized contracts. A standardized contract means there is a uniform process that determines the terms, which are designed to meet the needs of most traders and investors. By using standardized contracts, we lose some flexibility in terms (such as the number of shares, strike prices, and expiration dates) but increase the ease, speed, and security in which we can create the contracts.

In fact, if the exchanges find there is not sufficient demand for options on a stock, they will not even list those options. Most of the well-known companies have options available. If a stock has listed options, it is an *optionable* stock. Microsoft and Intel, for example, are optionable. There are currently over 2,300 optionable stocks so the list is quite large.

Another limitation of standardized contracts is the fixed strike price increments. If the stock price is below $50, you will find options available in $2.50 increments. If the stock price is between $50 and $200, options will be in $5 increments. And if the stock price is over $200, you will find option strikes in $10 increments. Notice that the strike price increments have nothing to do with the *current* price of the stock. The increments are based on the stock's price at the time the options start trading. If a stock's price has been greatly fluctuating, you might find different increments for different months. For instance, you may find $2.50 increments for the first two expiration months and $5 increments in later expiration months. This just tells you that the stock's price was above $25 when the later months started trading.

By having standardized strikes, we can quickly bring new contracts to market the meet the needs of the vast majority of people. Think how overwhelming the task would be if the exchanges tried to meet everybody's needs by creating strike prices at every possible price such as $30, $30.01, $30.02, etc. and then matched those with every possible expiration date such as June 1, June 2, June 3, etc. It would be a near impossibility. To solve these problems, the exchanges created standardized contracts so that we can have some flexibility while still keeping the list manageable.

What if you really want a customized contract? Is it possible to get one? Technically, there is nothing illegal about two people having a contract drawn up by an attorney that specifies the terms on which they agree to buy and sell stock. You could therefore have an attorney write a contract for you and another trader thus creating your own call or put option. A contract drawn in this manner is completely flexible - but it is also very time consuming and costly. In addition, even though you may have a legally binding contract, it is possible that the seller decides to not fulfill their obligation if the buyer wishes to exercise their option. If that happens, now you've got your hands tied up in court trying to get the seller to conform to the terms of the contract. In other words, customized contracts are subject to *performance risk*. That is, will the seller perform their part of the agreement if the buyer decides to exercise?

Standardized options solve the performance risk problem too since the OCC acts as the buyer to every seller and the seller to every buyer. If you exercise an option, the OCC decides who will be assigned by a random process. When you enter an options contract, you do not know who is on the other side of the trade. Nobody knows. It is strictly the person who ends up with the random assignment. Standardization increases confidence and influences the progress toward a smooth running, liquid market.

Besides having an attorney draw up a contract, there is another way to get flexible contracts. You can buy FLEX contracts through the *Chicago Board Options Exchange* (CBOE) that are totally customizable but they also require an extremely large contract size – usually over one million dollars. Because FLEX options are traded through the OCC they are not exposed to performance risk despite their large contract sizes. Because of the size requirements though, FLEX options are mostly used by institutions such as banks, mutual funds, and pension funds. The standardized market is the solution for the rest of us.

|||||||||||||||||||||||||||||||||||||||||||||||||||||||||||||||||||||||||||||||||||||||||||||||||||||

 Key Concepts

1. Options are derivative assets. Their prices are derived from the price of the underlying stock.

2. Your "lock in" price is called the "strike price" or the "exercise price."

3. If you decide to use your option, you must submit exercise instructions.

4. You are not required to ever buy or sell stock if you are trading options.

5. Your last trading day for options is the third Friday of the expiration month.

6. Options trade in units called "contracts."

7. The exercise price multiplied by the strike price equals the total contract value, or exercise value.

8. Options are standardized. You can only get them in a limited number of "flavors."

|||||||||||||||||||||||||||||||||||||||||||||||||||||||||||||||||||||||||||||||||||||||||||||||

Understanding a Real Call Option

Now that you know how call and put options work, let's take a look at some real call and put options. Let's pull up some quotes and see if we can make some sense of what we're looking at.

You can pull up option quotes for any optionable stock by going to www.cboe. com. That's the homepage for the Chicago Board Options Exchange (CBOE), which is one of the largest option exchanges in the world. Bear in mind that the options market is open from 9:30am to 4:02pm ET (it is open until 4:15pm ET for index options). If you are pulling up quotes after 4:02pm, you're looking at closing prices rather than live quotes. Also, options go through what is called an *opening rotation* every morning. This is simply an open outcry system that establishes option prices based on the current stock price openings. For this reason, you may not see live option quotes until 9:35 or 9:40 even though the options market is technically open at 9:30.

If you click on "Quotes" and then "Delayed Quotes" you will find a box where you can type your stock ticker symbol. If you are looking for options on eBay, for example, you'd just type the ticker symbol "EBAY" and hit enter. At this time, the shortest term options on eBay were July '05 (26 days until expiration) and the longest term was January '08 (943 days to expiration). The lowest strike is $22.50 and the highest is $80. So even though option contracts are standardized, there are many to choose from. Table 1-1 shows some of the shorter-term options available at the time of this writing:

Table 1-1: EBAY Option Quotes

EBAY **37.11 -0.94**

Jun 20, 2005 @ 14:43 ET (Data 15 Minutes Delayed)   Bid 37.10   Ask 37.11   Size 32x25   Vol 17121523

Calls	Last Sale	Net	Bid	Ask	Vol	Open Int	Puts	Last Sale	Net	Bid	Ask	Vol	Open Int
05 Jul 32.50 (XBA GZ-E)	4.40	-1.20	4.70	4.90	5	7319	05 Jul 32.50 (XBA SZ-E)	0.15	--	0.10	0.20	23	23943
05 Jul 35.00 (XBA GG-E)	2.50	-0.90	2.60	2.70	271	13510	05 Jul 35.00 (XBA SG-E)	0.45	+0.10	0.45	0.50	1811	24275
05 Jul 37.50 (XBA GU-E)	1.00	-0.55	1.00	1.05	909	21930	05 Jul 37.50 (XBA SU-E)	1.40	+0.45	1.35	1.40	633	18877
05 Jul 40.00 (XBA GH-E)	0.30	-0.20	0.30	0.35	613	34574	05 Jul 40.00 (XBA SH-E)	3.60	+1.15	3.10	3.20	206	13113
05 Aug 32.50 (XBA HZ-E)	5.00	--	5.30	5.50	100	0	05 Aug 32.50 (XBA TZ-E)	0.65	--	0.55	0.65	30	0
05 Aug 35.00 (XBA HG-E)	0	pc	3.40	3.60	0	0	05 Aug 35.00 (XBA TG-E)	1.25	-0.10	1.15	1.25	191	0
05 Aug 37.50 (XBA HU-E)	1.85	+0.10	2.00	2.10	82	0	05 Aug 37.50 (XBA TU-E)	2.45	-0.05	2.20	2.30	64	0
05 Aug 40.00 (XBA HH-E)	0.95	-0.10	1.00	1.10	64	0	05 Aug 40.00 (XBA TH-E)	0	pc	3.70	3.90	0	0

Before we continue, we need to cover some more terminology that has been deliberately withheld until now for the fact that it will be easier to understand at this point. There are three main classifications for options. First, there are two **types** of options, calls and puts. Second, all options of the same type and same underlying represent a **class** of options. Therefore, all eBay calls or all eBay puts (regardless of expiration) make up a class. Third, all options of the same class, strike price, and expiration date make up a **series**. For instance, all *July $32.50 calls* form a **series**.

At the time these quotes were taken, eBay stock was trading for $37.11, which you can see in the upper right corner of Table 1-1. The first column is labeled "calls" and several columns to the right you will find one labeled "puts." The first call option on the list is **05 Jul 32.50**. The "05 Jul" tells us that the contract expires in July '05 and the "32.50" designates that it is a $32.50 strike price. The last trading day for this option will be the third Friday in July '05. All you have to do is look at a calendar and count the third Friday for July '05 and that is the last day you can trade the option (which happens to be July 15 for this particular year). Remember, you can buy, sell, or exercise this option on *any* day but the last day to do so is July 15. All 05 July options will expire on the same date regardless of the strike price or whether they are calls or puts.

The **"XBAGZ-E"** notation is the symbol for that option. Just as every stock has a unique trading symbol, each option carries a unique symbol. However, you can forget about the "dash E" as the letter E is a unique identifier for the CBOE, which just tells us these quotes are coming from that exchange. If you wanted to buy or sell this option online, you'd enter the symbol "XBAGZ." Your broker, however, may require you to follow this symbol with ".O" to show that it is an option (for example, XBAGZ.O). Your broker will make it very clear if they have these requirements but the actual symbol (XBAGZ in this example) will always remain the same regardless of which brokerage firm you use.

 Your brokerage firm may list option symbols as "OPRA" codes. The committee named for consolidating all of the option quotes and reporting them to the various services is called the Options Price Reporting Authority or "OPRA." An OPRA code is the same thing as the option symbol. You can read more about OPRA at www.OpraData.com.

The $32.50 strike means that the owner of this "coupon" has the right, not the obligation, to buy 100 shares of eBay for $32.50 through the third Friday of Jul '05. No matter how high of a price eBay may be trading, the owner of this call option is locked into a $32.50 purchase price. Now this seems like a pretty good deal since the stock is trading much higher at $37.11. It appears that if you got the $32.50 call, you could make an immediate profit of $37.11 - $32.50 = $4.31. In other words, it appears that if we could get our hands on this coupon, we could buy the stock for $32.50 and immediately sell it for the going price of $37.11 thus making an immediate profit of $4.31. However, you must remember that call options, unlike pizza coupons, are not free. It will cost us some money to get our hands on it.

How much will it cost to buy this coupon? We can find out by looking at the "ask" column, which shows how much you will have to pay to buy the option. It shows a price of $4.90 to buy this call. This means the apparently free $4.31 is no longer free since you're paying $4.90 for $4.31 worth of immediate benefit. In fact, you will find that you must always pay for any immediate advantage that any call or put option gives you. The main point of this is that you cannot use options to collect "free money" in the market. When traders are first introduced to options, they often think they can buy a call option that gives them an advantageous price and then immediately exercise the call for a free profit. They overlook the fact that the price of the option will more than reflect that benefit. Why would someone pay $4.90 for $4.31 worth of immediate benefit? Because there is time remaining on the option. It is certainly possible that the option will, at some point in time, have more than $4.31 worth of benefit and traders are willing to pay for that time.

The $4.90 price is also called the *premium*. The premium really represents the price per share. Since each contract controls 100 shares of stock, the total cost of this option will be $4.90 * 100 = $490 plus commission to buy one contract. So if you spend $490, you can control 100 shares of eBay through the expiration date of the contract. That's certainly a lot less than the $3,711 it would cost to buy 100 shares of stock. If you buy two contracts, you would be controlling 200 shares and that would cost $980 plus commissions etc. Remember, we said that all options control 100 shares when they are first listed but it is possible for them to control more shares, which is usually due to a stock split. If that happens, it is possible for the contract size to change, which we will talk more about in Chapter Four. The main point to understand is that you always multiply the option premium by the number of shares that the contract controls in order to find the total price of the option. In most cases, you will multiply by 100.

Bid and Ask Prices

 Let's take a brief detour here to talk more about what the bid and ask represent since they can be confusing to new traders. Notice that the $32.50 call shows a *bid* price of $4.70 and an *ask* price of $4.90. You have to remember that the options market, just like the stock market, is a live auction. There are traders continuously placing bids to buy and offers to sell. The bid price is the highest price that someone is willing to pay at that moment. The asking price is the lowest price at which someone will sell at that moment. If these terms are confusing, think of the terms you use when buying or selling a home. If you wish to buy a home, you submit a bid. Buyers place bids. If you are selling your home, you'd say I am "asking" such-and-such a price for it. Sellers create asking prices. Sometimes you will hear the word "offer"

instead of "ask" but they mean the same thing. If the bid represents the highest price someone is willing to pay that means you can receive that price if you are selling your option. You are selling to a buyer and the trade can get executed. Notice that you cannot sell at the $4.90 asking price because that is a seller too and you cannot execute a trade by matching a seller with a seller.

Likewise, if you are buying this option, you should refer to the asking price to see how much it will cost you. Since the asking price shows the lowest price that someone will sell, we know you can buy the option for that price. In this case, you are buying from a seller and the trade can get executed. This is important to remember since the price you pay or receive depends on the bid and ask. Maybe this trade appears to be a good deal if you could sell for $4.90 but you would be disappointed if you find that you only received $4.70. You need to be aware of which price applies to your intended action. *In summary, if you are selling then you should reference the bid price. If you are buying, you should look at the asking price.* This is especially critical for options traders since the volume on options is not as high as it is for the stock and, consequently, options will have larger spreads between the bid and ask. For example, notice in upper right corner of Table 1-1, you can see that the stock is bidding $37.10 and asking $37.11, which represents a one-cent spread between the buyers and sellers. However, the $32.50 call option is bidding $4.70 and asking $4.90, which is a 20-cent spread. The bigger that spread, the more critical it is to understand what these numbers mean, otherwise you could be in for an unpleasant surprise when trading. We'll talk more about the bid and ask in Chapter Four when we discuss the Limit Order Display Rule and how you can use it to your advantage to lessen the effect of the spread.

> The "bid" price represents the highest price that a BUYER is willing to pay. It is consequently the price where you can sell the option.
>
> The "ask" price represents the lowest price that a SELLER is willing to receive. It is consequently the price where you can buy the option.

Okay, let's try the next call on the list in Table 1-1, which is the **05 Jul 35** call (notice that the strikes are in $2.50 increments since eBay is below $50, which is in agreement with what we said earlier). If you buy this call option, you have the right, not the obligation, to buy 100 shares of eBay for $35 per share through the third Friday in July '05. Since eBay is trading for $37.11, we know that anybody holding this option has an immediate advantage of $37.11 - $35 = $2.11 by buying this call and we now know that this advantage must be reflected in the price. You can verify that the asking price is $2.70, which shows the apparently free $2.11 benefit is not free. Again, the reason traders will pay more than the $2.11 benefit is because there is time remaining on the option and it certainly could end up with more value. If you want to buy this contract, it will cost you $2.70 * 100 shares = $270 per contract + commissions. If you buy two contracts, you would control 200 shares and that would cost $540 and so on.

While we're talking about the prices in Table 1-1, let's explain what the rest of the columns mean. The **LAST SALE** column records the price of the last trade of the option. Option traders rarely look at this since that price could have occurred during the last minute but it also could have been last week. We don't know when that trade took place. We just know that was the price when it last traded. For stock traders, the last sale will generally be very close to the bid and ask of the stock because optionable stocks generally have high volume but that is not necessarily true for their options. In Table 1-1, you can see that the last trade on eBay was $37.11 with the bid at $37.10 and the asking price at $37.11. The last sale for the stock is very close to the current bid and ask, which will usually be the case. But notice that the last trade for the $32.50 call was $4.40 with the bid and ask at $4.70 to $4.90. This shows that the last trade is somewhat stale and that's why option traders generally do not look at the last trade. If you were buying this option, the last sale would lead you to believe that it would cost $4.40 when it would really cost $4.90. If you were selling the option, the last sale may make you decide against it since it appears you would only receive $4.40 when, in actuality, you get $4.70.

The **NET** column shows the net change between prices for the two most recent trades just as it does for stocks. For the July $32.50 call, the last trade was $4.40 and that price was down $1.20 from its previous price, which means the previous trade was $4.40 + $1.20 = $5.70. If this option traded at $5.70 and the next trade was at $4.40 then that represents a $1.20 drop in price, which is what the **NET** column shows. Again, the reason for the apparent big drop in price is because there was a big time delay between those two trades.

The **VOL** column shows us the volume, which is simply the number of contracts traded that day. For the stock market, volume refers to the number of shares traded; for the options market, it refers to the number of contracts but the idea is the same. The **OPEN INT** column shows how many contracts are currently in existence, which is called the "open interest." We'll find out more about open interest in Chapter Four.

Understanding a Real Put Option

Now that we've looked at a couple of call options, let's take a look at some real put options. In Table 1-1, what does the **05 Jul 32.50** put option represent? If you buy this put, you have the right to sell 100 shares of eBay for $32.50 per share through the third Friday of July '05. For that right, you would have to pay 0.20 * 100 = $20 plus commissions. No matter how low of a price eBay might be trading, you are guaranteed to get $32.50 if you exercise this put option to sell your shares. Remember, you do not need to own the shares of stock to buy a put. By purchasing this put, you have the right to sell shares for $32.50 and somebody else will be very willing to buy this from you if eBay falls below $32.50. By purchasing the put, you're banking on eBay's price falling. If you think the price of eBay will fall, you can buy the put and then sell it to someone else thus capturing a profit without ever having the shares to sell. Notice that with this option, there is no immediate benefit in owning the $32.50 put. If you owned shares of eBay and wanted to sell, you'd just sell the shares in the open market for $37.11. Once again, the reason that there is any value to this $32.50 put at all is because there is time remaining and it may end up with a lot more value if eBay's price falls. Traders are willing to pay for that time.

Let's try the next one on the list, the July $37.50 put. If you buy this put, you have the right to sell 100 shares of eBay for $37.50 per share through the third Friday of July '05. Now this put does appear to have an immediate value since we could sell the stock for a higher price than it is currently trading. It appears that if we buy this put, we could buy the shares for $37.11 and immediately use the put option and collect $37.50 for an immediate guaranteed profit of 39 cents. As with our call option examples, any immediate benefit must be paid for and we can verify that by observing the 50-cent asking price. In other words, you're paying 50 cents for that 39-cent benefit. The market is willing to pay more than the immediate benefit since there is time remaining on the option. You cannot use options, whether calls or puts, to collect "free money."

|||||||||||||||||||||||||||||||||||||||||||||||||||||||||||||||||||||||||||||||||||||||||||

 ## Key Concepts

1) The price of an option is called the premium.

2) The "ask" price tells us how much we have to pay for an option. The "bid" price tells us how much we can sell it for.

3) To find the total price for one option contract, multiply the bid or ask by 100.

4) The last day to trade an option is the third Friday of the expiration month.

|||||||||||||||||||||||||||||||||||||||||||||||||||||||||||||||||||||||||||||||||||||||||||

Intrinsic Values and Time Values

In the previous section, we found out that some options have an "immediate value" or "immediate benefit" at the time they are purchased while others do not. It's time now to introduce some more terminology that will help you understand why.

We discovered that an option's price must reflect any immediate value in holding it. For instance, we found that the July $35 call could give a trader an immediate benefit of $2.11 since the stock is trading for $37.11. If the stock is trading for $37.11 and you have a call that gives you the right to buy the stock for $35, you're better off with the call by $37.11 - $35 = $2.11. That $2.11 worth of immediate benefit must be reflected in the price and we see that it is since that call is priced higher at $2.70. In option lingo, we'd say that the $35 call has $2.11 worth of *intrinsic value*. It will really help if you learn to substitute the word "immediate benefit" or "immediate value" for intrinsic value. If the stock is trading for $37.11, we know the $35 call must be worth at least $2.11 in the open market. In other words, options must be worth at least their intrinsic value.

If there is any value in the option over and above this amount, it is called *time value* or *time premium*. (Some texts will also refer to this as *extrinsic value*.) The time value is due to the fact that there is still time remaining on the option. Since the July $35 call was trading for $2.70 and the intrinsic value is $2.11 then the time value must be $2.70 - $2.11 = 59 cents.

Any option's price can be broken down into the two components of **intrinsic values** and **time values** and the following formula will help:

Formula 1-2:

Total Value (Premium) = Intrinsic Value + Time Value

Using the July $35 call example, we know that the intrinsic value is $2.11 and the time value is 59 cents so the total call value must be $2.11 intrinsic value + $0.59 time value = $2.70 total value. Figure 1-3 may help you to visualize the breakdown of time and intrinsic value:

Figure 1-3: Breakdown of Time and Intrinsic Values

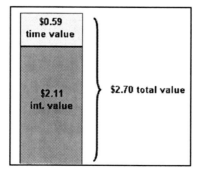

If there is no intrinsic value then the option's price is comprised totally of time value. For example, in Table 1-1, the July $37.50 is trading for $1.05. However, the stock is only $37.11. If you buy the $37.50 call, you're buying a coupon that gives you the right to buy the stock for a higher price than it is currently trading. On the surface, it may seem that the $37.50 call has no value. But the real way to say it is that it has no intrinsic value; the $37.50 call has no *immediate* value. There may be value in the future, but there's no immediate value at this time. The $1.05 premium on this call is made up of pure time premium. The only reason value exists on this call is because time remains.

Using Formula 1-2 for the July $37.50 call, we have $0 intrinsic value and $1.05 time value so the total value is $0 intrinsic value + $1.05 time value = $1.05 total value.

If you like mathematical formulas, you can find the intrinsic value of a call by taking the stock price minus the strike price (exercise price). If that number is positive, there is intrinsic value on the call option.

Intrinsic Value Formula for Calls:

Stock price - Exercise price = Intrinsic Value (assuming you get a positive number).

For example, the $35 call must have intrinsic value since $37.11 - $35 = $2.11. The $37.50 call, on the other hand has $37.11 - $37.50 = -39 cents. Since this number is negative, there is no intrinsic value on this call.

For puts, we use the same reasoning but in the opposite direction. In Table 1-1, the July $40 puts are trading for $3.20. There is obviously an immediate benefit in holding the $40 put since we could sell our stock for $40 rather than the market price of $37.11. The amount of that benefit is $40 - $37.11 = $2.89. The intrinsic value is therefore $2.89. Because the put is trading for $3.20, the remaining value must be time value. The time value is $3.20 - $2.89 = 31 cents. Once again, using Formula 1-2 we see that the $2.89 intrinsic value + $0.31 time value = $3.20 total value.

If you wish to use mathematical formulas to find intrinsic value for puts, we can just reverse the call formula (remember, puts are like calls but they work in the opposite direction). For put options, if the exercise price minus the stock price is positive then there is intrinsic value. For example, the July $40 put has intrinsic value since $40 exercise price - $37.11 stock price = $2.89 intrinsic value. We know this is the intrinsic value since the result is a positive number. The July $35 put, on the other hand, has no intrinsic value since $35 exercise price - $37.11 stock price = -$2.11 (negative number).

Intrinsic Value Formula for Puts:

Exercise price – Stock Price = Intrinsic Value (assuming you get a positive number).

We can rearrange Formula 1-2 to come up with another useful formula for finding time value. That is, Premium – Intrinsic Value = Time Value. We can abbreviate this formula as P – I = T, which looks like the word "pits." Just remember that option formulas are the "pits" and should have no trouble finding time values. What is the time value for the July $35 call? The premium is $2.70 and the intrinsic value is $2.11 so the time value is $2.70 - $2.11 = 59 cents.

Time Value for Calls and Puts:
Premium - Intrinsic Value = Time Value.

Intrinsic value is the key value to solve for. If you can find intrinsic value, you can find time value. We can't emphasize enough the importance of practicing by using the words "immediate benefit" or "immediate advantage" to determine if an option has intrinsic value. Formulas are nice if you are programming a computer but they do not allow you to understand why the formula works. Understanding why is important if you want to understand options. Use the formulas to check your answers.

Let's run through the thought process again for finding intrinsic value. For example, if someone asks you if the July $35 call in Table 1-1 has intrinsic value, you should ask yourself if there is an "immediate advantage" in being able to buy stock with the call for $35 when the stock is trading for $37.11. The answer is obviously yes. That means the $35 call has intrinsic value. How much intrinsic value? We just need to figure out the size of that advantage. If the stock is $37.11 and you can buy it for $35, there is $37.11 - $35 = $2.11 worth of advantage in the $35 call. The intrinsic value must be $2.11. Any remaining value in the option's price is due to time value. Because the option is trading for $2.70, there must be $2.70 - $2.11 = 59 cents worth of time value.

What about the $40 put? Again, we know there is an "immediate advantage" in being able to sell your stock for $40 rather than the current price of $37.11 so this put has intrinsic value. How much intrinsic value? Again, we just need to find out how big the advantage is. If the owner of that put can sell stock for $40 when the stock is trading for $37.11, there must be $40 - $37.11 = $2.89 worth of intrinsic value. Any remaining value in the option's price is due to time value. Because the option is trading for $3.20, there must be $3.20 - $2.89 = 31 cents worth of time value. Keep running through these steps and intrinsic and time values will become second nature to you.

Moneyness

We just covered the difference between time and intrinsic values and that allows us to understand some more option terminology. Options are generally classified by traders as *in-the-money*, *out-of-the-money*, or *at-the-money*, which are sometimes referred to as the "moneyness" of an option. An option with intrinsic value is in-the-money while an option with no intrinsic value is out-of-the-money. An option that is neither in nor out of the money is at-the-money.

The phrase "in-the-money" is generally used to imply that something is profitable. If someone says their new business is in-the-money, it means they are making money and that's really what this term is implying with options. For example, in Table 1-1, the $32.50 and $35 calls are in-the-money since both have intrinsic value. The owners of these calls are able to buy the stock for less than it is currently trading and therefore have some real value in holding the option. The $40 call is out-of-the-money since there is no immediate benefit in holding it; there is no intrinsic value. Technically speaking, an at-the-money option has a strike that exactly matches the price of the stock. But since it is rare that the stock price will exactly match a particular strike, we usually label the at-the-money strike as the one that is closest to the current stock price. In Table 1-1, we'd say that the

$37.50 strikes are at-the-money calls (even though they are technically slightly out-of-the-money).

If an option is very much in-the-money (usually by a couple of strike prices or more) the option is considered *deep-in-the-money*. If it is several strikes out-of-the-money it is considered to be *deep-out-of-the-money*.

For put options, the same definitions apply; all strikes with intrinsic value are in-the-money. For puts, this means that all strikes higher than the stock's price are in-the-money. In Table 1-1, the $40 puts are in-the-money since they have intrinsic value. The $35 puts are out-of-the-money since they have no intrinsic value. The at-the-money strike will be the same for calls and puts so the $37.50 puts would be considered the at-the-money strikes (even though they are technically slightly in-the-money).

The terms in-the-money, out-of-the-money, and at-the-money are used just for description purposes; it just makes it easier for option traders to describe types of options and strategies. For example, rather than tell someone that you bought some call options whose strike price is lower than the current value of the stock, it's easier to say you bought some in-the-money calls.

Table 1-4 describes the moneyness for calls and puts:

Table 1-4

CALL OPTIONS	
Moneyness	**Relationship to Stock**
In-the-money	Stock price > Strike price
At-the-money	Stock price = Strike price
Out-of-the-money	Stock price < Strike price

PUT OPTIONS	
Moneyness	**Relationship to Stock**
In-the-money	Stock price < Strike price
At-the-money	Stock price = Strike price
Out-of-the-money	Stock price > Strike price

Most option exchanges, such as the CBOE, always provide at least one in-the-money and one out-of-the-money option for each month. This means that as the stock moves to new highs (or lows) then new strikes will be added to each expiration month.

The moneyness of an option affects the amount of time premium present. In general, in-the-money and out-of-the-money options will have the smallest time premiums. At-the-money options have the greatest amount of time premium. In other words, at-the-money options contain the highest amount of time value and that value shrinks as we move toward the in-the-money or the out-of-the-money strikes.

 The at-the-money option has the highest time value. Time value shrinks as we move in-the-money or out-of-the-money.

For example, Table 1-5 shows the time values for the July calls and puts in Table 1-1:

Table 1-5

Strikes	Call Time Value	Put Time Value
$32.50	0.29	0.20
$35	0.59	0.50
$37.50	1.05	1.01
$40	0.35	0.31

Notice that the time values are relatively small for the in-the-money strikes ($32.50 call, $35 call, $40 put). The time values are also relatively small for out-of-the-money strikes ($40 call, $32.50 put, $35 put). It is the at-the-money strike ($37.50) that has the highest time value. Figure 1-6 shows the intrinsic and time values for only the call options in Table 1-4. You can see that the time value is very small for the $32.50 call because it is so far in-the-money. As we increase the strike price, the time premium gradually increases as well until we're only left with pure time premium.

Figure 1-6

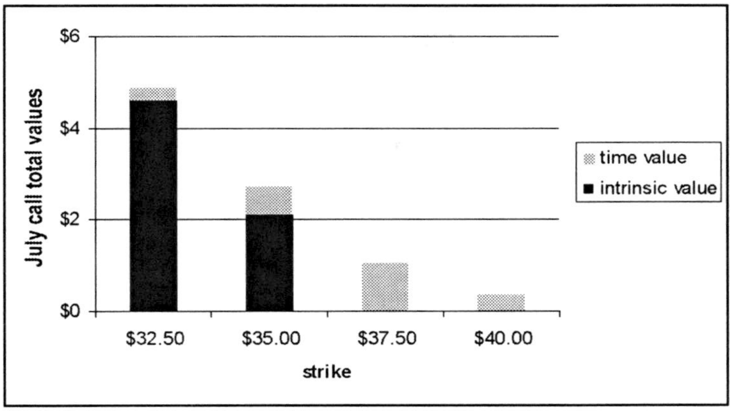

Parity

An option that is trading for purely intrinsic value (i.e., no time value) is trading at *parity*. For instance, assume that the underlying stock is trading for $46. If the $40 call is trading for $6 then it is comprised totally of intrinsic value and is therefore trading at parity. Options generally only trade at parity when there is little time remaining (usually a matter of hours).

Wasting Assets

We've learned that if you want a call or put option you must pay money for it. We also know that options expire at some time and that leads to an interesting question. Do options lose all of their value at expiration? After all, if the option is no longer good, how can it have any value?

While it is true that an option loses some of its value with each passing day, there is often a big misconception about how much of that premium is lost at expiration. There are traders who will tell you that *all* options become worthless at expiration and that is simply not true. In an earlier section "Intrinsic Values and Time Values," we said that all options must be worth at least their intrinsic value – and expiration time is no different. At expiration, all options lose only their *time value* but not their intrinsic value. It is only the time value portion of their price that slowly bleeds away with time. The intrinsic value remains intact. This is one of the reasons that it is so important to understand how to decompose an option into its intrinsic and time values. Certain strategies rely on the use of intrinsic values while others make use of the time values. If you want to trade, hedge, or invest with options, you need to know how much of each value is present at each strike price.

To make sure you understand this concept, let's look at the August \$35 call in Table 1-1, which is trading for \$3.60. We know there is \$37.11 - \$35 = \$2.11 worth of intrinsic value and that means that the remaining value, or \$3.60 - \$2.11 = 1.49 worth of time value. If you were to buy this call and eBay closed at the same price of \$37.11 at expiration, the \$35 call would still be worth the intrinsic value of \$2.11. It would not be worth zero. The only amount you would lose is the \$1.49 worth of time premium. Remember, traders are paying the additional \$1.49 over and above the immediate value because there is time remaining. Once time is gone (option is expired), then there can be no time value on the option but the intrinsic value will remain. In Figure 1-6, the intrinsic value is bold and the time value is shaded. It is only the shaded portion that erodes with time. (Bear in mind this doesn't mean that you cannot lose the intrinsic value. However, that value can be lost due to adverse stock movement only and not the passage of time.)

Because options lose some value with each passing day, they are called *wasting assets*. There are some traders who reject the use of options since part of the option's price deteriorates simply by the passage of time but that is a thoughtless reason. The car you drive loses value over time. The same is true for the fruits and vegetables you buy. What about the computer you use? It doesn't make sense to say that it's not worthwhile to invest in assets whose value depreciates over time. You just have to be careful in the way you use them. Nearly all assets deteriorate over time so don't back away from options just because a portion of their value depreciates over time. Even the expensive factories that General Motors, Dell Computer, or Intel has built all lose value with each passing day but the CEOs will tell you they have been very productive assets.

Time Decay

Time decay does not occur in a straight line over time. In other words, an at-the-money option with 30 days to expiration does not lose 1/30 of its value each day. Instead, it loses value slowly at first which then progressively accelerates more and more each day. This is called *exponential decay*. Figure 1-7 shows the price of a 90-day option where we assume that nothing changes except the passage of time.

You can see the rapid acceleration of decay as time gets near expiration – especially in the last thirty days.

Figure 1-7

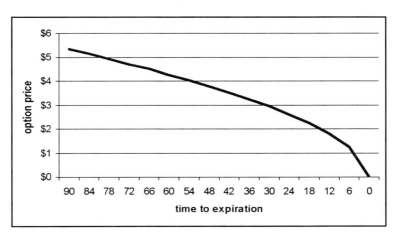

Some texts will show this chart in the reverse order with the numbers on the horizontal axis increasing from 0 to 90, which is probably more mathematically correct since the numbers are ascending as we move left to right. However, it makes it awkward to read since you must make time move from right to left as we approach expiration. It's usually easier for people to visualize time moving forward by moving from left to right. It's a matter of preference as to which type of chart you use. Just realize that as you continue reading about options that you may encounter time decay charts that appear backwards but it's just due to two different styles of presenting the same concept. The important point is that you understand that time decay is not linear. Because of this, it is usually to your advantage to buy longer periods of time and sell shorter periods of time. We will certainly revisit this concept later but just realize for now that an option's value does not decay in a straight line.

Before we leave this section, you might be wondering if there are any similarities between stocks and options. You might be surprised that options are similar to stock in many ways:

How Are Options Similar to Stocks?

- Options are securities.

- Options trade on national SEC (Securities Exchange Commission)-regulated exchanges.

- Option orders are transacted through market makers and retail participants with bids to buy and offers to sell and can be traded like any other security.

How Do Options Differ from Stocks?

- Options have an expiration date, whereas common stocks can be held forever (unless the company goes bankrupt). If an option is not exercised on or before expiration, it no longer exists and expires worthless.

- Options exist only as "book entry," which means they are held electronically. There are no certificates for options like there are for stocks.

- There is no limit to the number of options that can be traded on an underlying stock. Common stocks have a fixed number of shares outstanding.

- Options do not confer voting rights or dividends. They are strictly contracts to buy or sell the underlying stock or index. If you want a dividend or wish to vote the proxy, you need to exercise the call option.

||||||||||||||||||||||||||||||||||||||||||||||||||||||||||||||||||||||||||||||||||||||||

 Key Concepts

1) The intrinsic value of an option represents the "immediate benefit" in using the option.

2) Any value in the option above the intrinsic value is the time value.

3) In-the-money options have intrinsic value. Out-of-the-money options have no intrinsic value.

4) At-the-money options carry the highest time value.

5) You only lose your time value at option expiration. Any intrinsic value must remain.

||||||||||||||||||||||||||||||||||||||||||||||||||||||||||||||||||||||||||||||||||||||||

Chapter One Questions

1) **Call options give buyers the:**
   a) Obligation to buy stock
   b) Right to buy stock
   c) Obligation to sell stock
   d) Right to sell stock

2) **Put options give buyers the:**
   a) Obligation to buy stock
   b) Right to buy stock
   c) Obligation to sell stock
   d) Right to sell stock

3) **Option sellers:**
   a) Have rights
   b) Receive premiums
   c) Have obligations
   d) Both b and c

4) **One option contract generally controls how many shares of stock?**
   a) 25
   b) 50
   c) 75
   d) 100

5) **You bought an Intel $25 call. The "$25" figure is called the:**
   a) Contract value
   b) Moneyness
   c) Strike price or exercise price
   d) Intrinsic value

6) **The intrinsic value of an option represents the:**
   a) Time value
   b) Immediate benefit
   c) Contract value
   d) Strike price

7) **You are long an ABC $40 call. How much will it cost to exercise the call?**
    a) $40
    b) $400
    c) $4,000
    d) $40,000

8) **If you are "long" options:**
    a) You are not required to ever buy or sell the stock
    b) You are required to buy or sell the stock if assigned
    c) You are obligated to buy stock at some time
    d) You receive premiums

9) **Which of the following is true?**
    a) Long positions get assigned, short positions exercise
    b) Long positions exercise, short positions get assigned
    c) Long and short positions can exercise
    d) Long and short positions can get assigned

10) **XYZ is trading for $74. The XYZ $70 call is trading for $4.50. What are the intrinsic and time values?**
    a) $4 intrinsic, 50 cents time
    b) $4.50 intrinsic, $0 time
    c) 50 cents intrinsic, $4 time
    d) $0 intrinsic, $4.50 time

11) **ABC is trading for $107. The ABC $110 call is trading for $4. What are the intrinsic and time values?**
    a) $1 intrinsic, $3 time
    b) $3 intrinsic, $1 time
    c) $0 intrinsic, $4 time
    d) $4 intrinsic, $0 time

12) **An option is bidding $3 and asking $3.20. What does this mean?**
    a) The highest price that someone will pay is $3 and the lowest price at which someone will sell is $3.20.
    b) The highest price that someone will pay is $3.20 and the lowest price at which someone will sell is $3.

c)   You can currently buy the option for $3.20 and sell it for $3

d)   Both a and c

13) **The bid and ask represent the:**
a)   Lowest bidder and highest offer
b)   Highest bidder and highest offer
c)   Highest bidder and lowest offer
d)   Lowest bidder and lowest offer

14) **Microsoft is trading for $29 and the $30 put is trading for $2.50. This put is:**
a) $1 in-the-money
b) $1 out-of-the-money
c) $2.50 in-the-money
d) $2.50 out-of-the-money

15) **ABC stock is trading for $47. You just purchased an ABC $45 call for $3. If the stock remains at $47 at expiration, what is the amount, if any, you will lose on this option?**
a) $0
b) $1
c) $2
d) $3

16) **If you wish to exercise an option, you must:**
a)   Find a buyer or seller
b)   Do so only at expiration
c)   Submit assignment instructions
d)   Submit exercise instructions

17) **The OCC:**
a)   Guarantees an option's profit
b)   Is the buyer to every seller and seller to every buyer
c)   Acts as a mediator for disputes
d)   Requires you to become a member before trading options

18) **Options trade in units called:**
a)   Contracts
b)   Shares

c) Round lots

d) OCC units

19) **The last trading day for options is:**

a) The second Thursday of the expiration month

b) The second Friday of the expiration month

c) The third Friday of the expiration month

d) Saturday following the third Friday

20) **Because a portion of an option's value declines over time, options are referred to as:**

a) Physical delivery assets

b) Wasting assets

c) Linear assets

d) Cash delivery assets

21) **Which "style" are all equity options?**

a) Bermudan

b) Asian

c) European

d) American

22) **If you sell a put option, you have:**

a) The potential obligation to buy stock

b) The potential obligations to sell stock

c) The right to buy stock

d) The right to sell stock

23) **If you sell a call option, you have:**

a) The potential obligation to buy stock

b) The potential obligation to sell stock

c) The right to buy stock

d) The right to sell stock

24) **If you sell an option, you collect a premium. What happens to that premium if you are assigned?**

a) You only keep the premium if you are assigned

b) Option sellers do not receive the premium

c)   You keep the premium regardless of whether you're assigned or not

d)   You only keep the premium if you are not assigned

25)   If you buy or sell an option, you can escape your obligations by:

a)   Entering a reversing trade in a different month

b)   Entering a reversing trade at a different strike

c)   Entering the same trade again

d)   Entering a reversing trade

Chapter One - Answers

1)   Call options give buyers the:

b)   Right to buy stock

Long options always give the buyer some type of right. You will never incur an obligation by purchasing an option. Call options give buyers the right, not the obligation to buy stock. If you buy a call, you can purchase 100 shares of the underlying stock at any time for the strike price.

2)   Put options give buyers the:

d)   Right to sell stock

Put buyers have the right, not the obligation to sell stock. The put owner can sell 100 shares of stock and receive the strike price at any time through expiration.

3)   Option sellers:

d)   Both b and c

Option sellers receive a premium for accepting an obligation. The seller of a call has the potential obligation to sell shares of stock for the strike price while the put seller has the potential obligation to buy shares of stock for the strike price.

4)   One option contract generally controls how many shares of stock?

d)   100

When options are first issued, they generally control 100 shares of stock.

5)   You bought an Intel $25 call. The "$25" figure is called the:

c)   Strike price or exercise price

The price at which you are contracting to trade shares of stock is the exercise price. It is also called the strike price because that's where the deal was "struck."

6)   The intrinsic value of an option represents the:
b)   Immediate benefit

For call options, the intrinsic value is found by taking the stock price minus the strike price, assuming it is a positive amount. For put options, we take the strike price minus the stock price, assuming it is positive. With the stock at $55, a $50 call has $55 - $50 = $5 of intrinsic value. A $60 call has no intrinsic value since $55 - $60 = *negative* $5. Likewise, a $50 put has no intrinsic value since $50 - $55 = *negative* $5. The intrinsic value represents the amount of "immediate benefit" to the owner. If the stock is $55, the $50 call owner is better off by $5 since he can pay $50 for the stock rather than $55. The $60 put holder can sell his stock for $5 more than the current market price of $55 so is better off by $5 as well. Whenever you are trying to figure out the intrinsic value, think if there is an immediate benefit in owning that option. If there is, it has intrinsic value. The intrinsic value is also the amount that the option is in-the-money.

7)   You are long an ABC $40 call. How much will it cost to exercise the call?
c) $4,000

Each contract controls 100 shares of stock and you have the right to buy it for $40 per share. Therefore, it will cost 100 shares * $40 per share = $4,000 to exercise the call. In return, you will receive 100 shares of ABC.

8)   If you are "long" options:
a)   You are not required to ever buy or sell the stock

If you are long options, whether calls or puts, you have rights. This means you are not required to ever buy or sell stock. You can buy or sell stock if you choose. It is your *option* to do so.

9)   Which of the following is true?
b)   Long positions exercise, short positions get assigned

Long positions have the rights. It is the long position that decides whether or not to exercise. If the long position exercises then the short position must oblige. The short position has the obligation.

10) XYZ is trading for $74. The XYZ $70 call is trading for $4.50. What are the intrinsic and time values?
a) $4 intrinsic, 50 cents time

There is an immediate advantage in owning this call since it gives the buyer the right to pay $70 for a stock that is trading for $74. Specifically, there is a

$4 advantage so that is the intrinsic value. The remaining 50 cents of value is due to time.

11) ABC is trading for $107. The ABC $110 call is trading for $4. What are the intrinsic and time values?

   c) $0 intrinsic, $4 time

There is no immediate benefit in holding this call since it gives the buyer the right to pay $110 for a stock that is currently trading for $107. Therefore, there is no intrinsic value to this option. However, this does not mean the option has no value. Because time remains on the option, the stock does have a chance of rising above $110. All of this option's value is due to the fact that time remains on the option.

12) An option is bidding $3 and asking $3.20. What does this mean?

   d)   Both a and c

The bid represents the highest price that someone is willing to pay. In other words, it represents the highest bidder. The asking price represents the lowest price at which someone will sell. Because someone is willing to pay $3, this means we can sell to that person if we wish to sell this option. Likewise, because someone is willing to sell for $3.20, we can buy the option for this price.

13) The bid and ask represent the:

   c)   Highest bidder and lowest offer.

14) Microsoft is trading for $29 and the $30 put is trading for $2.50. This put is:

   a) $1 in-the-money

Put options give the holder the right to sell stock. Because this put allows the holder to sell for $30 when the stock is trading for $29, there is a $1 immediate benefit in holding this put. Therefore, this put is $1 in-the-money.

15) ABC stock is trading for $47. You just purchased an ABC $45 call for $3. If the stock remains at $47 at expiration, what is the amount, if any, you will lose on this option?

   b) $1

This call has $2 intrinsic value and $1 time value. If the stock is $47 at expiration, this option will be worth the $2 intrinsic value so the most you could lose is the $1 time value. Remember, the key to this question is that the stock remains at $47 at expiration. It is true that the most you could ever lose on this (or any) option is the amount paid, or $3 in this example. But the question is assuming the stock remains at $47. The only way you could lose more than the $1 time value is if the stock's price falls below $47.

16) If you wish to exercise an option, you must:

   d)   Submit exercise instructions

You are free to exercise an equity option at any time and the OCC guarantees the performance so there's no need to find a buyer or seller. The only thing you must do is submit exercise instructions to your broker which is done with a simple phone call.

17) The OCC:

   b)   Is the buyer to every seller and seller to every buyer

The OCC acts as a middleman to every transaction. If you buy an option, you are really buying it from the OCC. If you sell an option, you are selling it to the OCC.

18) Options trade in units called:

   a)   Contracts

Options trade in units called "contracts" because that's what they are – contracts between two people to buy and sell shares of stock. Stock trades in "shares" while options trade in "contracts."

19) The last trading day for options is:

   c)   The third Friday of the expiration month

The last trading day is the third Friday of the expiration month. Technically, options expire on Saturday following the third Friday but the last "trading" day is the third Friday.

20) Because a portion of an option's value declines over time, options are referred to as:

   b)   Wasting assets

A wasting asset is one whose price declines with the passage of time. Some options decline very little while others decline much more and much faster. Regardless, all options are classified as a wasting asset.

21) Which "style" are all equity options?

   d)   American

All equity options are American style, which means you can exercise them at any time prior to expiration. Bermudan and Asian options are actually styles too but they fall under the category of exotic options.

22) If you sell a put option, you have:

    a)   The potential obligation to buy stock

Put sellers have the potential obligations to buy stock. They must buy the stock only if the long put holder decides to exercise.

23) If you sell a call option, you have:

    b)   The potential obligation to sell stock

    Call sellers have to sell stock only if the long call holder exercises.

24) If you sell an option, you collect a premium. What happens to that premium if you are assigned?

    c)   You keep the premium regardless of whether you're assigned or not

Option sellers always keep the premium regardless of what happens. That is their fee for accepting some type of obligation (risk).

25) If you buy or sell an option, you can escape your obligations by:

    d)   Entering a reversing trade

You can always get out of an option contract by entering a reversing trade of the same month and strike. If you originally purchased an ABC $50 call you would enter a reversing trade by selling an ABC $50 call.

Chapter Two

Option Pricing Principles

We've just been introduced to real call and put options and now understand how to interpret their prices when looking at quotes. But did you notice in Table 1-1 that some options are more expensive than others? Why is that? And is there a pattern we should understand? This chapter takes you through some of the most important pricing principles of options. Understanding these principles is essential for mastering option strategies.

 Principle #1:
Lower Strike Calls (and Higher Strike Puts)
Must be More Expensive

If you look at the prices in Table 1-1, you'll notice that the lower strike calls are more expensive than the higher strikes. This will always be true assuming, of course, that all other factors are the same. That is, we must be looking at strikes on the same underlying stock and expiration month. For example, Table 2-1 shows the call prices for July from Table 1-1. Why do the prices get cheaper as we move to higher strikes?

Table 2-1

JULY CALL OPTIONS	
Strike	Price
$32.50	$4.90
$35	$2.70
$37.50	$1.05
$40	$0.35

There are many mathematical reasons why this relationship must hold and we'll look at one shortly. However, you already know enough to figure it out intuitively by thinking back to the pizza coupon analogy. Imagine that you walked in to buy a pizza and found the following two coupons lying on the counter:

Notice that both coupons control exactly the same thing (one large three-topping pizza) and have the same expiration date. The only difference is that the coupon on the left allows you to buy the pizza for $10.00 while the one on the right gives you the right to buy it for $20.00. If both pizza coupons allow you to do exactly the same thing but one just allows you to do it for a cheaper price, then obviously you would choose to pay the cheaper price. You should pick up the coupon that gives you the right to buy the pizza for $10.00.

The same thought process occurs in the options markets. For example, both the $32.50 call and the $35 call in Table 2-1 allow the trader to buy 100 shares of eBay so there are absolutely no differences in what those two coupons allow you to buy. However, the $32.50 allows you to buy the 100 shares for less money. Traders realize the benefit in paying $32.50 rather than $35 so will compete in the market for that coupon. It is a more desirable coupon so traders and investors will bid its price higher than the $35 coupon. The same process happens all the way up the line. Each successively lower strike is bid to a higher price. Or conversely, each higher strike is bid lower than the strike below it. When you get into strategies, there will be times when you need to figure out which call option is more valuable. You can always find the answer by asking yourself which is more desirable. The answer to that question is the one that has the *lower* strike price. As our first Pricing Principle states: Lower strike calls must be more valuable.

This same reasoning drives many decisions in the financial markets. If it is more desirable then it must cost more with all other factors constant. Consider government bonds. Why are government bond yields lower when compared to the same face amount and maturity as a corporate bond? The reason is that government bonds are guaranteed; corporate bonds are not. So if a government bond and corporate bond both mature to $10,000 at the same time, which would you rather have? Again, there is no difference in what either of these bonds promise. Both promise $10,000 to be delivered to you at the same time. However, there is a big difference in the ability to carry out that promise. The government bond is far more secure so it is *more desirable* to investors. Investors will therefore pay a higher price for the government bond. And when bond prices rise, yields fall. That's why government bonds will always have a lower yield than corporate bonds of the same face value and maturity.

When first attempting to understand option prices, you must remember that "more desirable" equates to more money with all other factors the same. If you do, you'll understand many aspects of strategies that many traders must memorize.

Now let's take a look at why *higher* strike puts are more expensive. Table 2-2 is a listing of the July put options from Table 1-1:

Table 2-2

JULY PUT OPTIONS	
Strike	**Price**
$32.50	$0.20
$35	$0.50
$37.50	$1.40
$40	$3.20

With the put options, the reverse appears to be true and the higher strike puts are more expensive. Why does this pattern occur? The reasoning is similar as it is for calls but you must remember that put options allow you to sell stock. If all prices were the same, which put option would you rather have? In other words, which strike price is more desirable? Obviously, it is more desirable to sell your shares for $40 than for $37.50 so traders will bid the prices of the $40 puts higher than that of the $37.50 puts and the $37.50 puts will be bid higher than the $35 puts and so on down the line. Higher strike puts will always be more expensive than lower strike puts with all other factors the same (same underlying stock and expiration).

To better understand the relationship between put strikes and price, think about insurance. If you have a $30,000 car and want to insure it for the full value, you will pay a certain premium. However, if you accept a $500 deductible and only want insurance for the remaining value, you will pay a lower premium. If you accept a $1,000 deductible, you will pay even less. In exchange for assuming some of the risk, you will pay a lower premium. In other words, the higher the value of your car insurance, the higher the premium you will pay.

This same relationship holds for put options. In Table 2-2, if a trader owns 100 shares of eBay and buys the July $37.50 put, he is attempting to insure the stock for more than its current value of $37.11. For that coverage he will pay $1.40 premium. However, if he chooses to assume some of the risk, he can pay a lower premium. How can he assume some risk? He can choose lower coverage by selecting a lower strike price. For instance, if he chooses the July $35 put, he will pay on 50 cents for the coverage. But in exchange for that lower premium, he is assuming the first $2.11 in damage since the protection on his stock does not start until a stock price of $35.

As we've said before, put options can be thought of as a form of insurance. If you want high coverage (high strike prices) you will pay a larger premium for that. If you choose to accept some risk (lower strike prices) you will pay a lower premium. In other words, high strike puts cost more than low strike puts.

There's another way to understand why lower strike calls and higher strike puts must be more valuable. We can do so by looking at different strikes from a probability standpoint. Let's assume that a stock can only move between $0 and $100 with all prices equally likely at expiration. If you own a $50 call, then there is a 50% chance that you will have intrinsic value at expiration. In other words, the $50 call acts as an asset to "catch" all stock prices to the right of the strike. Obviously, the more prices it can catch, the greater the value of the call. What can we do if we want to catch more strikes? We can shift to a lower strike price such as the $25 strike as shown in the following diagram:

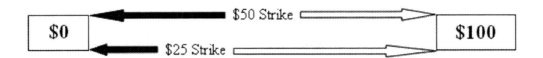

If we lower the strike from $50 to $25, you can see that we have far more area to the right for the stock price to land at expiration as shown by the white arrows. This shows that the $25 call must be more valuable than the $50 call because it allows the trader to potentially catch more intrinsic value. The reverse reasoning shows that higher strike puts must be more valuable since they catch more stock prices to the left of the strike price.

Stick with whichever method helps you to understand or visualize why lower strike calls and higher strike puts must be more valuable.

We've shown in two ways that lower strike calls and higher strike puts must always be the more expensive strikes. That's a pretty bold statement to make. While it may make sense as a practical argument, will these relationships always hold? The answer is yes. The reason is due to a process called *arbitrage*. Arbitrage is a process where "free" money can be made and that is a powerful incentive to keep a watchful eye on prices. Traders who search for these opportunities are called arbitrageurs (or arbs, for short). How does arbitrage work? Assume for a moment that the $32.50 call in Table 2-1 is $4.90 but that the $35 call is, instead, priced at $5.00. In other words, the $35 call is priced higher than the $32.50 call, which is something we said cannot be possible in the real markets. This is the perfect setup for an arbitrage opportunity since the more valuable call ($32.50) is cheaper than the less valuable one ($35).

In order to exploit this situation, arbitrageurs generally buy the underpriced option and simultaneously sell the higher priced option. Although simply buying the underpriced option or selling the overpriced one individually will provide a theoretical edge, it is not enough to complete the arbitrage. In this example, the $32.50 call is a cheaper *relative* to the $35 call; however, just buying the $32.50 call does not guarantee a profit because that option could still lose if the stock's price falls below $32.50 at expiration.

In order to capitalize on the mispricing, arbitrageurs would buy the $32.50 call and spend $4.90. Then they would immediately sell the $35 call and receive $5.00 for a net credit of 10 cents to their account:

Buy $32.50 call	=	- $4.90
Sell $35 call	=	+$5.00
Net credit	=	10 cents

A net credit of 10 cents may not seem like a lot of money but arbitrageurs do things on a very big scale. They may send hundreds of thousands or even millions of dollars worth of trades to take advantage of such a discrepancy. The sale of the $35 call more than pays for the $32.50 call so the arbitrageur has zero money invested. In other words, the sale of the $35 call more than financed his purchase of the $32.50 call. In fact, he was even paid 10 cents to take this trade. Now think about the arbitrageur's rights and obligations.

The arbitrageur now has the right to buy stock for $32.50 (since he bought the $32.50 call) and may have the obligation to sell for $35 (since he sold the $35 call), which means he could potentially make a $2.50 profit. But because he got paid 10 cents to execute the trade, his maximum gain is $2.60, which occurs if the stock price is greater than $35 at expiration. However, it's also possible for the stock price to fall below $32.50 at expiration so that both options expire worthless. That's okay too since the arbitrageur always keeps the 10-cent credit. (Remember, when you sell an option, the money you take in from the sale is yours to keep no matter what happens to the stock or option.) He might make as much as $2.60 but cannot earn less than the 10-cent credit. If the stock price closes somewhere between $32.50 and $35 at expiration then the arbitrageur's profit will fall somewhere between 10 cents and $2.60.

The arbitrageur cannot lose and has therefore capitalized on a trade that resulted in a guaranteed profit for no out-of-pocket expense – and that's the definition of arbitrage. We must include the phrase "for no out-of-pocket expense" otherwise the purchase of a government bond would qualify as arbitrage since it produces a guaranteed return. The difference between arbitrage and a bond purchase is that you must spend money on the bond and wait in order to get that guaranteed return. With arbitrage, you are paid to take the guaranteed trade.

Arbitrageurs will continue to execute the above trades – buy the $32.50 call and simultaneously sell the $35 call – as long as the opportunity is there. Unfortunately for the arbitrageur, their actions also guarantee that the opportunity will eventually disappear. As they buy the $32.50 calls they put upward pressure on its price. As they sell the $35 calls they put downward pressure on its price. Eventually the $32.50 calls will be more expensive than the $35 calls and that's when the opportunity disappears. It is the arbitrageurs who guarantee that lower strike calls will always be more valuable than higher strike calls (and that higher strike puts will be more valuable than lower strike puts).

 With all else being equal, LOWER strike calls and HIGHER strike puts must be more valuable.

Arbitrage is a high-stakes game involving computerized programs that search and execute the proper trades to exploit any mispricings. As a retail investor, you will never be able to participate in arbitrage. The speed at which arbitrage is carried out is too fast and complex for the tools and software that retail investors have to work with. In addition, the arbitrage opportunities that do arise are usually for pennies and retail investors pay too high of a commission to make arbitrage worthwhile. The big brokerage houses such as Merrill Lynch, Solomon Brothers, and JP Morgan are the ones doing the arbitraging. In fact, around 1995 there was an article in the *Wall Street Journal* about a Japanese firm engaged in *triangular arbitrage*. Triangular arbitrage is a currency arbitrage that is executed by purchasing one currency, converting it to another, and then immediately converting it back to the original currency. The speed at which these transactions is lightning fast and the article went on to say that this firm paid $23 million dollars to gain one second quicker access time to currency quotes. That's how big the stakes are and how fast the game is played. (So don't get any ideas of logging into your brokerage account and participating in arbitrage.)

There are many who feel that arbitrage is "unfair" because there's something that doesn't seem right about being able to make free money from the market. But the arbitrageurs provide an important economic function in that they make sure the relative prices stay fair for the rest of us. You don't need to understand the process of arbitrage to trade options. However, you do need to understand that lower strike calls and higher strike puts will always be more expensive. That's a big key to understanding many strategies.

Exercise

Go to www.cboe.com and check out option quotes on several stocks. Are lower strike calls always more expensive than higher strikes? Are higher strike puts always more expensive than lower strikes? What about for different expiration months? Explain in your own words why this happens.

Principle #2:
More Time Means More Money

Another principle of option trading is that longer term options will be more expensive than shorter term ones. As before, this assumes that all other factors remain constant; we must be talking about the same underlying stock and strike price.

Take a look at Table 2-3, which shows the July and August call options from Table 1-1. Notice that the July calls are more expensive that the August calls. Why are the August calls more expensive? (Hint: For any strike, think about which is more desirable.)

Table 2-3

CALL OPTIONS		
Strike	**July**	**August**
$32.50	$4.90	$5.50
$35	$2.70	$3.60
$37.50	$1.05	$2.10
$40	$0.35	$1.10

You guessed it. The markets realize there is an advantage in having time on your side since the price of the option has a better chance of increasing in value. Think about stock prices. If you buy a stock today for $50, is there a better chance for price appreciation after one day or after one month? Obviously, you have a better chance for the stock to increase in value over a one-month period. That's all this principle is saying. The market realizes that there is a better chance for the August $32.50 call to rise in value when compared to the July $32.50 call and so will place a higher value on it.

Since all other factors between the two calls are the same, the only difference between the July call for $4.90 and August call for $5.50 is the value of the additional time. Why 60 cents extra value? That's a question for which we will never know the answer. That is up to the market to decide; it's up to people like you and me. Every day we place orders to buy and sell options, we're either putting upward or downward pressure on their prices. At the time these quotes were taken, the market was placing 60 cents extra value on the August $32.50 call over the July $32.50 call. We can be sure that longer term options will always cost more than shorter term options but we cannot be sure by how much. All we can be sure of is that with all else constant (same underlying stock and strike price), longer term options will cost you more money.

Put options are also more valuable with additional time. The reason is that stock prices are equally likely to rise and fall. A $50 stock, for example, is equally likely to rise *or fall* by $5. Because put options act like all options but in the opposite direction, puts must also be more valuable with additional time.

Will longer term options always be more expensive than short term options? The answer is yes and the reason is arbitrage. Let's assume the July $32.50 call is $4.90 but that the August $32.50 call is $4.75. In other words, a longer term option is trading below that of a shorter term option, which is something we said should not happen. Arbitrageurs would sell the July $32.50 call and receive a $4.90 credit and then use $4.75 of that credit to buy the August $32.50 call thus taking in a credit of 15 cents:

Sell July $32.50	=	+$4.90
Buy August $32.50	=	-$4.75
Net credit	=	15 cents

Now think about their rights and obligations. They have the right to buy stock for $32.50 and may have to sell it for $32.50, which is a wash. If that happens, the arbitrageurs keep the 15-cent credit. However, it is also possible that the July contract expires worthless (the stock falls below $32.50) and the arbitrageur still owns the August contract, which could rise in value after July. This means that the arbitrageur is guaranteed to make at least 15 cents and could potentially make much more. This is a riskless opportunity for which the arbitrageur paid no money. As the arbitrageur buys the August calls and sells the July calls, he will put buying pressure on August and selling pressure on July eventually making August more expensive than July. At that point, the arbitrage opportunity disappears. A similar set of transactions occur for put options.

 With all else being equal, more time to expiration means higher option prices.

As before, you don't need to understand this arbitrage process to trade options. Just understand that there is a very real force that assures us that longer term options (calls or puts) will cost more than the shorter term ones assuming all other factors are the same (same underlying stock and same strike price). That part you do need to understand.

Square-Root Rule

While options get more expensive with increases in time, there is another mathematical boundary that option prices closely follow. That is, it takes about four times the amount of time in order to double the at-the-money option's price. For example, if a one-month, at-the-money option is trading for $1 then the four-month at-the-money option will be roughly $2. While it may seem that doubling time will double the option's price it actually takes a quadrupling of time. If you get more into the mathematics of option pricing, you will find that option prices are proportional to the square root of time. If time increases by a factor of four then the option's price doubles – a factor that is exactly the square root of four. If you double the time on an option then the option's price will rise by the square root of two, or about 1.41 times. If the one-month at-the-money option is worth $1 then the two-month at-the-money option is worth $1.41.

This means that if you are a buyer of an option that it is a progressively better deal for you to buy time. While options get more expensive over time, they get cheaper *per unit of time*. In our example, the one-month option costs $1 per month. The four-month option costs $2 for 4 months of time, or 50 cents per month. So while the four-month option is more expensive in total dollars, it is actually cheaper per unit of time. Think of it like buying soft drinks by the case at the grocery store. A case of Coke will cost more in terms of total dollars but is cheaper per can (per unit). The square-root rule implies that buyers should buy more time as they become progressively a better deal. Sellers should sell short-term options. With all else being equal, buyers are better off buying one four-month option rather than four one-month options. The opposite is true for sellers.

Exercise

Go to www.cboe.com and check out option quotes on several stocks. Are longer term options always more expensive than shorter term options? Explain in your own words why this happens.

Principle #3:
At Expiration, All Options Must be Worth either Zero or their Intrinsic Value.

At the end of the first chapter, we said that any intrinsic value must remain with an option at expiration. This means that if an option is in-the-money at expiration the price must be the difference between the stock price and the exercise price, or $S - E$. For example, if the stock closes at $53 at expiration, the $50 call must be worth exactly $3 since there is $3 worth of intrinsic value and no time value left. Because a long option cannot have negative value then all at-the-money and out-of-the-money calls expire worthless.

To restate it differently, a call option can only be worth one of two values at expiration: It is either worth the intrinsic value (intrinsic value + zero time value) or it is worth nothing (zero intrinsic value + zero time value).

Using our previous example, if the stock is $53, then how can we be sure the $50 call must be worth $53 - $50 = $3 at expiration? Once again, the answer is arbitrage. In order to understand the basics of the arbitrage, think back to the pizza coupons. Imagine that pizza coupons do have value and are traded in the streets (the marketplace). Now assume that pizzas are $15 and a $10 coupon is available, which means the coupon has $5 intrinsic value. However, let's assume the coupon is trading for only $4. Can anything be done to capitalize on the missing $1 intrinsic value? The answer is yes. The way the market corrects for this missing value is that enterprising individuals would buy the pizza coupon for $4 and then take it to the store and buy the pizza for $10. They would have spent a total of $14 to get the pizza ($4 for the coupon + $10 for the pizza). Then they'd walk out in the street and sell the pizza for $15, thus making a $1 guaranteed profit. This $1 profit is exactly the amount of the missing intrinsic value. As individuals figure this out, they will compete in the market for these coupons thus raising its price. At what point will the competition for coupons stop? When the price of the coupon reaches $5 (or more), which means that the full intrinsic value is now reflected in the price of the coupon.

At expiration, all in-the-money options must trade for their intrinsic value otherwise a similar set of transactions would take place in the market by arbitrageurs. For instance, assume that the stock is $53 and the $50 call is trading for $2 in the final minutes of trading, which means there is $1 missing from the intrinsic value. Arbitrageurs would short the stock and buy the call for a net credit of $51 to their account:

Short stock	=	+$53
Buy $50 call	=	-$2
Net credit	=	$51

Because they've shorted the stock, they have an obligation to buy it back and can do so by exercising the call and paying $50 out of the $51 credit they received. This leaves them with a guaranteed *minimum* profit of $1 for no out-of-pocket expense, which is exactly the amount of missing intrinsic value. Of course, if the stock price falls below $50, the arbitrageur would just let the call expire worthless and buy the stock in the open market to close out the short position. This would result in a profit greater than one dollar. So whether the stock price rises or falls, the arbitrageur is guaranteed a minimum profit of one dollar. As with all arbitrages, the arbitrageurs' actions restore the proper pricing relationship. In this example, the above transactions (shorting the stock, buying the call) will put selling pressure on the stock and buying pressure on the call until the full $3 intrinsic value is restored.

Expiration Values for Put Options

At expiration, put options must be worth either zero or their intrinsic value, which is found by taking the exercise price minus the stock price, or E - S. For example, assume the stock is $53. The $60 put must be trading for $60 - $53 = $7 at expiration. If the stock is above $60 at expiration, the put will expire worthless since there is no reason to exercise a put and collect $60 when you can just sell the stock in the open market for more money.

If a put option is in-the-money (stock is below the strike price) at expiration and not trading for the intrinsic value then arbitrage is possible. Assume the stock is $53 but that the $60 put is trading for only $5 thus missing $2 of intrinsic value. Arbitrageurs would buy the stock and buy the put for a net cash outlay of $58:

Buy stock   =   -$53
Buy $60 put   =   -$5
Net debit   =   -$58

The arbitrageur would then immediately exercise the put and receive the $60 strike price thus making an immediate, guaranteed *minimum* profit of $2 for no cash outlay, which is exactly the amount of missing intrinsic value. The missing intrinsic value can only be restored if the stock price rises to $55 or if the put price rises to $7 or some combination of the two. Notice that the above transactions (buying stock, buying puts) will place buying pressure on the stock and the $60 put and those are the forces necessary to restore intrinsic value.

So at expiration, options can only be one of two values: zero or intrinsic value. Now you see why all in-the-money options must retain intrinsic value at expiration. It is not a matter of courtesy or tradition by the market makers; it is forced through the process of arbitrage.

 All options must be worth either zero or intrinsic value at expiration.

Theory versus Reality

Okay, hopefully you're convinced that an option must always trade for at least its intrinsic value. Arbitrage is the theory that supports that conviction. However, the reality is that there are really two prices for an option – the bid and ask. The theory holds only for the asking price and not for the bid. For instance, assume that a $50 call option is close to expiration with the stock at $55. Because the option's price is approaching a pure intrinsic value of exactly $5, the market maker will not bid $5 for it. Instead, the market maker may bid $4.80 so that he can sell it for the $5 intrinsic value and make a 20-cent profit. If you sell this $50 call at the bid, there is 20 cents worth of missing intrinsic value. Most traders have observed this near expiration and just accept it as part of the way the system works. However, there is a way to get it back and it is similar to how the arbitrageurs do it.

Here's how to do it: If you are ever selling a call option that is bidding below intrinsic value, all you have to do is *short the stock and then immediately exercise the option*. Since you already own the call, you do not need to purchase it like the arbitrageurs do. However, the idea is the same. By selling the stock and exercising the option, you can gain back the missing intrinsic value.

Using our example, let's say you wish to sell 10 contracts of the $50 call that is bidding $4.80. If you sell at the bid, you'll receive $4,800. But if you short the stock and exercise the call, you'll get a net credit of $5,000:

Short stock	=	+$55,000
Exercise call	=	-$50,000
Net credit	=	$5,000

This represents a $200 difference from selling at the bid price of $4.80. The reason is that the bid price is missing 20 cents worth of intrinsic value, which equals 0.20 * 10 contracts * 100 shares per contract = $200. So in this example, for the commission of shorting the stock, you can pick up an extra $200.

You're probably thinking that this sounds good but with one problem. What if you don't have the $50,000 to exercise the call? The answer is you do have it. You'll get it from the $55,000 credit you'll receive from shorting the stock. The fact that there is intrinsic value in the option tells us that the value of the stock must be greater than the strike. Therefore, shorting the stock will always provide enough funds to pay for the exercise.

Also, there is no margin requirement on the short stock position since you own a long call with a lower strike price, which protects you from any upside movement in the stock. The point is that there is absolutely no reason to not grab the extra $200. For two small commissions – one to short the stock and another to exercise the option – you can restore your intrinsic value in the call option. Most firms today charge very low commissions to buy or sell stock but charge significantly higher commissions to buy or sell options. In most cases, you'll find that commission to short the stock and exercise the option will still be cheaper than the commission charged for selling the call. Exercising an option is normally charged as a regular stock transaction so it is usually worth your while to short the stock and then exercise the call to collect the missing intrinsic value.

If you have a put option with missing intrinsic value, you simply *buy the stock and then exercise the put.* For example, assume you have 10 $50 puts with the stock at $45 near expiration. The market maker might only bid $4.80 for this put even though it is theoretically worth $5. You can capture the missing 20-cents of intrinsic value by purchasing the stock and then immediately exercising the put:

Buy stock	=	-$45,000
Exercise put	=	+$50,000
Net credit	=	$5,000

By exercising the put, you collect the exercise price of $50. And because you only paid $45 for the stock, your net gain is the $5 difference. Once again, you may be wondering where you'll get the money to pay $45,000 for the stock. The answer is that you will receive it once you exercise the put. Because the OCC guarantees that the transaction will go through there is no reason for your broker to not allow it. In this example, for one small commission to buy the stock, you picked up an extra $200 for closing your $50 puts.

In the previous two examples, we assumed there was 20 cents worth of missing intrinsic value. How realistic is this figure? It's actually quite common and sometimes you'll find the options are missing much more. For example, Table 2-4 shows Cyberonics (CYBX) call and put quotes taken on expiration day June 18, 2004:

Table 2-4: CYBX Quotes Taken on Expiration Day

CYBX (Nasdaq)												37.55 -0.85
Jun 18,2004 @ 10:06 ET (Data 15 Minutes Delayed)							Bid 37.51	Ask 37.60	Size 2x8	Vol 1050155		

Calls	Last Sale	Net	Bid	Ask	Vol	Open Int	Puts	Last Sale	Net	Bid	Ask	Vol	Open Int
04 Jun 12.50 (QAJ FV-E)	25.50	pc	24.50	25.50	0	176	04 Jun 12.50 (QAJ RV-E)	0.05	pc	0	0.05	0	11018
04 Jun 15.00 (QAJ FC-E)	23.40	pc	22.00	23.00	0	1918	04 Jun 15.00 (QAJ RC-E)	0.05	pc	0	0.05	0	11925
04 Jun 17.50 (QAJ FW-E)	21.50	pc	19.50	20.50	0	3379	04 Jun 17.50 (QAJ RW-E)	0.05	pc	0	0.05	0	5805
04 Jun 20.00 (QAJ FD-E)	19.10	pc	17.30	18.00	0	10772	04 Jun 20.00 (QAJ RD-E)	0.05	pc	0	0.05	0	7436
04 Jun 22.50 (QAJ FX-E)	15.20	-1.00	14.50	15.50	4	8899	04 Jun 22.50 (QAJ RX-E)	0.05	pc	0	0.05	0	7303
04 Jun 25.00 (QAJ FE-E)	12.50	-1.50	12.10	13.00	2	13336	04 Jun 25.00 (QAJ RE-E)	0.05	pc	0	0.05	0	5990
04 Jun 30.00 (QAJ FF-E)	7.20	-1.80	7.10	8.10	1	17964	04 Jun 30.00 (QAJ RF-E)	0.05	pc	0	0.05	0	9275
04 Jun 35.00 (QAJ FG-E)	2.55	-1.25	2.50	3.00	101	4737	04 Jun 35.00 (QAJ RG-E)	0.10	-0.10	0.10	0.25	235	2853
04 Jun 40.00 (QAJ FH-E)	0.15	-0.25	0.05	0.15	774	5896	04 Jun 40.00 (QAJ RH-E)	2.60	+0.70	2.25	2.70	115	722

Notice that the stock was asking $37.60, which means the June $20 call should be worth $17.60. The bid price is only $17.30, which is 30 cents too low. Now look at the June $25 call, which should be worth $12.60 but is only bidding $12.10, which is 50 cents too low. The June $30 call is also bidding 50 cents below intrinsic value. The asking price for all of these strikes is greater than the intrinsic value, which is why you cannot arbitrage the prices. However, if you already own the call, you can short the stock and exercise to capture the missing intrinsic value.

Now look at the June $40 puts. With the stock at $37.60, these should be worth $2.40 at expiration but they are only bidding $2.25, which means they are missing 15 cents of intrinsic value. As with the calls, the $2.70 asking price more than reflects the intrinsic value so you cannot arbitrage these prices. But if you already own the put, you can buy the stock and immediately exercise the put to collect the full intrinsic value.

How bad can these discrepancies get? One day in 1999 while working on an active trader option's team, a client called in to sell 20 of his Juniper Networks (JNPR) Feb $50 calls. Table 2-5 shows the quotes and you can see that the Feb $50 calls were bidding $32 1/4 (this is when stocks and options were still quoted in fractions).

Table 2-5: JNPR Quotes Taken on Expiration Day

JNPR - JUNIPER NETWORKS							
LAST	NET CHG	BID	ASK	HIGH	LOW	VOL	TRADE TIME
83 5/8	-8 9/16	83 5/8	83 11/16	84 9/16	80 3/4	13,475,300	11:28:24

			BID	ASK	VOL	OPEN INT
Feb-50	2001	JUXBJ	32 1/4	33 1/2	0	61
Feb-55	2001	JUXBK	27 1/4	28 1/2	0	0
Feb-60	2001	JUXBL	22 1/4	23 1/2	0	0
Feb-65	2001	JUXBM	17 3/8	18 3/8	0	8
Feb-70	2001	JUXBN	12 3/8	13 3/8	2	82
Feb-75	2001	JUXBO	7 5/8	8 3/8	4	188
Feb-80	2001	JUXBP	3 3/8	3 7/8	1591	1,172
Feb-85	2001	JUXBQ	7/8	1	477	1,462
Feb-90	2001	JUXBR	1/8	1/4	92	6,049
Feb-95	2001	JUXBS	0	3/8	130	2,312
Feb-100	2001	JUYBT	0	1/8	66	4,389

I noticed that the stock was bidding $83 5/8, which means that his calls should be worth $83 5/8 - $50 strike = $33 5/8 rather than the $32 1/4 they were bidding. They were missing $1 3/8, or $1.375 worth of intrinsic value! What do you suppose we did? Hopefully you said short the stock and exercise the calls. Doing so brought in an additional 20 contracts * $1.375 * 100 shares per contract = $2,750 less some commissions for shorting the stock and exercising the call.

As you start trading options, you'll find that 20-cent (or greater) discrepancies occur all the time near expiration. You'll even find lesser, but still viable, discrepancies with as much as a week until expiration.

To capture this missing intrinsic value, some of the newer, more progressive, firms have an order called "exercise and cover," which automatically uses the technique we are describing. It's a way for you to quickly submit an order to sell the shares and then immediately exercise in order to capture any missing intrinsic value on your option. If you are trading even a few option contracts, this method of capturing intrinsic value near expiration day can be quite profitable. Depending on the commissions you're paying and the number of contracts you're closing it pays to check what your difference will be between the outright sale of the option versus trying to capture any missing intrinsic value. In many cases, you'll find that it is worth paying the extra commissions. Serious money can be hiding there and you now have the tools for picking it up.

Review of transactions

If call option is below intrinsic value:

    1) Short the stock

    2) Exercise the call

If the put option is below intrinsic value:

    1) Buy the stock

    2) Exercise the put

In either case, these actions provide the necessary funds to purchase the stock. You do not need to have any cash in the account.

 **Pricing Principle #4:**
Prior to Expiration, All At-the-Money and In-the-Money Call Options Must be Worth the Stock Price Minus the Present Value of the Exercise Price, or S – Pv (E).

The previous pricing relationship stated that all options must be worth either zero or their intrinsic value at expiration. Is there anything we can say about option prices *prior* to expiration? The answer is yes. Bear in mind that our previous pricing principle also applies prior to expiration and all options must be worth at least their intrinsic value. If not, arbitrage would be carried out exactly the same way as discussed for Principle #3. However, Principle #4 shows that prior to expiration we can make a stronger claim as to the minimum value. The relationship depends on whether we're talking about calls or puts. Let's start with the in-the-money call options.

Prior to expiration, all in-the-money call options must be worth at least the stock price minus the *present value* of the exercise price. In other words, all in-the-money call options must be worth their intrinsic value plus an amount equal to the cost of carry of the strike price. This may sound a little complicated but it's not so difficult once you understand what we mean by the cost of carry. In order to fully understand what this means, we need to take a little detour to talk about the financial concept of *present value.*

The Time Value of Money

One of the most important fundamental financial concepts is called the *time value of money.* Simply put, the time value of money states that a dollar today is worth more than a dollar tomorrow. This follows from the simple fact that a dollar today can be invested and earn the risk-free rate of interest. If someone owes you $10,000 in one year and offers to either pay you today or in one year, you'd rather have it today because you could invest that money at the risk-free rate and have more money in one year. The two payments are not the same. If $10,000 today is worth more in one year then it follows that $10,000 in one year must be worth less today. How much less? That depends on the risk-free interest rate.

Let's say you deposit $10,000 into an account that pays 5% interest. You will have $10,000 * (1.05) = $10,500 in one year. We call this the *future value* of money. In this example, the future value of $10,000 in one year is $10,500 if interest rates are 5%.

Now let's work the same problem backwards. If someone owes you $10,000 one year from now and interest rates are 5%, then you should be willing to accept $10,000/(1.05) = $9,523.80 today. In other words, it should make no difference to you by waiting one year and receiving $10,000 or collecting $9,523.80 today. The reason is that you can take the $9,523.80 today, invest it at 5% for one year, and still have your $10,000 a year from now. No matter which choice you take, you'd end up with $10,000 in one year.

It's important to understand that when dealing with present values and future values of money that you must be referring to *guaranteed* payments. You would be indifferent between taking $9,523.80 today and $10,000 in one year assuming the $10,000 payment in one year was guaranteed. If the person owing you the money is financially unstable and on the verge of bankruptcy, you would probably be willing to take substantially less than $9,523.80 today to settle the debt. In other words, before we can multiply or divide by the risk-free rate, we must be talking about risk-free payments.

In this example, we say that the *present value* of $10,000 is $9,523.80 if the risk-free rate of interest is 5%. Sometimes, as a simple notation, you might see this written as Pv ($10,000) = $9,523.80 and one we will use throughout the book[1]. To calculate the present value, we simply take the future value and divide it by 1 + risk-free interest rate.

We can use the concept of the time value of money to place even tighter restrictions on our call option price prior to expiration, which is what this fourth pricing principle states. If there is time remaining on the option then the in-the-money call option's price must be worth at least the stock price minus the present value of the exercise price, or S – Pv (E).

For example, let's assume we are looking at a one-year $50 call option with the stock trading for $55. We know there is $5 intrinsic value so the option must be worth at least $5. But because there is time remaining we know there is a higher minimum that it must be worth. Because you have the $50 call, you do not need to exercise it until the very end in one year, which means you can hang on to your $50 cash for one year and earn $50 * .05 = $2.50 interest. If you could earn an additional $2.50 in guaranteed interest in one year then that must have a value today of $2.50/1.05 = $2.38. This means that our $50 call has $5 intrinsic value ($55 stock - $50 strike) but also has an additional value today of $2.38 (the present value of the interest that is earned), which means the $50 call value today must be worth at least $5 + $2.38 = $7.38.

Now we find that there are two components to a call option's minimum value (we'll find out in Chapter Five that there is a third). The first is that all in-the-money call options must be worth the intrinsic value, or S - E. But in addition to this, they must also be worth the present value of the interest that could be earned on the strike price, or E - Pv (E). In other words, there is an interest rate component to an option's price.

To understand this second formula, the present value of the exercise price is $50/1.05 = $47.62. So the formula E - Pv (E) equates to $50 - $47.62 = $2.38 and is what we calculated previously. In other words, the difference between the exercise price and its present value is the today's value of the interest that could be

---

1 In some texts, you may see the notation Ee^{-rt} to denote the present value of the exercise price, where E = exercise price, e = the mathematical constant 2.7183…, r = rate, and t = time. The use of the mathematical constant e is just a way to accounting for continuously compounded interest and doesn't make a big difference in the calculations. To keep things simple and more understandable, we're going to use Pv (E) to mean the same thing.

earned on the exercise price. (Again, if the interest that can be earned is $2.50 then today's value is $2.50/1.05 = $2.38.)

Therefore, prior to expiration, all call options must be worth the sum of these two components: (S-E) + [E – Pv (E)]. If we remove the brackets, we see the expression reduces to S – E + E - Pv (E). The + E and – E cancel out, which further reduces to S – Pv (E). And that's exactly what Principle #4 tells us.

What would happen if a call option's price didn't reflect this minimum value? Let's say the one-year $50 call option is trading for $7 in the open market rather than the $7.38 minimum value we calculated. Once again, arbitrageurs would come to the rescue. Arbitrageurs would short the stock and buy the call for a net credit of $48:

Short stock	=	+$55
Buy $50 call	=	-$7
Net credit	=	+$48

The arbitrageur would hold on to this credit and allow it to earn interest. The $48 would grow to a risk-free value of $48 * 1.05 = $50.40. At the end of the year, the arbitrageur can exercise the $50 call to cover the short position and spend $50 from his credit balance thus leaving him with a 40-cent arbitrage profit. While 40 cents may not sound like much, you must remember that arbitrageurs would short enough stock and buy enough calls so that their final profit is potentially tens of thousands of dollars or more.

Even though the arbitrageur is shorting stock to take part in this arbitrage, he is never at risk of rising stock prices since he owns the $50 call and is therefore assured of never spending more than $50 to buy back the short stock. Of course, he could make more money if the stock falls during the year thus allowing him to purchase the stock back at a price cheaper than $50. But at a minimum, the arbitrageur will make 40 cents. Here's a good question to see if you understand the time value principle of money: Why does the arbitrageur make a 40-cent profit when only 38 cents were originally missing? The answer is that the 40-cent profit is made at the *end of the year* so the present value is 0.40/1.05 = 0.38, which is exactly the amount of missing value in the call.

This fourth principle that all in-the-money call options must be worth at least S – Pv (E) prior to expiration is just stating that there is an *interest component* to an in-the-money call option's price as well as an intrinsic value component. If you are looking at an at-the-money or out-of-the-money call option there is no intrinsic value but there is still an interest component. For example, if the stock is $55, we found the $50 call must be worth at least $7.38.

This fourth pricing principle holds for at-the-money calls as well. What is the minimum value for the $55 call? It is $55 – Pv ($55) = $2.62. With interest rates at 5%, the one-year $55 call must be trading for at least $2.62 otherwise arbitrage is possible. While out-of-the-money call options will have some time value prior to expiration, there is no minimum value we can state like there is for at-the-money and in-the-money calls as we have shown here. For instance, the formula shows that the $60 strike must be worth $55 - $60/1.05 = -$2.14. Because options cannot have negative value, this shows that there is really nothing we can say about this strike prior to expiration when it comes to an interest rate component.

Obviously, if you are looking at short-term options or if interest rates are low, there will not be a very big interest rate component. But if you're dealing in longer term options or if interest rates are high, these minimum values for calls may be much higher than you'd expect. If that value is not there, arbitrageurs will correct for it.

Minimum Value for a Put Option Prior to Expiration

Prior to expiration, a put option must be worth at least the exercise price minus the stock price, or E – S. Principle #3 showed us that a put option must be worth *exactly* E – S at expiration. But prior to expiration, we can only expand on that principle slightly by stating that a put must be worth *at least* that much. In other words, the put option must be worth its intrinsic value plus some additional value for the time remaining. Unlike the call option though, we cannot state a minimum amount for that time value.

The reason for this is that long call arbitrage involves short stock, which can earn interest. The arbitrageur is long the call and is fully hedged to short stock and earn interest. For the long put, however, the arbitrageur has the right to sell stock. He could fully hedge a long stock position but that means he would have to buy stock and that creates a cash outflow, which counteracts an arbitrage.

Prior to expiration, all in-the-money call options must be worth at least intrinsic value PLUS the interest that could be earned on the strike price. All in-the-money put options must be worth at least intrinsic value.

Principle #5:
The Maximum Price for a Call Option is the Price of the Stock. (The Maximum Price for a Put Option is the Strike Price.)

While stock prices may theoretically be unlimited, the same is not true for an option. Option prices are tied to the price of the stock and that stock price defines the maximum price of a call option. For example, assume that a stock is trading for $50. What is the maximum value for a $50 call? The maximum price it could ever be trading for is the same as the stock, $50. How do we know this is the maximum when we haven't said anything about the amount of time remaining on the option? It turns out that it doesn't matter. If the $50 call had a zero strike price (theoretically the lowest and best strike possible) with unlimited time remaining, it would be trading for the price of the stock. By now you've probably guessed that arbitrage is the reason. Let's assume that the $50 call is trading for $51 with the stock at $50. Arbitrageurs would buy the stock and sell the call for a net credit of one dollar:

Buy stock	=	- $50
Sell $50 call	=	+$51
Net credit	=	$1

By selling the call for $51, the arbitrageur has effectively been paid $1 to buy the stock. In the worst case scenario, the stock crashes to a price of zero, the short call expires worthless, and the arbitrageur keeps the dollar. What if the stock rises? Because the arbitrageur sold the $50 call, he also has the potential obligation to sell the stock for $50. If he is forced to sell the stock for $50, he will end up with an additional credit of $50 from the sale for a total credit of $51, which is the maximum profit from this arbitrage.

No matter what happens to the stock's price, the arbitrageur is guaranteed a minimum of one dollar profit, which is exactly the amount *over* the theoretical value of this hypothetical $50 call. The arbitrageur's actions puts buying pressure on the stock and selling pressure on the call until the stock is priced higher than the call. At that point, the arbitrage opportunity is gone and the option is priced less than the stock. (For those investors who have used the Covered Call strategy, you may have realized that your broker will only let you enter the trade for a net debit and this pricing principle shows why. The covered call strategy entails the purchase of stock and the selling of a call. Because the call option can never be more valuable than the stock, the covered call can only be executed for a debit.)

Maximum Value for Puts

For put options, the maximum value is the strike price. If you have a $50 put, the most it could ever be worth is $50 and that only happens if the stock's price is zero. Whenever you exercise a put, you give up the shares and receive the strike price. Because of this, the best you could ever do is surrender stock that is worthless and receive the strike price. And that means nobody would ever pay more than $50 for the $50 put.

How would the market correct for it if the put option's price did happen to exceed the strike price? Let's assume that the stock is $50 and the $50 put is trading for $51. Arbitrageurs would simply sell the put and receive $51 cash. By selling the put, they have the potential obligation to buy the stock for $50, which they can always do by using the $51 cash. Of course, they would receive stock in exchange for the cash, which they can always sell in the open market. The worst that could happen is for the stock's price to fall to zero in which case the arbitrageurs would still make a one dollar profit. If the stock should rise above $50 at expiration, then the put will be worthless at expiration and the arbitrageur is left with the $51 credit.

So $51 is the best that the arbitrageur can do and $1 is the worst. In other words, no matter what happens the arbitrageur is guaranteed to make money all from the fact that the put was sold for a higher price than the strike price. Arbitrageurs will continue selling the overpriced put until its price falls below the $50 strike at which point the arbitrage opportunity disappears.

We could extend this argument a little further and say that the maximum price for a put *prior* to expiration is the present value of the exercise price. The reason, of course, is that the arbitrageur earns interest on the cash balance from the sale of the put. While call and put prices can rise in value, these limits are not without boundaries. There are limits. Principle #5 shows us what those limits are.

 The maximum price for a call option is the price of the stock. The maximum price for a put option is the strike price.

Pricing Principle #6:
For any two Call Options (or any two Puts) on the Same Stock with the Same Expiration, the Difference in Their Prices Cannot Exceed the Difference in Their Strikes.

This relationship says that, for any two call options, the difference in their prices cannot be greater than the difference in their strikes. This is assuming that both options cover the same stock and have the same time to expiration. Say we see the following option quotes one day on the same underlying stock:

April $50 Call = $10
April $55 Call = $4

We know from the first pricing relationship that the $50 call should be worth more than the $55, and we see that it is. However, Principle #6 says that there cannot be this much of a difference. The difference in strikes is $5 yet the difference in price is $6. The difference in prices has exceeded the difference in strikes, which is a violation of this principle.

How will the markets correct for this? Arbitrageurs will buy the relatively cheap asset and sell the relatively expensive one. In this case, they will buy the $55 call and sell the $50 call for a net credit of $6:

Buy $55 call   = $4
Sell $50 call   =   +$10
Net credit   +$6

Now check the rights and obligations. The arbitrageur has the right to buy stock for $55 and the potential obligation to sell of $50, which would create a $5 loss as a worst case scenario. However, he was paid $6 to take the $5 loss, which leaves a $1 arbitrage profit. This profit would occur for any stock price above $55.

If the stock falls below $50 at expiration, both options expire worthless and the arbitrageur keeps the full $6 credit. If the stock closes between $50 and $55 the arbitrageur makes something between $1 and $6. For example, with the stock at $52, the arbitrageur will be assigned on the short $50 call and be required to deliver stock worth $52 and receive only $50 thus creating a $2 loss. He can pay for this loss out of his $6 initial credit, which leaves him a net gain of $4. No matter where the stock price may be at expiration, the arbitrageur is guaranteed to make at least $1 and as much as $6.

An easier way to understand Pricing Principle #6 is to think back to the pizza coupon examples. Assume two coupons are identical except that one allows you to pay $7 while another let's you pay $10. Now let's just say the market places a $1 value on the $10 coupon. What's the maximum value of the $7 coupon? We know the $7 coupon must be worth more than the $10 coupon so it is worth more than one dollar. But we also know that the maximum value is $4. The reason is that the $7 coupon gives you a *$3 advantage* over the $10 coupon so that is the maximum value it could ever have over the $10 coupon. For example, assume pizzas are selling for $20. The holder of the $7 coupon has a $13 advantage while the $10 coupon holder has a $10 advantage. The difference in these two advantages is $3. Run through this scenario with any price for the pizza and you will see that there is always an exact $3 advantage.

It just wouldn't make sense to bid the $7 coupon more than $3 above the price of the $10 coupon. Now, it is certainly possible that the market places *less* than a $3 difference between these two coupons. That would happen if the market didn't see any advantage in holding either one (the coupons are out-of-the-money). For instance, assume pizzas are selling for $6 and the market just doesn't think there's going to be much of a chance for a price hike. You may see a value of only 5 cents on the $10 coupon and 10 cents on the $7 coupon, which is only a five-cent difference.

Likewise, options must obey a similar principle. If you think about it, there really is no difference in owning a $50 call versus a $55 call other than the fact that the person with the $50 strike can pay $50 for the stock, while the person with the $55 strike can pay $55. The maximum difference in value between holding the

$50 call and the $55 call therefore cannot be more than $5. The market will never give you more than the difference in strikes for any option whether calls or puts (assuming the same underlying stock and time to expiration).

Just as with the pizza coupon example, option prices will expand to exactly the difference in strikes if the stock is well above both strike prices for calls (or well below both strikes for puts). For example, take a look at the Cyberonics (CYBX) quotes in Table 2-6:

Table 2-6: CYBX Option Quotes

CYBX (Nasdaq)   **37.55**   **-0.85**

Jun 18,2004 @ 10:06 ET (Data 15 Minutes Delayed)   Bid 37.61   Ask 37.60   Size 2x8   Vol 1050155

Calls	Last Sale	Net	Bid	Ask	Vol	Open Int	Puts	Last Sale	Net	Bid	Ask	Vol	Open Int
04 Jun 12.50 (QAJ FV-E)	25.50	pc	24.50	25.50	0	176	04 Jun 12.50 (QAJ RV-E)	0.05	pc	0	0.05	0	11018
04 Jun 15.00 (QAJ FC-E)	23.40	pc	22.00	23.00	0	1918	04 Jun 15.00 (QAJ RC-E)	0.05	pc	0	0.05	0	11925
04 Jun 17.50 (QAJ FW-E)	21.50	pc	19.50	20.50	0	3379	04 Jun 17.50 (QAJ RW-E)	0.05	pc	0	0.05	0	5805
04 Jun 20.00 (QAJ FD-E)	19.10	pc	17.30	18.00	0	10772	04 Jun 20.00 (QAJ RD-E)	0.05	pc	0	0.05	0	7436
04 Jun 22.50 (QAJ FX-E)	15.20	-1.00	14.50	15.50	4	8899	04 Jun 22.50 (QAJ RX-E)	0.05	pc	0	0.05	0	7303
04 Jun 25.00 (QAJ FE-E)	12.50	-1.50	12.10	13.00	2	13336	04 Jun 25.00 (QAJ RE-E)	0.05	pc	0	0.05	0	5990
04 Jun 30.00 (QAJ FF-E)	7.20	-1.80	7.10	8.10	1	17964	04 Jun 30.00 (QAJ RF-E)	0.05	pc	0	0.05	0	9275
04 Jun 35.00 (QAJ FG-E)	2.55	-1.25	2.50	3.00	101	4737	04 Jun 35.00 (QAJ RG-E)	0.10	-0.10	0.10	0.25	235	2853
04 Jun 40.00 (QAJ FH-E)	0.15	-0.25	0.05	0.15	774	5896	04 Jun 40.00 (QAJ RH-E)	2.60	+0.70	2.45	2.70	115	722

Look at the asking prices of the first two listed calls, the June $12.50 and $15 strikes. The asking prices are $25.50 and $23, respectively, which is a $2.50 difference. And that's *exactly* the difference in their strikes. Once the price of the $15 call is established by the market, the market will pay a maximum of $2.50 above that price for the $12.50 strike.

What's the difference in prices between the $15 call and the $20 call? Their prices are $23 and $18, which is exactly $5 and, again, the difference in strikes. Once the price of the $20 call is established, the market will not pay more than $5 above that price for the $15 call.

These prices expanded to the full difference in strikes because the stock price was so far above them at expiration. In other words, these strikes are very deep-in-the-money. With the stock at $37.55, the market didn't see a chance for any of these strikes to close out-of-the-money so their prices converged to the exact differences in strikes. (You may have noticed that the difference between the $35 and $40 strikes is $5.10 and this is simply a fluke. These quotes were probably in the process of being updated and you can be sure this fall to exactly a $5 difference in strikes.)

Now take a look at the $35 and $40 strikes. Their prices are $3.00 and 15-cents respectively, which is only a $2.85 difference. Here we have a five-dollar difference in strikes but only a $2.85 difference in price. Remember, this principle states that the difference in prices cannot *exceed* the difference in strikes. It does not say that it cannot be less. Because CYBX was trading for $37.55, neither the $35 strike or $40 strike are seen as being "guaranteed" to finish with intrinsic value at this time. That's why the market is not pricing a full five-dollar difference in their prices.

There are two conditions under which you'd see a $5 difference between the $35 and $40 strikes. First, if stock's price was sufficiently higher than these strikes, say $43, then you'd see a five-dollar difference between the $35 and $40 calls. The more time remaining until expiration (or the more volatile the stock) the higher that stock's price needs to be before you'd see a $5 difference between these two strikes.

The second condition under which we'd see a $5 difference is if these quotes were taken in the final seconds of trading and the stock was $40.01 or higher. The sole determining factor is the market's perception as to whether both of these options will expire in-the-money. If there is time remaining, then the stock's price needs to be well above both strikes. If there is little time, then the stock's price only needs to be just slightly above the higher strike in order for the difference in prices to be equal to the difference in strikes.

Now you should have a basic understanding of why this principle is true for any set of option quotes. If the option is deep enough in-the-money, the markets will view them as guaranteed to expire with intrinsic value, in which case the difference in strikes will equal the difference in price. Once risk is introduced though, the difference in their prices will be reduced to something less than the difference in strikes.

While option prices are free to fluctuate, there are invisible boundaries governing their prices. These are not rules set by exchanges or any person. Rather, they are economic and financial principles at work. Traders and investors who understand these six principles will be ahead of the game once we start talking about strategies.

 For any two calls (or any two puts) the difference in their prices cannot exceed the difference in their strikes.

 Key Concepts

1) Lower strike calls and higher strike puts are always more expensive (all else constant).

2) The longer the term to expiration, the more expensive the option (all else constant).

3) Options are either worth zero or intrinsic value at expiration. Long options cannot have negative value.

4) Prior to expiration, at-the-money and in-the-money calls are worth the intrinsic value plus an interest component.

5) The maximum price for a call is the stock price. For puts, it is the strike price.

6) The difference in two calls (or two puts) cannot exceed the difference in strikes (all else constant).

Up to this point, we have covered some basic principles about option prices. We have looked at some pricing examples assuming the prices have already been set by the market. Let's take the next step and ask a very important question: What gives an option its value in the first place?

What Gives an Option Value?

We've learned that an option's price, or premium, can be broken down into the two component parts of *intrinsic value* and *time value*. If there is any intrinsic value present in an option, it must be reflected in the price, otherwise arbitrage is possible. The arbitrageurs make sure that options will always have intrinsic value.

So for example, if you have a $50 call and the stock is currently $53, we know that the call option must be trading for *at least* $3.

In addition to that $3 though, there will be an additional value – time premium – that is due to the fact that time still remains on the option. Part of this time value is derived from the cost of carry as Pricing Principle #4 showed. But traders are willing to pay more than this cost of carry since it gives the stock more time to build intrinsic value into the option. So even though the time premium will *eventually* be zero, traders are willing to pay for time since it gives the stock more of a chance to move in a favorable direction thus making the option's price go higher.

So up to this point, we know there are at least two factors that give an option value. The first is favorable stock price movement and the second is time. Favorable stock price movement means that if you are holding a call option, you'd like to see the underlying stock price rise. Remember that a call option locks in a buying price for the stock. The higher the stock price, the more valuable a call option becomes. For example, with the stock at $55, a $50 call must be worth at least $5. But if the stock rises to $60, the $50 call must be worth at least $10.

If you are holding a put, you'd like to see the underlying stock fall. Since a put option locks in a selling price, the further the stock falls, the more valuable put options become. For example, with the stock at $55, a $60 put must be worth at least $5. But if the stock falls to $50 the $60 put must be worth at least $10.

The second action that gives an option value is time. What drives the value of the time premium other than the cost of carry? We can make the point clear by a little analogy. Imagine that someone makes you the following proposition: He will pay you $1 for every point scored above 20 by the end of an upcoming professional football game. For example, if the team scores 23 points, you are paid $3. If the team scores 32 points, you are paid $12 and so on. In exchange for this opportunity, you pay him a flat fee.

Now imagine that you are offered the same bet but for an upcoming basketball game. In either case, you're making money after 20 points but does that mean that both bets have the same value to you? Think about it for a moment, which would you pay more for, the football or basketball bet?

You probably realize that scores tend to be much higher for basketball than for football. It's pretty rare that a football team will score more than 40 points but not uncommon for a basketball team to score over 100. That means there is probably more money to be made from betting on the basketball team. In other words, because there is more "scoring potential" for basketball, the value of that bet should be worth more to you. No matter what you're willing to pay for the football bet, you should be willing to pay more for the basketball bet. In this example, your *perception* about the scoring abilities between football and basketball teams leads you to believe that the basketball bet is worth more. The key word here is "perception." It might turn out after the fact that the football bet was the better one to make. But prior to the games, your perception tells you that the basketball game is most likely the one that will produce the biggest reward.

As stated earlier, it is the "scoring potential" of the teams that drives the values of the bets. And that means that time plays a critical role since teams can produce higher scores the longer they are allowed to play. For example, if the basketball bet was only good for the first five minutes of the game then you should be willing to pay less than if it applied to the entire game.

It's exactly this same reasoning that drives the true time premium component (the component above the cost of carry) of an option. If you have a $20 call, it will have intrinsic value for every price above $20 at expiration. If the stock closes at $23 at expiration, the call will be worth exactly $3. If it closes at $32, the call will be worth $12. How much will you pay for this $20 call? As with the sports bet, the answer depends on the "scoring potential" of the stock. If you are dealing with a stock whose price fluctuates wildly, you will pay much more for the call than if the stock price hardly moves. If there is more ability to make money on the bet then the bet should be worth more money. In option trading, the "scoring potential" is known as *volatility*. A high volatility stock has large price fluctuations. It can be up or down several percentage points in a day. A low volatility stock, on the other hand, has almost no fluctuations in its price. *The time value portion of an option is solely determined by the market's perception as to the volatility of the stock between now and expiration.* There is no way to say for sure if the time premium is too high or too low. It is strictly a value that exists in the minds of the traders.

To further understand volatility using an everyday example, we would say that gas prices are more volatile than milk prices. We're pretty sure that a gallon of milk will cost about the same next week or next month but we're not nearly so sure about a gallon of gas. While there are many ways to measure the volatility of a stock, that's getting a little ahead of our goal. Just understand that the more volatile the stock's price – the more uncertain we are about it's price from day to day – the more money you're going to pay for an option. High volatility stocks have greater potential to move higher and traders are therefore willing to pay higher time premiums for the option. It is the high volatility stocks that carry the largest time premiums on their options.

For example, imagine that you are looking at two options:

ABC Jan. $50 call = $2
XYZ Jan. $50 call = $6

Both underlying stocks are $50 and both options expire at the same time. What can we conclude about the relative volatilities of these two stocks? We can conclude that XYZ must be more volatile than ABC and that's why traders are willing to pay more for that call option. XYZ is like a high-flying tech stock while ABC is more like a blue-chip company.

At the beginning of this chapter, Principle #2 told us that longer term options are worth more than shorter term options so we know the ABC or XYZ March $50 calls will be worth more than their January $50 calls. Now you should have little better understanding of why. For any given stock, the longer the timeframe, the better than chance for "high scores" or high stock prices and that makes the value of calls and puts rise. Remember that put options will rise too since stock prices behave a little differently from basketball and football games in that they can *rise or fall* with equal ease.

There is no way to place limits on what the time value will be that traders place on an option – it is a value that exists in their heads. It depends on how bullish or bearish traders are at that time. Obviously, if traders are extremely bullish they are willing to pay more for the time value. If they think the stock will just sit flat, they may not be willing to pay anything. The time value portion of an option is an indication of the volatility that traders believe the underlying stock will be exhibit through the life of the option.

Does this mean that you should only buy options on high volatility stocks? Although there are many traders who will tell you that you should only trade options on high volatility stocks that is actually a misconception. The reason is that those options, for reasons just stated, also have the highest time premiums and that makes it that much harder to earn a profit.

For example, assume you are looking at the ABC and XYZ $50 calls we saw previously. The XYZ $50 call was trading for $6 while the ABC $50 call was trading for $2. The XYZ $50 call certainly has more potential for greater profit but it also costs more.

We can show that the high volatility stock needs more movement to make a profit by calculating the break-even points for each option at expiration. To find the break-even point for a call, we simply add the cost of the option to the strike (we subtract it from the strike for a put option). For the ABC $50 call, this means the stock must close at $52 at expiration in order for the trader to break even. If the stock is $52 at expiration, the $50 call is worth exactly the intrinsic amount of $2. This means you paid $2 for the option and could sell it for $2 so you just broke even. The XYZ $50 call, on the other hand, must have the stock close at $56 at expiration in order to break even. If the stock is $56 at expiration, that $50 call is worth exactly the intrinsic amount of $6, which is the amount that was paid for it so you break even. Notice that the benefits of a high volatility stock are balanced by the higher break-even price. The market realizes the benefit in buying high volatility and prices those options higher.

When you hear traders tell you to only buy options on high volatility stocks, they are unknowingly making the assumption that both options will cost the same. If they did, you can be sure that the high volatility options would be the right choice. However, the financial markets will always bid the prices higher for options on high volatility stocks.

Let's return to our main idea about what gives an option value. We said the first factor was intrinsic value, which is determined by favorable price movement. The second is due to time, which is affected by traders' beliefs in the future volatility of the stock. This leads to a very important point about the characteristics of option prices: *Option prices can rise or fall with no movement (or with adverse movement) in the underlying stock.*

This can happen simply because of a change in traders' outlooks on the volatility of the underlying stock. For example, assume you buy a three-month $50 call option for $3. A month later the stock is still $50 and the option is trading for $2.

However, at that time, a buyout rumor starts circulating on the stock. We might see the $50 call trading for more than $3 even though less time remains on the option and the stock price hasn't moved. The reason is that traders now believe the "scoring potential" or volatility will be greater in the near future so are willing to bid the option higher than its price a month earlier.

Exercise

Go to www.cboe.com and check out option quotes on Google (GOOG) and McDonald's (MCD). Look at the prices for the at-the-money calls and puts. Which stock has the more expensive options? Why?

Now that you understand the concept of volatility, we can figure out why options have value while pizza coupons do not. Many are inclined to think that it's due to the prices; stocks are far more expensive than pizzas. That's partly true but the bigger reason is due to the *uncertainty* of prices. You can be pretty sure that pizza prices will be the same price next week or even next year. And as competitive as the pizza market is, there's even a good chance that prices may fall. Because we're pretty certain about the price we'll pay for pizza in the foreseeable and they don't make up a large portion of our incomes or net worth, there's no reason we'd want to "lock in" the price of a pizza. Consequently, pizza coupons have no value. With stocks, it's a different story. One day the stock is up 2%, the next it could be down 10% and we're never really sure what's going to happen. And because stock portfolios typically do make up significant portions of our wealth investors and traders are willing to pay to hedge those risks. They are willing to give options value. Options have value because stock prices fluctuate. Options were designed to control these fluctuations and therefore reduce risk.

Risk and Reward

While we're talking about options pricing, this is a perfect point to talk about one of the most misunderstood concepts in option pricing – risk and reward. It is, in fact, so misunderstood that you will find it misinterpreted even among professional traders. Because of this, it is also one of the biggest sources of option losses for new and seasoned traders. If you are to trade options successfully, you need to understand the indisputable relationship between risk and reward.

Will Rogers once said, "Why not go out on a limb? That's where the fruit is." This is one of the simplest ways of expressing the relationship between risk and reward. He was, of course, referring to the fact that in order to get the fruit (reward) you must venture out onto the tiny, unstable limbs. You must take some risk. The same concept applies to every financial decision you will ever make. In financial terms, if an investment is risky then we mean there is a chance you might lose some or all of your initial investment. The greater the chance for loss then the greater the risk of the investment.

Risk and reward is the inseparable dynamic duo of finance and always increase and decrease together. If the potential reward from an investment is great, you can be sure that it comes with a lot of risk. And if the risk is low, you can forget about making a lot of money.

While the concept of risk and reward may make intuitive sense, it is one of the most overlooked concepts among investors and causes many problems for those who only consider the reward side. If you want to succeed in investing, it is crucial that you understand the risk-reward relationship and why this pair cannot be separated. We can easily convince you why risk and reward go hand-in-hand by playing a simple game.

Pricing Game

Imagine that you are offered the chance to play the following three games. An auction is held to play each game for which there is a $100 cash prize. The highest bidder is allowed to play the game one time and does not get his bid amount back. Think about each of the games and then jot down your answers on a piece of paper:

1. For the first game, the highest bidder is guaranteed to win $100 cash. No risk. No hidden strings attached. If you are the high bidder, you walk up and collect $100. How much would you bid to play this game?

2. For the second game, you must correctly call heads or tails at the flip of a coin in order to win the $100 prize. How much do you bid to play the game now?

 3. For the third game, you must draw the ace of spades from a well-shuffled deck of cards in order to win $100. How much would you pay to play this game?

Even though we don't know the particular answers you chose for each game, we are 100% certain that you elected to pay the highest price for the guaranteed game, the next highest amount for the coin game, and the least amount for the card game. How do we know this? It's because of the relative risks involved in each game. The first game has no risk; we know that the winner always wins $100. And because of this, most people will bid this game up fairly close to the $100 reward. For the coin toss, we know that you would win $100 half the time and lose your bid amount half the time, which is certainly not as good as winning all of the time. In other words, we are less confident in the outcome – there is risk. There is no chance of losing with the first game but a significant chance of losing with the coin game. Because of this, you should be willing to spend less for this game. For the card game, we know you would win $100 only once out of every 52 tries, on average. This means you are almost certain to lose your money. On a comparative basis among the three games, this is the riskiest so you should be willing to spend the least to play it.

We just reviewed each game in terms of risk and find that the higher the risk, the lower the price you are willing to pay. We can also look at the three games in a positive light as we did when considering which strikes should cost more. We do that by simply asking which game is more *desirable* and that is the one that will carry the highest price. The guaranteed game is more desirable than the coin game and that's why its price is higher. Or conversely, the coin game is riskier (it is less desirable) than the guaranteed game so it is cheaper. It doesn't matter which dollar amounts you picked for each game but, just for the example, let's assume you bid the following amounts:

Guaranteed game: $99
Coin game: $49
Card game: $1

These are typical results that we get when this game is presented at Option University seminars. Once we have some prices to work with, we can look at the three games in a different light. If you were willing to pay $99 for the first game, that's the same thing as saying you were willing to invest $99 in order to make a $1 profit. The coin game, on the other hand, represents a game where you could invest $49 for the chance to make a $51 profit while the card game represents an opportunity to invest $1 in hopes of making a $99 profit. These costs and potential profit opportunities are summarized in Table 2-7:

Table 2-7

Game	Cost	Potential Profit
Guaranteed	$99	$1
Coin	$49	$51
Card	$1	$99

Notice the relationship between the prices and the rewards: The higher the price (cost), the lower the reward (potential profit). The guaranteed game carries the highest price of $99 and comes with the smallest reward of $1. The coin game has a lower price and a correspondingly bigger reward. The card game has the lowest price of all and also has the biggest reward. You can see why it would be easy for someone to just look at the prices and potential profits in Table 2-7 and wonder why they should play anything but the card game. After all, it doesn't seem to make sense to pay a high price to get a small reward when you can pay a tiny bit and possibly make a fortune. People who interpret the numbers in Table 2-7 this way are unintentionally assuming that the risks are equal across the board. That is easy to do if you're just looking at the numbers. But once you understand the nature of each game, you start to see why people are willing to pay higher prices for some of the games.

Price is the Equalizer

The market places a lower price on riskier assets as a way to equalize the demand. In the pricing game, you placed a higher price on the coin game than the card game. This doesn't mean that the coin game is necessarily the better game. If the coin game and card game were priced the same, then we could say for sure that the coin game is better. After all, it wouldn't make sense to pay the same price to play the card game. But because there is more risk with the card game, you will bid a lower amount. Once the prices are established for all three games, then all games are theoretically equally attractive. Your decision on which one to play just depends on how much risk you wish to take (or on how much reward you're looking for). If you don't like the $51 payoff of the coin game, you can certainly jump to the riskier card game and go for the $99 reward. Just understand that this decision means you are taking more risk and therefore have a higher chance of losing your investment. The important point to understand is that you cannot jump to a better payoff *and* take less risk. If you want more reward, you must be willing to take more risk.

Now let's go back and look at some of the eBay option quotes in Table 1-1, which have been reprinted below in Table 2-8:

Table 2-8

CALL OPTIONS		
Strike	**July**	**August**
$32.50	$4.90	$5.50
$35	$2.70	$3.60
$37.50	$1.05	$2.10
$40	$0.35	$1.10

As we pointed out before, the price of the call options get cheaper as we move to higher strikes. Notice that this is the same progression as with our pricing game when we move from the guaranteed game to the card game. The price gets cheaper as you move in that direction. This can only mean one thing for the options. *They must be getting riskier as we move to higher strikes.* However, most traders look at the quotes in Table 2-8 and think that all options could theoretically make an unlimited amount of money since they are all tied to the same underlying stock. It only makes sense to buy the cheapest one, which is the $40 strike. And this is usually a fatal mistake for options traders. Traders who use this line of reasoning are assuming that the risks are all the same and we now know that cannot be true since the prices are not the same. The market is bidding down the prices of the higher strikes due to the higher risk.

Our first pricing principle stated that lower strike calls must be more expensive. We said that a statistical reason for this is that lower strike calls are able to "catch" more intrinsic value and therefore must be more desirable. Lower strikes are more desirable because they are less risky. If it is less risky, it most cost more money.

We can show this effect by considering the break-even points for a call option. If you buy the $32.50 strike for $4.90, we showed that the stock would have to close at $32.50 + $4.90 = $37.40 in order to break even at expiration. Because CYBX is currently $37.11, you're only 29 cents away from your break-even point. However, if you elect to buy the cheapest option, the $40 strike, then the stock must climb to $40 + $0.35 = $40.35 just to break even at expiration. With the stock at $37.11, that means the first $40.35 – 37.11 = $3.24 worth of movement doesn't even count for you at expiration! The stock must climb higher than $3.24 by expiration before you make money. There is a very big difference between the $32.50 strike and the $40 strike – and that difference is the risk.

Using Table 2-8, many new traders still believe that the $32.50 call must be riskier than the $40 call since there is more money to potentially lose. If eBay falls from its current price of $37.11 to $32.50 at expiration, the $32.50 call buyer loses $4.90 while the $40 call buyer loses only 35 cents. However, if eBay falls to $32.50 at expiration then the stock has lost $4.61 worth of value. This means that the first $4.61 worth of loss on the $32.50 call is a risk that is common to both the stock and the option. It is not a risk that is unique to the option so should not be counted as a risk in the option. It is only the value above $4.61 – the 29 cents worth of time value – that is a risk of the $32.50 call. The $40 call loses only 35 cents but it does so if the stock falls, stays still, or even rises to $40 at expiration. It is far riskier than the $32.50 call.

Many traders feeling uneasy about putting much money into the trade when there are other strikes available for much less money. The key to trading options is to strike a balance between the two. We don't suggest buying an so far in the money that it's costing a fortune but, at the same time, we stay away from buying at-the-money and out-of-the-money options unless we are buying them with a lot of time remaining – perhaps more than a year to expiration. For the most part, you'll be better off buying options with intrinsic value.

Now let's look at the July and August calls in Table 2-8 above. Why do you suppose the July $32.50 is cheaper than the August $32.50? You should now understand that it is cheaper because it is riskier. As we stated before, the August call gives you more time for the stock to move higher – to build intrinsic value – and that means there is a better chance to make money. In other words, there is less risk with that option and that's why its price is higher. Many option traders make the mistake of buying the shortest-term, cheapest option available thinking they are reducing their risk and this is usually why most people lose with options. The short-term, high strikes should be treated like lottery tickets, not investments. Our basic risk-reward relationship can be found in many other areas outside of the financial markets too. As long as there is a price paid in exchange for a possible financial reward, the risk-reward relationship holds. Let's look at an example outside of the financial markets.

Lotteries

Why do you suppose that you can pay one dollar for a state lottery ticket for the chance to make $7 million or more? The reason is that the chance of making that huge reward is very small and so the price will also be low. It does not mean that it must be a great investment because of the "great risk-reward ratio" that so many traders talk about. If there is a great reward, there is a low price – and also a lot of risk.

As an example, Figure 2-9 shows two versions of the Florida lottery scratch-off Monopoly game: Instant Monopoly and Super Monopoly.

Figure 2-9: Florida Lottery's Instant Monopoly and Super Monopoly

Instant Monopoly costs $1 and offers a $5,000 grand prize while Super Monopoly costs $5 and offers a whopping $100,000 grand prize. Super Monopoly costs five times as much but offers twenty times the reward. Does it follow that Super Monopoly is the better game since it has a "better" risk reward ratio? Not necessarily. In order to answer that, we need to know the probabilities of winning each game. Depending on the probabilities, it may turn out that one is better than the other. However, the point is that you cannot just look at the "risk-reward ratios" and make that determination. What we do know for sure is that the Super Monopoly game must be more difficult to win. The higher payout is a reflection of the higher risk involved in that game. In fact, you can even verify this by going to the website www.FloridaLottery.com and looking at the odds. For Super Monopoly, the odds are 1:2,520,000 and are 1:890,000 for Instant Monopoly. Although you are not likely to win either game, there is no doubt that, on a relative scale, you are more likely to win at Instant Monopoly and that's why the payout is lower.

Comparing Returns among Funds and Managers

You will be persuaded by different types of investments or individual stock pickers to put your money with them because they "beat" the Dow or some other index. While their returns may be higher, it does not mean that they necessarily beat it on a *risk-adjusted* scale. As an example, assume the Dow increases 10% over the year but a money manager tells you to put your money with him since he earned 20%. On the surface, it seems like he did much better. However, we haven't considered the risk. What if this manager invested all his clients' money into Super Monopoly to get the 20% gain? Now it doesn't appear too impressive. If he is taking that much risk, you'd certainly want better than a 20% increase on your money. We'd say that, on a risk-adjusted scale, this manager *didn't* perform as well as the Dow even though his return is higher.

Traders and money managers who place their money in high-risk investments will do better than the Dow or S&P 500 or other broad-based index from time to time. But the chances that they will sustain that record are very low. People who place their money with a fund or manager just because they posted the highest numbers are mistakenly assuming that all of them took the same amount of risk. Before you place your money with them, find out *what* they are investing in before you get too impressed with the numbers. At any given time, there are thousands of speculators and hedge funds who speculate with high-risk investments. It shouldn't be a surprise that a great number of them will beat the Dow or S&P 500 during the course of a year. This doesn't mean that they are more skilled than the manager who *consistently* returns a smaller number.

Make sure you understand the risk-reward relationship before you start investing. Risk and reward never separate. They are joined together by a rational force – the same force that caused you to price the earlier games in the order you did. If you always seek the investments that have the highest potential for return, you are by default, seeking the ones with the highest risk. We have tried to give you many examples of how to use the risk-reward relationship so that you do not forget it, which is easy to do. For example, we just received an email promotion from an option's trader with the following advice:

Quote in Promotional email:

"Cheaper options are usually the best plays. They give you the most leverage, the percentage returns are better, and if the market or stock goes against you, you are risking less."

You can see that even this professional got it wrong. You are not "risking less" by purchasing cheap options – you are taking on more risk. It is true that if you buy a cheap option there is less money to lose but that is because you have a higher chance of losing it. And why are the percentage returns better? Because there is more risk. Why do cheap options give you the most leverage? Because there is more risk. But if you look at the quote, he is making it sound as if you're getting all the positive attributes (high leverage and higher percent returns) without any negative consequence since you are "risking less" for all of these benefits. That is simply not true. All of those positive attributes are a direct result of the higher risk in cheap options.

Understandably, it is and easy to make this mistake since we do not have little pictures (such as the coin and cards) off to the side like we did with the pricing game reminding us of the risk in each game. When you start trading options remember this one thing: Options are cheap for a reason. That reason is risk.

||||||||||||||||||||||||||||||||||||||||||||||||||||||||||||||||||||||||||||||||||||||||||||||||||||

 Key Concepts

1) The time value of an option is determined by the volatility of the underlying stock.

2) The time value is purely determined by what traders are willing to pay for additional time.

3) The higher the risk, the cheaper the price (and the higher the reward).

4) Higher strike calls (and lower strike puts) are riskier.

5) There is no inherent advantage in trading options on high volatility stocks because they will be priced correspondingly higher. Price is the equalizer.

||||||||||||||||||||||||||||||||||||||||||||||||||||||||||||||||||||||||||||||||||||||||||||||||||||

Option Price Behavior

One of the biggest mysteries to new (and experienced) traders is the way in which option prices move with changes in the underlying stock. For example, let's assume you buy a $50 call for $3 with the underlying stock trading for $50. Within a few minutes, the stock climbs up $1 to $51. What would you expect to happen to the price of your option? Would it climb $1 too? The answer is, unfortunately, no. Although it seems like it should be trading for $4 at that point, the option will rise something less than $1. Why is that?

This is a very difficult concept to explain to new traders and the explanation belongs in a more advanced book but it's important that you at least understand that options will generally not move dollar-for-dollar with the underlying stock. Please understand that the following details are not really necessary to understand in order to trade options. We're just showing you this to explain why options will usually not move dollar-for-dollar with the stock and so that you are not alarmed when you see it occur. Let's see if we can make some sense of why this might happen by going back to our pizza coupons.

Assume that pizzas are selling for $10 and you have a coupon that allows you to buy it for $7. If these coupons were actually traded in a market, we know that it must be worth at least $3. Why? Just as with our call options – arbitrage. Let's say the coupons were missing $1 of intrinsic value and trading for $2. Arbitrageurs could buy a coupon for $2 and then pay $7 for the pizza thus spending only $9 for the pizza. They could then sell it in the street for $10 thus making a free dollar. The buying pressure on the coupons will raise the price and the arbitrage opportunity will stop once the coupon is trading for at least $3.

Now let's assume that the storeowner announces that the price of pizzas will go up for certain by one dollar tomorrow to $11. Upon hearing the news, the market will immediately raise the price of the coupon from $3 to $4. If not, arbitrage is possible again for the same reasons as in the previous paragraph. In other words, if pizzas are now worth $11 then the $7 coupon must fully reflect the $4 intrinsic value. In this case, the pizza price rose one dollar and so did the coupon.

But now let's go back to the beginning when pizzas were $10 and change the situation a bit. Let's say that, instead, the storeowner announces that he will flip a coin tomorrow to decide whether or not to increase his prices by $1. If the coin lands heads, he raises prices to $11. If it lands tails, they stay the same at $10.

We know that when the storeowner announced that pizzas would definitely rise by one dollar that the coupons also rose by the same amount. In other words, because prices were *guaranteed* to rise, the market immediately priced that $1 increase into the coupons. With the coin flip though, the owner introduces some risk and we're now only 50% sure that pizza prices will rise. What should we pay for the coupon now?

Let's run through a couple of scenarios and see what happens. Let's assume that coupon prices do not change and they are still trading for $3. If we buy the coupon for $3, and the coin lands heads tomorrow, it will be trading for $4 and we will make one dollar. If the coin lands tails, the coupon still trades for $3 and we don't lose anything. So if we can buy the coupon for $3, we can't lose but we might make money. Everybody figures this out and buys coupons and their price rises. This shows that $3 is too low of a price given the fact that prices have a 50% chance of rising one dollar.

Is there a price that's too high for the coupon? The answer is yes. When the storeowner announced that prices would definitely rise, we know that the coupon immediately rose to $4. Now that we're not so certain of a price increase, $4 should be too much to pay. But just for argument's sake, let's assume that prices do rise to

$4 and we buy it. If the coin lands heads, the coupon is trading for $4 and we don't make any money. We paid $4 and could sell for $4 so we make nothing. However, if the coin lands tails, we could certainly lose since we paid $4 and it is now worth $3. By paying $4, we can't make money but we could certainly lose.

So now we know that $3 is a certainly a favorable price to pay since we can't lose but might win. We also know that $4 is too high since we can't win but might lose. This means there must be a price in between that a fair price to pay. It turns out that price is $3.50. If we pay $3.50 and the coin lands heads, we make 50 cents. If the coin lands tails, we lose 50 cents. If we were able to make such bets over long periods of time, we know that we'd win 50 cents half the time and lose 50 cents half the time and the price is considered fair at $3.50

In other words, even though there is an announcement of a possible $1 price increase, the coupons only increase in value by 50 cents. They do not move dollar-for-dollar under uncertainty. Only when the storeowner announced that he would definitely raise prices by one dollar does the coupon rise by that same amount.

This is really the simplest way to help you to understand why option prices will generally not move dollar-for-dollar with the underlying stock. If the stock rises one dollar, it is not guaranteed to stay there by expiration so the market will not price in the full dollar move. However, if we are in the final seconds of trading and the stock rises one dollar, then the market will price in the full dollar if the call option is in-the-money. It all hinges on the probability of the option retaining that intrinsic value at expiration.

Simplistic Stock Price Model

We can expand our understanding of why option prices generally do not move dollar-for-dollar with the underlying stock by considering an overly simplified model of stock price movements. Let's assume that a stock is currently trading for $100 and can only move in one-dollar increments. Further, assume the most it can only rise or fall is a maximum of five dollars and that all prices are equally likely. In the real world, all stock prices are not equally likely; a $100 stock has a much better chance of rising to $101 than it does to $105. But just to make the example easier, let's assume that all prices can occur with equal probability. With the current stock price at $100, this means the lowest it can move is $95 and the highest is $105. Now imagine that you have a $100 call option (at-the-money).

Under this scenario, your call option can only be worth one of the following values at expiration:

If stock price is:	At expiration, $100 call will be worth:
95	0
96	0
97	0
98	0
99	0
100	0
101	1
102	2
103	3
104	4
105	5

What is this $100 call option worth? Assuming that all final stock prices are equally likely, we know that the $100 call is worth the average of all possible prices. We simply add up all possible call values and divide by the total so the $100 call is worth 0+0+0+0+0+0+1+2+3+4+5 = 15 and the average is therefore $15/11 = $1.36. If you pay $1.36 for this call option hundreds and hundreds of times, you would just break even in the long run. If you try to buy this option for less money you can be sure that other traders will outbid you. Likewise, if the price rises above $1.36, traders will start selling thus bringing the price down. The end result is that the option's price should be $1.36 since that is the price at which neither the buyer nor the seller has a long run advantage. So in theory, if the market feels that the highest stock price is $105 and the lowest is $95 with all prices equally likely, then the option should be trading for $1.36.

Now let's assume that the stock rises by one dollar to $101. Under our assumptions, the stock can only rise or fall by five dollars so the new range of stock prices will be 96 to 106 and the range of possible option prices will be from $1 to $6:

If stock price is:	At expiration, $100 call will be worth:
96	0
97	0
98	0
99	0
100	0
101	1
102	2
103	3
104	4
105	5
106	6

The average price of the option is now found by summing up all the potential option values and dividing by 11. Our new $100 call price is 0+0+0+0+0+1+2+3+4+5+6 = 21 and 21/11 = $1.90

So if the stock rises from $100 to $101, the at-the-money call rises from $1.36 to $1.90. Notice that this is a $1 rise in the stock's price but only a 54-cent rise in the options price. Even with this simplistic price model, we are coming up with a very realistic price behavior for an at-the-money call option. Most at-the-money calls will have rise a little more than 50 cents on the dollar for the next one dollar move in the stock's price.

What would happen for the next dollar move in the stock's price? If the stock were to rise from $101 to $102, the call would rise by *more* than 54 cents. The reason is that each time we are dropping off one of the zeros and adding a bigger number. In the first situation, the highest call value was $5. In the second scenario, the highest call value was $6. So each time the stock rises, we add higher and higher values while dropping off zeros. The end result is that the option's price must rise by bigger and bigger amounts, at least up to a point. After some point, the option will move dollar-for-dollar with the underlying stock. Where is that point? When the option gets sufficiently in-the-money to a point where the market believes it will definitely have intrinsic value at expiration. Let's take a look at that scenario next.

Deep-In-The-Money-Options

Assume that the stock price is now $106 so that the $100 call is deep-in-the-money. Under our assumptions, the stock price can only move up or down a total of five points from its current price which means the expiration stock price will fall between $101 and $111. The total option price possibilities are as follows:

If stock price is:	At expiration, $100 call will be worth:
101	1
102	2
103	3
104	4
105	5
106	6
107	7
108	8
109	9
110	10
111	11

The option's price is now (1+2+3+4+5+6+7+8+9+10+11)/15 = $4.40. What do you suppose will happen if the stock rises another point to $107? Again, assuming the stock price can only rise or fall five points by expiration, the option values at expiration can range between $2 and $12 as follows:

If stock price is:	At expiration, $100 call will be worth:
102	2
103	3
104	4
105	5
106	6
107	7
108	8
109	9
110	10
111	11
112	12

To find the new option's price, we get to add the new, highest number 12 to the average but drop off the lowest number 1, which is a net gain of 11 to the average. Because we're dividing by 11, the option's price will rise by 11/11, which equals exactly one dollar. Using the same reasoning, if the stock rises again to $108, we'll add 13 to the average but drop off 2, which is again a net gain of 11 and the option's price will rise by one dollar again. This shows that once an option is sufficiently in-the-money, it will rise dollar-for-dollar with the underlying stock. Prior to that, the option's price will rise by something less than one dollar. The consequence of these actions is that an option's price will follow a curved path rather than the straight line, dollar-for-dollar action of the stock's price.

Out-Of-The-Money

In our previous examples, we saw that the at-the-money option will move about 54 cents for the next dollar move. Deep-in-the-money options, on the other hand, will move dollar-for-dollar with the underlying stock. What can we expect to happen with out-of-the-money options?

Let's assume the stock price is now $94 so that the final stock prices can fall between $89 and $99. In other words, the option has no chance for a payoff:

If stock price is:	At expiration, $100 call will be worth:
89	0
90	0
91	0
92	0
93	0
94	0
95	0
96	0
97	0
98	0
99	0

The option's price is now $0/11 = $0. If the stock rises one dollar to $95, we have removed a zero from the bottom and added a zero to the top so the option's price is still zero.

If stock price is:	At expiration, $100 call will be worth:
90	0
91	0
92	0
93	0
94	0
95	0
96	0
97	0
98	0
99	0
100	0

This shows that if your option is far enough out-of-the-money, its price may not even move even if the stock rises by a full dollar. Now let's take it a step further and assume that stock rises another point to $96:

If stock price is:	At expiration, $100 call will be worth:
91	0
92	0
93	0
94	0
95	0
96	0
97	0
98	0
99	0
100	0
101	1

Now the options price is (0+0+0+0+0+0+0+0+0+0+1)/11 = 9 cents. For a full point move in the stock, this option gained only nine cents in value. Further, if we make the comparison from a stock price of $94 then the stock moved two full points from $94 to $96 and yet the option only gained nine cents. This shows that far out-of-the-money options are relatively insensitive to stock price movements.

Deep-in-the-money options change respond nearly dollar-for-dollar with changes in the stock's price.

At-the-money options respond about 50 cents on the dollar.

Out-of-the-money option prices barely move with changes in the stock's price.

This is a very simple model of stock price movements. In reality, we'd assign higher probabilities for stock prices near today's price and lower probabilities for the extreme values. But to make the math easy, we just assumed that all stock prices were equally likely and still came up with similar option price movements as those observed in the real world. These fractional movements are in agreement with what we previously said will happen to the price of pizza coupons if we were less than 100% certain of a price increase. Notice that this simplified stock price model is also based on probabilities but in a more subtle way. When the stock was $100, the $100 call was worth $1.36. If the stock rises one dollar to $101, we cannot be sure of retaining the full value the highest option price possibility. With the stock at $101, the highest price possibility is $6. Since each price is equally likely, we should bid 1/11 * $6 = 54 cents higher for that option. And we did find that the new option price would be $1.36 + $0.54 = $1.90. The price of an option is ultimately determined by the probabilities for a particular range of stock prices.

What makes option pricing so unique is that it is based on an asymmetrical payoff schedule. If a stock trader buys stock, he gains dollar-for-dollar as the stock price rises and loses dollar-for-dollar as the stock price falls. Now look at the option prices in the previous tables. The options only have payoffs (values) for all stock prices above the $100 strike; all other values are zero. It is this asymmetrical payoff schedule that makes the options prices move less than dollar-for-dollar with the underlying (unless the option gets so far in-the-money in which case it moves dollar-for-dollar).

Now let's consider the July $32.50 call in Table 2-8. If the stock were to rise by one dollar right now, we are more certain that the $32.50 will retain intrinsic value at expiration when compared to the $35 call. The reason is that the stock has to fall much further to wipe out all of the intrinsic value on the $32.50 call. This means that the price of the $32.50 call will rise by a larger amount than the $35 call on the next dollar move in the underlying stock. If the stock were to move up one dollar from its current price of $37.11, we might see the $32.50 call rise by, say 85 cents, while the $35 call rise by only 70 cents. The $40 call, on the other hand, may not even budge in price. Once again, we see that the market is pricing the options according to risk. The $32.50 call gets bid up by a higher amount (in terms of dollars not percentages) than the $35 call because the $32.50 call is more certain to retain intrinsic value. In other words, the $32.50 call is *less risky* than the $35 call, which is what we stated earlier.

Delta of an Option

In the previous paragraph, we said that the $32.50 call may only rise by 85 cents for the next, immediate one dollar increase in the stock. An alternative wording is that the option is capturing 85% of the stock movement at this time. When traders talk about how an option's price moves in relation to the underlying stock, they are really talking about an advanced concept called *delta*. Delta is a measure of how much an option's price will move for the next, immediate one-dollar move in the underlying stock. We have to include the word "immediate" to remind us that the move must occur immediately and not later today or next week. Delta simply shows us how sensitive an option's price is to changes in the stock's price at that moment in time.

Most option trading software will show you the delta of an option. However, if your broker's platform does not, you can find them at a number of online resources, free of charge, such as at the Options Industry Council's (OIC) site at www.888Options.com, PC Quote at www.pcquote.com, or from the Philadelphia Stock Exchange at www.phlx.com.

Figure 2-10 shows our eBay options at this point in time with their corresponding deltas. Notice that the $32.50 strike has a delta of 0.90 (circled)[2]. This means that if

---

2 Sometimes you will see delta quoted as a whole number such as 90 rather than a decimal as 0.90 to reflect the fact that each option controls 100 shares. However, the concept is the same. A delta of 0.90 or 90 will rise about 90 cents for the next one-dollar move in the stock.

eBay were to immediately move one dollar that option will increase in price by 90 cents. Notice that the $35 call listed below shows a delta of only 0.39 so it will only increase in price by 39 cents on the next dollar move in the underlying stock.

Figure 2-10: Option Prices with Deltas

EBAY INC (EBAY)											
Symbol		Last		Time		Net	Bid	Ask	Reference price	Div freq	Div amt	Historical Volatility

| EBAY | 34.43 | 12.29 | -0.01 | 34.43 | 34.44 | 34.43 | 0 | 0 | 19.36% |

Calls							Jul 2005		Puts				
Ticker	Last	T-Val	Delta	Gamma	Theta	Implied Volatility	Strike	Ticker	Last	T-Val	Delta	Gamma	Theta	Implied Volatility
XBAGZ	2.45	2.07	0.90	0.108	-0.009	38.54%	32.5	XBASZ	0.45	0.08	-0.10	0.108	-0.006	35.41%
XBAGG	0.90	0.44	0.39	0.234	-0.015	34.13%	35	XBASG	1.46	0.94	-0.61	0.234	-0.012	32.56%
XBAGU	0.28	0.03	0.04	0.054	-0.003	35.18%	37.5	XBASU	3.30	3.02	-0.96	0.054	-0.000	31.70%
XBAGH	0.10	0.00	0.00	0.002	-0.000	37.21%	40	XBASH	5.70	5.49	-1.00	0.002	0.003	25.53%

We recently stated that the $32.50 call might move 85 cents while the $35 strike might move 70 cents, which is only a 15-cent difference. However, Figure 2-8 informs us that the $32.50 strike will move 90 cents while the $35 strike will move only 39 cents, which is a 59-cent difference. Why is there such a big discrepancy between what we previously said versus what Figure 2-7 is telling us? Why did we say there would be roughly a 15-cent difference when Figure 2-8 shows there is a 59-cent difference? The reason is that eBay has fallen from $37.11 to $34.43 when the quotes in Figure 2-9 were taken, which means the $35 strike is now out-of-the-money. It is no longer in-the-money as it was when the stock was $37.11. If eBay were still at $37.11, you'd see a much higher delta for the $35 call in Figure 2-9.

This shows that delta changes over time. Just because the $32.50 call delta is 0.90 right now does not mean that it will always be 0.90. Why does delta change? There is another interpretation of delta we can look to for a better understanding. Delta is mathematically an approximate measure of the probability that the option will expire with intrinsic value (in-the-money) at expiration. We must multiply that probability by the stock price move in order to see how the option will respond. In the pizza coupon example, we had a 50% chance of an increase in price and it's no coincidence that we figured out that the market would bid up the coupon by 50 cents because 50% of $1 = 50 cents.

If we define delta as the probability of the option expiring with intrinsic value, we can see that if there is a 90% chance of the $32.50 call expiring with intrinsic value then that call will increase by 90 cents for the next dollar move. The $35 call will only appreciate by 39 cents since it only has a 39% chance of expiring with intrinsic value. Since the $32.50 has a 90% chance of expiring with intrinsic value while the $35 call only has a 39% chance, this is yet another way to show that the $35 call is riskier than the $32.50 call. *The reason that deltas change is because the probability of an option expiring with intrinsic value changes.* Obviously, that probability hinges on the stock price and time to expiration. As time goes by or as the stock price moves, you will get different probabilities and therefore different deltas. The main point you want to understand about delta is that it does not remain the same throughout an option's life.

Put deltas are always shown as a negative number. This is not because there is a negative probability of them expiring in-the-money but rather it is a notation to remind us that a put *loses* value as the underlying stock rises and *gains* value as it falls. For example, in Figure 2-8, the $32.50 put has a delta of -0.10. If eBay were to rise by $1 right now, this put would lose 10 cents. But if the stock were to *fall* by one dollar, the put would gain 10 cents because -$1 * -0.10 delta = +0.10. The negative sign on a put delta is really a reminder that put option profitability moves opposite of the underlying stock.

Relationship Between Call and Put Deltas

If we know the delta of a call, is there anything we can say about the corresponding same-strike put? In other words, if we know the $32.50 call has a delta of 0.90, what can we conclude about the $32.50 put delta? The answer is easy with a little thought about probability. We know from basic probability theory that the sum of all mutually exclusive events must add up to one. This just means that if you break any event into two or more parts that cannot overlap (mutually exclusive) then the sum of all those probabilities must be one.

For example, if you have a 90% chance of passing an exam then that means there is a 10% chance you will fail since passing and failing are mutually exclusive – you can't pass and fail at the same time. You either pass or you fail. All probabilities must add up to one and, in this case, 0.90 + 0.10 = 1. If your favorite football team has a 60% chance of winning their next game then they must have a 40% chance of losing since they cannot win and lose. As before, all probabilities must sum to one and we see that 0.60 + 0.40 = 1.

Now think about stock prices. No matter where eBay is currently trading, it will either be above $32.50 at expiration or it won't. If the stock is above $32.50 then the $32.50 call will be in-the-money. If the stock is below $32.50 at expiration then the $32.50 put will be in-the-money. If there is a 90% chance (delta) that the $32.50 call will expire in-the-money then there must be a 10% chance the $32.50 put must be in-the-money. And that means that the delta of the $32.50 put must be 0.10. If you look at the delta of the $35 put in Figure 2-6, you'll see that it is, in fact, 0.10, or 10%. The delta for the call and put will nearly always add up to one (ignoring the minus sign of the put) since all probabilities must sum to one.

Exercise
Using Figure 2-9, check the sums of the deltas for the same-strike calls and put. Ignoring the minus sign of the put deltas, do they add up to one?

If the concept of delta has you confused, don't worry. Believe it or not, many professional traders confuse the definition and interpretation. *The key point to remember is that an option's price will generally <u>not</u> move dollar-for-dollar with the underling stock.* If you want to get a ballpark figure on how much the option will gain or lose with the next, immediate one dollar move in the stock you'll want to look up the delta of that option. The only time that an option will move nearly dollar-for-dollar is when the option is viewed by the market as being guaranteed to expire with intrinsic value. This means the option must either be very deep in-the-money or in-the-money with a very short time until expiration. If it is felt that the options are guaranteed to expire with intrinsic value, then the long call option will behave like long stock (delta = 1) and the put option will behave like short stock (delta = -1). The delta of a stock is always one since it rises and falls dollar-for-dollar with itself. (Consequently, the delta for short stock is always negative one since it loses dollar-for-dollar as the price rises and gains dollar-for-dollar as the price falls.) So once an option's delta reaches one, it is considered to be stock. If a put option's delta reaches negative one, it is considered to be short stock.

The relationship between call and put deltas should tell you that it's pretty difficult to have more than 50% of the options expire worthless. For instance, if all of the call options expire in-the-money then all of the put options must expire out-of-the-money. Because there are an equal number of call and put strike prices, this means that 50% of the options expired worthless. If the stock's price closes in the middle of all strike listed strike prices then, again, half of the calls and half of the puts expire worthless. Despite this relationship, there is a persistent myth that 90% of all options expire worthless. You will undoubtedly hear this figure quoted many times but you will never find a single study to substantiate it. In fact, the OCC (Options Clearing Corporation) publishes statistics on their website at www.OptionsClearning.com and you will find that historically the numbers are roughly as follows: 10% of all options are exercised, 30% expire worthless, and 60% are closed in the open market. There are obviously variations in these numbers but they rarely fluctuate by more than five percentage points in any direction.

 Roughly 60% of all options are closed in the open market. About 30% expire worthless and 10% are exercised. It is NOT true that 90% of all options expire worthless. It is a mathematical impossibility.

||||||||||||||||||||||||||||||||||||||||||||||||||||||||||||||||||||||||||||||||||||||||||||||

 Key Concepts

1) An option's price does generally not move dollar-for-dollar with the underlying stock.

2) An option's price will rise or fall by its delta on the next, immediate one-dollar move in the underlying stock.

3) Assuming the same expiration, calls and puts with the same strike will generally have deltas that add up to one (ignoring the minus sign of the put delta).

||||||||||||||||||||||||||||||||||||||||||||||||||||||||||||||||||||||||||||||||||||||||||||||

Chapter Two Questions

1) **ABC stock is trading for $76 near expiration and your $70 call is bidding $5.20. How do you capture the missing intrinsic value?**
   a) Buy the stock and short the call
   b) Short the stock and exercise the call
   c) Buy the stock and exercise the call
   d) Short the stock and short the call

2) **ABC stock is trading for $37 near expiration and your $40 put is bidding $2.80. How do you capture the missing intrinsic value?**
   a) Short the stock and exercise the put
   b) Buy the stock and exercise the put
   c) Buy the stock and short the put
   d) Short the stock and short the put

3) **What is the key factor that gives an option, whether a call or put, its value?**
   a) The strike price
   b) Price of the stock
   c) Volatility
   d) Open interest

4) **The higher the risk:**
   a) The higher the price, the higher the reward
   b) The lower the price, the lower the reward
   c) The lower the price, the higher the reward
   d) The higher the price, the lower the reward

5) **Out-of-the-money option prices move:**
   a) Dollar-for-dollar with the underlying stock
   b) About 50 cents on the dollar with the underlying stock
   c) Only a small fraction with the underlying stock
   d) About 75 cents on the dollar with the underlying stock

6) **The maximum value that a call option could ever be is:**
   a) The price of the underlying stock
   b) There is no limit

    c)   Only half of the underlying stock's price

    d)   The price of the put

7)   **Interest rates are 6% and you will definitely receive $5,000 six months from now. How much should you be willing to accept if the other party wanted to settle the debt today?**

    a) $4,716

    b) $4,854

    c) $4,981

    d) $4,622

8)   **You are looking at quotes on IBM March Calls. Which is more expensive, the $80 call or the $85 call?**

    a)   Cannot be determined with this information

    b)   They will be about the same price

    c) $85 call is more expensive

    d) $80 call is more expensive

9)   **You are looking at Dell Computer April $30 calls and July $30 calls. Which is more expensive?**

    a)   Cannot be determined with this information

    b)   They will be about the same price

    c)   April will be more expensive

    d)   July will be more expensive

10)   **You are looking at Intel December puts. Which is more expensive, the $30 put or the $40 put?**

    a)   Cannot be determined with this information

    b)   They will be about the same price

    c) $40 put is more expensive

    d) $30 put is more expensive

11)   **Delta measures:**

    a)   The intrinsic value of the option

    b)   The sensitivity of an option's price compared to the stock's price

    c)   The time value of the option

    d)   The sensitivity of an option's price compared to the overall market

12) **One interpretation of delta is:**
    a)   The probability that the option will expire out-of-the-money
    b)   The probability that the option will expire in-the-money
    c)   The probability that the option will expire without being exercised
    d)   The probability that the option will expire

13) **XYZ stock is trading for $44.50 near expiration. Your $40 call must be worth at least:**
    a) $4.00
    b) $4.50
    c) $44.50
    d)   There is no way to determine based on this information

14) **If the $50 call delta is 0.70, the $50 put delta is:**
    a) There is no way to determine based on this information
    b)   -0.50
    c)   -0.70
    d)   -0.30

15) **The ABC $50 call is trading for $7. What is the maximum amount the $45 call could be trading for?**
    a) $12
    b) $7
    c) $8
    d)   There is no way to determine based on this information

16) **What are the only two prices that are possible for an option to have at expiration?**
    a)   Premium or intrinsic value
    b)   Zero or intrinsic value
    c)   Zero or time value
    d)   Time value or intrinsic value

17) **You purchased a $40 call for $3. What is the breakeven point on the option?**
    a) $3
    b) $37
    c) $40
    d) $43

18) **You purchased a $70 put for $2. What is the breakeven point on the option?**
    a) $68
    b) $2
    c) $72
    d) $70

19) **Because high volatility stocks have a better chance for price appreciation, you should:**
    a)   Only place trades during highly volatile markets to increase your edge
    b)   Only trade options on low volatility stocks for more consistent profits
    c)   Not choose trades based on this fact because the volatility will be priced into the option
    d)   Only trade options on high volatility stocks

20) **If an 30-day option has a delta of 80 today:**
    a)   It will remain at 80 over the life of the option
    b)   It will change over time
    c)   It cannot fall below 80 but could rise above it
    d)   It can fall below 80 but not rise above it

Chapter Two - Answers

1) **ABC stock is trading for $76 near expiration and your $70 call is bidding $5.20. How do you capture the missing intrinsic value?**
    b)   Short the stock and exercise the call

With the stock trading at $76, the $70 call must be worth at the $6 intrinsic value at expiration. However, sometimes the bid-ask spreads can make the bid price slightly less than this intrinsic value. In this question, there is 80 cents missing from the intrinsic value. Rather than just sell your $70 call in the open market and receive $5.20, you can short the stock at $76 and immediately exercise the $75 call, which will leave you with a $6 gain.

2) **ABC stock is trading for $37 near expiration and your $40 put is bidding $2.80. How do you capture the missing intrinsic value?**
    b) Buy the stock and exercise the put

With the stock trading at $37, the $40 put should be worth the $3 intrinsic value at expiration. But just as for call options, sometimes there is some missing intrinsic value near expiration. In this question, you could place an order to buy shares of the stock for $37 and immediately exercise the put and sell the shares for $40 thus capturing a $3 rather than the $2.80 gain you'd get by selling the put in the open market. It does not matter if you don't have the cash to buy the shares of stock since the exercise of the put guarantees the funds.

3) **What is the key factor that gives an option, whether a call or put, its value?**

    c)   Volatility

The volatility of the underlying stock is the key factor in determining an options value. Volatility simply measures the fluctuations in a stock's price. The greater the fluctuations, the greater the uncertainty of prices and options become more valuable.

4) **The higher the risk:**

    c)   The lower the price, the higher the reward

If an investment is risky, the market will bid down its price to a level where it becomes desirable. If the price is low then the potential return, or reward, will be higher.

5) **Out-of-the-money option prices move:**

    c)   Only a small fraction with the underlying stock

Out-of-the-money options have a low delta, which means the option's price will only move a small percentage when compared to the move in the stock's price.

6) **The maximum value that a call option could ever be is:**

    a)   The price of the underlying stock

The maximum price a call option could ever reach is the price of the stock (Pricing Principle #5). If the price of any call option were to exceed the stock price then arbitrage would be possible.

7) **Interest rates are 6% and you will definitely receive $5,000 six months from now. How much should you be willing to accept if the other party wanted to settle the debt today?**

    b) $4,854

If interest rates are 6% per year then they are effectively 3% per six months. The present value of $5,000 would then be $5,000/1.03 = $4,854. This just means you should be indifferent between receiving $4,854 today and $5,000 in six months from now if interest rates are 6%. If you accepted $4,854 today, you could invest that money at the risk-free rate of 6% and it would grow to $5,000 in six months.

8) **You are looking at quotes on IBM March Calls. Which is more expensive, the $80 call or the $85 call?**

   d) $80 call is more expensive

   With all else being equal (that is, same underlying stock and expiration), lower strike calls must be more valuable than higher strikes (Pricing Principle #1). Although we don't know what the price of either call will be, we do know that the $80 call would be more valuable since it gives the holder the right to buy shares at a lower price.

9) **You are looking at Dell Computer April $30 calls and July $30 calls. Which is more expensive?**

   d)   July will be more expensive

   With all else being equal, longer term options will be more valuable than shorter term expirations (Pricing Principle #2). The reason is simply that more time allows the underlying stock to make bigger moves, whether higher or lower.

10) **You are looking at Intel December puts. Which is more expensive, the $30 put or the $40 put?**

   c) $40 put is more expensive

   With all else being equal, higher strike puts will be more valuable than lower strike puts (Pricing Principle #1). The reason is that the higher strike put allows the holder to sell stock at a higher price, which is more beneficial (valuable) than selling at a lower price.

11) **Delta measures:**

   b)   The sensitivity of an option's price compared to the stock's price

   If a call option has a delta of 0.50, then we know that the option's price will rise 50 cents for the next dollar move in the stock's price. If a put has a 0.50 delta, then its price will rise 50 cents for the next dollar fall in the stock's price. Delta therefore shows how sensitive an option's price is to movements in the stock's price.

12)   One interpretation of delta is:

   b)   The probability that the option will expire in-the-money

One mathematical interpretation is that it roughly shows the probability that an option will expire in-the-money at expiration. If an option has a delta of 0.70 then there is roughly a 70% chance that it will expire in-the-money at expiration.

13)   XYZ stock is trading for $44.50 near expiration. Your $40 call must be worth at least:

   b) $4.50

All options must be worth their intrinsic value at expiration. In this example, the $40 call must be worth $4.50. (If it were worth less than that, you'd simply short the stock an immediately exercise the call as in Question 1.)

14)   If the $50 call delta is 0.70, the $50 put delta is:

   d)   -0.30

Same-strike call and put deltas must sum to one (ignoring the minus sign of the put delta). If the call delta is 0.70, the corresponding put delta must be -0.30.

15)   The ABC $50 call is trading for $7. What is the maximum amount the $45 call could be trading for?

   a) $12

For any two calls (or puts) the difference in their prices cannot exceed the difference in the strikes (Pricing Principle #6). In this question, there could not be more than a five-dollar difference in their prices since there is a five-dollar difference in strike prices. We also know that lower strike calls must be more valuable than higher strikes so if the $50 call is $7, the $45 call could not be worth more than $12 otherwise arbitrage is possible.

16)   What are the only two prices that are possible for an option to have at expiration?

   b)   Zero or intrinsic value

An option will be worthless if it is out-of-the-money at expiration. If it is in-the-money, it will be worth exactly the intrinsic value. Remember, prior to expiration, out-of-the-money options will certainly have some value since time remains. But at expiration, they are worthless.

17) **You purchased a $40 call for $3. What is the break-even point on the option?**

d) $43

The break-even point for a call option is found by taking the premium and adding it to the strike price. In this question, the breakeven point is $40 strike + $3 premium = $43 stock price. If the stock is $43 at expiration, the $40 call is worth exactly $3, which is the same as the amount you paid – you have just broken even.

18) **You purchased a $70 put for $2. What is the breakeven point on the option?**

a) $68

The break-even point for a put option is found by subtracting the premium from the strike price. In this question, the break-even point is $70 - $2 = $68 stock price. If the stock is $68 at expiration, the $70 put is worth exactly $2, which is the amount you paid so you have just broken even.

19) **Because high volatility stocks have a better chance for price appreciation, you should:**

c)   Not choose trades based on this fact because the volatility will be priced into the option.

You will hear many traders tell you to only trade options on high volatility stocks since there is more room for price appreciation. But this is really a big myth. The reason is that the markets are well aware of that advantage so traders bid the prices of the high volatility options higher. The net result is that there is no net advantage in trading high volatility stocks.

20) **If an 30-day option has a delta of 80 today:**

b)   It will change over time

The delta of an option does not stay constant over the life of the option. The delta changes as other factors change. The key factors are time, volatility, and price of the underlying stock. But just because you buy an 80-delta option today does not mean that it will be the same next week. In fact, all in-the-money options approach a delta of 1.0 as expiration gets closer while all out-of-the-money options approach zero. The delta does not stay constant.

Chapter Three
Profit and Loss Diagrams

In the last chapter, we learned that options have an *asymmetrical payoff* structure and it is this property that makes them difficult to understand for new traders. As a refresher, if you buy stock, you have a symmetrical payoff structure. If you buy shares of stock, you make one dollar for every dollar it rises and lose one dollar for every dollar it falls. The gains and losses are symmetrical around the purchase price. However, these symmetrical profits and losses are not present for options. If you buy the $50 call, you will make one dollar at expiration for every dollar the stock rises above $50 but you will *not* lose one dollar for every stock price below $50. Option payoffs are not symmetrical around their purchase price.

Because of this unique asymmetrical payoff property, it can be difficult to understand how an option position will behave over a range of stock prices. Imagine how difficult it would be if you were dealing with two or more options!

Fortunately, there is a handy tool – the profit and loss diagram – that allows us to look at a picture to see how our profits and losses will be affected as the underlying stock price moves. Unfortunately, few investors or traders take the time to understand them and they end up missing out on a wonderful tool that will make their life easier and also adds insightful dimensions to their understanding of options. Profit and loss diagrams can also keep you out of a lot of trouble since they can alert you to potential risks of a particular strategy that you may have never considered. There is probably no better way to sum up the advantage of using profit and loss diagrams than with the saying, "A picture is worth a thousand words." The risks and rewards of any position, no matter how complex, are brought to life by looking at a simple picture. Even if you're not familiar with the particular names of strategies, if you can read a profit and loss diagram, you will have a good understanding of what the strategy is trying to accomplish.

Let's take a look at how to construct a profit and loss diagram and then we'll show you how easily they reveal the risks and rewards of various option strategies. Please understand that the work we are putting into these exercises is not necessary when trading options in the real world. Computer programs will draw the pictures for you and you will not need to actually create the tables and charts. However, if you run through the calculations by hand while learning, you will understand the pictures much better.

Profit and loss diagrams can be constructed for any asset, not just options. So let's start with a simple example and create a profit and loss diagram for one of the most basic of all positions, a long stock position.

In order to create any profit and loss diagram, we need two pieces of information. First, we need to know how much our asset in question will be worth at various stock prices. Second, we need to know how much was paid for the asset. With those two pieces of information, we can chart any profit and loss diagram.

Because we need to know what our asset in question is worth at various stock prices, we always start with a table consisting of various stock prices. That's always the first step. Next, we calculate what the profit and loss would be for our position in question if the stock were at each of those prices.

For instance, assume you purchased stock for $50 per share. To construct the profit and loss table, we'd start with a column of stock prices starting with the $50 purchase price and then extend the range somewhat above and below this center price. For example, we may consider a range of stock prices between $45 and $55 as in the first column of Table 3-1:

Table 3-1: Profit and Loss Table (Long Stock)

If the stock price is:	Cost of stock	Your profit/loss will be:
$45	$50	-$5
$46	$50	-$4
$47	$50	-$3
$48	$50	-$2
$49	$50	-$1
$50	$50	**$0 (break-even point)**
$51	$50	+$1
$52	$50	+$2

$53	$50	+$3
$54	$50	+$4
$55	$50	+$5

Next, we calculate what the profit or loss would be for our asset in question (long stock) for each of the listed stock prices. For instance, the first cell in Table 3-1 shows a stock price of $45. If the stock price is $45, you have a $5 loss since you paid $50 per share. If you look further down the list, you can see that if the stock price is $53, you'd have a $3 profit. If you like working with formulas, we can find the values for the profit/loss column by taking "Column 1 - Column 2."

Naturally, whether the profit/loss column represents a real loss or a "paper loss" depends on whether you actually sell the stock at that moment. For example, if you sell the stock at $45, you have a $5 "realized" loss. If you do not sell it, you have a $5 "unrealized" loss. Either way, if the stock is $45, there is some type of a five-dollar loss facing us and that's what Table 3-1 is showing us.

Once our table is constructed, we just need to plot this information on a graph. We will always use the "stock price" column as the horizontal axis (x-axis) and the profit/loss column as the vertical axis (y-axis). Once we do, we get a chart that looks like Figure 3-2:

Figure 3-2: Profit and Loss Diagram (Long Stock)

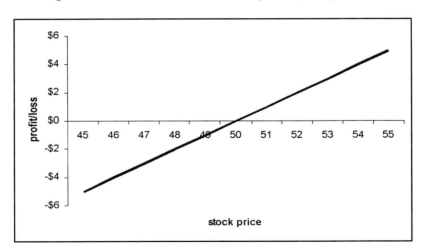

Figure 3-2 is the *profit and loss diagram* for a long stock position and is simply a picture of the information in Table 3-1. Notice that it is simply a straight line sloping upward to the right. To read the chart, you just select any stock price along the horizontal axis and then trace a line up to the profit and loss line. From there you follow it directly to the left axis and that tells you what your profit or loss would be for that particular stock price. For instance, what would our profit (or loss) be if the stock is $54? All we have to do is trace a straight line from the $54 stock price on the horizontal axis up to our profit and loss line and then over to the vertical axis on the left as shown by the dashed lines in Figure 3-3:

Figure 3-3

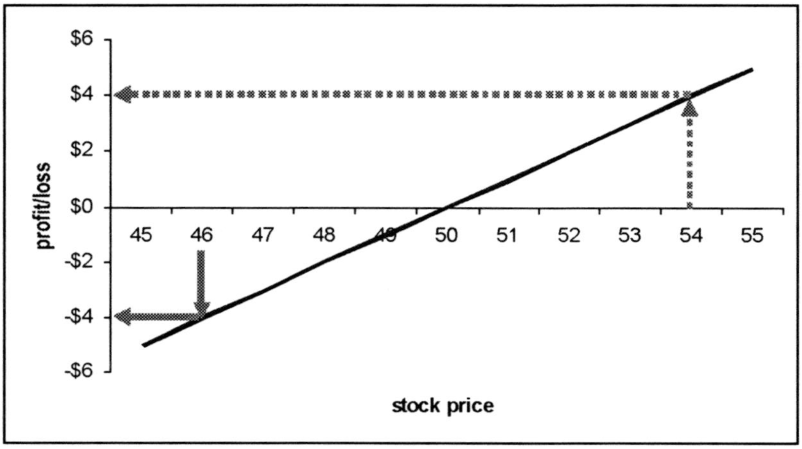

You can see that we land on a profit of $4. This tells us that if the stock is $54, then we have a $4 profit. Likewise, if the stock is trading at $46, we'd have a $4 loss, which is shown by the solid arrows.

Notice that the profit and loss line crosses the horizontal axis at $50. This tells us that at a stock price of $50, we have no profit or loss; we are just breaking even. Anytime a profit and loss line intersects the horizontal axis that shows a breakeven point. (For some strategies, there will be more than one break-even point.)

Figure 3-3 shows that we break-even at $50 and make one dollar if the stock is $51, two dollars if it is $52, etc. Likewise, it shows that we lose one dollar if it falls to $49, two dollars if it falls to $48, etc. In other words, if we own stock, we make dollar-for-dollar as the stock price rises and lose dollar-for-dollar as the stock price falls.

Even though Table 3-1 and Figure 3-2 are two different ways of expressing the same information, the picture is easier to follow. It is much harder to visualize the profit and loss behavior by looking at the table. Now, if you are familiar with graphing, you probably figured out that the information in Table 3-1 would plot as a straight line. However, as we move to the asymmetrical payoffs of options and add more complex strategies, the table will be nearly impossible to follow. A picture becomes a much easier way of understanding how your profit or losses will be affected with changes in the underlying stock and that's why we want to understand how to read profit and loss diagrams.

Let's take the next step and try a little harder problem by creating a profit and loss diagram for a long $50 call option that we purchased for $5.

Remember, we always start with a column of stock prices. However, when dealing in options, we pick the stock prices based on the *strike price* of the option (or options) rather than the purchase price as we did for the long stock example. Because we're trying to figure out the profit and loss diagram for a $50 call, we would create a column of stock prices starting $50 and then select a few stock prices above and below $50 such as shown in the first column of Table 3-4:

Table 3-4: Profit and Loss Table (Long $50 Call)

If the stock price is:	At expiration, $50 call is worth:	$50 call cost	Profit/ Loss
$35	$0	$5	-$5
$40	$0	$5	-$5
$45	$0	$5	-$5
$50	$0	$5	-$5
$55	$5	$5	$0
$60	$10	$5	$5
$65	$15	$5	$10

Notice that our stock prices are in five-dollar increments rather than one-dollar increments we used for the previous long stock example. In actuality, it doesn't matter which increments you use since all methods produce the same picture. But in order to keep the tables small, we generally count by five-dollar increments when dealing with options.

The second column in Table 3-4 shows what the $50 call will be worth *at expiration*. It's important to understand that when drawing profit and loss diagrams for options, we are drawing them at expiration of the option. For example, we know that if the stock is $50 or less at expiration that the $50 call expires worthless. However, if the stock is $55, the $50 call would be worth exactly $5 at expiration. If the stock is $60 at expiration, the $50 call is worth $10 and so on.

The third column in Table 3-4 shows us the cost of the call, which we assumed was $5 for this example. In this were a real-life example, we may just use the $5 premium for the option or we may be more realistic and include commissions. Either decision will not change the shape of the profit and loss diagram but it would change the profit or loss values. Whether you decide to include commissions or not, the cost you come up with does not change as the stock's price changes. That's why the third column in Table 3-4 is the same answer ($5) for the entire column.

Now we have our two necessary pieces of information to draw the profit and loss diagram: (1) We know the value of the $50 call at various stock prices by looking at column 2 and (2) We know the cost of the $50 call by looking at column 3. Now we just need to figure out what our profit or loss will be for the various stock prices in the table. We figure out the profit or loss just as any business would by taking "revenues minus costs." In this example, if the stock closed at $35 at option expiration, your revenues would be zero from the sale of the option since it is worthless. Because you paid $5 for the option, you'd have a $5 loss with the stock at $35. The formula for the profit/loss column is simply Column 2 - Column 3.

Once we have the necessary pieces of information, all we have to do is plot the profit/loss column against the stock prices (bold columns in Table 3-4) and we get the following profit and loss diagram shown in Figure 3-5:

Figure 3-5: Profit and Loss Diagram (Long $50 Call)

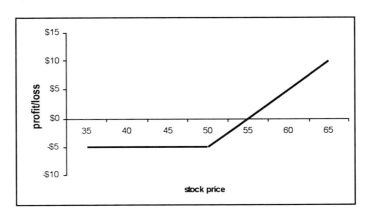

We read this profit and loss diagram in the same way as we did for the long stock profit and loss diagram. How much would we make or lose if the stock closed at $60 at expiration? We just need to find $60 on the horizontal axis and draw a line to the profit and loss curve. From that point, we just look directly to the left axis to find the answer, which is $5, as shown by the dashed arrows in Figure 3-6:

Figure 3-6: Profit and Loss Diagram (Long $50 Call)

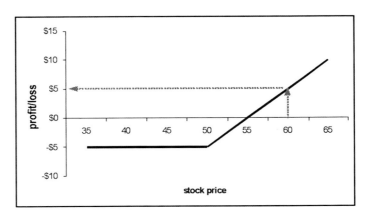

We can check the answer by hand. If the stock were $60 at expiration, the $50 call would be worth exactly $10. Because we paid $5 for it, our profit must be $5. Hopefully you are convinced that it is much easier it is to look at the picture to arrive at this answer rather than going through all of the steps by hand.

The picture immediately tells us that a long call is a bullish asset since it makes money as the stock price rises. Further, there is no limit to the amount of money that could be made since the chart continues to rise with increasing stock prices. Even if you do not understand a particular strategy, a quick glance at its profit and loss diagram immediately shows what the trader would like to have happen to the stock price.

Notice that the profit and loss diagram for a long call looks more like a "hockey stick" rather than the straight line we saw for a long stock position. This is because the holder of a long call can only lose the purchase price no matter how low the stock's price may fall below the strike price. If the stock is $50 or lower at expiration, the long call holder loses a maximum of five dollars and that's why the curve flattens out for all stock prices below $50. Anytime you see a "flat" segment (running parallel to the horizontal axis) of a profit and loss diagram, it tells you that particular range of stock prices has no effect on your profit or loss at expiration.

But if the stock is above $50 at expiration, the long call holder makes dollar-for-dollar just as the long stock owner does. This demonstrates one of the most important characteristics about long call options. That is, long calls allow traders and investors a way to participate dollar-for-dollar as the stock price rises but not lose dollar-for-dollar if the stock price falls. In other words, long calls provide traders and investors with some downside protection. The diagram visually demonstrates the asymmetric payoff structure of options.

Characteristics of Profit and Loss Diagrams

There are three important characteristics that are common to all profit and loss diagrams:

- A "bend" will occur at every strike price
- There will be a portion above and below zero
- The curve will cross zero at one or more points (the break-even point)

Let's go through each of these in a little more detail. First, all profit and loss diagrams will "bend" at each strike price of the option(s). In Figure 3-5, the $50 call bends upward at the $50 strike but that will not always be the case. Depending on the option, whether it is long or short, and how it is paired with other assets, the profit and loss diagram may bend up, down, or even sideways. But you can always be sure that it will bend at every strike price involved in the strategy.

The second characteristic of all profit and loss diagrams is that every one will have a portion of the diagram that falls above and below zero. The reason is simple. Every strategy has a potential reward and that is the portion that is represented in the chart as the area above the horizontal zero mark. If there is a reward then there must be a potential risk in attempting to gain that reward and that is the portion that lies below zero. This is important to understand because it will help you to decide if a particular strategy has a risk-reward ratio suitable for your tastes. Train your eye to see the profit areas (area above zero) as well as the loss areas (area below zero).

The third characteristic is that all profit and loss diagrams will have at least one break-even point. This follows from the fact that if a portion of the profit and loss diagram must lie above and below zero then it follows that the diagram must *cross* zero at some point. The point where it crosses the zero on the horizontal axis is the break-even point. In Figure 3-6, our long $50 call purchased for $5 crosses zero at a stock price of $55. This tells us that if the stock closes at $55 at expiration, we will have no profit and no loss (not counting commissions). If the stock is $55, the $50 call can be sold for $5. Because we paid $5, we break even on the trade. Remember, the break-even point for a call position (long or short) is found by adding the strike price and the premium. In this example, $50 strike + $5 premium = $55 break even and that's exactly what the chart is showing us. Figure 3-7 highlights these three important characteristics:

Figure 3-7

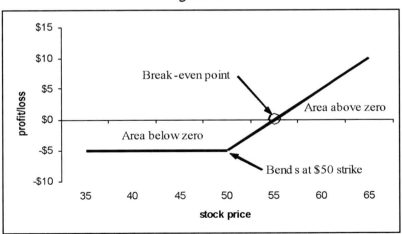

II

 Key Concepts

1) The area below zero on a profit and loss diagram represents the risk.

2) The area above zero represents the reward.

3) The point(s) where the profit and loss curve crosses zero is the break-even point.

4) A "bend" in the curve will always occur at a strike price.

IIIIIIIIIIIIIIIIIIIIIIIIIIIIIIIIIIIIIIIIIIIIIIIIIIIIIIIIIIIIIIIIIIIIIIIIIIIIIIIIIIIIIIIIIIIIIIIIIIIIII

Closing an Option

In Chapter One, we showed that you can effectively escape any option contract by entering a "reversing" trade. This just means that in order to get out of the contract that you do the opposite set of actions that got you into it. So if you own an option, you can simply sell it. If you sold an option, you can buy it back. These actions effectively get you out of the contract. Now that you understand profit and loss diagrams, you will have a better appreciation as to why this works.

Assume you buy a $50 call "to open" for $4 and later sell it "to close" for $6. What has effectively happened? Take a close look at the two trades forgetting about the opening or closing notations:

Buy a $50 call = -$4
Sell a $50 call = +$6

These transactions are really no different from buying and selling stock. If you buy 100 shares of Intel for $30 and sell 100 shares of Intel at $35, you no longer have any Intel shares. All you're left with is the difference in cash (whether a gain or a loss). The same idea is true for the options. If you buy a $50 call for $4 and then sell a $50 call for $6, you no longer have the call but only the cash difference; in this case, a $2 profit.

We can use profit and loss diagrams to get a better understanding as to why this works mathematically. Assume for a moment that the above two transactions were "opening" transactions; that is, you bought the $50 call for $4 "to open" and the sold $50 call for $6 "to open." In the real world, you're not allowed to be long and short the same contract in the same account and the reason for it will be apparent shortly. But for now, just assume that we could do these transactions in the same account. Figure 3-8 shows a profit and loss diagram for each of these two transactions:

Figure 3-8: Long $50 Call for $4 (solid line) and Short $50 Call for $6 (shaded line)

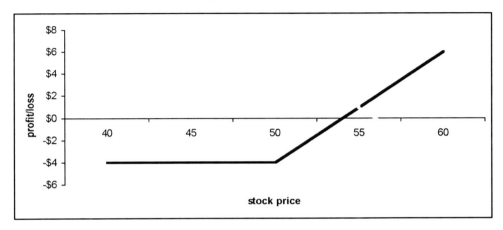

The solid line shows the starting position of purchasing a $50 call for $4. The shaded line shows our profit and loss from selling the $50 call for $6. If we actually held these two positions separately in our account then our profit and losses from this point forward will be the vertical summation of these two lines. In other words, for any stock price you'd just find the profit or loss of each position and combine them. For example, at a stock price of $45, the green line shows +$6 while the red line shows -$4. The result must be a profit of $2. At a stock price of $55, the red line shows a +$1 gain and so does the green line so the total profit is $2. At a stock price of $60, the red line shows a profit of $6 while the green shows a loss of $4, which is another gain of $2. We can actually combine these two profit and loss diagrams into one, which gives us Figure 3-9:

Figure 3-9

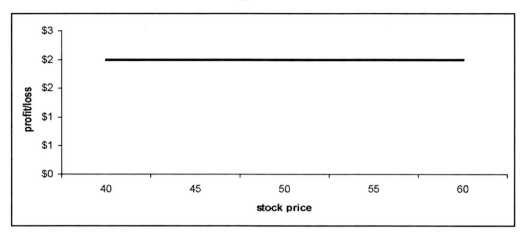

Notice that buying and selling the same option creates a flat line from a profit and loss perspective. That is, your profits or losses are *not in any way affected by stock price movement*. So theoretically, you could buy the $50 call "to open" and then sell the $50 call "to open" and you'd be out of the contract. However, if you have two "opening" contracts then this creates additional "open interest" that really isn't there. It is for this reason that the OCC (Options Clearing Corporation) does not allow you to be long and short the same option in the same account. Effectively there's nothing there. That's why you must either buy the contract "to open" and then sell it "to close" or do the reverse and sell the contract "to open" and then buy it "to close." One action just undoes the other and you're effectively out of the contract and hopefully holding onto a profit as a result.

What's the Best Strategy?

One of the biggest benefits of using profit and loss diagrams is that they allow us to compare strategies or positions. For instance, Figure 3-10 compares the previous two profit and loss diagrams we've discussed. It compares long stock purchased at $50 with the long $50 call purchased for $5:

Figure 3-10: Comparison between Long Stock (solid line) and Long Call (shaded line)

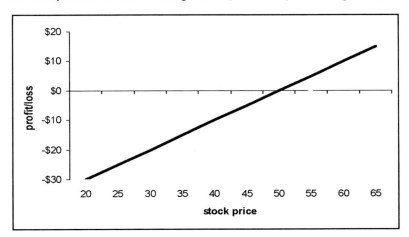

We've extended the range of stock prices to cover from $20 to $65 so that you can really see that the $50 call provides downside protection. The long stock holder can lose the entire $50 investment while the long call holder can only lose $5. If the stock is trading above $50 at expiration, both the call and stock owner participate dollar-for-dollar. The long call holder participates fully to the upside but does not lose as much to the downside. So why would anybody trade anything other than options? The reason is that this "favorable" risk-reward of the call option does not come for free. Notice in Figure 3-10 that the long stock position intersects the long call position at a stock price of $45. This is called the *crossover* point. This shows that both strategies are equal at expiration at a stock price of $45. If the stock closes at $45 at expiration, the long stock holder loses five dollars and so does the long call holder.

However, below the crossover point, the long call performs better since its line lies above that of the long stock position. Even though both positions lose in this region, the long call has a fixed loss of five dollars while the long stock position continues to lose all the way down to a stock price of zero.

On the other hand, above the crossover point, the long stock position performs better for all stock prices since its line lies *above* the $50 call line. In other words, the profit is higher for the long stock holder for all stock prices above $45 at expiration. How much better off is the long stock position? For all stock prices above $50, the long stock holder will have five dollars more profit than the long call holder. The reason is that the long call owner paid a five-dollar time premium thus making his breakeven point $55 while the long stock holder breaks even at $50. So the distance between those two lines above $50 is exactly $5, which is the cost of the call.

This shows that options are all about tradeoffs. Whenever you compare two (or more) strategies on the same graph, you will always find that one strategy is better than the other for certain areas while it is worse off in others. *No strategy can be superior to another for all areas on the profit and loss diagram (otherwise arbitrage is possible)*. In Figure 3-10, you can see that the long stock position performs better for all stock prices above the $45 crossover point and worse for all stock prices below. It is up to the option trader or investor to decide if the cost of the option is worth the benefit it provides. Profit and loss diagrams are the easiest way to visualize exactly what the tradeoffs are.

Let's now draw a profit and loss diagram for a long $50 put position purchased for $3. Hopefully, you're now starting to understand the steps and know that we need to know what the $50 put would be worth for various levels of the stock at expiration. Second, we need to know the cost of the put. With those two pieces of information, we can draw the profit and loss diagram. We'll start by making a profit and loss table to show us the various values for our chart:

Table 3-11: Profit and Loss Table (Long $50 Put)

If the stock price is:	At expiration, $50 put is worth:	$50 put cost	Profit/ Loss
$35	$15	$3	$12
$40	$10	$3	$7
$45	$5	$3	$2
$50	$0	$3	-$3
$55	$0	$3	-$3
$60	$0	$3	-$3
$65	$0	$3	-$3

The explanations of the numbers in this table should be fairly obvious to you now. Reading across the first row, if the stock price is $35 at expiration, the $50 put is worth exactly $15. Because we paid $3 for it, we'd have a $12 profit. For all stock prices above $50, the put expires worthless and we lose our $3 investment. If we plot the profit/loss values against the stock prices, we get Figure 3-12:

Figure 3-12: Profit and Loss Diagram (Long $50 Put)

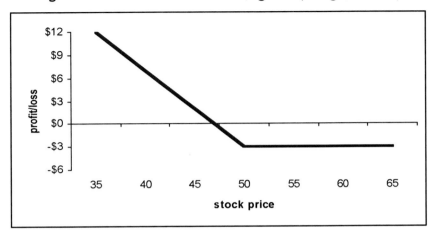

We can see in this chart that long put options gain value as the stock price falls, which tells us this is a bearish position. The chart "bends" at the $50 strike price and all area to the right of $50 results in a maximum loss while all area below the $47 break-even brings a profit. Remember, the break-even for a put option (long or short) is found by taking the strike minus the premium. In this case, a $50 strike - $3 premium = $47 break-even. The trader who buys a $50 put for $3 needs the stock to be below $47 at expiration in order to profit. Now, this does not mean that a profit cannot be made *prior* to expiration even if the stock never falls below $47. The reason is that quick movements in the stock can cause the option to increase in price even if the stock is not below the strike price. It is certainly possible that we pay $3 for this put and the stock quickly falls to $49 thus making the put worth more money. However, remember that these charts are drawn "at expiration" and that's why Figure 3-12 shows that we need to have the stock below $47 in order to make a profit.

As we said before, profit and loss diagrams are invaluable for understanding strategies or comparing different strategies. We have just looked at two simple strategies, a long $50 call purchased for $5 and a long $50 put purchased for $3.

Let's make a small change and see if you can answer a tricky question. Which do you think is better, a long $50 call for $5 or a *short* $50 put for $3? Many traders might be led to believe that the long call is a superior strategy since it makes more money if the stock rises and loses less if the stock falls. What do you think is the correct answer? Hopefully you now understand that the answer can be found by checking the profit and loss diagrams for each and the answer will be readily apparent. Figure 3-13 shows the two strategies plotted on the same chart:

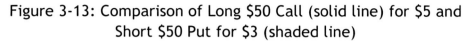

Figure 3-13: Comparison of Long $50 Call (solid line) for $5 and Short $50 Put for $3 (shaded line)

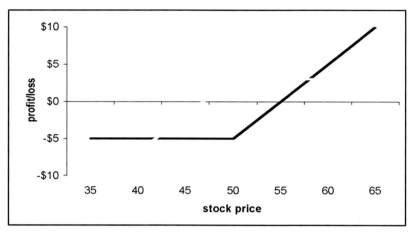

Now it is easy to see that the long call is not superior over *all* ranges. Yes, it's true that the long call makes more money if the stock rises substantially and loses less if the stock falls substantially. However, we can see there are two crossover points at $42 and $58. (Recall that the crossover points are where the two graphs intersect.) This means that the short put will be the superior strategy if the stock closes between $42 and $58 at expiration. And because the stock is currently $50, that is an eight-point swing, or 16%, on either side of the current price, which is a pretty big move. So even though the long call may have some nice qualities in that it makes more than the short put if the stock rises and loses less if it falls, those qualities come at a price. In this example, that price is that the stock must rise or fall more than 16% in order to beat the short put strategy. Once again, note how easy this is to see when you look at a picture rather than trying to figure it out in your head or by hand.

Profit and loss diagrams can also show one of the most fateful characteristics about options. If you look at Figure 3-14, you'll see the profit and loss diagram for a long $50 call at $5 (solid line) and a short $50 call at $5 (shaded line).

Figure 3-14

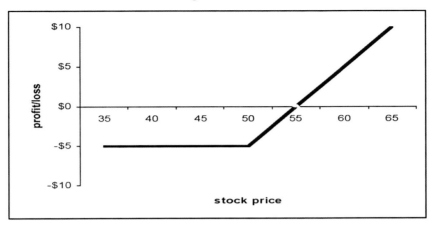

Notice that the two profit and loss lines are mirror images of each other; that is, the gains to one trader are exactly the losses to the other. We say that options are a *zero-sum game*, which simply means that no new money is created in the markets by their use as there is for stock. For instance, if Intel rises one dollar, then all holders of stock make money. The increase in the value of the stock creates wealth for all investors. There will be some speculators who will lose from the increase in share price; however, the number of short sellers is far less than the number of stock owners. Remember that corporations issue physical shares of stock and there are far more people who own those shares than are short. Therefore, an increase in the stock's price creates overall wealth to stockholders. Option contracts, however, are not issued by the company. For the options market, it takes a long and short position to create a contract and that's why options are a zero-sum game. If Intel rises one dollar, then all long call owners benefit at the expense of the short call writers.

At the same time, Figure 3-14 shows that options do not create a "black hole" where money is funneled out of the financial system inevitably leading to its collapse, which is a theory that many steadfastly believe. Instead, money just shifts from the pockets of the losers to those of the winners. The options market only redistributes the wealth but it does not destroy it.

Let's revisit a question we posed at the beginning of this chapter: Why do we have an option's market? The reason is that the "risk" one investor is trying to avoid by purchasing options might be willingly accepted by the investor who sells the option. For example, if you wish to speculate on a fall in the stock's price, you might buy a $50 put for $3 to avoid the upside risk of a short stock position. The person who sells you that $50 put might be very willing to buy stock for $50. Now let's assume the stock falls to $45 at expiration. You could exercise the put and receive $50 for your stock rather than the current $45 market price. This means you have a $5 gain for a $3 cost for a 66% gain. The short put seller must buy your stock for $50 but was willing to do that anyway. The fact that he received $3 for selling the put just offset his losses. Rather than being down $5, he is now only down $2. So you gained $2 on the put while the short put seller lost $2 from the sale. However, both of you see yourselves as better off. This shows that just because one investor "loses" on the option it doesn't mean that he is truly worse off than if he hadn't entered the trade. Options were designed as a way to accept or reject risks in the market. If another party is willing to accept risks you do not want then all investors can be made better off.

Okay, let's finish this section with one final example to really show the power of profit and loss diagrams. We're going to name an advanced strategy that you've probably never heard of and one that we're not even going to discuss in this book. That strategy is the *Short Iron Condor*. This particular example will be constructed by selling the $55 put and $60 call. Next, we will buy the $50 put and $65 call. We will assume that these transactions bring in a $3 credit to the account. Now for the hard part. Can you tell if this a bullish or bearish strategy? What are the maximum gains and losses? Where will the strategy break even? You can see that these questions are nearly impossible to answer without the visual aid of a profit and loss diagram. Figure 3-15 shows the profit and loss diagram for a short iron condor established for a $3 credit:

Figure 3-15: Short Iron Condor

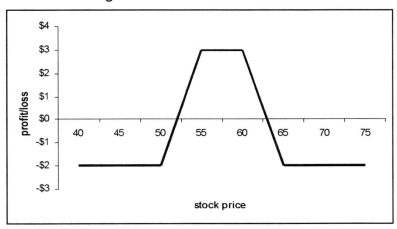

Now that you have a picture, you should readily see the answers. You can see that the strategy outlined in this example can make a maximum of $3, which occurs if the stock price is between $55 and $60 at expiration. The maximum loss is $2 and that occurs if the stock's price is below $50 or above $65 at expiration. This strategy is not looking for big price moves in either direction. Instead, it needs the stock to stay relatively quiet between $55 and $60. It is not bullish or bearish – it is a neutral strategy. This strategy has two break-even points. The first is at $52 and the second is at $63. Even though the ideal situation is to have the stock close between $55 and $60, it can actually close between $52 and $63 at expiration and still be profitable. Below $52 and above $63 is losing territory.

Notice how much we could tell about a strategy that we knew nothing about just by looking at its profit and loss chart. They are invaluable tools for learning strategies and assessing the risks and rewards of any position. As you start trading options, computer software will draw these charts for you. The important thing is that you know how to read them. In fact, most programs will even draw profit and loss diagrams *prior* to expiration. This requires the aid of an option pricing model to help with theoretical calculations (that's why we draw them at expiration by hand). The pictures will change but the way you read them is the same. If you take the time to work with profit and loss diagrams, you will have a much better understanding if a particular strategy really is right for you.

Chapter Three Questions

1)   What is a profit and loss diagram?
- a)   A picture of the maximum losses
- b)   A picture of your profits or losses at various stock prices
- c)   A picture of the break-even points
- d)   A picture showing the risks and rewards of long stock

2)   One of the most insightful observations we can get from profit and loss diagrams is that:
- a)   No strategy is superior to another for all stock prices
- b)   Long call options are definitely better than long stock positions
- c)   Call options have no risk
- d)   Some option strategies perform better than others for all stock prices

3)   For any profit and loss diagram, the area that lies above zero represents:
- a)   The potential losses
- b)   The potential rewards
- c)   The breakeven point
- d)   The value of the contract if exercised

4)   Which two pieces of information do you need to construct any profit and loss diagram?
- a)   The breakeven point and the price at which the asset was sold
- b)   The price paid for the asset and the price at which it was sold
- c)   The price paid for the asset and the breakeven point
- d)   How much the asset is worth at various stock prices and the price paid for the asset

5)   The profit and loss diagram for a long stock position shows that:
- a)   Long stock positions carry a large amount of downside risk
- b)   Long stock has an asymmetrical payoff
- c)   Long stock has multiple break-even points
- d)   Long stock has little reward

6)   When drawing profit and loss diagrams without theoretical values, you always calculate the option values:
- a)   Based on the bid-ask spread
- b)   Prior to expiration

c)   At expiration

d)   By subtracting the delta from intrinsic value

7)   **The break-even point for any profit and loss diagram is always where:**

a)   The curve bends at the strike price

b)   The curve lies above zero

c)   The curve lies below zero

d)   The curve crosses the horizontal axis at zero

8)   **The profit and loss diagram for a long call option shows that:**

a)   Long calls have two break-even points

b)   Long calls have a symmetrical payoff

c)   Long calls are better than long stock

d)   Long calls have limited downside risk and unlimited upside potential

9)   **The area below the zero horizontal axis for any profit and loss diagram represents:**

a)   The strike price

b)   The risk

c)   The reward

d)   The break-even point

10)   **For any profit and loss diagram, a "bend" will always occur at:**

a)   Every break-even point

b)   Every strike price

c)   The maximum gain

d)   The maximum loss

11)   **If you compare any two strategies, you will always find there are points where the two intersect. These intersections are called:**

a)   Break-even points

b)   Crossover points

c)   Maximum gain points

d)   Maximum loss points

12)   **The profit and loss diagram for a long put shows that:**

a)   Long puts have limited upside risk

b)   Maximum upside risk

c)   Long puts have two break-even points

d)   Make money if the underlying stock rises

13) **Which of the following best summarizes the reason for using profit and loss diagrams?**
   a)   They allow you to clearly see the risks and rewards for any strategy
   b)   They can locate superior strategies
   c)   They allow you to reduce your losses
   d)   They help you find undervalued stocks

14) **The axes for any profit and loss diagram are always:**
   a)   Vertical = option theoretical value, Horizontal = option price
   b)   Vertical = option price, Horizontal = option theoretical value
   c)   Vertical = stock price, Horizontal = profit and loss
   d)   Vertical = profit and loss, Horizontal = stock price

15) **Profit and loss diagrams show that the profit to the long position is exactly the loss to the short position and vice versa. This is another way of saying that options are:**
   a)   A way to create wealth in the markets
   b)   More lucrative by selling
   c)   A zero-sum game
   d)   A losing proposition

16) **The profit and loss diagram for a long call position shows that:**
   a)   Long calls have limited downside risk
   b)   Long calls have unlimited downside risk
   c)   Long calls are superior to long stock for all stock prices
   d)   Long calls have no downside risk

17) **If you plot the profit and loss diagram for a $50 call purchased at $4, it will cross the zero line at:**
   a) $54
   b) $50
   c) $4
   d) $46

18) **If you plot the profit and loss diagram for a $100 put purchased at $3, it will cross the zero line at:**
   a) $100
   b) $97

c) $103

d) $3

19)   **If you plot the profit and loss diagram for a $50 call sold at $4, it will cross the zero line at:**

a) $54

b) $50

c) $4

d) $46

20)   **If you plot the profit and loss diagram for a $100 put sold at $3, it will cross the zero line at:**

a) $100

b) $97

c) $103

d) $3

Chapter Three - Answers

1)   **What is a profit and loss diagram?**

b)   A picture of your profits or losses at various stock prices

Profit and loss diagrams provide a picture of where profits and losses will occur at various stock prices. Further, they show the size of those profits and losses.

2)   **One of the most insightful observations we can get from profit and loss diagrams is that:**

a)   No strategy is superior to another for all stock prices

For any two strategies, you will always find that neither is superior to the other across all stock prices. Profit and loss diagrams clearly show that no strategy is superior to another in all respects. It is up to the investor to figure out which attributes are desirable based on the outlook.

3)   **For any profit and loss diagram, the area that lies above zero represents:**

b)   The potential rewards

Profit and loss diagrams show us the range of potential rewards and potential losses. All areas that lie above the horizontal "zero" line (the break-even point) represent gains.

4) **Which two pieces of information do you need to construct any profit and loss diagram?**

    d)   How much the asset is worth at various stock prices and the price paid for the asset

Profit and loss diagrams are constructed by plotting the various profits or losses against various stock prices. Because of this, we must know how much the asset (option) is worth at the various stock prices as well as the price paid for the asset (option).

5) **The profit and loss diagram for a long stock position shows that:**

    a)   Long stock positions carry a large amount of downside risk

Profit and loss diagrams show that long stock positions carry unlimited downside risk – all the way down to a stock price of zero. Options, on the other hand, have a limited amount of downside risk.

6) **When drawing profit and loss diagrams without theoretical values, you always calculate the option values:**

    c)   At expiration

Because we don't know the values of a particular option prior to expiration, we usually draw profit and loss diagrams based on the option values at expiration. At expiration, we know that an option must be worth either zero or the intrinsic value. If you wish to plot a profit and loss diagram prior to expiration, you must use a theoretical pricing model to generate option values. Profit and loss diagrams drawn prior to expiration are almost always generated by a computer.

7) **The break-even point for any profit and loss diagram is always where:**

    d) The curve crosses the horizontal axis at zero

If the profit and loss diagram crosses the "zero" axis then that's telling you that the position produces no profit or loss. In other words, it breaks even at that point.

8) **The profit and loss diagram for a long call option shows that:**

    d)   Long calls have limited downside risk and unlimited upside potential

9) **The area below the zero horizontal axis for any profit and loss diagram represents:**

    b)   The risk

Any space below the "zero" horizontal mark represents losing territory so it therefore represents the risk of that position at various stock prices.

10) For any profit and loss diagram, a "bend" will occur at:

   b)   Every strike price

Because options create rights or obligations, there are changes that occur at each strike price of any profit and loss diagram.

11) If you compare any two strategies, you will always find there are points where the two intersect. These intersections are called:

   b)   Crossover points

Crossover points simply show where the two strategies are equal. You will always find that one strategy does better than the other to the right of the crossover and vice versa.

12) The profit and loss diagram for a long put shows that:

   a)   Long puts have limited upside risk

The risk of short selling a stock is the unlimited upside risk. Option traders can effectively short stock without this risk by simply buying a put.

13) Which of the following best summarizes the reason for using profit and loss diagrams?

   a)   They allow you to clearly see the risks and rewards for any strategy

14) The axes for any profit and loss diagram are always:

   d)   Vertical = profit and loss, Horizontal = stock price

15) Profit and loss diagrams show that the profit to the long position is exactly the loss to the short position and vice versa. This is another way of saying that options are:

   c)   A zero-sum game

A zero-sum game is any game where one person wins at the loser's expense. If you make a $5 profit on an option then somebody had to lose $5 on that same option. In the option's market, money simply shifts hands from the losers to the winners. No new capital is created in the market by using options (but none is destroyed either).

16) The profit and loss diagram for a long call position shows that:

   a)   Long calls have limited downside risk

Profit and loss diagrams easily show that call options have limited downside risk, which is one of the biggest advantages of owning call options.

17) If you plot the profit and loss diagram for a $50 call purchased at $4, it will cross the zero line at:

  a) $54

The breakeven point for a $50 call purchased at $4 is $54. As learned in the first chapter, the reason is that if the stock is $54 at expiration, the $50 call would be worth exactly the $4 intrinsic value. Because the zero line represents the breakeven point, the profit and loss diagram would cross zero at $54.

18) If you plot the profit and loss diagram for a $100 put purchased at $3, it will cross the zero line at:

  b) $97

The breakeven point for a $100 put purchased at $3 is $97. Put options become more profitable as the stock falls. In this case, the stock must fall $3 by expiration just to breakeven. If the stock is $97 at expiration, the $100 put will be worth exactly $3. Because you paid $3 for it then you would just break even at this stock price.

19) If you plot the profit and loss diagram for a $50 call sold at $4, it will cross the zero line at:

  a) $54

Remember that options are a zero sum game. Therefore, the break-even points for the long and short position must be the same. If you sell a $50 call at $4, you'd receive $4 up front but would have the obligation to sell stock for $50. If the stock is $54 at expiration, you'd have a $4 loss since you'd have to buy stock for $54 and deliver it for only $50. Because you received $4 up front, you'd just break even at a stock price of $54.

20) If you plot the profit and loss diagram for a $100 put sold at $3, it will cross the zero line at:

  b) $97

As with Question 19, options are a zero sum game, which means the break-even points for the long and short position must be the same. If you sell a $100 put at $3 you'd receive $3 up front but would have the obligation to buy stock for $100. If the stock is $97 at expiration, you'd have a $3 loss since you'd have to buy stock for $100 that is only worth $97. Because you received $3 up front, you'd just break even at a stock price of $97.

Chapter Four
Option Market Mechanics

The first three chapters introduced you to options, critical pricing principles, and profit and loss diagrams. With these tools, you now understand what an option is, how its price behaves and why, and how to read what the profits or losses will be at various stock prices. Our next step is to dive into the market mechanics of options. In this chapter, you will discover practical skills on placing orders, reading symbols, understanding option cycles, trading between the bid and ask, leaning against the book, stock splits, and many other topics you need to master options trading. Let's start by taking a look at option symbols.

Option Symbols

In Table 1-1, we saw that each option has a unique identifying symbol. For example, the symbol for the July $32.50 call was XBAGZ. Although the letters may appear random, there is actually an organized structure to their makeup. Understanding the symbol structure is important for one critical reason. It serves as a backup that you have, in fact, entered the correct symbol for your option order. Believe it or not, entering the wrong symbol is one of the top mistakes year after year for retail traders (and brokers as well). Most of the time this is due to a simple typing mistake; however, many of these could have been prevented had the traders understood option symbols. Entering wrong symbols creates numerous problems. First, you must pay extra commissions to get out of the wrong trade and into the correct one. Second, the erroneous trade may move against you thus providing a loss in addition to the extra commissions. Third, you may miss out on any favorable price movement in the option intended to buy. All of these provide reasons for understanding option symbols. In this section, we'll take a closer look at how these symbols are created and what they mean.

All option symbols follow the format of XXX – MS where "XXX" represents the *root symbol*. The root symbol is a code that identifies the underlying stock and can be any length from one to three letters. The "M" designates the "month" and "S" tells us the strike price. When you are learning option symbols, train your eye to look at the last two letters of any option symbol; they represent the month and strike, respectively. All other letters make up the root symbol.

If a stock is listed on an exchange such as the New York Stock Exchange or American Stock Exchange for example, the root symbol will usually be the same as the ticker symbol. It is easy to spot a listed security as it will always have a symbol of three or fewer letters. So IBM, GE, and T are all listed securities, and their option root symbol will usually be the same as the stock ticker (although it may be different from splits, mergers, or acquisitions).

For any Nasdaq traded stock (any stock with four or more letters in the ticker symbol), the option root symbol will usually be reduced to three letters. In many cases it will be similar to the original symbol but with the addition of the letter "Q" to designate Nasdaq. For example, the root symbol for DELL is DLQ, INTC is INQ, and MSFT is MSQ.

Once you have the root symbol, it is fairly easy to find the letters that represent the month and strike. For call options, the letters A through L (the first 12 letters of the alphabet) represent each month of the year. For puts, the letters M through X (letters 13 through 24) are used:

Option Month Symbols

	Jan	Feb	Mar	Apr	May	Jun	Jul	Aug	Sep	Oct	Nov	Dec
Calls	A	B	C	D	E	F	G	H	I	J	K	L
Puts	M	N	O	P	Q	R	S	T	U	V	W	X

For the strike prices, a similar coding system is used. The letter A represents $5, B is $10, C is $15 etc. Once you reach $100 (letter T), a new root symbol is created and you start back at letter A, which is now $105. Here is a partial list showing the sequence of option strikes:

Option Strike Price Symbols

A	B	C	D	E	F	G	H	I	J	K	L	M	N	O	P	Q	R	S	T
5	10	15	20	25	30	35	40	45	50	55	60	65	70	75	80	85	90	95	100
105	110	115	120	125	130	135	140	145	150	155	160	165	170	175	180	185	190	195	200

Obviously, this pattern can continue for stocks priced higher than $200. In addition to the above letters strikes, the letters U through Z are usually reserved for $2.50 strike intervals:

Option Strike Price Symbols for $2.50 Increments

U	V	W	X	Y	Z
7.50	12.50	17.50	22.50	27.50	32.50
37.50	42.50	47.50	52.50	57.50	62.50
67.50	72.50	77.50	82.50	87.50	92.50

It may look confusing but it is actually very easy. Say you want to buy a Microsoft October $45 call. The root symbol is MSQ. The October call symbol is J and the $45 strike symbol is I. So the call option symbol for the option will be MSQJI. Of course, you are not expected to drum up this symbol on your own to enter the trade. When you are looking at a list of option quotes, they will have the symbols listed as in Table 1-1. Most brokerage firms allow you to click on the option to enter an order on that specific option, which means the symbols is automatically entered for you. However, it is still possible to click on the wrong one. Further, some brokers require that you type the symbol into its own field when entering the order. And there is obviously lots of room for error there. Understanding how option symbols are created can keep you out of trouble. If you were comfortable with the symbol construction, you would realize that the letters "JI" in this example represent an October $45 call and this serves as a double check for your order. Just understanding the last two letters will tell you three important pieces of information. They tell you the month, strike, and option type (call or put). Even as a basic check, if you are buying a call option, you know that the "month" designator (second to the last letter of the option symbol) should fall between A and L. If you're buying a put, that letter should fall between M and X.

Remember, this is only a guideline. You should always check with your broker or with some of the resource sites at the CBOE (www.cboe.com) if you are unsure about an option symbol. The reason is that option root symbols change for different reasons. For example, MSQ is the root symbol for short-term Microsoft options but that root symbol will be different for the LEAPS, which are simply longer-term options. LEAPS is a registered trademark of the Chicago Board Options Exchange and stands for **L**ong-term **E**quity Antici**P**ation **S**ecurities (as if that wasn't obvious) and have expiration dates nearly three years in length.

Standard root symbols and strikes can change for a number of reasons but splits, mergers, acquisitions, and special dividends are probably the most common. For example, on July 30, 2004, Microsoft declared a special $3 dividend and the option strike prices and root symbols were adjusted to reflect this payment. If any option you are holding goes through a symbol change, it will automatically change in your account. The main point is that you should *always check your symbols before entering the trade.* Just because MSQ may have been the root symbol for Microsoft while you were last trading those options does not mean that it is still the same the next time you trade. This is especially true if the stock has made recent highs or lows and new strikes are being rolled out. For example, JDS Uniphase (JDSU) currently uses UQD for strike prices up to $65, XXZ for strikes $70 to $90, UCQ for $95 to $140, and YSU for strikes $145 and higher. Don't try to memorize all the root symbols or to construct them on your own based on past experience. Use your understanding of option symbols covered in this section as a *backup* measure to ensure you have entered the correct symbol.

As mentioned before, entering the incorrect symbol is always one of the top three errors – even among professional brokers (the others are *wrong quantity* and *wrong action* (buy vs. sell). With today's low commissions and traders entering their own orders online, brokers are very unforgiving if you enter a wrong symbol.

Try the following few examples to make sure you have the hang of it. Which options do the following symbols represent? Remember, the last two letters always represent the month and strike. The remaining letters represent the underlying stock, which you will probably recognize. If not, at least try to figure out the month, strike, and whether it is a call or put:

1) FAH
2) DLQOE
3) IBMCE
4) GEXD

5) XBAHH (Hint: "XBA" is the root symbol for eBay)

Okay, let's see how you did:

1) FAH. We know that all option symbols use the last two letters to designate the month and strike. In this example, we only have one letter remaining, which is F and that must be used to designate the underlying stock. The symbol F is for "Ford" so this symbol represents the Ford January $40 call.

2) DLQOE. We said earlier that DLQ is the root symbol for Dell Computer. This option represents the Dell March $25 put.

3) IBMCE. The last two letters represent the month and strike so the remaining IBM letters are used for the underlying stock, which is obviously IBM. This represents the IBM March $125 call (IBM was trading near $125 at the time so the letter "E" would represent $125 rather than $25).

4) GEXD. Again, the last two letters are used for the month and strike, which means that only GE remains to identify the underlying stock, which is obviously General Electric. This option represents the GE December $20 put.

5) XBAHH. We are told that XBA represents eBay and the last two letters tell us this is an August $40 call. Table 1-1 is reprinted below and you can see that this is the symbol for the August $40 call. (Recall that the "dash E" represents the exchange, which is the CBOE and is not part of the symbol.)

EBAY 37.11 -0.94

Jun 20, 2005 @ 14:43 ET (Data 15 Minutes Delayed)   **Bid** 37.10   **Ask** 37.11   **Size** 32x25   **Vol** 17121523

Calls	Last Sale	Net	Bid	Ask	Vol	Open Int	Puts	Last Sale	Net	Bid	Ask	Vol	Open Int
05 Jul 32.50 (XBA GZ-E)	4.40	-1.20	4.70	4.90	5	7319	05 Jul 32.50 (XBA SZ-E)	0.15	--	0.10	0.20	23	23943
05 Jul 35.00 (XBA GG-E)	2.50	-0.90	2.60	2.70	271	13510	05 Jul 35.00 (XBA SG-E)	0.45	+0.10	0.45	0.50	1811	24275
05 Jul 37.50 (XBA GU-E)	1.00	-0.55	1.00	1.05	909	21930	05 Jul 37.50 (XBA SU-E)	1.40	+0.45	1.35	1.40	633	18877
05 Jul 40.00 (XBA GH-E)	0.30	-0.20	0.30	0.35	613	34574	05 Jul 40.00 (XBA SH-E)	3.60	+1.15	3.10	3.20	206	13113
05 Aug 32.50 (XBA HZ-E)	5.00	--	5.30	5.50	100	0	05 Aug 32.50 (XBA TZ-E)	0.65	--	0.55	0.65	30	0
05 Aug 35.00 (XBA HG-E)	0	pc	3.40	3.60	0	0	05 Aug 35.00 (XBA TG-E)	1.25	-0.10	1.15	1.25	191	0
05 Aug 37.50 (XBA HU-E)	1.85	+0.10	2.00	2.10	82	0	05 Aug 37.50 (XBA TU-E)	2.45	-0.05	2.20	2.30	64	0
05 Aug 40.00 (XBA HH-E)	0.95	-0.10	1.00	1.10	64	0	05 Aug 40.00 (XBA TH-E)	0	pc	3.70	3.90	0	0

Every time you enter an option order, go through the motions of checking those last two letters and the patterns will eventually become second nature. With one quick glance, you will know the month, strike, and type of option (call or put).

It is a relatively simple thing to learn over time and it will increase your confidence and speed at which you can enter order.

Option Expiration Cycles

 As you start trading options, you will notice that not all stocks have the same expiration months available. For example, it is now July and Dell Computer has November options listed but Intel does not. Why is that? When will November options become available for Intel? In order to answer these questions, you need to understand *option expiration cycles*. Understanding the expiration cycles is important for option traders and investors. The reason is that you might wish to trade an option in a particular month and find that it is not available. Obviously, it would be nice to figure out when it will start trading.

When options started trading in 1973, the Chicago Board Options Exchange (CBOE) decided that there would only be four months of equity options traded at any given time. (This is one of the limitations of having standardized contracts that we talked about in Chapter One.)

Originally, all optionable stocks were assigned to one of three cycles: a **January**, **February** or **March** cycle. (These cycles are also called Cycle 1, Cycle 2, and Cycle 3, respectively.) The assignment was purely random and had nothing to do with earnings cycles of a company or any other reason you might hear; it was purely a random assignment.

Under the original rules, A January cycle (Cycle 1) meant that options would have expirations matching the first month of each quarter. So if a stock were assigned a January cycle, options on that stock could *only* have the first months of each quarter available:

Jan Feb Mar   **Apr** May Jun   **Jul** Aug Sep   **Oct** Nov Dec

A February cycle stock could only have option expirations for the middle months of each quarter available:

Jan **Feb** Mar   Apr **May** Jun   Jul **Aug** Sep   Oct **Nov** Dec

And, of course, the March cycle would have expirations for the end-months of each quarter available:

Jan Feb **Mar**   Apr May **Jun**   Jul Aug **Sep**   Oct Nov **Dec**

Because these expirations are arranged at equal intervals in each quarter, they were called *quarterly expirations*. Because of these positions, sometimes you will hear the cycles referred to as front-month (January), mid-month (February) or end-month (March) cycles. Once a stock is assigned a particular cycle, it does not change. For example, a January cycle stock always trades as January cycle stock.

As we just showed, when options started trading in 1973, if you were deciding on an option to buy on a January cycle stock, you would only have four months to choose from: January, April, July, and October. For a February cycle stock, you would only have February, May, August, and November expirations to choose from. A March cycle stock would only have March, June, September, and December expirations.

As options gained in popularity, traders were looking for ways to trade or hedge with shorter-term options, which weren't always available due to the way the cycles were structured. For example, assume it is now January and you were trading options on a January cycle stock. If you did not want to trade the January expiration then the next month available would be the April contract – more than three months into the future. To insure that there would always be shorter-term options, the CBOE decided to change the rules around 1984.

New Rules Create Shorter-Term Contracts

Under the new rules, there would still be four option expiration months listed at any given time but two must be reserved to represent the *current month* and the *following month* (these two contracts are also called the "front month" and "near-term" contracts, respectively). The remaining two months would remain from the original quarterly cycle. The current and following months are referred to as *serial* months.

Let's take a closer look at how these rules work. Assume it is now January and we are looking at a stock that trades options on a January cycle. Which months will be traded under the new rules? Remember, under the new rules, the CBOE decided that there would always be the current month plus the following month available. Because it is January in our example, then January and February *must be* available. Because four months must trade, the remaining two months will be from the original quarterly cycle, which would be April and July:

Jan Feb Mar   **Apr** May Jun   **Jul** Aug Sep   Oct Nov Dec

So if it was now January and we were looking at a stock that was assigned a January expiration cycle, we would find January, February, April, and July options to choose from. January and February are the serial months (or the serial contracts) while April and July are the quarterly contracts.

What happens when January expires? Looking at the expiration months above, you can see that when January contracts expire we will be left with only three expiration months – February, April, and July. However, we know that we must have four expiration months listed and we also know that we must have February and March listed. This means the March expiration must be added to the list:

Jan **Feb <u>Mar</u>**   **Apr** May Jun   **Jul** Aug Sep   Oct Nov Dec

After the March contracts are added, we have four contracts with the current month (February) and following month (March) on the list – exactly what the new rules say we should have.

When February expires, we are left with only three contracts: March, April, and July. However, this time we *do* have the current month and following months available by default (March and April). Even though April was originally issued as a quarterly contract, it now serves as a serial month. So once February expires, we will add the next quarterly contract, October, to the list:

Jan Feb **Mar**   **Apr** May Jun   **Jul** Aug Sep   <u>**Oct**</u> Nov Dec

Once the October contracts are rolled out, we are left with the current month plus following month (March and April) along with two quarterly contracts (July and October).

This pattern continues regardless of which cycle we're on. The current month and the following month must always be made available. No matter which cycle a stock may be trading, it will always have the current month and following month contracts available. The remaining two contracts will be from the corresponding quarterly cycle.

One problem many investors face is trying to figure out when a particular contract will be traded. For instance, let's continue with our above example using the January cycle and see if we can figure out when the November contract will be traded. This is easy once you understand option cycles. The first thing you want to ask is this: Is November one of the January cycle months? No, it is part of the February cycle. This means that November can never be added to the list unless it is a serial month. It can never be added months in advance as a quarterly contract. The <u>only</u> time it will become available is when October starts trading (September contract expires). When September expires, October will be the current contract and November will be added to the list as a serial contract.

Ok, here's where it gets a little tricky. See if you can answer the following question still assuming a January cycle. It is now April and we have April, May, July and October trading as shown below. When will the January contracts start trading?

Jan Feb Mar   **Apr May** Jun   **Jul** Aug Sep   **Oct** Nov Dec

Because we're asking about a month that *does* fall on the January cycle, this contract may open for trading months in advance. Again, this is because it is a quarterly contract and not a serial month.

If you run through the steps outlined above, you will see that the January contract will start trading when May expires. Once May is expired, June will become the current month so there will be a June, July and October for a total of three months. The fourth month will be the addition of January. The steps are outlined in the following box:

We started with April, May, July and October contracts traded and are wondering when the January contract will begin trading:

Jan Feb Mar   **Apr May** Jun   **Jul** Aug Sep   **Oct** Nov Dec

When April expires, June will be added to the list since we must always have the current month and the following month available:

Jan Feb Mar   Apr **May Jun**   **Jul** Aug Sep   **Oct** Nov Dec

When May expires, we will only have the following three contracts traded: June, July, and October. This means we must add a fourth. However, by default, we have June and July contracts traded (the current month and following month):

Jan Feb Mar   Apr May **Jun**   **Jul** Aug Sep   **Oct** Nov Dec

This means we must add the next quarterly contract. October is the next quarterly contract but it is already traded so we must move to the next quarterly month, which is January:

Jan Feb Mar   Apr May **Jun**   **Jul** Aug Sep   **Oct** Nov Dec

So the January contracts will start trading once May expires.

LEAPS

As options gained in popularity, investors showed an interest in choosing from contracts that included longer times to expiration. In 1990, the CBOE answered by creating LEAPS. While the name makes them sound complicated, they are simply options but with longer lives. When options first started trading, they were available up to nine months in the future. But with the addition of LEAPS, you can find options nearly three years forward. If a stock has LEAPS options traded, there will be more than four contracts listed at any given time. So while your local newspaper or other sources may only print three expiration months to conserve space, understand that there are always at least four different contract months traded at any given time.

How do option cycles work with the addition of LEAPS? Once you understand the basic option cycle, adding LEAPS into the rotation is not too difficult.

As mentioned earlier, LEAPS usually trade in January for a maximum of three years forward although there are exceptions. If a stock trades LEAPS, then new LEAPS will be issued sometime between May and July. This is difficult to explain without the use of examples so let's go back to our Intel options.

It is currently July '05 and Intel has the following months trading: July, August, October, January '06, January '07, and January '08 as shown by the "Xs" in the table below:

Jan	Feb	Mar	Apr	May	Jun	Jul	Aug	Sep	Oct	Nov	Dec
$X_{'06}$						x	x		x		
$X_{'07}$											
$X_{'08}$											

At this point, January '07 and January '08 are LEAPS contracts. The January '06 is considered a quarterly contract since it is less than nine months until expiration.

When July expires, September will be added. We will then have August, September, October, and January '06, thus providing four months of regular contracts (nine months or less):

Jan	Feb	Mar	Apr	May	Jun	Jul	Aug	Sep	Oct	Nov	Dec
$X_{'06}$							x	x	x		
$X_{'07}$											
$X_{'08}$											

When August expires, we will have September, October, January '06 thus providing *only three* different months of regular contracts:

Jan	Feb	Mar	Apr	May	Jun	Jul	Aug	Sep	Oct	Nov	Dec
$X_{'06}$								x	x		
$X_{'07}$											
$X_{'08}$											

At this point, the next January cycle month will be added, which is April:

Jan	Feb	Mar	Apr	May	Jun	Jul	Aug	Sep	Oct	Nov	Dec
$X_{'06}$			x	x				x	x		
$X_{'07}$											
$X_{'08}$											

This process continues and eventually the date will become May '06. The January '06 options will have been expired for four months and we will have the following months traded (Notice that the January '06 options are no longer listed):

Jan	Feb	Mar		Apr	May	Jun		Jul	Aug	Sep		Oct	Nov	Dec
X$_{07}$					x	x		x						
X$_{08}$														

When May options expire, we will only have three contracts in existence (not counting the LEAPS January options). These months will be June, July, and October. This is where we need to add another January contract since it is the next January cycle month. It is at this point where the January '09 contract will be rolled out:

Jan	Feb	Mar		Apr	May	Jun		Jul	Aug	Sep		Oct	Nov	Dec
X$_{07}$						x		x				x		
X$_{08}$														
X$_{09}$														

At the same time, the January '07 contracts will lose their LEAPS designation because they have less than nine months to expiration. The root symbol will change to show that it is no longer a LEAPS option. If you are holding this option, the symbol will automatically change in your account and there is nothing that you need to do. Just be aware that this can happen as some investors are puzzled when there is a symbol change on some of their LEAPS. This will happen in May, June, or July when the current year LEAPS option becomes a regular option. This process is called *melding*. Melding is when LEAPS options become regular options. Technically speaking, LEAPS options do not expire; instead, they meld to a regular option and then it is the regular option that expires.

So, depending on which cycle your stock is on, look for new LEAPS to be added sometime in late May, June or July.

Which Cycle is My Stock On?

As mentioned earlier, there will be times when you will need to know when a particular month will be added to the list. Before you can find out, you will need to know on which cycle your stock is traded. This is easy to find out once you understand the expiration cycles. For example, let's see if we can figure out which cycle Intel is on. It is now July and Intel has the following months being traded:

- July
- August
- October
- January '06
- January '07
- January '08

From what we learned earlier, we know there must be a July and August contract and we see that there is. You can never tell which cycle a particular stock is on just by looking at the first two months since all options will have these months being traded. But we can find out which cycle the stock is on by looking at the third month and fourth months. The reason we cannot just look at the third month is that it may be January and we would not be sure if it is a LEAPS contract or not. In this case, the third month is October:

- July ⎫
- August ⎭ | These contracts must be traded |
- **October**
- January '06
- January '07
- January '08

Now we just need to ask which cycle October falls under? It is part of the January cycle (it is the first month or the "January "position of the fourth quarter). So we just figured out that Intel trades on a January cycle.

Let's try another. Which cycle is Dell Computer on? It is still July and Dell has the following contracts traded:

- July
- August
- November
- January '06
- February '06
- January '07
- January '08

Once again, we know that the current and following month must be traded for all stocks so the first two months tell us nothing about which cycle the stock is on. However, the third month is November and that does reveal the cycle.

Because that month is November, we know that Dell Computer trades on a February cycle (because November is the middle month or "February" position of the fourth quarter).

- July ⎫
- August ⎬ These contracts must be traded
- **November**
- January '06
- February '06
- January '07
- January '08

Let's try one more example but this time we'll show why you cannot consider January if it falls in the third month. We'll still use Dell Computer but now assume that the July options have expired. If so, we'd see the following contracts traded:

- August
- November
- January '06
- February '06
- January '07
- January '08

We know to not look at the first two month of August and November since all stocks will have those months listed. However, in this instance, if we look at the third month, we'd find January and we'd be led to believe that Dell is on a January cycle. Remember, all stocks that have LEAPS options will have them listed in January so we cannot be sure if this is a January cycle stock or not. To be sure, we'd need to move down to the fourth month, which is February and now we know that Dell is on a February cycle. In order to find which cycle your stock is on, you can never do so by looking at the first two expiration months. All stocks have those months traded. You must find the next quarterly contract (with the exception of January) that is listed and that will guide you to the cycle on which your stock is traded. Once you know which cycle your stock is on, it never changes. You will always be able to determine which months will be traded and which will be added at expiration.

However, if you should need a reference, the following tables will tell you which contracts will be traded during which months:

JANUARY CYCLE

Contracts that will be traded:

Current Month	**Jan**	Feb	Mar	**Apr**	May	Jun	Jul	Aug	Sep	**Oct**	Nov	Dec
Jan	x	x		x			x					
Feb		x	x	x			x					
Mar			x	x			x			x		
Apr				x	x		x			x		
May					x	x	x			x		
Jun	x*					x	x			x		
Jul	x*						x	x		x		
Aug	x*							x	x	x		
Sep	x*			x*					x	x		
Oct	x*			x*						x	x	
Nov	x*			x*							x	x
Dec	x*			x*			x*					x

Bold represents months in the following year

FEBRUARY CYCLE

Contracts that will be traded:

Current Month	Jan	**Feb**	Mar	Apr	**May**	Jun	Jul	**Aug**	Sep	Oct	**Nov**	Dec
Jan	x	x			x			x				
Feb		x	x		x			x				
Mar			x	x	x			x				
Apr				x	x			x			x	
May					x	x		x			x	
Jun						x	x	x			x	
Jul		x*					x	x			x	
Aug		x*						x	x		x	
Sep		x*							x	x	x	
Oct		x*			x*					x	x	
Nov		x*			x*						x	x
Dec		x*			x*						x	x

Bold represents months in the following year

			MARCH CYCLE									
					Contracts that will be traded:							
	Jan	Feb	**Mar**	Apr	May	**Jun**	Jul	Aug	**Sep**	Oct	Nov	**Dec**
Jan	x	x	x			x						
Feb		x	x			x			x			
Mar			x	x		x			x			
Apr				x	x	x			x			
May					x	x			x			x
Jun						x	x		x			x
Jul							x	x	x			x
Aug	x*							x	x			
Sep	x*								x	x		x
Oct	x*									x	x	x
Nov	x*		x*								x	x
Dec	x*		x*			x*						x
				Bold represents months in the following year								

By the way, you can always find out which contracts will be available for any stock going to www.cboe.com and then clicking on "Trading Tools" and then "Cycles and Strike Month Codes."

You can also find similar tools at the homepage for the Options Industry Council (OIC) at www.888options.com. Click on "Tools and Literature," "Pricing Calculators," and then "Cycles."

Double, Triple, and Quadruple Witching

Now that you understand option cycles and how the contract months are determined, let's talk about the terms *double witching* or, more commonly, *triple witching*. These are days when multiple derivative products expire on the same day. For example, if stock futures, stock index options, and stock options all expire on the same day then that is a triple witching day. Typically, stock futures expire on the quarterly expiration (the last month of each quarter) months of March, June, September, and December so triple witching occurs only in these months. Double witching occurs when any two of the three assets expire at the same time. Less commonly knows is quadruple witching, which occurs when single-stock future contracts expire on the same day as well. It is widely believed that volatility in the market is much greater on these days as traders scramble to close positions. The truth is that few professional traders wait until the very last day to close positions so these witching days are probably not as disruptive as many believe. Still, it is worth knowing what these terms mean as you will definitely hear them once you start trading or investing in options.

Contract Size (The Multiplier)

In the first chapter, we said that options generally cover 100 shares of stock. In this section, we're going to show you why we said "generally." When options first start trading, the contract size is always 100 shares. This 100 share-sized lot is also referred to as the *multiplier* because that is the amount we must multiply the option premium by to find the total cost of the contract. For example, if a call option is asking $3, you will pay $3 * 100 = $300 (plus commissions). It is also the amount we must multiply by to find the total contract value. If you exercise a $30 call, you will pay $30 * 100 = $3,000 and receive 100 shares of stock. So the "contract size" and "multiplier" are two different ways of expressing the *unit of trade* of the option.

While all options start with a contract size of 100, there are corporate actions that can change that. The most common event is a stock split. Stock splits generally occur when the price of the stock is perceived to be too high so the company will split the stock to bring down the price.

A stock split is really a cash dividend, which means the company pays you a dividend in shares of stock rather than cash. With a 2:1 stock split, the company pays you one share of stock for each that you own thus doubling the number of shares you own.

However, because the company is paying a dividend (whether in cash or shares) the price of the stock must be reduced to reflect the fact that some value of the company has been paid out to shareholders. A stock split therefore will always increase the number of shares outstanding (and therefore in your account) and the stock price will always fall.

How many shares will you have and by how much will the stock price fall? These questions are easy to answer once you understand the mechanics of a stock split. Anytime a split is announced, it is always reported as the ratio of two numbers such as 2:1. If you take the first number divided by the second, you get the "split ratio," which is 2 for this example. The number of shares will always be multiplied by this ratio and the stock price will be divided by the same number.

There are many types of splits with 2:1 being the most popular. However, you will also see variations such as 3:1, 4:1 and so on. We will refer to these as "whole number" splits since you always end up multiple 100-share lots after the split. In addition to whole number splits, you may see "fractional" splits such as 3:2, 5:4, 8:7, and so on. Any split ratio where the second number is greater than one creates a fractional split. These types of splits increase the number of shares you own just as whole number splits; however, that new number will not be evenly divisible by 100. For instance, a 3:2 split means that you will receive 3 shares for every 2 that you have thus increasing the number of shares by 50%. If you had 100 shares prior to the split, you will have 150 shares after the split. A 5:4 split leaves you with 125 shares for every 100 shares you previously held.

For instance, assume ABC stock is trading for $180 per share. At this price, the company may think its share price is too expensive as it is difficult for many investors to buy shares, at least in round lots of 100, since that will cost $18,000. In order to bring the price per share down, the company may announce a 2:1 split. If you own 100 shares of ABC prior to the split, you will own 200 shares at a price of $90 after the split. Notice that we multiplied the number of shares by two (split ratio) and divided the price by two as well.

Because we doubled the number of shares but cut the price in half, the total number of dollars invested does not change. If you have 100 shares of ABC at $180, then the position is worth $18,000. After the split, you'd have 200 shares at $90, which is still $18,000 worth of stock.

A 3:1 stock split would give you 300 shares at a price of $60 per share after the split ($18,000 worth of stock). A 4:1 split yields 400 shares at a stock price of $45 ($18,000 worth of stock).

Now let's take a look at some fractional split examples. If the same stock had a 3:2 split, then the split ratio is 3/2 = 1.5. If you had 100 shares prior to the split, you'd have 100 * 1.5 = 150 shares after the split and the price would fall to $180/1.5 = $120. Again, notice that after the split you still have 150 shares * $120 = $18,000 worth of stock. A 5:4 split provides a split ratio of 5/4 = 1.2 so you'd end up with 100 * 1.2 = 120 shares at a price of $180/1.2 = $150 per share. In both of these cases, you still own $18,000 worth of stock.

So a stock split doesn't change the total value of your investment but only the way in which it's packaged. It's no different than when you exchange *one* $10 bill for *two* $5 bills. You have twice as many pieces of paper (shares) at half the value so the total value of your wallet hasn't changed. When viewed in this light, stock splits aren't really a big deal even though they are often met with much fanfare by the investing public. After a stock split, it is true that the company may create more demand by the public to own it and that certainly can put upward pressure on the price. However, the stock price is now twice as hard to move because there are twice as many shares outstanding so there are drawbacks to splitting a stock. But regardless of whether stock splits are good or bad, they do occur and they can change the contract size.

The key to understanding stock splits is that the stock split cannot change the total value of the company and therefore cannot change the total value of your position. If it did, companies could create unlimited value by continually splitting their stock which doesn't make any more sense than you being able to create infinite wealth by continually splitting ten dollar bills into two fives.

The key to understanding how stock splits *affect your options* is to understand that if a stock split cannot change the total value of the stock then it cannot change the total *exercise value* of your options.

Let's now see how various stock splits will affect your option contracts. Assume you own one $180 call option that is trading for $6. If the stock does a 2:1 split, the split ratio is 2/1 = 2. You will then control twice as many contracts, or two for this example. The strike price will be reduced to $180/2 = $90. In addition, the price of the option will be $6/2 = $3. Your options are packaged a little differently but the total exercise value is the same. You are controlling $18,000 worth of stock before and after the split. In addition, the value of your options is $600 before and after the split.

If the stock does a 3:1 split, the split ratio is 3/1 = 3. You then own three times as many calls. The strike is $180/3 = $60 and you still control $18,000 worth of stock. The price of the option will drop to $6/3 = $2 and the value of your options is still $600.

Now let's look at how fractional splits affect your option contracts. Recall that fractional splits are any where the split ratios have a last digit greater than one such as 3:2 and 5:4, and 8:7 for example. Fractional splits affect options in a similar way as the whole number splits we just reviewed. However, they create a small problem because the number of shares is not increased in units of 100. To alleviate the problem, the exchanges decided to adjust the number of shares each contract controls.

For instance, if you own one $180 call trading for $6 and the stock does a 3:2 split then the split ratio is 3/2 = 1/5. After the split, you will still own one contract; however, it will now control 150 shares of stock and the strike price will be $180/1.5 = $120. After the split, you still control 150 shares * $120 = $18,000. In this case, the "multiplier" is increased to 150 since that is how many shares the option controls. The option's price will fall to $6/1.5 = $4. So if you see this option quoted at $4, you must remember to multiply it by 150 to find its total value.

If the stock does a 5:4 split then the split ratio is 5/4 = 1.2. After the split, you will own one contract that controls 100 * 1.2 = 120 shares with a strike price of $180/1.2 = $150 and you will still control 120 * $150 = $18,000 worth of stock. The option's price would fall to $6/1.2 = $5. All options, calls and puts, are adjusted in the same way. In addition, all short positions are adjusted in the same way as the long positions. After all, the short position is simply on the other side of the trade from the long position.

For any "whole number" split (2:1, 3:1, 4:1 etc.) the number of contracts you own increases by the split ratio. The multiplier stays the same.

For any "fractional" split, (3:2, 5:4, 8:7, etc.) the number of contracts stays the same but the number of shares it controls is multiplied by the split ratio.

The market price of the stock, the strike price of your option, and the market value of the option is always reduced (divided) by the split ratio regardless of the type of split.

The following chart may help you to see the differences. Notice that the procedures for the strike price and market price are the same regardless of the type of split.

Market Adjustments	Whole Number Splits (2:1, 3:1, etc.)	Odd Number Splits (3:2, 5:4, etc.)
# Contracts	Increased by split ratio	Remains same
Strike	Reduced by split ratio	Reduced by split ratio
Stock price	Reduced by split ratio	Reduced by split ratio
Multiplier	Remains same	Increased by split ratio

Reverse Splits

There is another type of split called a reverse splits, which are done for the opposite reasons of a stock split. Companies whose share price is very low may vote for a reverse split to lift the price in hopes of getting it "recognized" as a viable investment. Many times this is done so that the company meets certain listing requirements so that they can trade on a nationally recognized exchange.

Reverse splits are most often seen in the penny stocks or other troubled stocks looking for a boost in price (and hopefully awareness). Because of this, you will rarely see reverse splits on optionable stocks since they must be above $10 to meet listing requirements to trade options. However, they can occur. If they do, the math previously described works exactly the same way but in the reverse direction.

For example, assume that XYZ is trading for $4. The company may vote for a 1:3 reverse split. The split ratio is then 1/3 = 0.33. This just means that shareholders will receive one share for every three they currently own and the price will rise by a factor of three. If you own 300 shares today, you have $1,200 worth of stock. After the split, you'll have 300 * 0.33 = 100 shares after the split. The stock price will rise to $4/0.33 = $12. Once again, this doesn't affect any the value of your position because the value of your position will still be $1,200 after the split.

Let's see how the reverse split would affect your option contracts. Assume you own 20 XYZ $10 calls trading for $1 and the company announces a 1:5 reverse split. The split ratio is 1/5 = 0.20. The number of contracts you own is now 20 * 0.2 = 4 and the strike price is increased to $10/0.20 = $50. The price of the option rises to $1/0.2 = $5. Let's check the math to make sure we got the right answer. The original position was worth $1 * 20 contracts * 100 shares per contract = $2,000 and had an exercise value of $10 * 20 contracts * 100 shares per contracts = $20,000. After the split, it is worth $5 * 4 contracts * 100 shares per contract = $2,000 and the exercise value is 4 contracts * $50 * 100 shares per contract = $20,000. Nothing has changed; only the packaging.

Whenever an option undergoes an adjustment, you'll probably see a notation stating "adjusted option" or "adj opt" while placing the trade. You may see this in the final "readback" screen where you verify the order before sending it or you may see it next to the symbol when looking up symbols. Whenever you see this notation, be sure to check the number of shares it is controlling.

For example, when we get to strategies, we will talk about the "Covered Call" where we will buy 100 shares of stock and then sell one call controlling 100 shares. If you inadvertently sell a call that controls 150 shares rather than 100 there could be potential problems if the stock price rises substantially. That's because you own 100 shares but may have to deliver 150 shares if the stock's price rises above the strike. In essence, you would be short 50 shares of stock.

Just as you should develop habits of checking option symbols when entering orders, you should also check to see if the total cost of the trade is roughly what you think it should be *before* sending the order. For example, assume you are placing an order to buy one ABC $50 call trading for $4. If you place an order to buy one contract and the computer tells you the estimated cost of the trade is over $600 including commissions, you should realize that something isn't right. One contract at $4 should cost $400 plus commissions so the $600 price is obviously too high. Assuming you entered the right quantity (one contract) you can be sure this discrepancy is a sign that you're dealing with an option that controls 150 shares.

As with any option adjustment, there is nothing you need to do as all adjustments and symbol changes will automatically take place in your account.

There is nothing necessarily wrong with trading adjusted options; in fact, in some situations you have no choice. If the ABC $180 call undergoes a 2:1 split, it will be adjusted to a $90 strike. This is technically an adjusted option because it was once a $180 strike and it is now the $59 strike. However, it still controls 100 shares and in all other ways behaves just like a regular unadjusted option. If you wish to trade the $90 strike, you may have no choice but to trade the "adjusted" contract. Just be sure that you understand what that contract represents and that it matches your goal.

Stock splits are not the only event that causes option adjustments. Mergers, acquisitions, special dividends, and other forms of corporate activity and restructuring will cause adjustments. Under these scenarios, some adjusted options can get complex and control differing amounts of shares plus shares of another company plus cash. For example, in 2004, Motorola (MOT) announced that all owners of record on November 29 would receive a distribution of Freescale Semiconductor (FSL.B). All options affected by the distribution would be adjusted to control 100 shares of Motorola, 11 shares of Freescale Semiconductor, and 76 cents cash. Most traders avoid adjusted options that control numerous assets like this because the liquidity (the number of contracts available in the market) tends to be low. After all, why would you want the right to buy or sell 100 shares of Motorola, 11 shares of Freescale Semiconductor, and 76 cents in cash? So as a general rule, avoid entering into adjusted options with *complex* structures unless there is a very good reason you need that specific contract.

Contract Adjustments for Special Dividends

Many stocks pay dividends, which are simply a cash payment to shareholders usually made on a quarterly basis (sometimes they are paid semiannually). In some cases, dividends may cause strike price adjustments so it's important to understand when and why these adjustments occur.

If a stock pays an eight-cent dividend that really means eights cents per share per year. If you own 100 shares, you'd receive a total cash deposit of $.08 * 100 = $8 per year. But because dividends are usually paid on a quarterly basis, you'd actually receive four payments of $2. Dividend payments are usually deposited electronically to your brokerage account.

The stock's price is always reduced by the amount of the dividend on the date the dividend is paid, which is called the *ex-date*. The ex-date is simply the date that the stock trades "ex," or "without" the dividend. For example, assume a $100 stock pays a $1 dividend tomorrow. The stock will open tomorrow for trading at $99 *unchanged*. Even though the stock's price is technically lower, that is due to the payment of the dividend and not a factor between supply and demand. Think about it this way: If you have a jar of 100 one-dollar bills, it is worth $100. If you take one dollar out, the jar is now worth only $99. This is exactly what happens with corporations when they pay a dividend. The value of the stock is comprised of all assets of the company, one of which is cash. If one dollar is paid to each stockholder, the total value of the stock must be reduced by the amount of that payment, which means the stock would now be worth $99. Just remember that the value of the stock is always reduced by the amount of the dividend on the ex-date.

Most companies that pay dividends pay them on a regular basis. These regular dividends do not cause option strikes to be adjusted. The reason is that the market knows about these dividends well in advance and they automatically get factored into the option's price.

Sometimes, however, corporations pay a special one-time dividend and, in these cases, they do cause adjustments to option strikes. Whenever a special dividend is announced, all call and put strikes are *reduced* by the amount of the dividend. For example, on July 20, 2004 Microsoft announced a special $3 cash dividend. This was a special one-time dividend so the option strikes – calls and puts – were adjusted downward by the amount of the dividend. If you were holding the $30 call, it became a $27 strike. If you were holding the $30 put, it also became a $27 strike. Why does this happen? Again, any adjustment in option strikes is done to assure that option investors are not financially hurt (or unfairly rewarded) because of a corporate action such as a split, merger, or even a special dividend.

By reducing all strike prices by the amount of the dividend, calls and puts retain all of their intrinsic value after the split. To show how, imagine that Microsoft is trading for $35 and that you own the $30 call that is worth exactly the $5 intrinsic value just prior to the payment of the $3 dividend. On the ex-date, the stock's price will be reduced by the dividend and will open for trading at $32. With the stock at $32 though, your $30 call will only be worth $2, which means the value of your call dropped from $5 to $2 for no reason other than the fact that a special dividend was paid (call prices fall with a drop in stock price). In order to keep the $30 call holders from unfairly losing $3, the strike is reduced by the amount of the dividend to $27. With the strike at $27, your option is still worth the $5 intrinsic value when the stock opens at $32.

Now let's run through an example with a put option. Think about a $40 put that is trading for the intrinsic value of $5. On ex-date, the stock price is reduced from $35 to $32 and, the option's price jumps to the $8 intrinsic value. In this case, the put holder unfairly benefits from the reduction in the stock's price (put options benefit from a drop in the stock's price). However, if that strike is reduced by the dividend to $37, it will be worth $5 with the stock at $32.

In both cases, the calls and puts are worth $5 before the ex-date and after due to the adjustment. In other words, the special dividend does not affect their pricing. When you think about it, the special dividend should not affect option prices since it doesn't really affect the holder of the stock. While it appears that the owner of 100 shares of Microsoft gets a nice $3 "bonus," you must remember that the price of Microsoft will also fall by $3 on ex-date. The owner of Microsoft receives $300 cash but loses $300 in stock value, which is a wash. In other words, stock holders were not really affected negatively or positively but only the form of their wealth has changed. If stock holders are not really affected by the special dividend then why should option holders be subjected to unfair increases or decreases in wealth? The answer is they shouldn't and that's why the strike prices are adjusted.

You might be wondering if there's a way to get some "free money" from the markets by buying a call and then exercising it to collect the dividend. The answer is no since you will always pay a time premium for the call. Once you exercise the call, you lose the time premium so you'd always be better off just buying the stock in the open market. For instance, let's assume the Microsoft $50 call is trading for $2. If you pay $2 and then immediately exercise it, you will pay $50 and receive 100 shares of stock. However, you paid $2 for the option, which means you effectively paid $52 to gain the stock. You could have just purchased the stock in the open market for $50 and paid one commission to do so. Whenever special dividends are announced, especially large ones, you will hear all kinds of option "strategies" that allow for some type of arbitrage. These are simply false rumors and the reason they won't work is twofold. First, time premiums make it more costly to buy the stock. Second, the strike prices are reduced on ex-date.

Just remember that stock prices are *always* adjusted when dividends are paid. In the case of special dividends, option strike prices will be adjusted too. The previous section talked about stock splits, which we said are technically dividends. Rather than receiving cash though, investors receive shares of stock. If a stock does a 2:1

split that is really recorded through the brokerage firm as a one share dividend for every share owned. What does that do to the stock's price? Just as with cash dividends, it reduces the price of the stock. If you receive one share of stock for every share you have, the company has, in fact, paid half of its value back to shareholders and that means the share price must fall in half.

Open Interest

In the first chapter, we mentioned that the column labeled "Open Int" in Table 1-1, which has been reprinted below as Table 4-1, represented *open interest*. Now it's time to take a closer look at what those numbers represent.

Table 4-1: EBAY Option Quotes

EBAY								Jun 20, 2005 @ 14:43 ET (Data 15 Minutes Delayed)					Bid 37.10 Ask 37.11 Size 32x25 Vol 17121523 **37.11 -0.94**	

Calls	Last Sale	Net	Bid	Ask	Vol	Open Int	Puts	Last Sale	Net	Bid	Ask	Vol	Open Int
05 Jul 32.50 (XBA GZ-E)	4.40	-1.20	4.70	4.90	5	7319	05 Jul 32.50 (XBA SZ-E)	0.15	--	0.10	0.20	23	23943
05 Jul 35.00 (XBA GG-E)	2.50	-0.90	2.60	2.70	271	13510	05 Jul 35.00 (XBA SG-E)	0.45	+0.10	0.45	0.50	1811	24275
05 Jul 37.50 (XBA GU-E)	1.00	-0.55	1.00	1.05	909	21930	05 Jul 37.50 (XBA SU-E)	1.40	+0.45	1.35	1.40	633	18877
05 Jul 40.00 (XBA GH-E)	0.30	-0.20	0.30	0.35	613	34574	05 Jul 40.00 (XBA SH-E)	3.60	+1.15	3.10	3.20	206	13113
05 Aug 32.50 (XBA HZ-E)	5.00	--	5.30	5.50	100	0	05 Aug 32.50 (XBA TZ-E)	0.65	--	0.55	0.65	30	0
05 Aug 35.00 (XBA HG-E)	0	pc	3.40	3.60	0	0	05 Aug 35.00 (XBA TG-E)	1.25	-0.10	1.15	1.25	191	0
05 Aug 37.50 (XBA HU-E)	1.85	+0.10	2.00	2.10	82	0	05 Aug 37.50 (XBA TU-E)	2.45	-0.05	2.20	2.30	64	0
05 Aug 40.00 (XBA HH-E)	0.95	-0.10	1.00	1.10	64	0	05 Aug 40.00 (XBA TH-E)	0	pc	3.70	3.90	0	0

Because of the way options are traded, the OCC (Options Clearing Corporation) must account for the total number of outstanding contracts. The reason is that options are created out of thin air when two traders enter into opposite sides of the agreement. There is not a fixed number of option contracts like there is for shares of stock. Because there is a fixed number of shares of stock, you only need to use the words "buy" or "sell" when you trade shares of stock. However, when you trade an option, the OCC needs to know if you are entering into the contract or getting out of it. So if you are buying a call option to *enter* (or increase) the position, you need to enter the order as "buy to open." When it comes time to exit (or reduce) that position, you would enter an order to "sell to close."

We can also enter into an option contract by selling it first. If you sell a call option to enter (or increase) the position, you would enter the order as "sell to open." When closing (or reducing) the position, the words "buy to close" would be use.

This can be a little confusing to new traders but it is actually quite simple. Just remember the key words "entering the contract" or "exiting the contract." If you are entering, you are "opening" the contract. If you are exiting the contract, you are "closing." When you enter an option order online, the computer will prompt you to either "buy" and "sell" and another section will ask you to specify "to open" or "to close." You will need to check off one from each section.

Let's take a look at a few examples. Let's say you currently have no Intel options in your account and you buy 5 Intel $30 calls. You would enter the order as "buy to open." Now assume that, at a later date, you wish to buy two more contracts. This is still an opening transaction since you are *increasing* the size of the position. You have simply "opened" or entered into two additional agreements. At this point, you would be long 7 Intel $30 calls. Now let's say you decide to sell 4 contracts. Because you are reducing the size, this would be entered as "sell to close." At a later time, if you sell the remaining 3 contracts, it would also be a "closing" trade since you are exiting or eliminating the position. It's important to understand that "buying" does not necessarily mean you are entering the position. The reason is that you could enter an option position by selling it first. For example, if you sell a call to open, you are accepting money in exchange for the potential obligation to sell shares of stock. This is a common strategy called the "covered call" and one we'll look at in depth in Chapter Seven. The point is that you can enter into an option agreement by either buying it or selling it. It just depends on whether you want to pay money for the right to buy or sell or receive money for the obligation to buy or sell.

The "open interest" column in Table 4-1 keeps track of how many open contracts there are for that particular option. To do so, one could either tally all long positions *or* all short positions to get the total number of outstanding contracts. This is because each contract has a buyer and a seller (a long and a short position). Some people mistakenly believe that the open interest is the total number of long *and* short positions. However, this would double count the actual number of open contracts.

For example, let's say today is the first day a particular call option starts trading so that the open interest is zero. You wish to buy 10 calls and another trader wishes to sell 10 calls. You would enter the order as "buy to open" while the other trader would enter an order to "sell to open."

The total open interest is now 10 contracts. Note that we can get this answer by either counting all 10 long positions or all 10 short positions. But if we count all long *and* short positions then we get a total of 20, which exactly doubles the correct answer. The reason 20 is not correct is because each contract requires two people. Think of it like buying a house. If you buy a house then someone else must sell that house to you. You have two "traders" but only one house has been sold. For the same reason, if you buy 10 contracts and another trader sells 10 contracts then only 10 contracts changed hands and not 20.

Whenever both traders are entering "opening" transactions then open interest will increase. The reason is the both traders are "entering the positions" so open interest must be increasing.

Now let's assume that you wish to sell five of your contracts. You would enter an order to "sell to close." The trader on the other side must be buying since a buyer is required to complete your sales transaction. But depending on whether he's opening or closing will determine what happens to open interest. For example, if the trader is buying to close, then open interest will decrease by five since both of you are closing positions. However, if the other trader is buying to open, then one trader is opening while the other is closing and open interest remains unchanged.

Table 4-2 will help to summarize what happens to open interest based on the actions of both traders:

Table 4-2

Trader #1	Trader #2	
	Opens	Closes
Opens	Increases	Unchanged
Closes	Unchanged	Decreases

Another way to interpret the chart is that if both traders are opening then open interest will increase. If both are closing then open interest will decrease. And if one is opening and the other closing then open interest remains unchanged.

Let's now go back to Table 4-1 and interpret the open interest numbers. The first call option listed is the July $32.50, which shows and open interest of 7,319. This means that there are 7,319 open contracts for this month and strike in existence at this time. Because each contract represents 100 shares of stock, we know there are really 7,319 * 100 = 731,900 shares of stock being controlled by this one contract.

We see from Table 4-1 that the volume for this contract today (so far) is five. Assuming this is the total volume by the close of trading, what will be the new open interest tomorrow? Many new traders believe that the open interest must be 7,319 + 5 = 7,324. However, from what we previously learned, we know that is not necessarily true. The reason is that we have no idea whether the five contracts were "opening" transactions or "closing" transactions. If one trader bought five contracts "to open" and the other sold five contracts "to open" then open interest will, in fact, increase to 7,324 tomorrow. But if one trader bought five contracts "to close" and the other sold five contracts "to close" then open interest will *decrease* to 7,319 − 5 = 7,314. And if one trader bought "to open" and the other sold "to close" then open interest will remain at 7,319 tomorrow (it would also remain unchanged if one trader bought "to close" and the other sold "to open").

Open interest tends to be highest for the at-the-money contracts. In Table 4-1, we would probably consider the $37.50 calls the at-the-money but, in this case, they do not have the highest open interest. Part of the reason is that traders were very bullish on eBay at this time and were buying the higher strike $40 call. For the puts, the highest open interest doesn't match with the $37.50 contracts either. Instead, the highest open interest contracts are the $35 and $32.50 puts. This is often typical for puts if they are used for insurance. Remember, most traders were bullish on eBay at this time so relatively few were buying at-the-money puts as a bearish bet. However, when traders and investors use puts for insurance reasons, they typically buy out-of-the-money contracts because they are cheaper and still protect a significant part of their holdings. But generally speaking, you will find the highest volume and open interest for the at-the-money contracts.

Here's an interesting question: Why do you suppose that the open interest is zero for all of the August calls and puts? The reason is that the last trading day for the June options was June 17 (third Friday of that month). From our discussion on expiration cycles, you know that once the June contracts expire that we must have July and August contracts traded (current month plus following month). This means that August must not have been trading and they were rolled out on the same date that these option quotes were taken (July 20). In other words, July 20 is the first trading day for the August options and that's why their open interest is zero.

Open interest is generally used as a liquidity guide for trading purposes, especially if you are placing large dollar amounts into a particular option. For example, McDonald's is currently $29.02 and the July $30 call (one week to expiration) has an open interest of 6,692, which is a relatively large number when comparing absolute open interest figures. It might appear as though this option is very liquid. However, a better method is to take the 669,200 shares that it represents and multiply it by the market price of the option. Whether you use the bid, ask or last trade usually won't make a huge difference unless there is a very high bid-ask spread. The asking price on this July contract is five cents. In terms of total dollars represented in the contract, that's only 6,692 open interest * 100 shares per contract * $.05 = $33,460, which by market standards, is not too liquid.

Conversely, the Nasdaq 100 Index (NDX) is currently trading around 1,550 with the December $1550 call trading about $108 (yes, this index is extremely expensive due to the volatility!). There open interest is "only" 1,578, which doesn't appear to be too liquid especially when compared the 6,692 for McDonald's. But if we take 1,578 * $108 * 100, we see there is over $17,000,000 represented in this option. When you compare this number to the $33,460 in the McDonald's contract, you can see that total dollar value is probably a better measure of true liquidity in an option. If you are placing a large order, you may wish to check the open interest figure to gauge the liquidity. In other words, if your order is substantially large relative to the amount of contracts at that strike, it is possible that your order could significantly move the market price. If that looked possible, we would say the option doesn't appear to be too liquid. This is why many traders wish to check the actual number (by looking at the open interest column) as well as the *total dollars* represented in that option.

However, despite the apparent justification for checking open interest, you must realize that market makers and others stand by ready, willing, and able to provide liquidity. Just because an option may appear to be illiquid does not mean that it is. Chances are any order will get executed quickly and within reasonable limits of the current price. The reason we make this clarification is because we find that many new traders get caught up in deciding if the open interest is sufficiently large for their order. Unless you are entering an order for 50 or more contracts, we wouldn't even suggest considering the open interest; it's just not going to matter.

Early Exercise

Equity options, that is, options on stock are an American style option, which means they can be exercised at any time prior to expiration. To many traders, the exercise restriction that comes with European options seems like a negative feature. It seems sensible that there must be times when you would like to exercise a call option early to gain the stock. For example, what if you're holding a call option and the stock makes a sudden large move up above the strike price? Wouldn't it be to your advantage to exercise the option and then sell the stock for a sure profit? Many traders believe this and do so every day. But it is one of the biggest mistakes in options trading and traders who exercise call options early end with more risk while literally throwing money away, which is certainly not a winning strategy. When the drawbacks to early exercise are mentioned in many of our seminars, it is often met with heated debates but the participants quickly find that there are better choices once we give a few examples. The point is that it is instinctual at times to want to exercise a call option early but it is, in most cases, the wrong move to make.

To further confuse the early exercise issue, traders who exercise put options early may actually be better off at times. This section fully explains the differences to make sure you are not throwing money away due to illusory beliefs about options and early exercises.

Call Options

With only one exception, we can say that it is never advantageous to exercise a call option early. The exception would be for those investors who wish to collect an upcoming dividend on a stock. Because option holders do not collect dividends, if they wish to collect it, they must exercise the option in order to take control of the stock. However, most dividends are relatively small and are usually not worth the risk of holding the stock – even if just overnight. For the few times when early exercise might be warranted, we'll show you when to exercise in the next section.

For now, let's just concentrate on why it's usually not in your best interest to exercise a call option early if no dividend is being paid.

Early Exercise on a Non-Dividend Paying Stock

We'll compare two investors: One buys stock for $50 while the other buys a $50 call for $2. There is no limit as to the amount of money that either trader could make. Either trader's windfall depends on how high the stock's price rises above $50. Of course, the call option trader's profit will always be $2 less than the stock holder since the call trader pays $2 for the right to buy stock at $50, which would make his cost basis $52 if he uses the call to buy the stock. But aside from that difference, both traders have unlimited upside potential.

If the stock is trading for $60 at expiration, the stock holder makes $10 while the $50 call is worth $60 - $50 = $10 as well. After subtracting the $2 cost, the $50 call trader makes $8. No matter how high the stock's price may rise above $50, both traders continue to profit dollar-for-dollar with the underlying stock near expiration. At no point near expiration is one trader better off than the other when considering stock price increases. But now let's look at the downside; that is for all stock prices below $50. If the stock falls, the stock holder loses dollar-for-dollar all the way down to a stock price of zero. The $50 call holder, on the other hand, can only lose $2 so there is a very big difference in the way the $50 call and long stock positions behave for decreasing stock prices. Call options have a very small, limited downside risk (the price paid for the option) when compared to that of the stock trader. At expiration, call options win dollar-for-dollar to the upside, but do not lose dollar-for-dollar to the downside.

The second chapter showed that this asymmetrical property is one of the main reasons that traders buy calls in the first place. In other words, traders buy call options to *avoid* holding the risky stock. Traders are naturally drawn to this beneficial feature of calls. They should be. Short-term traders and speculators survive by using stop orders or other types of risk-management techniques and the asymmetrical payoffs of call options provides an automatic risk management tool; the most you can lose is the amount you paid for the option.

Traders are completely disregarding this benefit when they exercise a call early. Once you submit exercise instructions, you are swapping the call option for the stock and are now accepting the full downside risk of the stock. That alone should be enough to convince you to not exercise a call early. But there's more to the early exercise story than just increasing your downside risk.

The second part has to do with the time value remaining in the option. Chapter Two (Pricing Principle #3) showed us that an option's price must always contain the intrinsic value, or S − E. However, prior to expiration, the call option must be worth at least S − E plus some time value (Pricing Principle #4). When you exercise an option, you are only left holding the value between the stock and exercise price, or S − E. For example, if the stock is $53 and you exercise a $50 call, you are better off by $3. However, we know that the option's price must be worth more than $3. So if you just sell the call rather than exercise it you would be better off.

By exercising a call option early, not only do you accept full downside risk in the stock but you also throw away the time value of that call option. To put it in a more distressing way, you throw money away in exchange for accepting more risk! It does not matter how short of a time period you intend to hold the stock either. Even if you plan to sell the stock the next day, you're still at risk of some serious negative news announced before the opening bell. It's important to remember that, with a call option, your purchase price is locked in. It doesn't matter how high the stock's price may rise; you will always be able to purchase it for the strike price so there really is no need to take delivery of the stock early.

Let's take a look at a real example. Below are actual option quotes on September eBay calls with 32 days to expiration. The last trade on the stock is $79.21:

Strike	Bid	Ask
$70	9.90	10.10
$75	5.90	6.10
$80	2.90	3.00

If you were holding the $70 call and exercised early, you'd receive stock worth $79.21 by paying $70, which nets a gain of $9.21. However, if you just sold the call, you'd get the bid of $9.90, which is certainly better than $9.21 and it keeps you from holding the downside risk of the stock. If you were holding the $75 call, you'd gain $4.21 by exercising early but $5.90 by selling to close. As an extreme example, if you were holding the $80 call and exercised, you get stock worth $70.21 by paying $80, which leaves you in for a loss of 79 cents. Selling the $80 call to close though would bring in $2.90. It doesn't matter how you cut it, it does not pay to exercise a call early. Early exercise only causes you to lose the time premium *and* take additional risk by holding the stock.

If that's not enough to convince you, there is yet a third reason for not exercising a call early: You are giving up the time value of money. If you exercise 10 $50 calls that have three months remaining on them, you will pay $50,000 today in order to gain that stock. If, instead, you had waited until expiration, you would have held onto that $50,000 for an additional three months on which to earn interest. In either case, your purchase price does not change so there is no rush to pay for it early.

Mathematical Examples

So far, we have covered three rationales for not exercising early:

1) Increase your risk

2) Discard the time value in the option

3) Lose interest by paying for the stock early

While these are pragmatic arguments, there are some people who like to see the math behind the arguments. While mathematical proofs are convincing, they are often difficult to follow. But for those who are mathematically inclined, we'll show you a mathematical proof for not exercising early.

Start by considering two traders. One holds the stock while the other holds a call option plus some cash. How much cash does he hold? He holds just enough so that, after the interest has been paid on that cash balance, he will have exactly the amount of the strike price. For example, if interest rates are 5% and the trader is holding a one-year $50 call then he would need to hold $47.62 in cash. In one year, he will have $47.62 + 5% interest = $50 in cash. He could then take this $50 and buy the stock by exercising his call option. This amount of cash is the *present value* of the $50 strike. While the trader must pay $50 to exercise the call in the future, that payment is worth only $47.62 today if interest rates are five percent. If, instead, he were holding a three month, $50 call he would need $49.38 in cash since that amount would grow to $50 in three months at five percent interest. The two important points to understand are:

1) The cash held by the trader will always equal the exercise price at expiration.

2) The amount of cash necessary to hold is always less than the exercise price.

Keeping these points in mind, the two portfolios are as follows:

Trader #1: Stock

Trader #2: Call option + present value of the exercise price in cash

Now, at expiration, the value of the first trader's position is always the value of the stock, which we can write as Trader #1 = S. No matter what happens to the stock's price, Trader #1 is always worth S at expiration.

What about Trader #2? At expiration, this trader will be holding a call option plus cash that has grown to the exercise price, or +E. This trader has a choice. If the stock's price happens to be above the strike price, then the second trader will exercise the call and will pay the exercise price, -E. His portfolio with then be worth S – E + E = S. In other words, no matter how high the stock's price might be trading, Trader #2 can always gain the stock by simply paying the exercise price. That is, Trader #2 can always match the performance of Trader #1 for high stock prices.

However, prior to expiration, Trader #2 has cash that is worth Pv (E). This means that if he exercises early, his portfolio is worth (S-E) + Pv (E), which is *less* than S. (Remember, the Pv (E) is less than E so S-E + Pv (E) must result in a number less than S). So if the second trader exercises early, he underperforms Trader #1. This means the second trader is better off not exercising until expiration.

Notice too what happens to the second trader by keeping the present value of the cash as long as possible. If the stock should fall below the strike, the second trader loses the value of the call but always has the cash. In the worst case, the stock could become nearly worthless, but the second trader will always walk away with the full exercise price in cash. We can't say the same for the first trader. He will have lost everything.

We could also view the early exercise error in another light. Let's say the second trader exercises early and does not have the cash in the account. He would need to borrow the exercise price and will owe the future value of the exercise price (E + interest). He buys the stock on borrowed funds, which means his portfolio is immediately worth S – future value of E after the exercise. However, this value is always less than the value of the call since an in-the-money call must be worth at least S – E at any time. Remember, the future value of E is a bigger number than just E. Therefore S – future value of E must be a smaller value than S – E and our goal is to make our positions worth more money, not less. By exercising early, the trader lessens the value of the call.

Hopefully you're convinced that it is not to your advantage to exercise a call early. But it is still one of the biggest mistakes in option trading. While working for an active trading team for a large firm, I received a call from a client who had an account value of $124,000 at the close of trading and $120,000 the very next morning. All of his stocks were basically unchanged and certainly not down enough to create a $4,000 shortfall. He wondered what happened to the money. I found out that he exercised 10 call options the day before. When I looked up the previous day's quotes, I found those options had four points of time premium in them. By exercising the 10 calls early, he literally threw away the $4,000 and there is no way to get that money back. It's gone for good.

Exercising a Call to Collect a Dividend

The previous section showed that exercising a call option early for the sole reason of gaining the stock is never to your advantage. However, exercising a call to collect a dividend is a viable strategy despite the fact that it is designed to offset a loss and not for a financial gain. To understand why, consider a simple example where the option is trading at parity (intrinsic value). Assume that the stock is trading for $50 and pays a $1 dividend. You own a $40 call that is trading at parity for $10. The day the dividend is paid, the stock price drops to $49 and the call option immediately becomes worth the $9 intrinsic value thus causing a $1 loss in value for you.

If you exercise the call, you will receive stock worth $50 and pay $40 thus gaining $10 of unrealized value. When the dividend is paid, your stock position becomes worth $49 but you also collect the $1 dividend, which still provides $10 of value for you ($9 unrealized plus a $1 dividend). So if you do not exercise your option, your value falls from $10 to $9. If you exercise the option, you maintain the $10 value. If you wish to collect a dividend to offset a loss then only do it if the value of the dividend exceeds the time value of the call you are sacrificing.

Despite the advantage of collecting a dividend, you must consider whether offsetting a small loss is worth holding the downside risk of the stock

 Do not exercise a call option early except to capture a dividend. Even in this case, be sure the size of the dividend is worth letting go of your downside protection!

Put Options

Hopefully you're now convinced that exercising a call option early is not a healthy thing for your account. However, the opposite may be true for put options. For puts, if the stock is sufficiently in-the-money, then it does make sense to exercise early. Why the difference between calls and puts? When you exercise a call, you're receiving the risky stock and giving up the secure cash. With puts, however, you're getting rid of the risky stock and receiving cash. It's the opposite set of transactions so it has the opposite characteristics.

Imagine that you are holding stock along with a $50 put that you bought as insurance. The stock is now $35 and you see no hopes of it moving above $50 before expiration. If you did, you'd be better off holding the stock hoping that it shoots above $50 and let the put expire worthless. But if you don't see the possibility, then you have two choices: Exercise now and collect the money or exercise at expiration and collect the money. Obviously, take the money now. What stock price is satisfactory for early exercise? Mathematically, it will occur where the delta equals one, where the put is gaining dollar-for-dollar with each fall in the stock's price. Of course, this doesn't mean that you must wait for the delta to equal one in order to exercise but it should serve as a precautionary check. Even though you may not think that the stock has a chance of coming back, the delta may reflect something different. Delaying the exercise of a put only costs you the interest that you could have earned on the cash; you will always be able to get the strike price no matter how long you wait. And if interest rates are low, there's not much of an advantage to exercising the put early. So if you're in doubt as to exercise the put option early, check the delta. If it's not close to one (say 95 or higher), then you're probably better off waiting.

As an example, assume you are holding 100 shares of stock plus a $50 put with three months to expiration. The stock has fallen to $45 and your broker pays you 3% on cash balances. You decide to exercise early, sell your stock and take the $5,000 today, which will then earn interest and grow to $5,037 in three months. However, at a later time, the stock is trading for $51, which means you would have been better off holding the stock and letting the put expire worthless. In fact, we can even calculate a breakeven point for the decision. If the best you can do is $5,037 in three months with the cash, where does the stock's price need to be at expiration to make the two choices equal? It would need to be at $50.37. At a stock price of $50.37, the $50 put is worthless and we can sell the stock for $5,037, which is exactly what we'd have from exercising early and earning interest. If you think the stock has a decent chance of rising to $50.37 by expiration, you're probably better off to not exercise the put. Remember, you will always be able to get the $5,000 by exercising the put. The only difference is that you may collect something less than the $37 of interest if you delay your decision, which should obviously not be a critical point. On the other hand, if interest rates are high and you have 20 $100 puts, then that's a different story. Just always be aware what the tradeoffs are and make your choices appropriately.

We've shown that exercising a call option early is never to your advantage with the exception of collecting a dividend. If that's true, then why are so many traders tempted to do so? It is usually the result of strong desire to pay a low price for the stock that is trading relatively high above the strike. For example, if a hot stock is suddenly trading for $65 and you're holding the $50 call, it just seems like you should take advantage of that "deal" before the stock falls. And it's that mindset that causes traders to buy the stock while not realizing exactly what happened in the exchange. If you want to buy the stock, you can either pay $65 or pay $50 by exercising the call. The higher the stock price is above the strike, the better the deal. So once the stock seems to be getting relatively high, many traders erroneously think they had better exercise to take maximum advantage of the call option. But they never realize that they just increased the downside risk – and paid money to do so. Even with something as simple as exercising a call, traders can stumble in making the right decision. This is why it is so important to understand profit and loss diagrams, the price behavior of options, and market mechanics if you're going to get involved in options. What appears to be a simple decision can easily be clouded by a number of factors that are not so easy to see.

There are many persistent myths in options trading. They survive because many of the technicalities seem so obvious that it's hard to change our perception. Early exercise is perhaps one of the most difficult viewpoints to shake. Hopefully, this section has changed your perception.

Mechanics of Exercising a Call to Collect a Dividend

We previously learned that it is not optimal to exercise a call option early in order to gain the stock with the exception of collecting a dividend.

If you wish to collect a dividend you must exercise the call to gain control of the stock and only then can you get the dividend. However, you cannot just exercise it at any time and be assured of getting the dividend. The reason is that the dividend is only paid to those stock holders as of a specific date called the *record date*. If you are the owner of stock after the record date, you will not receive the dividend. For this reason, it is important to understand the mechanics of how dividends are paid and when to exercise the call option if you should decide to collect a dividend.

As with any exercise of a call, you do not want to exercise it any earlier than you must and this standard still applies when exercising to get the dividend. Exercise too early and you're exposing yourself to unnecessary downside risk. At the same time, if you exercise too late, you will miss out on the dividend. The key to collecting the dividend is to exercise the option on the correct date. In order to understand when that correct date is, you must understand the *ex-dividend* date.

What Is The Ex-Dividend Date?

The ex-dividend date, also called the *ex-date*, is the date the stock trades *without* the dividend. Just remember that "ex" means "without" and you will not be prone to one of the most common mistakes made by investors and brokers.

For example, let's say a stock is about to pay a dividend and the ex-date is June 8. If you buy the stock on June 8 or later, you will not get the dividend. Remember, "ex" means without. If you buy the stock on the ex-date (or later), you are buying the stock without that dividend. On the other hand, if you buy the stock on June 7 (or earlier) you will get the dividend. On the flip side, if you sell stock on the ex-date or later, you will get the dividend. If you sell stock before the ex-date, you will not collect it. If investors would just focus on the ex-date, it is very easy to determine who gets the dividend and who does not.

Why Is There So Much Confusion In Practice?

Although it appears to be an easy task to figure out who gets the dividend, many investors find that it's not so easy. Many times they buy the stock in anticipation of the dividend only to find that they are not entitled to it. The reason for the confusion is that when a dividend is announced, there are usually three dates associated with it:

• Record date

• Payable date

• Ex-date

Corporations usually only publicize the *record date* and *payable date* in newspapers, financial websites, and television shows. The record date is the only date that matters to the company. Before the company pays the dividend, they look up a list of names of all investors who are owners of their stock as of the record date and pay the dividends to those names. Using the previous example, if a company announces a June 10 record date and your name is on the list then you get the dividend. The payable date is when the payment is actually made, which may be a week or more after the record date. They may announce, for example, that they will pay a 20-cent dividend to all stock holders as of record of June 10 and payable on June 15.

Here's where the confusion sets in for most investors...

In order to be the owner of record, the stock transaction must be *settled* by the record date. There is currently a *three-business day* settlement period, which is also called "T+3" settlement and stands for "trade date plus three business days." In order to find the settlement date, you just add three full business days to your purchase date, not counting the trade date. For instance, if you buy stock on Monday, it will settle on Thursday since Thursday is three full business days from the trade date (assuming none of the days in between are holidays). If you buy stock Wednesday, it will settle on Monday.

Continuing with our previous example, if you want to own the stock as of a June 10 record date, you need to purchase it on June 7 or before. If you purchase the stock on June 7, the stock transaction will settle on June 10 and you will be owner of record as of June 10. If you purchase the stock on June 8 or later, you will not be owner as of the record date. In this example, June 8 would be the ex-date. Now you can see where all the confusion comes from. It all has to do with the timing of the settlement period. Many investors think that you just need to purchase the stock on or before the record date in order to collect the dividend and that is not true. You must purchase the stock three full business days before the record date.

The ex-date is an artificial creation by brokerage firms to mathematically figure out the purchase date that makes you owner by the record date. In the previous example, we figured out that June 8 would be the ex-date. If you purchase on June 8 or later, you will not be owner of record by June 10 and will not get the dividend. (Of course, you would be entitled to the following dividend assuming you were still holding the stock.)

Corporations are not stockbrokers and they are not, in many cases, even aware of the three-business day settlement period. They only publish the record date. This is why most corporations will not even be able to tell you when the ex-date is even if you call their investor relations department. Hopefully you see how much easier it is if you just focus on the ex-date, which you may have to call your broker to get.

Now that you understand the stock settlement process, adding call options to the picture is not difficult. If you have a call option and wish to exercise it in order to collect a dividend, you must exercise the call the *day before* the ex-date. This is exactly the same as if you were buying the stock in the open market. In our example, that would be June 7. Once you submit exercise instructions, the Options Clearing Corporation (OCC) has you listed as of that date. If you submit exercise instruction on June 7, the OCC recognizes that you bought stock on June 7 and it will settle on the June 10 record date. This is sometimes referred to as "E+3" settlement, which just designates that the settlement date is "exercise date plus three business days."

Does It Really Matter If Stock Holders Get The Dividend?

While some stock investors are adamant about collecting a dividend, it doesn't really matter mathematically if you get the dividend or not. Many new to investing find this hard to believe. After all, it certainly seems like you'd be better off buying the stock and getting the dividend rather than not getting the dividend.

The reason there is not a mathematical difference is that the stock price is reduced by the amount of the dividend on the ex-date. We saw this effect when discussing stock splits and said that any payment made by the company must be deducted from the price of the stock. Whether the company pays stock dividends (stock split) or cash dividends, the stock price must be reduced.

For instance, say a stock closes at $100 on June 7 and is scheduled to pay a $2 dividend with the ex-date being June 8. On June 8, the stock will open at $98 *unchanged* to reflect the $2 dividend that was paid. The reason the stock will show its price as unchanged is because the drop in price from $100 to $98 was due to the dividend and not changes in supply and demand for the stock.

Let's compare two investors each starting with $100 cash in their account. One buys one share of stock before the ex-date and another buys one share on the ex-date.

The investor who buys before the ex-date will pay $100 for the stock and receive a $2 dividend. The stock, however, will trade for $98 on ex-date and the total value of the account will still be $100 ($98 in stock and $2 in cash). This investor is down $2 in the value of the stock, which is offset by the $2 dividend.

The second investor buys the stock on ex-date will only pay $98 for the position and not receive the dividend. While he did not receive the $2 dividend, he paid $2 less for the stock. His account has stock worth $98 and $2 in cash. Both investors are holding $98 in stock and $2 in cash so it doesn't really matter mathematically whether you get the dividend or not (although there could be tax benefits to one choice over the other).

Rules Violation: Selling Dividends

Many brokers take advantage of investors by touting an immediate return on your money by purchasing stock just before the ex-date. Using the previous example, a broker may call saying if you buy this stock for $100, you will get an immediate 2% return on your money the very next day. By now you should see why this is not true.

If you buy the stock for $100, it will be worth $98 the next day and you will have $2 in cash for a total position value of $100, which is neither a gain nor loss. If this were really an immediate return of 2%, the total position would be worth $102 the following day.

Further, buying the stock just to get the dividend is a bad idea for tax reasons. If you buy one share of stock for $100, you are paying with *after-tax* dollars; you do not owe taxes on the $100. However, if you buy the stock, the very next day your position is still worth $100, yet you owe taxes on $2. Basically, the dividend represents an immediate taxable return of capital (where previously there was none) and not a return on your money.

For these reasons, the NASD (National Association of Securities Dealers) prohibits brokers from selling you stock *solely* for the reason of getting the dividend. Obviously, if the broker thinks the stock is going to be much higher in the next day or two and recommends buying it for that reason, that's okay. They just cannot sell you the stock based solely on the immediate return of the dividend. If they do, they are guilty of "selling dividends" and in violation of NASD rule 2830, which states:

NASD Rule 2830 (e): No member shall, in recommending the purchase of investment company securities, state or imply that the purchase of such securities shortly before an ex-dividend date is advantageous to the purchaser, unless there are specific, clearly described tax or other advantages to the purchaser, and no member shall represent that distributions of long-term capital gains by an investment company are or should be viewed as part of the income yield from an investment in such company's securities.

This NASD rule is further proof that collecting a dividend is not mathematically better to an investor who waits until after the ex-date to purchase the stock. The only reason to exercise a call option early is to collect the dividend in order to offset a (usually) small loss and even that must be questioned when you consider all of the other negative features that are attached with early exercise.

A Real Life Example

The following is an excerpt from a *Business Wire* news article. Notice that they mention the payable date, record date, and ex-date.

FAIRFIELD, Conn.--(BUSINESS WIRE)--Dec. 14, 2001--The Board of Directors of GE today raised the Company's quarterly dividend 13% to $0.18 per outstanding share of its common stock and increased its share repurchase program to $30 billion from $22 billion.

"GE has paid a dividend every year since 1899," said GE Chairman and CEO Jeff Immelt. "Today's increases, in both our dividend and our share repurchase program, signal our confidence in our ability to extend this track record of returning value to shareowners."

The dividend increase, from $0.16 per share, marks the 26th consecutive year in which GE has increased its dividend. The dividend is **payable** January 25, 2002, to shareowners of **record** on December 31, 2001. The **ex-dividend** date is Thursday, December 27.

If you own a call option and wish to receive an upcoming dividend, you should wait as long as possible and exercise the call option *the day before* the ex-date date and no sooner. If you're unsure as to when that date is, ask your broker. Also remember that collecting a dividend doesn't really change your overall portfolio value since the value of the stock is reduced by the dividend. If you do exercise that call to get the stock, you're letting go of the downside protection that call options provide, which is usually a bigger benefit than the value of the dividend. However, for those times that you wish to get the dividend, especially a large one-time payment, make sure you understand the mechanics of the ex-dividend date otherwise you may end up missing the payment simply due to the mechanics of the market. When we get to Chapter Five, we'll talk about synthetic positions and show you a potentially better way to collect a dividend.

Types of Option Orders

Once you decide to buy or sell an option, you must place an order online or with a broker. When we discuss strategies, we'll show you specifics on how to enter the orders but for now we want to get some of the terminology out of the way. It is crucial that you understand the many terms associated with placing orders especially in today's market where most people place trades online and there is no interaction with a broker. While trading online does provide you with a greatly reduced commission, the drawback is that you are 100% responsible for the trade. If you are not fully aware of what a particular order or qualifier means, you could end up with a very different outcome than what you were expecting.

Making the Trade

Whenever you buy or sell options, you must specify five basic pieces of information:

- Action (Buy or Sell)

- Quantity (Number of contracts)

- Symbol

- **Price** (Market or Limit)

- **Time** (Day or Good-til-Cancelled (GTC))

The action, quantity, and symbol are all straightforward and really don't need any detailed explanation. These fields are simply telling your broker whether you wish to buy or sell, how many contracts, and of which option. But the price and time fields are the ones that create the most questions – and unexpected surprises – for new traders so that's what we're going to focus on. Each of the possible orders carries a different set of possibilities and, depending on the situation, one will probably be a better choice than the other. We'll go through each so that you understand them fully.

Price

When you place an order to buy or sell, you must provide some information about the price at which you're willing to make the deal. There are two ways to provide price information: *market order* or *limit order*.

Market Order

A market order guarantees that your order will be filled but does not guarantee the price at which the transaction will be made. If you place an order to buy five $30 Intel calls "at market," then you know for sure that you have purchased the five calls. But in order for this transaction to be guaranteed, it means that you must be flexible on the price. The reason you must be flexible on price is because option prices can change nearly every second of the day; they do not stay constant throughout the day such as when shopping at a retail store!

If the option is trading for $3 when you place your order, it's quite possible that your purchase price will come back at a different price (whether higher or lower) than $3 even though it may only take a few seconds for the trade to get filled. When you place a market order, you're really stating that you want to be filled at the best price (which is the prevailing price at that moment) when your order reaches the trading floor. The simplest way to describe a market order is this: *A market order guarantees the execution but not the price.*

New traders often wonder why they cannot guarantee that the deal goes through but at a predetermined price. After all, whenever you buy a house or car, you can guarantee the deal at a stated price. The reason for the apparent inconsistency is due to the fact that the stock market is one continuous live auction where traders place bids to buy and offers to sell. The stock's price (and therefore the option's price) depends on the supply and demand of the stock at that moment in time. If you place an order "at market," you're telling the broker to fill the order but the price at which the order is filled depends on the time your order arrives. There is no way to be sure to get the contracts while also stating a maximum or minimum price. Think about it this way: Imagine that you are a buyer for a multi-millionaire who sends you to an auction to purchase a specific Picasso painting. There is no way he can tell you to definitely come back with the painting but, at the same time, not to spend more than $10 million. If you must buy something at an auction, you must be flexible on price.

Multiple Fills

If you place a market order, it is possible that the order comes back filled at multiple prices. This just means the traders were only able to get a certain number of contracts at one price and had to fill the balance at one or more prices. For example, assume Intel $30 calls are trading for $3. If you place an order to buy 10 $30 calls at market, it is possible that your order comes back as follows: bought 7 contracts at $3 and bought 3 contracts at $3.10. When you are filled at more than one price, it is called a *multiple fill*. These happen for the sheer fact that market orders must fill and, just as there's no guarantee as to the price. There's also no guarantee that the price will be the same for all contracts (or shares for that matter) traded.

Despite the small risk of adverse price movements, if you *must* get in or out of a trade, then the market order is still your best choice. It is the only way to be sure you are in or out of the trade. However, there may be times when you want to ensure that your buy price does not rise past a certain point or that your sell order does not fall below a certain price. If so, then you can use another type of price called a limit order.

Limit Orders

A limit order is one where you specify a price. If you are buying options, your order cannot be filled at a price higher than your limit price. If you are selling options, your order cannot be filled at a price lower than your limit price. But if that limit price cannot be realized, then your order remains open, which means it is possible you never get filled. *Limit orders guarantee the price but not the execution.*

For example, if you place an order to buy 10 Intel $30 calls at a limit price of $3 then the order will only be filled if the market maker can fill it for $3 or less. If your order is to sell the 10 contracts at a limit price of $3 then the order can only be filled for $3 or higher.

Most traders use limit orders to buy options at a lower price (or sell it at a higher price) than the current market price. If the Intel $30 call is $3 and you think its price will fall in the near future, you might place a trade to buy contracts at a limit of $2.50, for example. That way you'll have a standing order on the books if the price should hit $2.50. If the option never hits that price (or lower), the trade goes unexecuted. If you place the order with the limit price equal to the current market price, it is called a *marketable limit order*. In this example, if you placed an order to buy the $30 calls at a limit price of $3, it is called a marketable limit order.

This just means that you are willing to pay the current price or lower but will not get filled it if should move above $3 when your order reaches the floor.

Limit orders are a great tool for discipline. If you just purchased the 10 $30 calls for $3 and are willing to sell them for $4, you can immediately place an order to sell the contracts at a limit price of $4. The only way the trade will get executed is if the call option's bid price hits $4 or higher. Limit orders are a handy tool since they allow you to have a standing order on the books, which keeps you from having to watch the prices at every moment of the day.

Tick Size

Whenever you submit option orders, there are certain minimum amounts that a price can change. These minimum amounts are called the *tick size*. Currently, all option orders priced below $3 can be submitted in five-cent increments and all option orders above $3 must be submitted in ten-cent increments. In other words, all option limit orders must fall somewhere on the following list of possible prices:

.05, 0.10, 0.15, … $2.95, $3.00, $3.10, $3.20… etc.

This means that there is a five-cent tick size for option orders at $3.00 and below and a ten-cent tick size for all option orders above $3.00. If you try to submit an order above $3 in five-cent increments, such as $3.15, it would be rejected and returned to you! At the time of this writing, the Nasdaq has filed to list options trading in pennies so these tick size rules are likely to be changed in the near future.

Why Can't I Guarantee the Execution and Price?

It is important to understand that when you place orders you can either guarantee the execution (market order) or the price (limit order) but you cannot guarantee both. Why can't a trader guarantee both the price and execution? That would be too good to be true. If we could guarantee both, we would be guaranteed to buy an expensive option for a very low price and guaranteed to sell it for a very high price, which is simply not possible. You only get one choice between price and execution. If you must have the order executed then use a market order and be flexible on price. If you must have a certain price, then use a limit order and accept the risk of not getting filled.

Or-Better Orders

The price risk associated with market orders leaves some traders uncomfortable especially if they have a relatively small account and do not wish to risk having to send additional money to pay for a trade. Placing a limit order alleviates this risk but then you run the risk of not getting filled. Is there some way to blend the two orders? Is there a way we can be reasonably certain of getting filled but, at the same time, not be at risk for a price we find unsatisfactory? The answer is yes and we can do that with an "or-better" qualifier. An or-better qualifier is a type of limit order where your buy price is stated above the current market price and your sell limit is placed below the current market price.

For example, assume that the Intel $30 call is trading for $3 and you want to buy 10 contracts but do not want to be totally flexible on price. You could place an order, for example, to buy the 10 contracts at $3.20 *or-better*. By selecting the or-better designation, in this example, it means that you are willing to pay *up to* $3.20 per contract even though the current price is $3. This order qualifier gets its name from that fact that you are willing to buy the contracts at $3 or at a better price, which is lower. Some new traders think the "or better" qualifier is suggesting that you will buy the contracts at $3 "or higher" and that's not true. That would be better for the seller, not you. You're telling the broker you'll buy for the $3.20 price "or better" for you. If they can fill the order for $3 they will certainly do it.

By using the or-better qualifier, if the price should move up a bit after you send the order, at least you'll get filled assuming the price doesn't move above $3.20. The or-better qualifier allows for some price fluctuation between the time you send the order and the time it is filled. Of course, this is still a type of limit order so it is possible (although less likely) that you do not get filled. By using the or-better qualifier, you have a much better chance of being filled as compared to a trader that places a marketable limit at $3 per share.

You can use or-better qualifiers on the sell side too. If the Intel $30 call is $3 and you place an order to sell 10 contracts for $2.90 or-better, you could get filled for any price of $2.90 or higher. The or-better designation on the sell side just tells the broker you're willing to take less than the current market price if necessary to get the trade executed.

When entering an or-better order online, most firms require that you check off a little box that says "or better" at the order entry screen so they know that you are willing to buy above the current price (or sell below the current price). The reason they require you to check off the box is because, otherwise, they're not sure of your intentions. For instance, if the current price is $3 and you place an order to buy for $3.20 it appears that you might be trying to *sell* the option (since most traders would place a limit order above the current price if they are selling). By checking off the or-better box, it lets your broker know that you are not making a mistake in the order and that you are, in fact, willing to buy at a higher price than the current market price. If you do not see a check-box for the or-better qualifier, you can just enter the order and you will likely get a pop-up message that states something like this: "You have entered an order to buy at a price above the current market. If you wish to place this trade, it will be entered as an or-better order."

Some traders find or-better orders a little unsettling to use. They feel that the market makers will take advantage of them and fill the order at the higher price. That's not true since the market makers are bound by the *time and sales*, which is a recording of all sales (trades) and the times they occurred. Market makers cannot arbitrarily fill your order at the higher price just because you're willing to pay it. They could only do so if the time and sales recording shows that was the going price for the option at the time your order was filled.

Another fact about limit orders is that you are really stating to buy or sell *up to* that many contract at the limit price. If you place an order to buy 10 Intel $30 calls, you could get filled for any number of contracts up to and including 10. If your order is filled for fewer contracts than you requested, it is called a partial fill.

All-or-None (AON)

If you do not wish to get a partial fill, you can place an *all-or-none (AON)* restriction on your order. This is simply done by checking off the AON box at the order entry screen when you enter the trade. This just tells the market makers to not fill your order unless they can fill the entire number of contracts you requested. While this may sound like a good restriction to place on all orders, there are many drawbacks. First, your order is handled differently and market makers are not required to show your orders to the public if they are marked AON. This means that you may reduce your chance of getting filled. Second, multiple fills are not a possibility with AON orders. For instance, assume you place an order to buy 30 call options for $3. It's possible that all 30 contracts could have been filled but at different times of the day. However, if you marked the trade AON, then you would get none of them filled unless all 30 could be filled at once. Third, you must ask yourself if a partial fill is really a bad outcome. Will you be upset that you only bought 25 out of 30 call options if the stock really takes off? There are times for AON restrictions but, for most traders, it acts as a hindrance. Also, all option quotes must be good for at least 20 contracts. For example, if you see an option that is bid $2.95 and asking $3.10 then you know that you can sell at least 20 contracts for $2.95 and can buy at least 20 contracts for $3.10. If your order is for fewer contracts than 20, the all-or-none restrictions can only hurt the order. Except for certain circumstances, we wouldn't consider using an all-or-none restriction for fewer than 50 contracts. But just be aware of the AON restriction as it can be very useful at times.

Time Limits

In addition to setting a price when entering your order, you must also specify a time limit for which the order is good. This is true for any bid to buy or offer to sell. If you place a bid on a new home and the seller rejects it, he or she cannot come back a week later and force you to accept it. There is only so long that a bid or offer can stand. In the same way, when you place an order to buy or sell stock, you must specify for how long the order is valid. There are two basic choices for time limits: *Day Order* and *Good 'til Cancelled* (GTC). There are two others, which are *Immediate or Cancel* (IOC) and *Fill or Kill* (FOK) but those are rarely used, especially if you are new to trading so we'll only consider the day order and GTC.

Day Orders

A day order is good only for the trading day. If you place a day order after the market close, then it will be good only for the following business day. Any market order can only be entered as a "day order" for the fact that market orders are guaranteed to fill. There is no reason that the order would roll over to another day. Most computer programs will automatically select the "day order" time limit if you enter a market order. However, if it doesn't and you manually select GTC, the order will likely be rejected since it raises questions for the floor traders; they are not sure if you meant to use a limit order or meant to make the time period good for the day.

We just found out that a day order is the only acceptable time limit for a market order. However, if you enter a limit order, then the "day" time limit makes the trade only good for the trading day and is cancelled at the end if it is not filled. If you wish to reenter the trade, you must retype a new order and submit it. Rather than go through these motions everyday, the exchanges created the *good-til-cancelled* order.

Good 'til Cancelled Orders (GTC)

Good 'til cancelled order may only be used for limit orders. GTC orders can be a handy tool that keeps you from having to retype orders that do not fill. If a GTC limit order does not fill today, it will automatically renew itself the following business day.

A GTC order can be good for a period of time not to exceed six months. However, it is up to your broker as to how long a GTC order lasts. Brokers are always allowed to make any rule stricter and most brokers only hold GTC orders for about 60 calendar days (and not trading days).

The quantity automatically adjusts if you get partial fills. For instance, assume you place an order for 30 call options at a limit of $3, GTC. If you get 10 filled today, the order will automatically reinstate tomorrow to buy 20 calls at a limit of $3. The time remaining on the new GTC order starts from you place the original order; the time does not reset because of a partial fill.

At the end of the GTC time period, all remaining open orders are cancelled for good. If you wish to continue with the order, you would have to enter a new one, which you could elect to do as GTC again. Brokers generally require this because they do not want orders floating around the books for very long periods of time so that traders forget about them. That's why most will only hold them for 60 days, which is probably in your best interest. We've seen many bad cases where investors forgot about open orders on the books.

Due to the rapid price changes of options, most traders use day orders so they know for sure that nothing is open the following day. *If you use GTC orders, it's important to check your account on a daily basis so you are aware of any new fills that may have occurred.*

Stop and Stop Limit Orders

As you start investing with options, you'll find there are many types of conditional orders and order qualifiers that help you manage risks. Most of the orders that can be used for stocks can also be used for options. For example, stops, stop limits, all-or-none, not held, or-better, are all types of conditional orders that can be used with stocks and options.

We're not going to cover the numerous types of orders that can be placed with the exception of *stop orders* and *stop limit orders.* The reason is that there is probably more confusion, even among brokers, about the mechanics of these two orders. Further, there is a subtle difference for the way these orders work for options versus stocks and you need to be aware of that difference.

Stop orders are *conditional orders* to buy or sell "at market." Your "stop price" is simply a price at which point the trade is "triggered" (technically "elected") thus making it a live market order. As with any market order, the execution is guaranteed but not the price. It is crucial to understand that your order will be triggered if the stock trades at *or below* your stop price.

Let's take a look at an example of how stop orders work by considering a stock position. Assume you purchased 200 shares of Microsoft (MSFT) at $36 and later place the an order to sell 200 MSFT at a stop price of $35.

This tells your broker that if Microsoft trades at $35 *or lower,* to sell your 200 shares at market. Notice that stop orders convert to "market" orders, which means your shares are sold at the current prevailing price, *which may be very different from your stop price.* In other words, just because the stop price is $35 does not mean that's the price you'll receive for your shares.

For example, assume Microsoft closes at $35.50 tonight and then opens tomorrow morning at $27 on bad news. In that case, your stop price of $35 *or lower* has been reached, the order is activated, and your 200 shares are sold at the market price of $27. If the stock's price slowly drifts lowers, stop orders can work great. But if the stock gaps down, stop orders may leave you with a large loss. Years ago, stop orders used to be called "stop loss" orders and you will still hear some investors refer to them as such. But as we just demonstrated, stop orders are not at all guaranteed to prevent losses. It is for this reason that the SEC (Securities and Exchange Commission) does not allow professionals to use the term "stop loss" anymore.

 Stop orders do not in any way *prevent* losses.

Stop orders for options work the same way as they do for stocks with one exception. If you place a stop order on a stock, the "last" trade dictates whether the stop order is triggered or not. If you place a stop order on an option, it is the asking price that triggers the stop order. Once the order is triggered, the option is then sold at the bid price.

Stop Limit Orders

A stop limit order is an extension of a stop order. The difference is that stop limit orders convert to a limit order, which means your shares will be sold only if the limit price or higher can be and guarantee a price. But as with any limit order, if you guarantee the price, you cannot guarantee the fill.

Key Differences Between Stops and Stop Limits

Stop Orders = Become a live "market" order if stop price is triggered. Guarantees that the order will be filled but cannot guarantee the price.

Stop Limit Orders = Become a live "limit" order if stop price is triggered. Guarantees the price but cannot guarantee that the order will be filled.

In order to place a stop limit order, you must specify two prices. The first price is the stop price. Once you specify the stop price, you must then specify a stop limit price (which must be less than or equal to your stop price).

Let's use the previous example but now apply a stop limit. Assume you purchased 200 MSFT at $36 and have now placed the following order:

Sell 200 MSFT at a stop price of $35 with a stop limit of $34.50.

Notice that two prices must be entered. The first price ($35) is the stop price. This just tells the computer when to activate the order. If the stock trades at $35 *or below*, the order will become activated and becomes a live *limit order* to sell 200 shares of MSFT at the stop limit price ($34.50) or higher. The stop limit price you enter (second price) you enter must be less than or equal to the first price. Many traders like to reduce the second price a bit to allow for some market fluctuations if the order is triggered.

Now let's go back to your stop limit order and assume that MSFT opens at $27. The order is activated because the stock traded at or below $35. You now have a live limit order to sell at $34.50. Obviously, the order cannot be executed since you are requiring a price of $34.50 or higher. This shows that stop limit orders do not prevent losses any more than stop orders. However, stop limit orders will keep you from selling at prices you consider unfavorable.

Which should you use, stop or stop limits? That depends on the situation and you may find that you use both at different times. The one question you need to answer is this: If MSFT opens below my stop price do you want to sell the shares at any price? Is your goal to simply get rid of the shares regardless of price? If the answer is yes then use a stop order. However, if there is a price at which you'd rather hold onto the shares rather than sell then use a stop limit order.

Option Stop Orders

The key point you want to understand with stop and stop limits when applied to options is that the orders are "triggered" if the *asking price* equals the stop price or lower. Option stop orders and stop limits are not based on the last trade. The reason is that it is possible to not have any trades on the option even if the stock's price is falling. In other words, there might not be any activity and therefore no last trades. However, the bid price and asking prices on the options will definitely change in response to the falling stock price. That's why the exchanges trigger stop and stop loss orders on the asking price for options and execute the orders on the bid price.

Limit Order Display Rule

In Chapter Two, we how the bid-ask spread near expiration can make a big difference on your profits especially if the bid price falls below intrinsic value. In a similar fashion, the spreads at any time during the option's life can have a dramatic negative impact on profitability even if the bid price represents the full intrinsic value. For example, assume a stock is trading for $51 and the $50 call is bidding $2 and asking $2.25. Both the bid and ask prices contain the $1 intrinsic value. However, if you were to buy at the asking price of $2.25 and immediately sell at the $2 bid price, you would instantly lose over 11% of your money just because of the spread. Many traders dream of making a quick 10% on their money but notice how the spread can quickly eat that away. The spread causes buyers to pay a higher price and sellers to receive a lower price than the theoretical fair value and is a serious threat to profitability especially when you consider the relatively low prices of options when compared to stocks.

But there is an effective way we can trade between the bid and ask to reduce this detrimental effect. The effectiveness of this technique hinges on an exchange rule called the *Limit Order Display Rule*. In order to understand how we can use this rule to our advantage, we must first understand how the quotation system works.

Understanding the Quote System

Let's say you see an option with the following quote:

Bid: $2.00 **Ask**: $2.25

What exactly does this mean? We learned in the first chapter that the bid price represents the price at which you can sell while the asking price represents the price at which you can buy. In many ways, this is like the difference between retail and wholesale; you can buy this option for $2.25 but you can sell it for only $2.00.

While this is a correct interpretation of the bid and ask prices, it hides the source. Chapter One showed us that the bid price represents the highest bidder among a list of many bidders while the asking price (also called the offer price) is the lowest selling price among a list of many sellers. In order to understand this bid-ask interpretation better, it helps to see how option orders are accumulated by market makers. Whenever you submit an order to your broker, it is received by a market maker who will stack all orders according to price and time.

Here's how the process works: Let's assume the market is not open yet and the maker has no orders on the books. When orders are placed through the various brokerage firms, the market maker will accumulate them in a specific manner. Assume that the first order is an order to buy 5 contracts at a limit of $1.90. Because this is an order to buy, the market maker will list it under the "bid" column (remember, buyers place bids):

Bid	Ask
1.90 (5)	

The number in parenthesis shows the number of contracts at that price. Assume that the next order is an order to buy 10 contracts at a limit of $2.00. Because this is another buy order, the market maker will place it under the "bid" column as well. However, this trader is considered a "stronger" buyer since his buy price is higher than the person at $1.90. The markets are only concerned with the highest bidder and lowest offer. Because of this, the market maker will place the order *above* the $1.90 price as follows:

Bid	Ask
2.00 (10)	
1.90 (5)	

Assume the next order is an order to sell 8 contracts at a limit of $2.35. Because this is a sell order, the computer will place it in the "ask" column (remember that sellers submit "asking" prices). As a matter of convention, asking prices are generally stacked on the top for reasons we will see shortly:

	2.35 (8)
Bid	Ask
2.00 (10)	
1.90 (5)	

The next order is an order to sell 4 contracts at a limit of $2.25. This trader is considered a "stronger" seller since the selling price is *less* than the previous order at $2.35. Because of this, the market maker will place this order below the previous order:

2.35 (8)

2.25 (4)

Bid   **Ask**

2.00 (10)

1.90 (5)

Notice how the orders are being stacked. The bids are being stacked in descending order from strongest to weakest; that is, from highest to lowest. The sellers are stacked in ascending order from strongest to weakest; that is, from lowest to highest. Let's say the next order is to buy 6 contracts at a limit of $1.95. This trader is the stronger than the buyer at $1.90 but not as strong as the one at $2.00 so that order will get placed between the two:

2.35 (8)

2.25 (4)

Bid   **Ask**

2.00 (10)

1.95 (6)

1.90 (5)

To finish the example, assume that the next order is to sell 2 contracts at a limit of $2.30. This trader is a stronger seller than the one at $2.35 but not as strong as the one at $2.25 so that order will get placed between those two:

2.35 (8)

2.30 (2)

2.25 (4)

Bid   **Ask**

2.00 (10)

1.95 (6)

1.90 (5)

If any order matches a previous order it will be placed in line according to the time it arrived. For instance, if the next order is to sell 6 contracts at a limit of $2.25

This process continues until all the orders are on the books. Of course, the final list will be quite long but the entire system is automated so it happens very quickly. Once all orders are in, only the highest bid and lowest offer are located at the center of the computer screen. When you access an option quote, you are looking at only the highest bid and lowest offer, which is called the *inside quote*. In this example, you would see the option quoted as bid $2.00 and asking $2.25 as shown in Table 4-3:

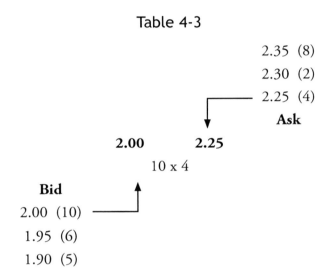

Table 4-3

The numbers 10 x 4 below the quote are called the *size* of the market. The size is always stated as two numbers; the first is the number of contracts available at the asking price and the second is the number available at the bid. Whenever you look at an option quote, you're looking at the inside quote; you just see the highest bidder and the lowest offer at that point in time. The market maker's book may contain hundreds or thousands of orders but you'll only see the orders that are at the front of each respective line.

The difference between the bid and ask is called the *bid-ask spread* or, more simply, the *spread*. In this case, there is a 25-cent spread on the option quote.

Notice that all orders in our example were limit orders. That's because we are assuming the market is not open yet but traders are placing orders. Any market orders placed prior to the open will get filled at the market price at the open but we don't know what that price is until all limit orders are in. Anytime you place a market order to buy (sell) you are really stating that you will take the current asking (bid) prices. In trading terminology, this is called "lifting" the offer or "hitting" the bid.

In our discussion on limit orders, we said it was possible to get a partial fill. Let's now take a look at how that happens. Let's say you place an order to buy 10 contracts "at market." If there were no market makers to provide liquidity, you would buy the 4 contracts available at $2.25, buy the 2 available at $2.30, and buy the remaining 4 (of the 8 available) at $2.35. This is called a *multiple fill* since the order is filled at multiple prices.

The trader selling the 8 contracts at 2.35 would receive a confirmation saying that 4 contracts were sold at 2.35 and have an open order to sell the remaining 4 at 2.35 (assuming he does not have an all-or-none restriction). This is called a *partial fill*. While multiple fills do occur, in most cases, market makers step in and take up some of the slack in size so your order is less likely to come back with multiple fills. In fact, as we will find out later, all option quotes must be good for at least 20 contracts on each side of the market. This just means that market makers must make sure that at least 20 contracts are available at the bid and 20 at the ask. So in the real world, your order for 10 contracts would not come back as a partial fill. But if the order was much larger than that (say 50 contracts) then it is certainly possible that you'd get multiple fills.

 All option quotes must be good for at least 20 contracts on the bid and 20 contracts on the offer.

In Table 4-3, notice that the quote of bid $2.00 and asking $2.25 is not from the market maker, which is what a lot of traders think. The market makers must be ready to keep a liquid and orderly market when one is not available. If the market is quite liquid and competitive, it is possible that the inside quote is strictly due to retail traders. While the market makers usually have some presence at the bid and ask, it is possible that it is represented by only retail traders at certain times.

Now, it used to be the case that market makers did *not* have to allow you to compete with them. In our example, if you submitted a more competitive sell order, say $2.15, the market makers did not have to let you jump in front of the line and show that order. They could have let your order sit out in the wings and kept the asking price at $2.25. Obviously, this is not fair to the rest of the traders and it certainly hurts the efficiency of the market since higher bids and lower offers will reduce the spread between the bid and ask. Higher bids attract sellers and lower offers attract buyers; both create more contracts traded in the marketplace. In order to ensure that higher bids and lower offers would be shown, the exchanges created the "Limit Order Display Rule," which we can use to our advantage once you understand how it works.

Limit Order Display Rule

The Limit Order Display Rule, sometimes called the "Show or Fill Rule" (the official name is "Exchange Act Rule 11Ac1-4), is not a rule that the market makers make very well known for obvious reasons, as we shall soon see. However, knowing this rule can make a big difference in your option profits. Here's how it works: Using our above quote setup in Table 4-3, let's assume you wish to place an order to buy 2 contracts. You don't wish to pay the current asking price of $2.25 so you put in an order for something between the bid and ask, say $2.15. When the market maker receives the order, he now has one of two choices: He can either *fill the order* or *show the order*. If he chooses to not fill the order, he must show it by allowing you to jump in front of the line as shown in bold below:

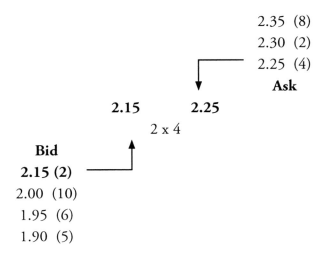

Notice that by showing your order, the bid-ask spread has been reduced from a 25-cent spread (2.00 to 2.25) to a 10-cent spread (2.15 to 2.25). The narrower the spread, the more efficient the market and the Limit Order Display Rule was created for that very reason. Before the rule, market makers could hide your order from the public and just leave the quote at bid 2.00 and ask 2.25. Under the new rule, the market maker must either fill it or show it – even if your order is for just one contract,

Having the ability to compete with market makers and their quotes is certainly an advantage. By raising the bid from $2.00 to $2.15, you have now provided a stronger incentive for someone to sell at the new higher price and there is a better chance that you will get filled. But aside from being able to compete with the market makers, there's an additional advantage you can gain. As we said earlier, there is an exchange policy that all quotes must be good for *at least twenty contracts*. In this example, you have submitted an order to buy 2 contracts for $2.15. How can you do that if the exchanges require all quotes to be good for at least 20 contracts? The reason is that it is up to the market makers to make sure that all quotes are good for at least 20 contracts and we can use that to our advantage.

If the market maker chooses to not fill your two-contract order, he must show it, which means the new bid price becomes $2.15. However, that also means that the market maker must be willing to buy an additional 18 contracts at $2.15 since he must ensure that all quotes are good for at least 20 contracts. In other words, if another trader decides to sell 20 contracts at the new bid of $2.15, the market maker must fill the order. He will give two of those contracts to you but must buy the remaining 18 contracts at $2.15. And that's where you get the advantage. Since the market maker was only willing to buy at $2.00, you are, in effect, forcing him to potentially buy 18 contracts for $2.15. *In order to prevent this liability, the market maker will most likely fill your order to get you out of the queue!*

Think of what a difference that trading between the bid and ask can make on your trades, especially when you consider that it works for the sell side too. Whether you are buying or selling a small number of contracts, you have an advantage of submitting limit orders between the bid and ask. Although the difference may appear small, even a five-cent difference on both the buy side and sell side can really add up. In many cases, it can cover the commissions on the trade.

Remember this rule when you are trading options. If you are trading small numbers of contracts, say up to seven, there is a very good chance you can trade between the bid and ask and get filled for no other reason than the market maker wanting to avoid the additional liability of having to complete the 20-contract exchange rule. Of course, this can still work for any number of contracts less than 20 but there's far more pressure on the market maker if you are trading smaller numbers. The bid-ask spread can have a significant negative impact on your option profits but you now have a way that reduces your chances of having to pay the asking price or sell for the bid price.

Now you should have a clearer understanding why we said to be careful when using all-or-none (AON) restrictions, especially for less than 50 contracts. If you place an order with an all-or-none restriction, that's telling the market maker that he can only fill the order in its entirety; he cannot come back with a partial fill. Because of this, many option traders believe that they should mark all orders with an all-or-none restriction to prevent partial fills. However, there is a big danger in using this restriction. That is, the market maker is not required to show your order if it is marked all-or-none. And if your order is for 20 contracts or less, the quote size must be good for at least 20 so it's redundant to mark it with an all-or-none restriction. You're really hurting yourself by not allowing your order to be shown according to the Limit Order Display Rule. Again, use all-or-none restrictions sparingly. In most cases, they will only work against you.

Leaning Against the Book

 We just learned how to gain an advantage against the market makers when trading small numbers of contracts. However, there is a tactic used by market makers that can hurt you if you are trading larger numbers of contracts, say 20 or more. Let's use the above example and assume the quote is bid $2.00 and ask is $2.25. You place an order to buy 20 contracts for $2.15. If your order is not filled, you would expect the quote to move to $2.15 to $2.25. But the very second you send the order you see the quote move to $2.20 to $2.25. What happened? How did someone manage to jump in front of your order so quickly? While it could have happened by chance, the more likely answer is that it was the market maker placing a new higher bid in

response to yours. Why would he do this? The reason is that you now have enough contracts to cover the 20 contract minimum required by the exchange.

If the market maker is filled at $2.20, he has effectively purchased a call option for only five cents rather than the $2.00 price he was previously willing to pay. Here's why: If he is filled at $2.20 and the market rallies, then all is well and the market maker will make money from the long call options. But if the market falls, he can always get rid of his contracts by selling them to you for $2.15, which leaves him with a five cent loss. In effect, the market maker is using you as his stop order! He has, "leaned" against his "book" of business for support. So if you're placing larger quantities of contracts (20 or more) it's best to do one of two things: First, you can feed your contracts into the market in smaller lots perhaps placing four trades of five contracts each. Many brokers though will charge four separate commissions to do this so it may not be advantageous. But if your broker aggregates all order by symbol and side (buy or sell) at the end of the day, this may be a viable choice for you. The second thing you can do is mark your order with a "not held" qualifier. If you trade online, you should be able to check off a box that says "not held" or "NH" and that just means you are not holding the floor broker accountable to "time and sales." Time and sales is just a running record of all transactions, which shows the execution prices and the time it was filled. Time and sales is the modern version of the "ticker tape" or just "tape."

If you do not mark an order as "not held," you can hold the broker accountable to time and sales. For example, say you have an order to buy at $2.15 and later see the *asking* price on time and sales moved below this price, say to $2.10. The only way for the asking price to fall to $2.10 is if all buyers at $2.15 were filled. If your order was not filled but you discovered this on time and sales, you could notify your broker and the order must be filled. This is a very rare occurrence but it does happen. However, if you mark an order as "not held," that qualifier is stating that you will not hold the floor broker to the prices on time and sales. Still, a "not held" qualifier can be beneficial. When an order is marked this way, the floor traders do not have to show the order and can work it manually on the floor. In most cases, you will get a better fill than if you didn't mark it "not held."

Learn to use the Limit Order Display Rule and the twenty-contract minimum exchange rules to your advantage. If you don't, the market makers certainly will.

The Economics of Large Bid-Ask Spreads

We previously said that the difference between the bid and ask is called the bid-ask spread. Take a look at the bid-ask spreads in Table 4-1, which are reprinted below as Table 4-4:

Table 4-4

EBAY												37.11	-0.94

Jun 20, 2005 @ 14:43 ET (Data 15 Minutes Delayed)   **Bid** 37.10   **Ask** 37.11   **Size** 32x25   **Vol** 17121523

Calls	Last Sale	Net	Bid	Ask	Vol	Open Int	Puts	Last Sale	Net	Bid	Ask	Vol	Open Int
05 Jul 32.50 (XBA GZ-E)	4.40	-1.20	4.70	4.90	5	7319	05 Jul 32.50 (XBA SZ-E)	0.15	--	0.10	0.20	23	23943
05 Jul 35.00 (XBA GG-E)	2.50	-0.90	2.60	2.70	271	13510	05 Jul 35.00 (XBA SG-E)	0.45	+0.10	0.45	0.50	1811	24275
05 Jul 37.50 (XBA GU-E)	1.00	-0.55	1.00	1.05	909	21930	05 Jul 37.50 (XBA SU-E)	1.40	+0.45	1.35	1.40	633	18877
05 Jul 40.00 (XBA GH-E)	0.30	-0.20	0.30	0.35	613	34574	05 Jul 40.00 (XBA SH-E)	3.60	+1.15	3.10	3.20	206	13113
05 Aug 32.50 (XBA HZ-E)	5.00	--	5.30	5.50	100	0	05 Aug 32.50 (XBA TZ-E)	0.65	--	0.55	0.65	30	0
05 Aug 35.00 (XBA HG-E)	0	pc	3.40	3.60	0	0	05 Aug 35.00 (XBA TG-E)	1.25	-0.10	1.15	1.25	191	0
05 Aug 37.50 (XBA HU-E)	1.85	+0.10	2.00	2.10	82	0	05 Aug 37.50 (XBA TU-E)	2.45	-0.05	2.20	2.30	64	0
05 Aug 40.00 (XBA HH-E)	0.95	-0.10	1.00	1.10	64	0	05 Aug 40.00 (XBA TH-E)	0	pc	3.70	3.90	0	0

Why do some option quotes have relatively small spreads, say 5 cents, while others have much wider spreads such as 20 cents? Many traders believe this is the market maker "playing games" or trying to "squeeze out" extra money from the more active options. The fact of the matter is that the market – people like you and me trading – create the spread. The spread is simply a reflection of the volume. Lower volume options have higher spreads while higher volume options have narrow spreads.

In order to understand why this happens, you must understand some basic economics about prices. First, the higher that bid prices rise, the more that sellers are willing to come to the market. Figure 4-5 shows this relationship:

Figure 4-5: Higher Bids mean More Sellers Coming to Market

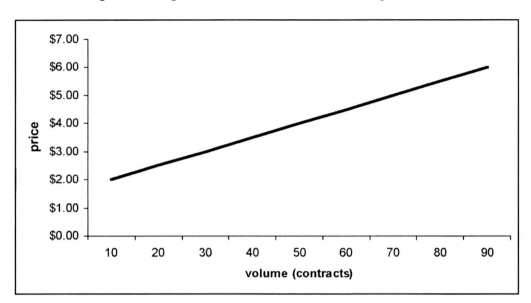

Figure 4-5 shows the volume (number of contracts) along the horizontal axis with the price on the vertical axis. The chart just shows that as the price rises, so does the volume.

This is another way of showing how the "supply" for an option is created. If you want more supply, you (or the market maker) must bid the contract higher. The higher the price, the more that sellers will step in and unload contracts. Traders often have difficulty understanding how they can control the supply. Price is the answer. Rising prices act as a signal to the market that supply is needed. As prices rise, eventually someone will step in and sell. Figure 4-5 is a graphical representation of this process. Of course, we can never be sure of the number of contracts that will become available as the price continues to increase but we just need to understand that it will increase.

Conversely, the lower the asking price falls, the more buyers will come to market as shown in Figure 4-6:

Figure 4-6: Lower Asking Prices mean More Buyers Coming to Market

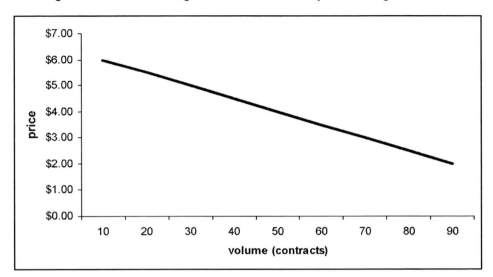

Figure 4-6 shows the "demand" side of the equation. As the asking price continues to fall, more and more buyers come to market in response to the lower price.

Figure 4-7 is an overlay of Figures 4-5 and 4-6. You can see there is a point where these two supply and demand lines intersect. We know from basic economics that they must intersect at the *market clearing price*, which is shown to be a volume of 50 contracts at a price of $4.00:

Figure 4-7: The Market Clearing Price is $4.00 with 50 Contracts Traded

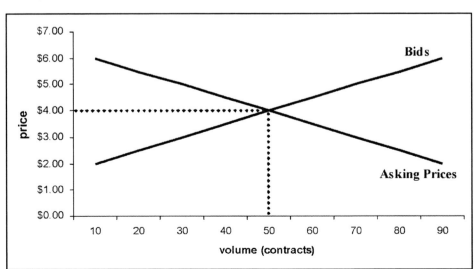

A market clearing price is the price where all who want to buy and sell at that price can do so. In our example, a price of $4 means that 50 contracts will be purchased and sold. If the price were higher, we'd get more sellers than buyers. If the price were lower, we'd get more buyers than sellers. At a price of $4, there is an equal number of buyers and sellers and the market clears.

In the real world of options, we do not just have a single price. Instead, we have a bid-ask spread, which tends to reduce the volume. For instance, if we charge a higher price for those willing to buy, say $4.50, and are willing to pay a lower price to those wishing to sell, say $3.50, we will get fewer buyers and sellers. However, because of the two-price system, we can find an equilibrium point and the market can clear as shown by the shaded line in Figure 4-8:

Figure 4-8: Bid-Ask Spread Creates Lower Volume

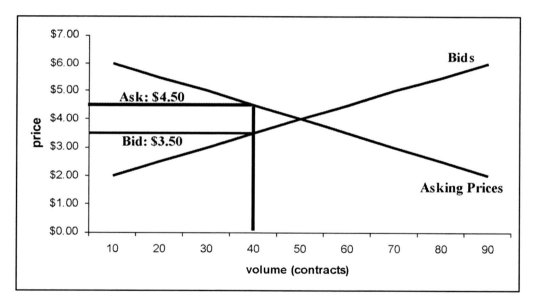

Notice that the introduction of a spread shifted our market clearing volume of 50 down to 40. Bid-ask spreads create three major inefficiencies in the market:

- Buyers must pay more than the market clearing price ($4.50 in this example)

- Sellers must receive less than the market clearing price ($3.50 in this example)

- Less volume is created

It is for all these reasons why the market regulators create rules such as the Limit Order Display Rule to allow investors to compete in the market. The rules create smaller spreads, higher volumes, and a more efficient market.

The wider the spread, the lower the volume. Conversely, the lower the volume, the wider the spread must be to balance supply and demand. So the bid-ask spread is purely a function of the supply and demand for an option. If there is a heavy amount of supply and demand such as for at-the-money options, you'll tend to find narrow bid-ask spreads. On the other hand, if you have deep-in-the-money or deep-out-of-the-money options then the spreads tend to widen for the fact that there is very low volume in these contracts. The bid-ask spread is simply an economic reflection of the supply and demand for any particular strike. Remember, if you feel that a particular bid-ask spread is too wide, you are always free to tighten it up by either bidding higher or offering to sell for less. If your order is not filled, it must be posted due to the Limit Order Display Rule, which creates smaller bid-ask spreads. But if you're not willing to bid higher or offer for less then you shouldn't be too concerned that market makers are leaving the spreads wide. It's not their job to determine the spread but rather to balance supply and demand.

Chapter Four Questions

1) **You have 5 Dell Computer options in your account with the symbol DLQDE. Which month and strike do they represent?**
    a)   April $25
    b)   May $20
    c)   May $25
    d)   April $27.50

2) **For any option symbol, the last two letters always designate (in order):**
    a)   Month and style
    b)   Month and strike
    c)   Strike and Month
    d)   Strike and type

3) The "month code" for an option identifies if it is a call by using which set of letters?

a) A through L
b) M through X
c) U through Z
d) A through T

4) When a stock if first assigned an option trading cycle, it is assigned to one of which three cycles?

a) January, February, May
b) January, June, December
c) January, June, September
d) January, February, March

5) It is now April and you find that ABC stock has April, May, August, and November options. Which cycle is ABC on?

a) March cycle
b) December cycle
c) January cycle
d) February cycle

6) It is now April and ABC has April, May, August, and November options. When will February options start trading?

a) When April expires
b) When May expires
c) When June expires
d) February options will never trade for this cycle.

7) When equity options are first issued, they control how many shares of stock?

a) 50
b) 100
c) 150
d) 1,000

8) You own 10 ABC $50 calls. ABC goes through a 2:1 split tomorrow. How many contracts will you have and which strike price after the split?

a) 20 contracts, $50 strike

b)   10 contracts, $50 strike

c)   10 contracts, $25 strike

d)   20 contracts, $25 strike

9)   **The open interest for a particular option is 3,000. Today you notice that 50 contracts traded but the open interest is still 3,000 tomorrow. How could this happen?**

a)   This is a mistake and the open interest should be 3,050

b)   All were closing trades

c)   All were opening trades

d)   50 were opening and 50 were closing

10) **You bought one $40 call when the underlying stock was $40. The stock has quickly risen to $45 with two months remaining before your option expires. If you wish to own the stock, you should:**

a)   Exercise the call immediately to take advantage of the $40 purchase price

b)   Wait until expiration and only exercise if it is advantageous

c)   Exercise immediately if there is sufficient open interest

d)   Wait until expiration and exercise the call regardless of the stock's price

11) **You own a call option and the underlying stock is about to pay a large surprise dividend. You wish to exercise the call so that you can collect the dividend. When should you exercise the call?**

a)   Exercise on the payable date

b)   Exercise the day after the ex-date

c)   Exercise the day before the ex-date

d)   Exercise on the ex-date

12) **You own 300 shares of Dell Computer and have placed a stop order at $25. How will this order be handled? The order:**

a)   Becomes a market order if Dell trades at $25 or higher

b)   Is filled at $25 if Dell trades at $25 or below

c)   Becomes a limit order at $25 if Dell trades at $25 or below

d)   Becomes a market order if Dell trades at or below $25

13) You own 300 shares of Dell Computer and have placed a stop order at $25 with a stop limit of $24.50. How will this order be handled? The order:
   a)   Is filled for $24.50 if Dell trades at $25 or higher
   b)   Is filled for $24.50 is Dell trades at $25 or lower
   c)   Becomes a limit order at $24.50 if Dell trades at or below $25
   d)   Becomes a market order if Dell trades at or below $24.50

14) Stop and stop limit orders:
   a)   Are guaranteed to fill within 5% of your stop price
   b)   Are never guaranteed to prevent losses
   c)   Are guaranteed to prevent losses
   d)   Are guaranteed to fill within 10% of your stop price

15) XYX stock is trading for $37 and pays a $1 dividend tomorrow. What will happen to the stock tomorrow assuming all else being constant?
   a)   The price of XYZ will remain the same
   b)   The price of XYZ will be reduced by $1
   c)   The price of XYZ will be increased by $1
   d)   The stock will halt trading until all options are exercised

16) When a stock splits, the exchanges adjust option strikes and possibly the contract sizes. What is the purpose of these adjustments?
   a)   They keep the total value of the contract the same
   b)   They increase the value of the contract to reflect the higher demand for the stock
   c)   They decrease the value of the contract to reflect the decreased demand for the stock
   d)   They are strictly a way for the exchanges to make money

17) No matter which cycle a stock may be trading, there will always be which two contracts traded?
   a)   The current month plus the first cycle month
   b)   The current month plus the following month
   c)   The current month plus the second cycle month
   d)   The first months of the following quarterly cycles

18) **You own a $50 call option. If the underlying stock undergoes a 5:4 split tomorrow, which adjustments will be made to the contract?**

    a)   The strike will be adjusted to $40 and the contract will control 125 shares

    b)   The strike will remain at $50 and the contract will control 125 shares

    c)   The strike will be adjusted to $40 and the contract size remains at 100 shares

    d) T he strike will be adjusted to $62.50 and the contract will control 125 shares

19) **Large bid ask spreads are the result of:**

    a)   Fraudulent market maker activity

    b)   Leaning against the book

    c)   High volume

    d)   Low volume

20) **An option is currently bidding $5 and asking $5.30. You place an order to sell 20 contracts at $5.10 and find that the bid immediately jumps to $5.20. This is most likely due to the market maker:**

    a)   Not receiving your order

    b)   Leaning against the book

    c)   Filling your order

    d)   Dishonestly jumping in front of your order

Chapter Four - Answers

1) **You have Dell Computer options in your account with the symbol DLQDE. Which month and strike do they represent?**

    a)   April $25

Notice that you do not even need to know the root symbol for the underlying stock if you are only trying to determine the month and strike. The month and strike are always determined by the last two letters of the option symbol, which are D (April) and E ($25 strike) in this example.

2) **For any option symbol, the last two letters always designate (in order):**

    b)   Month and strike

As stated in the answer to the previous question, the last two letters always represent the month and strike in that order. Train your eye to separate the last two letters from the option symbol as those are the month and strike. The remaining letters make up the root symbol.

3) **The "month code" for an option identifies if it is a call by using which set of letters?**

   a)   A through L

The first 12 letters of the alphabet (A through L) designate the 12 months of the year for call options.

4) **When a stock if first assigned an option trading cycle, it is assigned to one of which three cycles?**

   d)   January, February, March

These cycles are also known as Cycle 1, Cycle 2, and Cycle 3 respectively. Once a stock is assigned a cycle it never changes.

5) **It is now April and you find that ABC stock has April, May, August, and November options. Which cycle is ABC on?**

   d)   February cycle

Because it is April, we know that April and May options must be traded for all contracts regardless of which cycle it may be on. So those two months tell us no information about the cycle that this stock is on. To determine that we need to look to the following month for the answer and that is August. August is the middle month or "February" position for that quarter so this is a February cycle stock.

6) **It is now April and ABC has April, May, August, and November options. When will February options start trading?**

   c)   When June expires

Start with April, May, August, and November contracts. When May expires June will be added as the near-term contract. When May expires, July will be added as the near-term contract. When June expires, the near-term contract (July) is already trading. The exchange will roll out the next quarterly month, which will be February.

7) **When equity options are first issued, they control how many shares of stock?**

   b)   100

8) **You own 10 ABC $50 calls. ABC goes through a 2:1 split tomorrow. How many contracts will you have and which strike price after the split?**

    d)   20 contracts, $25 strike

As with shares of stock, a 2:1 split will double the number of shares that you own and cut the market price in half. The same is true for options. You will end up with double the number of contracts and the strike will be cut in half. Another way to check this is to understand that the total contract value must remain the same. If you have 10 contracts of the $50 calls, you have a total exercise value of 1,000 shares * $50 = $50,000. If the strike is cut in half to $25, the total contract value must still remain the same and that means that there must be $50,000/$25 = 2,000 shares, or 20 contracts.

9) **The open interest for a particular option is 3,000. Today you notice that 50 contracts traded but the open interest is still 3,000 tomorrow. How could this happen?**

    d)   50 were opening and 50 were closing

Open interest only increases if both parties – the buyer and seller – are entering into opening transactions. The reason this open interest remained the same is because one trader was opening while the other trader was closing so the net result was unchanged.

10) **You bought one $40 call when the underlying stock was $40. The stock has quickly risen to $45 with two months remaining before your option expires. If you wish to own the stock, you should:**

    b)   Wait until expiration and only exercise if it is advantageous

It is never advantageous to exercise your call option early to simply gain the stock. The reason is that you are "throwing away" the time premium of the option when you exercise and then you are exposed to the total risk of the stock. You should wait until expiration before you exercise. If the stock's price is still above the strike price then go ahead and exercise the option. However, if the stock's price is below the strike price then just purchase the shares in the open market and let the call option expire worthless.

11) **You own a call option and the underlying stock is about to pay a large surprise dividend. You wish to exercise the call so that you can collect the dividend. When should you exercise the call?**

    c)   Exercise the day before the ex-date

12) **You own 300 shares of Dell Computer and have placed a stop order at $25. How will this order be handled? The order:**

   d)   Becomes a market order if Dell trades at or below $25

13) **You own 300 shares of Dell Computer and have placed a stop order at $25 with a stop limit of $24.50. How will this order be handled? The order:**

   c)   Becomes a limit order at $24.50 if Dell trades at or below $25

14) **Stop and stop limit orders:**

   b)   Are never guaranteed to prevent losses

15) **XYX stock is trading for $37 and pays a $1 dividend tomorrow. What will happen to the stock tomorrow assuming all else being constant?**

   b)   The price of XYZ will be reduced by $1

   The stock's price is always reduced by the amount of the dividend. XYZ would open at $36 "unchanged" assuming that no other factors created buying or selling pressure.

16) **When a stock splits, the exchanges adjust option strikes and possibly the contract sizes. What is the purpose of these adjustments?**

   a)   They keep the total value of the contract the same

   Option contracts are always adjusted so that the total value of the contract (exercise value) remains unchanged. You will find examples of this in Question 5 and Question 15.

17) **No matter which cycle a stock may be trading, there will always be which two contracts traded?**

   b)   The current month plus the following month

18) **You own a $50 call option. If the underlying stock undergoes a 5:4 split tomorrow, which adjustments will be made to the contract?**

   a)   The strike will be adjusted to $40 and the contract will control 125 shares

   A 5:4 split increases the number of shares by a factor of 5/4 = 1.25. If you own 100 shares, you will have 125 shares after the split. The strike must also be reduced to $50/1.25 = $40. Notice that the total contract value remains the same. Prior to the split, the contract controls 100 shares at $50, or $5,000 total contract value. If the strike is reduced to $40, it must control $5,000/$40 = 125 shares. The point to remember is that any adjustment made to an options contract leaves you no better or worse off. It is simply an adjustment made to reflect the current prices without adversely affecting your option contract.

19) Large bid ask spreads are the result of:

d)   Low volume

21)   An option is currently bidding $5 and asking $5.30. You place an order to sell 20 contracts at $5.10 and find that the bid immediately jumps to $5.20. This is most likely due to the market maker:

b)   Leaning against the book

Chapter Five

Put-Call Parity &
Synthetic Options

Up to this point, calls and puts appear to be polar opposites. Calls represent the right to buy while puts represent the right to sell. And if you look at option quotes, there doesn't appear to be any connection between the price of the call and the same-strike put. However, call and put prices are highly dependent and are not arbitrarily chosen. Although it may not appear possible, there is a strong, mathematical relationship that describes the connection between calls and puts known as *put-call parity*. This is one of the most important concepts for beginning and advanced option traders alike so we will devote an entire chapter to it. Once you understand put-call parity, you'll find that calls and puts are really one in the same; it just depends on how they're paired with the underlying stock. So, strange as it may sound, calls are really puts and puts are really calls if properly paired with the underlying stock. In fact, when options were first introduced in 1973, only call options were traded on 16 stocks. Put options did not appear until 1977. The reason is that puts were created by "put-call brokers" who created puts by properly pairing calls with the underlying stock and put-call parity show them how to do just that.

The word "parity" means "equivalence." There are many types of parity relationships in the financial world such as *purchasing power parity* and *interest rate parity*, for example. Parity relationships simply show the connections between two or more variables. As stated before, put-call parity just shows that calls and puts are "equivalent" when properly paired with the underlying stock. Once you understand put-call parity, you will have increased insights into the mechanics of the options market and how options are priced. As you gain experience, you will

215

also find more efficient ways of trading options by using this simple relationship between calls and puts.

There are many ways to present the put-call parity relationship. But perhaps the easiest way to understand it is by looking at how option orders are filled on the floor of an exchange. Once we get the basic put-call parity relationship, we can alter it to get some intriguing looks at how call and put prices are connected.

Filling an Option Order

Let's say you want to buy 10 calls to open of the ABC $50 strike at market. ABC stock is also trading at $50. In order to make the calculations easy, we'll assume there is one year to expiration.

When this buy order is received on the floor, the market maker must become the seller so that the transaction can be completed. This means the market maker must be willing to be *short* a call. While you may be totally comfortable in speculating by buying 10 calls, the market maker may not be so eager to be on the short side of the transaction. We found in Chapter Three that the call owner's gains are the call seller's losses. If you buy a call, you have the potential for unlimited gains and that means the call seller is exposed to unlimited losses.

If the market maker is to be on the short side of 10 one-year calls, his risk is that the stock price rises. In order to protect himself from this risk, he can purchase 1,000 shares of ABC stock. Now, no matter how high the stock moves, he will always be able to deliver 1,000 shares of stock (represented by the 10 calls) at expiration.

However, because the market maker now owns the stock, there is now a new risk; the stock price may fall. To protect himself from this risk, he can buy 10 $50 puts with one year to expiration.

Our market maker is now long 1,000 shares of stock, long 10 $50 put options and short 10 $50 call options. By using these options, the market maker is now fully hedged (protected) against any stock price movement at expiration. This means he is guaranteed to receive $50 per share ($50,000 total) for his stock no matter what happens one year from now. How is this possible?

Think back to the first chapter when we talked about rights and obligations. The market maker paid $50 for the stock and has the *right to sell* it for $50 by exercising the put. The market maker will exercise the put if the stock price is below $50 at expiration and receive $50 per share. By selling the call, he has the *obligation to sell* the stock for $50 at expiration. Of course, the only time someone would exercise the call is if the stock's price is above $50 at that time. If the stock is above $50 at expiration, the market maker will be assigned ("called away") on the short call and receive $50 per share. What happens if the stock is exactly $50 at expiration? In this case, both options expire worthless and the market maker can sell the stock in the open market for $50. So no matter what happens to the price of the stock at expiration, the market maker is guaranteed to receive $50 per share in one year. It is kind of ironic that, using these speculative derivatives of puts and calls, we can actually create a *risk-free* portfolio. This is perfect proof of our statement in the first chapter that options are not necessarily risky; it all depends on how they're used.

The market maker can now sell you the 10 calls with confidence knowing that all stock price risk has been removed. But what price should he charge you for the 10 calls?

We said the market maker is *guaranteed* to receive $50,000 in one year regardless of the stock price. Because this is guaranteed, we can easily figure out what the value of this package is worth today. Let's assume that the risk-free interest rate is 2%. Chapter Two showed us that the present value of $50,000 in one year is $50,000 / (1.02) = $49,020 today. The market maker should therefore pay $49,020 today for the package containing long stock, long put and short call positions. If he pays $49,020 and receives $50,000 in one year, his return on investment will be 2%, which is exactly the interest rate he should receive for a risk-free investment.

The market maker will spend $50,000 for the 1,000 shares of stock trading at $50. Let's also assume he pays $3 for the put. Now he will spend an additional $3,000 for the put for a total cash outlay of $53,000. We already figured that the fair price for this package of three assets should be worth $49,020 yet he's paying $53,000 for it.

The market maker has overpaid by $53,000 - $49,020 = $3,980, so he will need to bring in a credit for this amount. How can the market maker receive a credit of $3,980? Easy, he will fill your order on the 10 $50 calls for roughly $3.98.

Doing so, he will receive the necessary credit to make his $53,000 cash outlay equal to $49,020. Of course, the market maker will try to make a little profit and quote a price of $4.00 or $4.10 on the $50 calls (remember, options above $3 must quote in ten-cent increments so $3.98 or $4.05 would not be allowed but $3.98 would be the theoretical price). Why won't he scalp you and charge a much higher price, say $10? The reason is competition. If the market maker quotes too high of a price, somebody else will step in and offer a lower price. Market makers get very competitive with risk-free packages. The reason is they can, in this example, borrow at 2% and loan it risk-free at a higher percent. The reason their rate of return is higher than 2% is because of the additional few cents they tack on for profit, which is reflected in the bid-ask spread. In effect, they end up buying the put for less than the theoretically fair price and sell the call for a little more than the theoretically fair price thus paying less for the package than the present value would suggest it is worth. However, if they are able to borrow at 2% and are earning a much larger risk-free return, market makers will want to create more of these packages and put buying pressure on the puts and selling pressure on the calls until the rate of return is much closer to the risk-free rate.

To summarize, the market maker's initial position looks like this:

Buy 1000 shares at $50	=	-$50,000
Buy 10 $50 puts at $3	=	-$ 3,000
Sells 10 $50 calls at $3.98	=	+$3,980
Equals		-$49,020 cash outlay by market maker.

This is guaranteed to grow to a value of $50,000 in one year since $49,020 * 1.02 = $50,000 because of the full hedge provided by the long put and short call.

This three-sided position (long stock + long put + short call) established by the market maker is called a *conversion*. If he had done the reverse (short stock + short puts + long calls) then it is called a *reverse conversion* or *reversal*. Reversals are one of many "locked" trades. A locked trade simply means that it cannot lose. In this case, the market maker buys the three assets at a discount from the exercise price and will receive the full exercise price at expiration.

The Put-Call Parity Equation

 We have shown that the market maker's three-sided position (conversion) is guaranteed to be worth the present value of the exercise price. No matter what happens to the stock's price, the market maker is guaranteed to receive the $50 exercise price at expiration. Because he's guaranteed the $50 exercise price, the long stock + long put + short call position must be worth the *present value* of the exercise price ($50 in this example).

If we use S for stock price, P for put price, C for call price, and Pv (E) for the present value of the exercise price, then we can write the relationship of long stock + long put + short call equals the present value of the exercise price more concisely:

Formula 5-1:

$$S + P - C = Pv (E)$$

Notice the use of plus and minus signs. The long positions are denoted by a plus sign while any short positions are indicated by a minus sign. (If no sign precedes a letter such as with the "S" then it is assumed to be a plus sign.) This formula is stating that values of long stock + long put + short call are equal to the present value of the exercise price. Using our previous example, Formula 5-1 is stating that $50,000 + $3,000 - $3,980 = $49,020. *Formula 5-1 is one variation of the put-call parity.* If Formula 5-1 or any of the upcoming algebraic variations do not hold in the real world then arbitrage is possible.

Let's see if the formula works by using the above example. If we have a portfolio consisting of stock purchased at $50, a long $50 put, and a short $50 call, what will happen at expiration to the value of the portfolio at different stock prices?

Table 5-2

Portfolio				
Stock price	Stock	$50 put	$50 Call	Total Value
35	35	15	0	50
40	40	10	0	50
45	45	5	0	50
50	50	0	0	50
55	55	0	5	50
60	60	0	10	50
65	65	0	15	50

The last column in Table 5-2 shows the total value of the portfolio at expiration, which is found by adding the "stock" column to the "$50 put" column and then subtracting the "$50 call" column, which is what Formula 5-1 tells us to do. Reading row one for example, if the stock price is $35 at expiration (column one) then your stock position must also be worth $35 (column two). The $50 put would be worth $15 (column three) and the $50 call would be worthless (column four). This means that your total portfolio would be worth $35 + $15 + $0 = $50 if the stock closes at $35.

The "total value" column shows us that this portfolio always sums to $50 no matter what happens to the stock's price at expiration and is exactly what we expected to happen. Of course, these are not the only stock prices that could occur at expiration. But you can check for yourself that *any* stock price results in a final portfolio value of exactly $50.

If the value of this package of long stock, long put, and short call is guaranteed to be worth $50 at expiration then that package today must be the present value of $50, which is what Formula 5-1 tells us.

As stated before, Formula 5-1 is just one variation of the put-call parity formula. We can rearrange it algebraically and come up with other forms that will provide different views of the pricing connections between calls and puts. We will present some of the more interesting forms but, as you read through these, *don't worry so much about the formulas as much as the insights they provide.* Formula 5-3 shows an algebraic rearrangement of Formula 5-1 that was created by adding the call option (C) to both sides of the equation:

Formula 5-3:

$$S + P = C + Pv\,(E)$$

This form tells a very interesting story. The left-hand side of the equation represents an investor who owns stock plus a protective put. The right-hand side represents an investor who owns a call option plus a deposit of cash, Pv (E), which will grow to the exercise price at expiration by earning the risk-free rate. You can think of the deposit of cash as an investment into a Treasury bill or CD or other guaranteed security. Formula 5-3 tells us that an investor who buys stock and a put is financially doing the same thing as someone who buys a call and deposits sufficient cash to grow to the exercise price at expiration by earning the risk-free rate. *In other words, owning stock with the right to sell it is financially the same thing as someone who has enough cash at expiration with the right to buy stock.*

Let's see if that's true by comparing two investors; one owns the stock + put (left side of equation) while the other owns a call plus the present value of the exercise price in cash (right side). If the stock is above the exercise price at expiration the investor on the left side of the equation will let the put expire worthless and be left with the stock. The investor on the right side will exercise the call and pay for the stock with the cash that has grown to the exercise price. In other words, both investors will be holding the stock. However, if the stock price is below the exercise price at expiration, the investor on the left-hand side of the equation will exercise the put and receive the strike price in cash. The investor on the right side will let the call expire worthless and be left holding an amount of cash equal to the exercise price. No matter what happens to the stock's price, both investors are equal at expiration.

What's most interesting about Formula 5-3 is that it refutes one of the most persistent myths in options trading. That is, most brokerage firms view investors who buy stock and a put as insurance (left hand side of equation) as being responsible, conservative investors while those who buy calls (right hand side of equation) as being risk takers and reckless. Formula 5-3 shows that as long as the call buyer has enough cash to buy the stock at expiration, both investors are doing exactly the same thing. Both investors are either conservative or reckless but not one of each. Yet most brokerage firms maintain a split view on each even though they are identical strategies.

Let's take a look at another variation:

Formula 5-4:

$$C - P = S - Pv\,(E)$$

Formula 5-4 is saying that the *difference* between the same-strike call and put prices (left side of equation) must be separated by the same difference as the stock and present value of the exercise price (right side). In Chapter Two, Pricing Principle #4 showed us that the right hand side, $S - Pv\,(E)$, is the minimum value for a call option. This variation tells us that the call and put prices must be separated by an amount equal to the minimum value for a call option.

For example, assume the stock is $50 and interest rates are 5% with one year to expiration. The cost-of-carry on the stock is $50 * .05 = $2.50. In other words, if you buy the stock, you will miss out on $2.50 worth of interest in one year. In turn, the value of this missed opportunity is $2.50/1.05 = $2.38 today.

Formula 5-4 tells us that the difference between the call and put prices must be *at least* $2.38. If you were looking at a $50 call and a $50 put with one year to expiration and 5% risk-free interest rates, you would find that the call price is $2.38 higher than the put price. The volatility of the underlying stock changes the total prices but their difference will be exactly $2.38. For instance, if the put were priced at $2 then the call must be $2 + $2.38 = $4.38. If the put were worth $10 then the call must be worth $10 + $2.38 = $12.38.

What happens if the stock and strike prices are not equal? Assume the stock is $55, the strike is $50 ($5 intrinsic value), and interest rates are 5% with one year to expiration. Formula 5-4 tells us that the difference between the call and put prices must be $55 − ($50/1.05) = $7.38. This price arises from the fact that we must immediately pay for the $5 intrinsic value plus the cost of carry, or $5 + $2.38 = $7.38. Hopefully, you're starting to see that call and put prices are tied together.

Formula 5-4 shows that all call options must be priced higher than the puts by the cost-of-carry on the exercise price. New traders often confuse this relationship and think that call options are priced higher by the cost-of-carry on the *stock price*. The reason it is the cost-of-carry on the exercise price and not the stock price is because it is the exercise price that is effectively being borrowed when you buy a call option. If you buy a call and exercise it to get the stock then you get to defer the payment of the *exercise price* until expiration. It is the exercise price that determines the cost-of-carry.

If call and put prices are separated by the cost-of-carry on the exercise price then they must be separated by the difference between the stock and exercise price at expiration. The reason is that, by definition, the present value of the exercise price must grow to the exercise price at expiration. Remember, the negative Pv (E) on the right side of the equation tells us that the investor *sold* the present value of the exercise price, which means he receives the present value of the exercise price in cash and must repay the strike price at expiration. This is similar to the issuance of Treasury bills. The government sells them at a discount from face value and receives cash. In return, the government must pay the holder the face value at maturity. So anytime we see a negative Pv (E) in a put-call parity equation that just means the investor *borrowed* money and must repay the strike price at expiration. For example, if the exercise price is $50 and the risk-free rate is 5% then the present value is $50/1.05 = $47.62. The investor would borrow $47.62 and owe $50 at expiration.

Conversely, anytime we see a positive Pv (E) that means the person has deposited cash into a risk-free account and will receive the strike price at expiration. Using the previous example, the investor would deposit $47.62 into a risk-free account and receive $50 at expiration.

At expiration, the value of the right hand side of Formula 5-4 must always be the stock price minus the exercise price, or S − E. This is evident since the Pv (E) always grows to E at expiration. The left hand side is not so easy to see but let's step through the actions. If the stock price is above the exercise price at expiration then the investor will receive stock (+S) by exercising the call and paying the exercise price (-E). In other words, his portfolio will be worth S − E.

But if the stock price is below the exercise price, the investor will be assigned on the short put and buy stock (+S) and pay the exercise price (-E). If the stock price is below the strike price at expiration, the portfolio is still worth S-E. No matter what happens to the stock's price at expiration, the left and right hand sides of Formula 5-4 are worth S − E.

Let's test the formula and see if it works. We'll assume two portfolios. Portfolio A contains a long call and short put (left side of Formula 5-4) while Portfolio B contains long stock and the borrowing of the present value of the exercise price in cash (right side of Formula 5-4), which means the investor owes $50 at expiration:

Table 5-5

Stock price	Portfolio A				Portfolio B		
	$50 Call	$50 put	Total Value		Long stock	Repay $50	Total Value
35	0	15	-15		35	50	-15
40	0	10	-10		40	50	-10
45	0	5	-5		45	50	-5
50	0	0	0		50	50	0
55	5	0	5		55	50	5
60	10	0	10		60	50	10
65	15	0	15		65	50	15

In Table 5-5, you can see that the "total value" columns for either portfolio are equal at expiration. The total value for Portfolio A is found by taking the "$50 call" column minus the "$50 put" column, which is what the left hand side of Formula 5-4 tells us to do. The "total value" for Portfolio B is found by taking the "long stock" column minus the "Repay $50" column, which is what the right hand side of Formula 5-4 says to do at expiration. Notice that the total values for Portfolio A and B are worth the stock price minus the $50 exercise price, or S – E, which is what we calculated.

\Let's put Formula 5-4 to the test and look at some real option quotes using Affymetrix (AFFX) in Figure 5-6:

Figure 5-6: AFFX Option Quotes

Calls	Last Sale	Net	Bid	Ask	Vol	Open Int	Puts	Last Sale	Net	Bid	Ask	Vol	Open Int
AFFX										**46.70**	**-0.22**		
Aug 02, 2005 @ 16:36 ET (Data 15 Minutes Delayed)							Bid 46.68	Ask 46.73	Size 2x1	Vol 784247			
05 Aug 40.00 (FIQ HH-E)	6.70	pc	6.70	6.90	0	1566	05 Aug 40.00 (FIQ TH-E)	0.15	pc	0.05	0.15	0	2430
05 Aug 45.00 (FIQ HI-E)	2.20	-0.15	2.25	2.45	16	1126	05 Aug 45.00 (FIQ TI-E)	0.50	pc	0.50	0.65	0	3545
05 Aug 50.00 (FIQ HJ-E)	0.30	-0.15	0.25	0.35	8	3237	05 Aug 50.00 (FIQ TJ-E)	3.50	--	3.40	3.60	79	6520
05 Aug 55.00 (FIQ HK-E)	0.05	-0.10	0	0.10	56	3960	05 Aug 55.00 (FIQ TK-E)	7.50	pc	8.20	8.40	0	2648
05 Sep 40.00 (FIQ IH-E)	7.40	pc	7.10	7.30	0	38	05 Sep 40.00 (FIQ UH-E)	0.40	pc	0.30	0.40	0	928
05 Sep 45.00 (FIQ II-E)	4.10	pc	3.20	3.40	0	734	05 Sep 45.00 (FIQ UI-E)	1.65	+0.35	1.35	1.50	10	1195
05 Sep 50.00 (FIQ IJ-E)	1.20	pc	1.00	1.15	0	3728	05 Sep 50.00 (FIQ UJ-E)	4.10	pc	4.10	4.30	0	266
05 Sep 55.00 (FIQ IK-E)	0.55	pc	0.25	0.35	0	1084	05 Sep 55.00 (FIQ UK-E)	9.90	pc	8.30	8.60	0	217

When these quotes were taken, interest rates were low (about 3.5%) and there were 16 days until expiration so the interest value of the options is not too great. Formula 5-4 states that the difference in call and put prices should equal the stock price minus the present value of the exercise price. But because there is not a lot of time remaining and interest rates are low, the present value of the exercise price will not be too different from just the exercise price. We should therefore expect that the difference in the call and put prices to be roughly the difference between the stock and exercise price, or $C - P \approx S - E$.

Take a look at the August $40 call and put prices in Figure 5-6. To make our calculations a little more precise, we'll split the bid and ask prices since the bid price tends to be below theoretical value and the asking price tends to be above. The August $40 call is $6.80 and the August $40 put is 10 cents. The difference is $6.80 - 0.10 = $6.70. This difference should be roughly equal to the stock price minus the exercise price, or $46.70 - $40 = 6.70. In this case, it's a perfect match.

Now look at the August $45 calls and puts. They are $2.35 and 0.575 respectively, which is a difference of 1.77. The difference between the stock and exercise price is $46.70 - $45 = $1.70, which is pretty close.

Let's try one more. The August $50 calls and puts are 0.30 and $3.50 respectively, which is a difference of -$3.20. The stock price minus the exercise price is $46.70 - $50 = -$3.30, which again is pretty close. There are many reasons why we're not coming up with exact matches but it's partly due to the fact that we don't know the true theoretical prices. For example, the August $45 calls are bid $2.25 and asking

$2.35, which has a midpoint price of $2.30. It may seem reasonable to think that the theoretical price is $2.30 with the bid five cents below and the asking price five cents above. However, it's also possible that the theoretical price is $2.32 or any other number between the bid and ask. It's difficult to know since options below $3 must trade in five-cent increments.

Another reason we're not coming up with exact matches is because the time premium gets bigger as we approach the at-the-money calls and then diminishes again. That's why we got an exact match for the $40 strike, were off by seven cents for the $45 strike, and off by 10 cents for the $50 strike. Even though these options are close to expiration and interest rates are low there is still *some* cost of carry (interest that could be earned on the strike price). Since we're not accounting for interest, we will be off by a little in our calculations.

The important point to see is that call and put prices are definitely tied together by the invisible force of put-call parity. These prices are not arbitrarily chosen by the market makers. Once a put price is determined by the market, the call price is automatically determined and vice versa.

Put-call parity can also show us some invaluable insights as to why investors and traders are attracted to options. Let's rearrange the put-call parity formula to solve for a long call option:

Formula 5-7:

$$C = S - Pv\,(E) + P$$

Formula 5-7 shows us that a long call option is the same thing as owning stock (+S), borrowing money, -Pv (E), and also owning a put (+P). In Chapter Three, we said that call options provide downside protection and Formula 5-7 shows why. When you buy a call, you are borrowing money to buy stock and *also* buying a put option! The total value of the put option is really the time value of the call option over and above the cost of carry on the exercise price. In Chapter Two, we also said that in-the-money call options contain intrinsic value plus an interest component, which are shown by S – Pv (E). Now you see that there is a third component to a call option's value and that is the value of the put option.

Of course, there's nothing that says the put must have value. Let's assume the put is worthless. If the put has no value then Formula 5-6 reduces to S – Pv (E), which is what we previously found to be the bare minimum price for a call option. We can show why by comparing a long $50 call with a portfolio of long stock at $50 and the borrowing of the present value of the exercise price as shown in Table 5-8:

Table 5-8

| Stock price | $50 call | Portfolio A | | |
		Stock	Pay $50 Exercise	Total Value
35	0	35	50	-15
40	0	40	50	-10
45	0	45	50	-5
50	0	50	50	0
55	5	55	50	5
60	10	60	50	10
65	15	65	50	15

The $50 call performs better than Portfolio A for stock prices below $50.

The $50 call performs equally well as Portfolio A for all stock prices above $50.

Table 5-8 shows that the $50 call performs the same as Portfolio A for stock prices above $50 at expiration (shown in bold). However, the $50 call performs better if the stock is below $50 at expiration since it does not lose dollar-for-dollar with the stock. So we know that the call option's value is either greater than or equal to Portfolio A. In other words:

$$C \geq S - Pv\ (E)$$

This tells us that an in-the-money call option's minimum price is the intrinsic value plus the cost of carry, which is exactly what we found in Chapter Two (Pricing Principle #4). The call's price must be at least this great otherwise arbitrage is possible.

How can we get Portfolio A to equal that of the call option? We must insure the stock prices below $50 by purchasing a $50 put. If we purchase the put, the two portfolios are now equal and we're right back to Formula 5-7:

$$C = S - Pv\ (E) + P$$

Formula 5-7 shows that an in-the-money call option's minimum value is S - Pv (E). The difference between the exercise price and the Pv (E) contributes to the time premium of the call, E – Pv (E). Now we see that the remaining time premium comes from the value of the put.

Put-call parity can show us the most efficient ways to trade based on the confidence in our outlook on the stock. For example, if you were absolutely 100% certain that a stock's price was going to rise, what would you do? (Perhaps you're Gordon Gekko from the movie *Wall Street*.) Most investors would just buy the stock and be happy with that. Some that are familiar with options would just buy the calls. But if you really understand options and the put-call parity formula, you'd see a different angle. Formula 5-7 has been reprinted below and let's take a closer look at what it's telling you:

$$C = S - Pv (E) + P$$

It says that if you buy a call, you're really buying stock with borrowed funds and then buying a put option for insurance. If you're certain that a stock is going to rise and wish to use stock then buy the stock with *borrowed funds* (S – Pv (E)). In other words, buy the shares on margin as it will provide financial leverage (you'll be able to buy more shares with the same amount of money). However, if you plan to buy call options, notice that you're also implicitly buying a put option, which is an unnecessary expense if you're sure the stock is going to rise. Instead, buy the call and *sell the put*. Purchasing the call is the same as borrowing money to buy the shares but it also includes the insurance value of the put in its price and there's no sense in paying for that. In the movie *Wall Street*, Gordon Gekko purchased 1,500 July $50 calls once he gained insider knowledge that Anacott Steel was being acquired. He would have done much better if he had also sold 1,500 of the July $50 puts. We can look at these put-call parity relationships graphically:

Figure 5-9

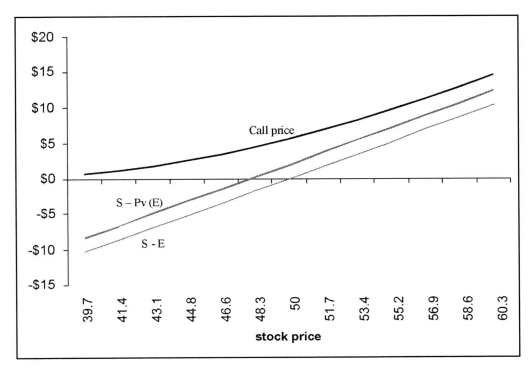

Figure 5-9 shows the call price prior to expiration. Notice that it is curved rather than the "hockey stick" formation we are used to seeing. The reason is that this chart is drawn *prior* to expiration rather than at expiration. Figure 5-9 also shows the values for the stock price minus the exercise price (S-E) as well as the stock minus the present value of the exercise price, E – Pv (E).

Now let's see what the various sections between the curves represent. The value for any space between two curves in Figure 5-9 can be found by simply subtracting the curve below from the curve above as in Figure 5-10:

Figure 5-10

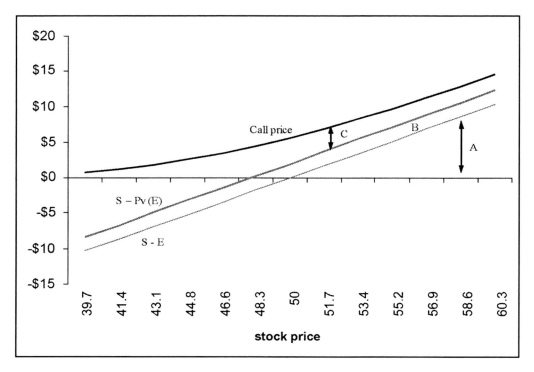

For example, the space labeled "C" is found by taking the curve above it, S – E, and subtracting the horizontal axis, 0, below. This is S – E – 0, which is simply, S – E, the intrinsic value of the call.

Distance B is also found by the difference between the two lines above and below it. This distance is (S – Pv (E)) – (S – E), which factors out to S – Pv (E) - S + E. The positive and negative S cancels out thus leaving E – Pv (E), which is simply the interest that can be earned on the exercise price. In reality, the distance between these two lines (above and below Area B) is very small. Figure 5-10 is drawn for a 20% risk-free rate just so we could get some separation between the two lines.

Area C is the space between the call price and the S – Pv (E) line. The value of this area is found by the call price, C, minus the S – Pv (E) line. This is C – (E – Pv(E)), which factors out to C – E + Pv (E). We know from put-call parity that this is the value of the put option.

We can see from the diagram that the total value of the call option is composed of these three areas:

Area A	Area B	Area C

$$\text{Call} = \quad (S - E) \quad + \quad (E - Pv(E)) \quad + \quad \text{Put}$$

Of course, Areas B and C make up the time value of the option since these are the areas above and beyond the intrinsic value of S - E. This shows that the time value portion of a call option's price is really comprised of two components. One is the cost of carry and the other is the value of the put. Once they're gone, we're just left with Area A, which is the intrinsic value, or $S - E$. If there is no value to the put, this shows that the minimum time value of the call option is comprised of the cost of carry on the exercise price (Area B). Once again, this minimum value is $S - E + E - Pv(E)$, which is simply $S - Pv(E)$, which is what we said previously. *Any additional time premium must be equal to the value of the put (Area C).*

Additional Insights from Put-Call Parity

In Chapter Four we said that it is not optimal to exercise a call option early. Areas A, B, and C show why. When you exercise a call, you're left with Area A, the intrinsic value. But because you exercise the call and didn't sell it, you throw away Areas B and C. Area B represents the interest we could have earned on our money by not spending the exercise price early. Area C represents the time value in the call. Another way of looking at Area C is that you throw away the value of the put option by exercising early; that is, you are accepting the full downside risk of the stock.

Notice the curved line in Figure 5-10 that represents the price of the call option. If the stock rises sufficiently, that curved line eventually runs parallel to the line represented by $S - E$. At that point, the call option is behaving like stock. The reason is that $S - E$ obviously runs parallel to the profit and loss line for just plain stock (not shown in diagram) because that line is simply stock reduced by the value of the exercise price. Another way of understanding it is that if the call is in-the-money at or very near expiration, it will be worth $S - E$ and gains point-for-point with the underlying stock. If the call option is deep enough in-the-money prior to expiration, the curved line runs parallel to the $S - E$ line so must also gain point-for-point with the stock. This is a graphical representation drawing the same conclusion as our simplistic mathematical model we found in Chapter Two. The point to understand is that deep in-the-money calls behave like stock.

Now look at Area C. It shows the value of the put option, which is the same as the time value of the call (remember that the call price is bounded by zero and S – E). As the stock rises, the value of the put decreases, which is equal to saying that the time value of the call decreases. This observation is handy for trading applications. For example, say you wish to find a call option with a delta near one, which means that it is effectively behaving like stock at that point. All you need to do is look at the option quotes for a put option that it bidding zero. If the corresponding put is bidding zero then that call must have a delta near one. This aggress with the relationship between call and put deltas we discovered in Chapter Two and will be important once we discuss strategies for buying long calls and puts.

Put-call parity lends many insights into option pricing and theory. But it goes far beyond theory because there is a practical application to the formula that is used by all professional traders. It is the formula that provides the foundation for synthetic options.

Synthetic Options

Synthetic options are not a type of option such as calls or puts. As the name implies, synthetic options are ways of creating positions that look, feel, and behave like one asset but are constructed from entirely different assets. By using the put-call parity equation, we can create one asset from another. The benefit to us is that one form may be more liquid or more efficient than another.

For example, let's say we want to create a *synthetic long call* option. All we have to do is refer to any of our put-call parity formulas and algebraically solve for the call option. We might choose to use our original formula:

$$S + P - C = Pv\ (E)$$

If we are to solve for the call option, we must get C to one side of the equal sign with the other variables on the other. Using the above formula, in order to get the "C" by itself, we must add C to both sides and then subtract Pv (E) from both sides. This result is:

$$C = S - Pv (E) + P$$

This is the same formula we saw earlier in Formula 5-6. In other words, if you borrow the present value of the exercise price and buy stock plus buy a put, you have exactly created a call option – you have created a *synthetic call* option.

When we say that one position is the synthetic equivalent of another, we really mean that the two positions have exactly the same profit and loss profiles at expiration. Let's see if these two positions are truly equal. Assume one investor buys a $50 call while another holds Portfolio A, which contains long stock at $50, long $50 put, and borrows the present value of the $50 exercise price. The borrowed funds mature to $50, which means the investor holding Portfolio A owes $50 at expiration. According to Formula 5-6, the profits and losses to either investor should be identical at expiration regardless of the stock's price. Table 5-11 compares the two investors:

Table 5-11

Stock price	$50 Call	Portfolio A			Total Value
		Long stock	Long $50 Put	Repay $50	
35	0	35	15	50	0
40	0	40	10	50	0
45	0	45	5	50	0
50	0	50	0	50	0
55	5	55	0	50	5
60	10	60	0	50	10
65	15	65	0	50	15

For example, if the stock price is $35 at expiration, the $50 call is worthless. Portfolio A has stock worth $35 and a long put worth $15 for a total of $50. However, the holder of Portfolio A must also repay $50 at expiration thus leaving him with zero. Notice that the two bolded columns have exactly the same values. No matter which stock prices we might try, both columns will always match. This shows that a call option can be synthetically created by borrowing the present value of the exercise price to buy stock and then protecting that investment with a put option. So if the two positions are equal, which should we choose? That all depends on which is more cost effective.

For instance, in Figure 5-12, Google (GOOG) was trading for $293 and the January $290 calls with 529 days to expiration (1.47 years) were asking $58. The $290 put was asking $39.40.

Figure 5-12

Calls	Last Sale	Net	Bid	Ask	Vol	Open Int	Puts	Last Sale	Net	Bid	Ask	Vol	Open Int
07 Jan 250.0 (OUW AJ-E)	88.60	pc	79.30	80.40	0	1682	07 Jan 250.0 (OUW MJ-E)	23.10	pc	22.30	22.80	0	3996
07 Jan 260.0 (OUW AL-E)	74.10	-1.90	73.20	74.30	5	2009	07 Jan 260.0 (OUW ML-E)	27.40	pc	25.80	26.60	0	1080
07 Jan 270.0 (OUW AN-E)	69.70	pc	67.50	68.50	0	993	07 Jan 270.0 (OUW MN-E)	30.00	pc	29.70	30.30	0	1298
07 Jan 280.0 (OQD AP-E)	61.70	pc	62.00	63.00	0	1263	07 Jan 280.0 (OQD MP-E)	32.60	pc	34.00	34.50	0	903
07 Jan 290.0 (OQD AR-E)	60.30	pc	56.90	58.00	0	1134	07 Jan 290.0 (OQD MR-E)	38.40	pc	38.50	39.40	0	767
07 Jan 300.0 (OQD AT-E)	54.60	pc	52.20	53.30	0	5841	07 Jan 300.0 (OQD MT-E)	43.80	pc	43.50	44.00	0	2218

GOOG 293.07 +0.72. Aug 08, 2005 @ 15:04 ET (Data 15 Minutes Delayed) Bid 293.04 Ask 293.11 Size 7x1 Vol 3482811

Our synthetic relationship tells us there is no difference between the long call and long stock + long put + borrowed funds portfolio. However, many investors get trapped into thinking that the $290 call is obviously a better deal at $58 rather than spending $293 for the stock plus $39.40 for the put. If you do not plan to purchase the stock at expiration then it may be best to spend less money and buy the $290 call. However, if you are planning to buy the stock at expiration, we need to find out which is our most efficient method. If you buy the call and the stock price is greater than $290 at expiration, you will pay $58 today for the call and $290 in 1.47 years when you exercise the call. Alternatively, you could buy the stock for $293 and the $290 put for $39.40 today and accomplish the same thing. While it may appear that the call is the better deal, we need to consider the financing rates.

If you buy the stock plus put combination it will cost you $293 + $39.40 = $332.40 today. If you buy the call, it will only cost $58 today. However, if plan to buy the stock at expiration, you will have a payment of $290 due in 1.47 years. The question we need to answer is this: Is it cheaper to pay $332.40 today or $58 today and $290 nearly a year-and-a-half in the future? In order to compare these two cash flows, we need to line them up at the same time. In this example, it's easiest to line them up at today's prices. We know the stock + put will cost $332.40 today and the call will cost $58, which is a difference of $274.40. Now we just need to figure out which interest rate makes a future payment of $290 equal to $274.40 today. In other words, if we deposit $274.40 into a risk-free account today, what risk-free interest rate is necessary for our money to grow to $290 at expiration?

We can solve this from the basic principle and interest relationship:

interest = principal * rate * time

In this example, the interest is the difference between the $290 future value and the $274.40 present value, or $15.60:

$15.60 = $274.40 * r * 1.47

r = $15.60 / ($274.40 * 1.47)

r = .0387, or 3.87%.

If your broker pays a risk-free rate of 3.87% on cash balances then there is no difference between buying the call or the stock plus put combination. If your broker pays more than 3.87%, you should keep your cash and buy the call. If your broker pays less, you should buy the stock and put combination. So while the cheapest combination today may seem to make the most sense that may not be true once we consider the financing rates.

Whenever we consider a true synthetic equivalent, we must consider all four variables in the put-call parity equation. However, in the world of trading, synthetic positions usually ignore the present value of the exercise price. This means that synthetic positions are usually not calculated on total values but, instead, they are figured out on *net changes* between the two positions. For instance, let's look at our previous positions but this time we're not going to account for the borrowed funds.

In other words, we're going to make Portfolio A the combination of long stock and a long put and forget about the borrowed funds. Table 5-13 shows that the two portfolios are not equal in terms of total value. Reading the first row, if the stock price is $35 at expiration, the $50 call is worth zero while the stock plus put combination of Portfolio A is worth $50. Reading the last row, if the stock is $65, the $50 call is worth $15 while the stock and put combination for Portfolio A are worth $65 so they are clearly not equal. However, look at the "total value" column for Portfolio A. If you consider the *net changes* for this column in relation to the "total value" column, you'll find they match the expiration values for the $50 call and are shown in the last column:

Table 5-13

		Portfolio A			
Stock price	$50 Call	Long stock	Long $50 Put	Total Value	Net change from $50 purchase price
35	0	35	15	50	0
40	0	40	10	50	0
45	0	45	5	50	0
50	0	50	0	50	0
55	5	55	0	55	5
60	10	60	0	60	10
65	15	65	0	65	15

So if our only concern is to make the net changes of two positions behave the same then we can forget about the borrowed funds. This means that any synthetic position can be calculated by only considering the stock, put, and call in the put-call parity equation.

Our first version of put-call parity was:

$$S + P - C = Pv (E)$$

We can rewrite this by subtracting Pv (E) from both sides:

Formula 5-14:

$$S + P - C - Pv (E) = 0$$

Formula 5-14 is just another variation of put-call parity. It tells us that if we buy stock, buy a put, sell a call, and borrow the present value of the exercise price, we are effectively doing nothing. This also means this portfolio should cost nothing. If we are going to ignore the borrowed funds portion, we can just drop off the Pv (E) variable to get:

Formula 5-15:

$$S + P - C = 0$$

And it is Formula 5-15 that provides our basic synthetic option formula. Notice that the combination of long stock, long put, and a short call is a conversion and are the same assets used by the market maker to create the risk-free position that we started with in this chapter. Consequently, this is sometimes referred to as a *synthetic T-bill* (Treasury Bill). If you buy stock, buy a put, and sell a call, you are guaranteed to receive more money than you spent – just as if you purchased a T-bill.

To find the synthetic version of any of these three assets, all we need to do is reference Formula 5-15 for the answer.

To start, we need to get the asset that we're trying to replicate (either the stock, put, or call) by itself and with the correct sign. Let's stick with our same example and find the synthetic equivalent value of a long but this time we'll use Formula 5-15. To do so, we need to get a +C (remember, we are using "+" to denote a long position) on one side of the equation. Using some basic algebra, if we add C to both sides of the equation we get: S + P = C and there's the answer; long stock plus long put (left side of the equation) will behave just like a long call (right side of equation). Therefore, if you hold long stock and a long put, you have a synthetic call position.

Shortcut method:

Rather than adding or subtracting variables in the equation, it's easier to just imagine that you are moving the letters (assets) to one side of the equal sign or the other. If you change sides of the equal sign, the sign of the asset will change:

Using the above example, we were trying to get C by itself:

$$S + P - C = 0$$

The quickest way to envision that is to move the C from the left side of the equal sign to the right side:

$$S + P - C = +C$$

Because the C changes sides of the equal sign, its sign will change too. In this case, it changes from negative to positive.

According to Formula 5-15, an investor who owns stock and a put will share the same profit and loss diagram as one who is long a call. Remember, this does not mean that both investors will have the same portfolio values since we're not accounting for the borrowed funds. But the two portfolios should respond the same way to stock price changes at expiration. Let's assume one investor buys stock plus a $50 put for $5 while another buys a $50 call for $5 and check the profit and loss diagrams to see if we're correct:

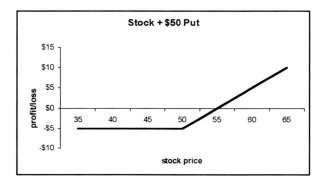

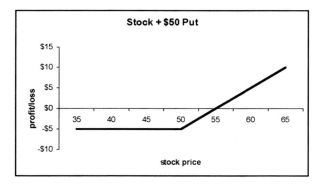

As you can see, there is no difference between long stock + long $50 put purchased at $5 (left chart) and the long $50 call purchased at $5 (right chart). The person holding the long stock and long put raised the cost basis of their stock from $50 to $55, that's why their break-even point is now $55. However, they still participate in all of the upside movement of the stock. What if the stock falls?

The investor is protected for all prices below $50, which is the strike of the put. The worst that can happen is for the stock to fall to zero. This investor will exercise the put and receive $50 effectively only losing on the $5 they paid for the put; therefore the maximum loss is $5.

For the call holders (right chart), they paid $5 so their maximum loss is also $5 but they too participate in all of the upside of the stock. The stock will have to be $55 at expiration in order for the call holders to break even since they have the right to buy stock at $50 but paid $5 for that right. This makes their breakeven price $55 as well.

We can use this information to gain some trading advantages. For example, most firms do not allow investors to buy call options in their IRA (Individual Retirement Account) but now you know that it can be done in a roundabout way with synthetics. You simply buy the stock and put and you are effectively long a call option. Now, your return on investment will be much lower using long stock plus a long put as compared to the person who buys only the call. This is due to the difference in capital required to purchase the stock but the two positions will behave the same in terms of net gains or losses at expiration.

Synthetics are useful for understanding option pricing behavior as well. In Chapter Two we showed that out-of-the-money options respond slower to changes in stock prices because of the number of zeros used in the averaging process. Synthetics can show us another view as well. Assume that a stock is trading for $100. We can create an out-of-the-money call, such as the $105 strike, by purchasing the stock for $100 and also buying the $105 put. Remember that the "bend" in any profit and loss diagram occurs at the strike price so a long stock position plus a $105 put will look exactly like a $105 call in a profit and loss diagram. As the stock rises from $100 toward $105, the long stock position will obviously make dollar-for-dollar. However, the long $105 put is losing intrinsic value or nearly dollar-for-dollar up to the $105 stock price. The net result is that the long stock and long put positions nearly cancel each other out and there is no change in value. In other words, the long stock plus long $105 put combination will hardly budge in value as the stock climbs toward $105. But once the stock price rises above $105 then the put has no more intrinsic value to lose but only some time value. The stock, on the other hand, continues to increase dollar-for-dollar and the long stock plus long $105 put combination now starts to increase in value if the stock continues to climb above $105. This is exactly how a long $105 call would behave. The next time you're tempted to buy an out-of-the-money call because it's cheap think about synthetics. If you're really bullish and want to buy the stock, would you buy an in-the-money put (that's going to lose dollar-for-dollar) to protect it? If not, then think twice about that out-of-the-money call because it is the same thing.

Using Formula 5-15, we can figure out any synthetic position. Notice that there are only three assets in the equation – stock, puts, and calls. A very simple property of synthetics is that the synthetic equivalent of any one asset will be some combination of the other two. In other words, stock can be formed by some combination of puts and calls. Calls can be replicated by some combination of stock and puts. The synthetic equivalent will never include the asset you're trying to replicate. For example, a synthetic long call will not include a call option in the answer. If you come up with that, a mistake has been made. The only thing left now is to figure out whether those combinations are long or short and that's where Formula 5-15 helps.

Now that you have Formula 5-15, let's work through some examples to see how to figure out – and understand – synthetic options.

Synthetic long stock

Can we use the basic put-call parity formula (Formula 5-15) to see if there's a way to own stock synthetically? Without looking ahead, see if you can use the equation $S + P - C = 0$ and solve it for long stock.

Because we have +S on the left side already, let's move the C and P to the other side, which changes their signs. Once we do, you will find that $S = C - P$. This tells us that a trader holding a long call and short put (right side of equation) is doing the same thing as someone holding stock (left side). That is, a long call plus a short put is synthetically equivalent to long stock.

Let's check the profit and loss diagrams for each and see if we're correct:

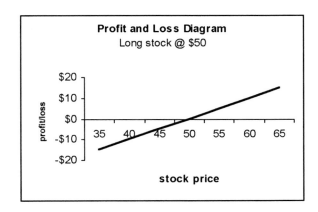

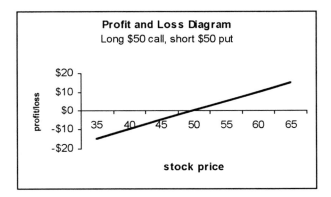

Again, we see there is no difference between the two positions. The long stock purchased at $50 (left chart) will gain and lose point-for-point to the upside as well as the downside. The same is true for the long $50 call and short $50 put (right chart). The $50 call will gain point-for-point at expiration while the short put will become a liability (loss) point-for-point if the stock should fall. Many traders wonder how these two positions can be exactly the same. Isn't there some time premium on the call option and doesn't that change the profit and loss diagrams? Refer back to Figure 5-10, which is reprinted below:

| Area A | Area B | Area C |

$$\textbf{Call} = \quad \textbf{(S} - \textbf{E)} \quad + \quad \textbf{(E} - \textbf{Pv (E))} \quad + \quad \textbf{put}$$

This showed that the time value of the call (over the cost of carry) is equal to the value of the put. If you buy the call and sell the put, you have eliminated the entire time premium in the call.

Another way to understand why the long call plus short put combination is equal to long stock is to think back to our discussion on the deltas of calls and puts. We said that the absolute delta values must sum to one. If the call delta is 60 then the put delta is -40. So if you bought this call and sold the put, you are long 60 deltas and short 40 deltas, or +60 – (-40) = 100 deltas. The delta of stock is always 100 since it always gains and loses point-for-point with itself. Buying a call and selling a put is exactly the same thing as owning stock from a profit and loss standpoint. Of course, it is much different on a leveraged basis since we are not accounting for the cost of carry since we ignore the Pv (E) from our original put-call parity equation. In an earlier section, we mentioned that Gordon Gekko would have done much better had he purchased the calls *and* sold the puts. Now you see why; he would have been holding synthetic long stock.

Synthetic Short Stock

If synthetic stock is just a long call plus a short put what would synthetic short stock be? Once again, all we have to do is change the signs of our previous answer and find out that a long put plus a short call will behave just like a short stock position. This is great to know for all traders involved in short selling. With synthetic options, it is now possible to short stock without an uptick or when stock is not even available for shorting.

Question

You wish to short a stock, which is trading for $100. Your broker informs you that the stock is not marginable and therefore cannot be shorted. How can you effectively enter a short sale?

Answer

Enter a synthetic short by selling the $100 call and buying the $100 put.

How much will it cost to enter an at-the-money synthetic short stock trade? Think back to put-call parity. One variation was:

$$C - P = S - \text{Present value E}$$

This tells us that if we buy the call and sell the put (left side) it should be worth the difference between the stock price and present value of the exercise price (right side). Because we are doing the reverse and buying the put and selling the call, the transaction should result in a slight credit.

Realistically though, because of bid-ask spreads and commissions, the trade may result in a slight debit. Regardless, it will not be a major cash outlay to enter this position (please keep in mind that there will be significant margin requirements to do so). However, they should not exceed (and will usually be much less) than the 150% Reg T margin required to short a stock. So not only can synthetics allow trades that otherwise cannot be done, they usually allow it to be done in a more efficient way by requiring less capital to take the same position.

Example

Figure 5-16 shows a chart of the S&P 100 (OEX). Between May 17 and June 3, 2002 (the area to the right of the dotted vertical line), the OEX took another. While there is usually no way to short the OEX index through the stock market, you could have done it synthetically in the options market.

Figure 5-16

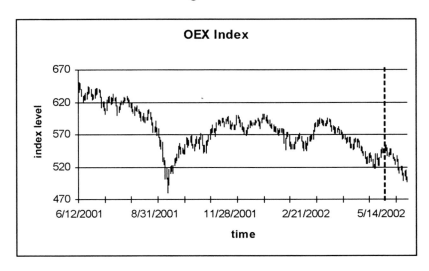

On May 17, the index was trading at 550 and the 550 calls were $13.00 with the 550 puts at $11.80. As we showed earlier, an at-the-money synthetic short will usually result in a slight credit, which was the case here. Selling 20 calls and buying 20 puts would result in a net credit of 20 contracts * 100 * $1.20 credit = $2,400. Just 17 days later, at the close of the trading, the puts were worth $38.20 and the calls 0.80. The synthetic short position could have been closed out for a credit of $37.40 * 20 * 100 = $74,800. For no money down (in fact, a credit of $2,400) you could capture a $70,000 profit in a relatively short time. Of course, this trade does not come without risk. The risk is that the index traded higher, which would have left you with an equally big loss if the index had risen by the same amount. We're just trying to show that synthetics allow you to initiate positions that others will tell you cannot be done. The more agile and efficient you are at establishing positions, the better trader and investor you will become. Synthetics give you those abilities.

Added Insights into Synthetics

All combinations of synthetics can be created by Formula 5-15 which is:

$$S + P - C = 0$$

Now that you understand synthetics, it is easier to see why the formula works. Assume you are long stock and also have another asset in your portfolio. You don't know what this asset is but you are told that it makes your long stock position risk free. What does that tell you about the other asset? If you have no risk, then the other assets must be short stock. If you are long stock and short stock then you are effectively flat and have no risk. Now think about our synthetic formula. If you are long stock and have other assets (shown by the box) and are also told that you have no risk then the boxed assets (long put + short call) must be equal to short stock and that's exactly what we found out.

$$S \boxed{+ P - C} = 0$$

To find any synthetic equivalent, all you need to do is isolate the variable(s) you're trying to solve for and the answer will be immediately visible. Let's try another. If you want to find out the synthetic equivalent to a long put, just isolate that +P position:

$$S \enclose{circle}{+ P} - C \ = 0$$

If that long put is paired with other assets so that it has no risk then the other assets must be equal to a short put. This immediately shows that long stock plus a short call must be equal to a short put.

It turns out that no matter which asset you pick, the other two are the synthetic opposite and fully hedge the risk. It should follow that we could also pick any two assets and know that the third will fully hedge those two.

All Combinations of Synthetics

It is great practice to run through Formula 5-15 and figure out the various combinations of synthetic trades. If you are really motivated, try to draw the corresponding profit and loss diagrams. All of the combinations are listed below for your reference. Note that the short positions are exactly the opposite of the long positions.

Asset	Synthetic Equivalent
Long stock	Long call + Short put
Short stock	Short call + Long put
Long call	Long stock + Long put
Short call	Short stock + Short put
Long put	Short stock + Long call
Short put	Long stock + Short call

Synthetic trades may seem complex at first but, in reality, are actually quite simple. Many think they are a needless academic exercise and of no practical use but nothing could be further from the truth. If you plan to actively trade options, it is crucial to understand synthetics. Market makers make their living with the put-call parity relationship so don't think it's a waste of your time to gain a basic understanding. A little time invested will make option investing worth your time.

 All combinations of synthetic positions are derived from the put-call parity equation.

Real Applications for Synthetics

Are synthetics really useful? In Chapter Four we found that it is never advantageous to exercise a call option early except to collect a dividend. When you exercise a call option, you give up the rights with the call option in exchange for the stock. If you exercise a call to gain the stock, you are holding all of the downside risk of the stock in exchange for collecting the dividend. Now that you understand synthetics, we can perhaps find a better way to do this. When you are long the call, rather than exercising it, you could, instead, sell the same strike put. This creates a synthetic long stock position (since you are long the call and short the put), which is effectively the same position you were going to have if you exercised the call. While the synthetic long stock position does not allow you to collect the dividend, it does let you collect the premium of the put. In many cases, this put premium will be of greater value than the dividend on the stock while either choice exposes you to the same downside risk. In addition, by choosing the synthetic long call position, you can hold onto the exercise value of the cash a little longer to earn interest. In other words, if you choose to exercise the call, you must pay for the stock today.

By entering the synthetic long stock position, you will end up buying the stock at the same price but at a later date. Why? For the synthetic long stock position, you are long the call and short the put. If the stock price is above the strike at expiration, you will exercise the call and buy the stock for the exercise price. If the stock's price is below the strike, you will be assigned on the put and buy the stock for the strike price. No matter where the stock's price is at expiration, you will pay the strike price and receive the stock, which is exactly what you would have done had you exercised the call only at a later date. This allows you to hold onto the cash for a longer period of time to earn interest. As long as the put premium plus interest earned exceeds the value of the dividend, you are better off with the synthetic long stock position. This means that it may still be advantageous to use the synthetic stock strategy even if the put premium is less than the dividend. You must compare the put premium plus interest earned to the dividend. Only when the dividend exceeds the value of the put plus interest should you exercise the call for the dividend. Please keep in mind that we are not saying that you should always capture either the dividend or put premium. In many cases, neither choice may warrant holding all of the downside risk of the stock whether synthetically or not.

We're just saying that if you have decided that it is worthwhile then you should consider the synthetic long stock version before exercising the call.

The mathematics behind put-call parity work no matter how you may choose to attack a particular problem. For example, we could have solved the problem of early exercise by considering what would happen if you actually exercised the call to get the dividend. If you exercise the call, you are buying stock and *effectively* selling your call. If you buy stock and sell a call, what have you done synthetically? You have sold a put. Different investors and traders see synthetics in different ways. But no matter how you view them, you'll arrive at the same answer.

Creating a Call Option

Synthetic options provide tremendous insights into the role of options in the marketplace. Assume you wish to buy a stock but are either afraid to because of the recent volatility or simply for the fact that you do not have enough money. So rather than buy the stock, you decide to buy a call option.

When your order is received, the market maker must create a call option. Remember, call options are simply contracts between two people; they do not exist in actual form such as shares of stock. In order to create that long call, the market maker must buy stock and buy a put, which is a synthetic long call. He can then transfer that over to you buy selling the call. Note what these actions by the market maker create:

Market maker buys stock
Market maker buys the put
Market maker sells you the call

Hopefully you remember these three actions – long stock, long put, short call – as a conversion, which is a risk-free, or "locked" trade. Because you did not want to take the risk of holding the stock, the market maker bought the stock for you and then bought a put to protect that downside risk. Doing so, he created a synthetic call. When he sells you the call, he has effectively transferred the long stock plus long put positions over to you.

So the reason you were able to buy a call is because the market maker was able to buy a put. The person who sold him that put must be willing to buy the stock (that's the obligation of the short put). By purchasing the call, you have the right to buy the stock. This means that the market maker has a guaranteed sale of stock at expiration.

If the stock's price is above the strike price, he will be assigned and required to sell the stock. If the stock's price is below the strike, he will exercise his put and sell the stock. The market maker is fully protected from any adverse movements in the stock's price. Notice that the option's market created a sale of stock (to the market maker) when nobody wanted to buy it at that point in time. *It was only because of the option's market that stock was traded.*

The options market creates more buyers of stock. If you buy a call option, somebody else is buying stock. The options market just creates an easy way to "find" these other people. If you want to buy a call, all you have to do is look at the quote board and see if the price is right. If you buy it, somebody somewhere in the world must be taking the other side of the trade and you will never know who that person is.

Are Options Bad for the Market?

Put-call parity provides powerful insights for option traders. Despite this quality, there is perhaps a bigger problem that it solves. That is, put-call parity formula can shed some light on one of the most polarizing debates in finance: Are options bad for the market? One group adamantly says yes; the other says no with equal conviction. Can put-call parity help solve the debate?

There are many investors who adamantly refuse to buy or sell options because they hear how "speculative" they are. They insist on holding only stocks. However, if you refuse to use options, you are speculating. Options were created as hedging tools or a way to decrease risk. Whenever you hedge your long stock, perhaps by purchasing a put or selling a call, you give up some upside profits in exchange for some downside protection. So if you buy stock and refuse to buy or sell options, you are speculating that nothing will go wrong with your long stock position. You are willing to hold out for more profit at the expense of downside exposure to a price of zero. It can be argued that investors who don't use options are among the most speculative of all! However, if you're still in doubt, would you believe that stock can be viewed as an option?

Valuing Corporate Securities as Options

Advanced option traders know to consult with an option pricing model of some kind before entering a trade. We'll talk more about option pricing models and why we use them in Chapter Six. For now, just understand the most famous of pricing models is the Black-Scholes Option Pricing Model developed by Fisher Black and Myron Scholes. When Black and Scholes developed this option pricing model, they were certain there were many uses for it other than just valuing call options. One of the uses they suggested was in valuing corporate securities.

Consider a firm that has issued one zero-coupon bond that matures to a value of $1,000,000 in five years. A zero-coupon bond just means that the corporation doesn't make quarterly payments; instead, they make one lump-sum payment of 1,000,000 in five years. In exchange, they receive less money than the 1,000,000 face value. With this money, the firm produces products and hopes to have a value in excess of this $1,000,000 in five years and pay off their debt leaving the stockholders with whatever remains in value. However, if the firm's value is less than $1,000,000 at maturity of the bond, the stockholders will simply turn over the assets to the bondholders and will be free of further liability.

Let's look at the payoffs for stockholders and bondholders at maturity:

If value of the firm is *less* than $1,000,000, say, $800,000:
Bondholders get: $800,000
Stockholders get: $0
Total value of firm = $800,000

If the value of the firm is *greater* than $1,000,000, say $1,200,000 at maturity:
Bondholders get: $1,000,000
Stockholders get: $200,000
Total value of firm is $1,200,000

We see with the above payoffs that the total value of the firm is partitioned between the stockholders and bondholders. Notice how the stockholders get nothing at expiration if the value of the firm is below the value of the matured debt. But if the value of the firm is greater than the matured debt, stockholders receive the *excess value*.

Now compare this bondholder and stockholder relationship to options. Assume you own 100 shares of stock and have sold, or written, a $100 call option against it. This means that you have been paid for the potential obligation to sell your shares. (If this sounds like a nice arrangement, it is a strategy called the "covered call" and we'll talk much more about it in Chapter Seven.)

At expiration, if the value of the stock is less than $100, say $80:
You get: $80
Call buyer gets: $0
Total value of your position is $80

In other words, if the value of the stock is below the strike at expiration, you end up holding the stock at its current value of $80. The long call owner receives nothing since it expires worthless.

However, if the value of the stock is greater than $100, say $120 at expiration:
You get: $100
Call buyer gets: $20
Total value of positions is $120

If the value of the stock is above the strike at expiration, you will be assigned and receive the $100 strike price; that's the most you will ever receive. The call owners will receive the stock and pay the strike for a value of the stock price minus the strike price. The call owners, in this case, receive what's left over after you have been paid. If you look closely, you will see that the payoff for the call option above exactly resembles the payoffs to the stockholders for the corporation discussed earlier.

Using the Black-Scholes Model

Recall the put-call parity formula:

Stock + Put - Call = Present value of the exercise price

We can rewrite this for the above corporation as:

Stock + Put - Call = Present value of the debt

Which can be rewritten *at maturity* as:

Stock + Put - Call = Total value of debt

Stock - Call = Total value of debt - Put

So the Black-Scholes Option Pricing Model tells us the value of the covered call position (left side of equation) is equal to the debt at maturity with a put written against it (right side of equation).

This means the bondholders have, in essence, written a put against the firm. In other words, if the value of the firm is less than the debt that is due at maturity, the stockholders "put" the firm back to the bondholders and walk away losing only what you paid for the stock – just as when you buy a call option. *The value of this "put" is part of what gives your stock its value.*

If you like owning stocks for this reason then there's no reason you should feel that options are bad for the market. In fact, Pricing Principle #5 from Chapter Two showed that the price of an option with a zero strike price and an unlimited time to expiration would equal the price of the stock. Options allow you to do what stockholders have always done – but for a lot less money. Why? Because they have strike prices. They allow you to partition the unlimited range of possible stock prices into segments that you wish to control. Options can also be used to create downside hedges in exchange for upside profits. Because of these uses, investors can create better risk-reward profiles that are simply not possible with stock alone.

||||||||||||||||||||||||||||||||||||||||||||||||||||||||||||||||||||||||||||||||||||||||||||||||||||||||

 Key Concepts

1) Stock + Put – Present value of the exercise price = Risk-free position (Conversion).

2) The opposite of a Conversion is a Reversal (Short stock – Put + Present Value of the exercise price).

3) The value of a put option equals the time value of the call (above the cost of carry).

4) Any synthetic position can be found by solving the formula $S + P - C$ = Present value of E for a single variable.

5) Buying calls is synthetically equivalent to buying stock on margin and buying a put for insurance.

||||||||||||||||||||||||||||||||||||||||||||||||||||||||||||||||||||||||||||||||||||||||||||||||||||||||||||||||

Chapter Five Questions

1) **Which of the following represents a synthetic long call?**
   a) Long stock + short call
   b) Short stock + long call
   c) Long stock + short put
   d) Long stock + long put

2) **The put-call parity formula shows us that an at-the-money call will be priced higher than the at-the-money put. How much higher will the price of the call be?**
   a) Stock – Pv (E)
   b) Stock + Pv (E)
   c) Stock – call
   d) Stock – put

3) **A call option's price can be broken down into three components. The first is the intrinsic value. The second is the cost of carry on the exercise price. What is the third component?**
   a) Present value of the exercise price
   b) Short put
   c) Long stock
   d) Long put

4) **Which of the following is a synthetic T-bill (or long bond)?**
   a) Long stock + long put + short call
   b) Short stock + short put + long call
   c) Long stock + long call + long put
   d) Short stock + long put + short call

5) **Which of the following is a synthetic long put?**
   a) Long stock + long call
   b) Long stock + short call

    c)   Short stock + long call

    d)   Short stock + short call

6) **Which of the following is synthetic long stock?**
   a)   Short call + long put
   b)   Long call + short stock
   c)   Long call + long put
   d)   Long call + short put

7) **Which of the following is synthetic short stock?**
   a)   Short call + long put
   b)   Long call + short stock
   c)   Long call + long put
   d)   Long call + short put

8) **Which of the following is a variation of the put-call parity equation?**
   a) $S + P - C = Pv (E)$
   b) $S + P + C = Pv (E)$
   c) $S - P - C = Pv (E)$
   d) $S - P + C = Pv (E)$

9) **Which of the following is one of the biggest advantages of the put-call parity equation? It can identify:**
   a)   Guaranteed trades
   b)   Superior strategies
   c)   The most efficient trades
   d)   Market direction

10) **When using the put-call parity equation, you will end up with plus and minus signs with each variation. What do these signs represent?**
    a)   Plus = long position, Minus = short position
    b)   Plus = high probability trade, Minus = low probability trade
    c)   Plus = market ends up, Minus = market ends down
    d)   Plus = hedged position, Minus = unhedged position

11) **In the put-call parity formula, what does S + P – C equal?**
    a)   The present value of the exercise price
    b)   The exercise price

c)   The future value of the exercise price

d)   The present value of the stock price

12) **Which of the following is the technical name for the three combined position: S + P – C?**

a)   Conversion

b)   Reversal

c)   Parity

d)   Arbitrage

13) **Which of the following is a synthetic short put?**

a)   Short call + long put

b)   Long stock + short call

c)   Long put + short stock

d)   Long call + short put

14) **Which of the following is a synthetic short call?**

a)   Short stock + short put

b)   Short stock + short call

c)   Long put + short stock

d)   Long call + short put

15) **Put-call parity shows that call options are really put options and vice versa depending on:**

a)   How the calls or puts are paired with the underlying stock

b)   How the calls or puts are exercised

c)   The length of time until expiration

d)   Any arbitrage opportunities that may exist

16) **Anytime you see the negative of the present value of the exercise price, – Pv (E), in the put-call parity formula that represents:**

a)   Loaning of funds

b)   Borrowing stock

c)   Shorting stock

d)   Borrowing of funds

17) Before exercising a call early to collect a dividend, you should check the bid of the corresponding (same strike as the call) put. If the bid price is higher than the dividend, you should:

a)   Exercise the call and short the stock

b)   Buy the put and sell the call

c)   Buy the put

d)   Sell the put

18) Put-call parity can show us why it is not optimal to exercise a call option early. When you exercise a call option early, you are throwing away the value of the:

a)   Put option

b)   Stock

c)   Interest that could be earned on the exercise price

d)   Both a and c

19) Interest rates are 5%. You observe that ABC stock is trading for $20 per share. The one-year, $20 call is $3 and the one-year $20 put is $1. Using put-call parity, what would you expect to happen to the call and put prices?

a)   Call prices should rise and put prices fall

b)   Call prices should fall and put prices rise

c)   Call prices and put prices should remain the same

d)   Call and put prices will both fall

20) Interest rates are 5%. You observe that ABC stock is trading for $20 per share. The one-year, $20 put is $1. Using put-call parity, what would you expect to see the one-year $20 call trading for?

a) $1.95

b) $2.15

c) $0.85

d) $0.75

Chapter Five - Answers

1)   Which of the following represents a synthetic long call?

d)   Long stock + long put

Using the basic formula $S + P - C = 0$, we can rearrange it to solve for a long call. This can easily be done by simply taking the $- C$ to the other side of the equal sign. Once we do, we see that a long call is synthetically equivalent to long stock plus a long put.

2)   The put-call parity formula shows us that an at-the-money call will be priced higher than the at-the-money put. How much higher will the price of the call be?

a)   Stock – Pv (E)

The put-call parity formula can be arranged to show that $C - P = S - Pv (E)$. This shows that the difference between a call and put (same strike) is equal to the difference between the stock and present value of the exercise price. In other words, the call will cost more than the put by the interest that could be earned on the exercise price. *explain why doesn't work with pricing model *

3)   A call option's price can be broken down into three components. The first is the intrinsic value. The second is the cost-of-carry on the exercise price. What is the third component?

d)   Long put

Call options have an implicit put option built into their price. It is this put that gives the call the limited downside risk.

4)   Which of the following is a synthetic T-bill (or long bond)?

a)   Long stock + long put + short call

The combination of long stock, long put, and a short call behave just like a T-bill. You will purchase the three assets at a discount from the exercise price and will collect the full exercise price at expiration.

5)   Which of the following is a synthetic long put?

c)   Short stock + long call

Using the basic formula $S + P - C = 0$, we can rearrange it to solve for a long put. Since the put is already "+" or long on the left side, we just need to bring the S and C over to the right side of the equal sign and change their signs in the process.

The result is P = -S + C, which means that a long put is equal to short stock plus a long call.

6) Which of the following is synthetic long stock?

   d) Long call + short put

The formula S + P – C = 0 can be rearranged to solve for long stock. Since the stock is already long on the left side, we just need to bring the P and C over to the right side of the equal sign and we end up with S = C – P. This tells us that the synthetic equivalent to long stock is a long call plus a short put.

7) Which of the following is synthetic short stock?

   a) Short call + long put

Once again, we just need to rearrange the formula S + P – C = 0 to solve for short stock, which we can do by moving the S to the right side of the equal sign thus changing its sign to negative. The result is P – C = - S, which means that a long put plus a short call is the synthetic equivalent to a short stock position.

8) Which of the following is a variation of the put-call parity equation?

   a) S + P – C = Pv (E)

9) Which of the following is one of the biggest advantages of the put-call parity equation? It can identify:

   c) The most efficient trades

10) When using the put-call parity equation, you will end up with plus and minus signs with each variation. What do these signs represent?

   a) Plus = long position, Minus = short position

11) In the put-call parity formula, what does S + P – C equal?

   a) The present value of the exercise price

12) Which of the following is the technical name for the three combined position: S + P – C?

   a) Conversion

These three positions together make up a conversion, which is a "locked" trade meaning that it has no risk. If the opposite set of transactions were taken (-S, -P, +C) then it is called a "reverse conversion" or reversal.

13) Which of the following is a synthetic short put?

b)   Long stock + short call

If you buy stock and sell a call you are doing exactly the same thing as someone who sells (shorts) a put.

14) Which of the following is a synthetic short call?

b)   Short stock + short put

If you buy stock and sell a put you are doing exactly the same thing as someone who sells (shorts) a call.

15) Put-call parity shows that call options are really put options and vice versa depending on:

a)   How the calls or puts are paired with the underlying stock

16) Anytime you see the negative of the present value of the exercise price, – Pv (E), in the put-call parity formula that represents:

d)   Borrowing of funds

If you are short the present value of the exercise price this means that you have borrowed the present value and must repay the exercise price at expiration. It is similar to selling a bond. Bond sellers receive cash up front (borrow money) but must repay the higher face value at maturity (pay back with interest).

17) Before exercising a call early to collect a dividend, you should check the bid of the corresponding (same strike as the call) put. If the bid price is higher than the dividend, you should:

d)   Sell the put

By selling the put, you have created a synthetic long stock position, which is effectively what you are doing by exercising the call. However, because the bid of the put is higher than the dividend, you have more money for not taking on any additional risk when compared to exercising the call.

18) Put-call parity can show us why it is not optimal to exercise a call option early. When you exercise a call option early, you are throwing away the value of the:

d)   Both a and c

If you exercise a call option early, you are effectively throwing away the interest that could have been earned on your money by paying for the stock too early. In addition, you also throw away the protective value of the put option.

19) **Interest rates are 5%. You observe that ABC stock is trading for $20 per share. The one-year, $20 call is $3 and the one-year $20 put is $1. Using put-call parity, what would you expect to happen to the call and put prices?**

b) Call prices should fall and put prices rise

This one is tricky. You could borrow money and buy 1,000 shares of stock for $20,000. Then you could sell 10 $20 calls and receive $3,000 and buy 10 $20 puts for $1,000. The net cost to you is $18,000, which you could borrow at 5% thus owing $18,000 * .05 = $900 in interest for a total of $18,900 at the end of one year. However, the position (conversion) is guaranteed to have a value of $20,000 at expiration thus paying back far more money than you own. At these prices, you could create a risk-free money machine. As traders discover this, they will continue to demand conversions thus putting buying pressure on the puts and selling pressure on the calls. This means that the call prices will fall and put prices will rise.

20) **Interest rates are 5%. You observe that ABC stock is trading for $20 per share. The one-year, $20 put is $1. Using put-call parity, what would you expect to see the one-year $20 call trading for?**

a) $1.95

Put-call parity tells us that S + P − C must equal the present value of the exercise price. In this case, a one-year $20 call has a present value of $20/1.05 = $19.05 if interest rates are five percent. We now know that the three-sided package containing S + P − C must be worth $19.05. The stock is worth $20 and the put is $1 so $21 − C = $19.05. Solving, we find that the call must be worth $1.95. You should have recognized that answers C and D could not be correct as they are less than the value of the put and we know that the same-strike call must always be more than the put by the cost-of-carry.

Chapter Six

An Introduction to Volatility

In Chapter Two, we talked briefly about volatility and how it affects an option's price. It was there we found out that the uncertainty of stock prices – the volatility – is what gives an option its value. The higher the volatility of the stock, the higher the option's price. However, the definition alone is not enough to trade options successfully. New and experienced traders must understand the role it plays in determining the fair value of the option as well as how it is possible to lose with options even though the underlying stock moves in their favor.

The Frog and the Roo

To understand the role of volatility and option prices, imagine that you are at a carnival with a very unusual game – a frog jumping game. A frog starts in the middle of a floor and can only jump left or right. The frog moves randomly, jumping right or left with equal probability. At the end of one minute, the frog's final destination is marked and you are paid $1 for every foot the frog is to the *right* of the starting point. If the frog happens to land anywhere to the left of the starting point, you win nothing:

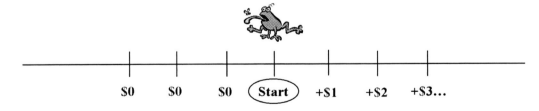

How much would you pay to play this game? There is no right or wrong answer but think about it for a moment and pick a number that you think sounds reasonable. Now let's change the mechanics of the game a bit. Imagine there is another game that is played with the same set of rules except this one uses a kangaroo:

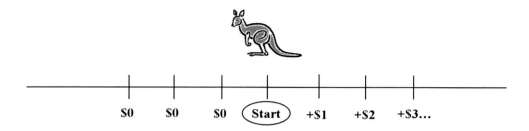

$0 $0 $0   (Start)   +$1   +$2   +$3...

How much would you pay to play this game now? As before, there is no right or wrong answer but think again for a moment and come up with your best estimate as to what this game is worth to you. It should be obvious that no matter which price you chose for the frog you should be willing to pay a higher price to have it replaced by a kangaroo. Why? Because the kangaroo has the ability to jump further and that means you could win far more money so the game is worth more to you. Notice that while both games offer potentially different rewards, neither has a mirror-image downside risk. In other words, you do not lose one dollar for every foot to the left of the starting point. The reason is that once you place your bet that's the most you can lose. So the only thing that matters to you is the *upside* potential. The game with the most upside is the one that is worth the most. It is the asymmetrical payoffs of these games that makes the kangaroo game more valuable.

In order to understand how volatility affects options prices, just replace the frog and kangaroo with at-the-money calls on two different stocks. One stock hardly moves like a big blue-chip stock such as General Electric (GE). The other bounces all over the board like Google (GOOG). Which call is more valuable to you? It's the one that has the highest ability to move; in other words, it is the stock with the highest volatility. If you own a call option, you're not as concerned with the downside risk as you are when holding a stock. If you own a stock, you can make dollar-for-dollar on the upside but also lose dollar-for-dollar on the downside. Put-call parity showed us that when you buy a call option, you are doing the same thing as someone who buys stock and buys a put option. In other words, call options provide downside protection so we are not concerned with the downside in the same way as when you own stock. Likewise, if you own a put option, you are doing the same thing as someone who shorts stock and also buys a call to protect them from the upside risk. Therefore, when you own an option, your maximum loss is limited. What determines the value of the call (or put) is the likeliness for the stock to make large moves – the volatility.

We can mathematically measure the volatility of a stock. The calculation is quite easy, although tedious, but is not really necessary to understand for our purposes. Just be aware that we can measure how far a stock price typically moves from its average. Volatility is typically measured in percents; the bigger the percentage, the more volatile the stock. A high volatility stock is one that exhibits large price swings throughout the day or over time. Conversely, low volatility stocks are those whose prices do not move much. The volatility range is not limited to 0 and 100 like many might suspect when dealing in percentages. Most stocks will probably fall in the 15% to 30% categories while 50% and higher would probably constitute a relatively high volatility stock. However, ranges can extend into the thousands during unusual circumstances.

One of the exercises in Chapter Two asked you to look up at-the-money quotes for Google and McDonald's and see which is more expensive and then asked why. If you did that exercise, you found that the options on Google were far more expensive than for McDonald's. From the brief discussion on volatility in that chapter, you should have realized that Google options are more expensive because the stock is more volatile. Now let's see if we can gain a better understanding of what we meant. Take a look at Figure 6-1, which shows historic price charts for Google and McDonald's over the same six-month time frame:

Figure 6-1

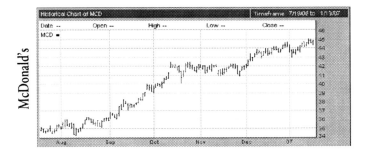

Think of the pictures as roller coasters. You can see the Google is a much "wilder ride" since there are bigger drops between the peaks and valleys. McDonald's, on the other hand, had a relatively steady climb and doesn't exhibit price swings like Google. Another way we can tell that Google is more volatile than McDonald's over this time period is by the heights of the individual bars. The heights of those bars are determined by the high and low stock prices during the day. It is evident that the bars are much taller for Google than for McDonald's, on average, and that means Google had much larger price swings during the day. So whether you look at the charts intraday or across time, Google had bigger price fluctuations than McDonald's and that means we'd expect it to have a higher volatility number. Granted, these two charts are on different scales but they still give a good visual representation of the concept of volatility. If we were to look up actual volatility numbers during this time frame, we'd find that Google had 40% volatility while McDonald's had 20%, which confirms what we just visually interpreted.

It's important to understand that high volatility does not necessarily mean better performance. Higher volatility just means that there are larger price fluctuations over the time period; it says nothing about the performance of the stock. In fact, in Figure 6-1, you can see that Google had a low around $360 and a high of about $490 over the time period, or a 36% increase. McDonald's had a low and high of $34 and $45 respectively, or 32%. So the performances are similar even though the volatilities are vastly different. The higher volatility for Google just means that the movements across the chart exhibited bigger "jumps" than were realized for McDonald's.

In the same way, the kangaroo game is more volatile than the frog game. This simply means that the *sizes of the jumps* are much bigger for the kangaroo so there is more potential for upside gains. But this doesn't necessarily mean that the kangaroo will always win. It is certainly possible for the frog to win. High volatility just means there are bigger fluctuations during the day and across time; it says nothing about performance.

A Simple Pricing Model

The size of the jumps – the volatility – in a stock's price is the key to determining what an option is worth. In order to gain a better understanding of how volatility affects an options price, let's make a very simple model and assume that a stock is trading for $50 and that it can only rise or fall by $5 at expiration with equal probability. (To make the calculations simple, we'll assume there is no cost of carry; that is, interest rates are zero.)

This means that only two final prices are possible, $45 and $55. What is the $50 call option worth? We can figure that out intuitively. Half the time it will be worth $5 (the call has $5 intrinsic value) when the stock ends at $55 and half the time it would be worth nothing when it ends at $45 (the $50 call expires worthless).

Now let's consider some prices to pay for the call. If you pay $5 for the $50 call then half the time you'll break even and half the time you'll lose $5. This means you can't win but could certainly lose so $5 is too much to pay for the call. What if you paid $1? In this case, you'd make a $4 profit half the time and lose $1 half the time, which means you'll make money for sure over the long run. This price is certainly a good deal for you but that also means you'll likely get outbid by another trader so will be too low of a price in an actual market.

It turns out that $2.50 is the price you should be willing to pay. If you do, you'll win $2.50 half the time and lose $2.50 half the time thus breaking even in the long run. This is called the *fair value* of the option. The fair value of an option is the price at which you will neither gain nor lose over the long run. It's very important to understand that when we talk about the fair value of an option, we're talking about the price where you would break even if you were allowed to play this exact option hundreds and hundreds of times. In this example, if you were able to buy this call option over and over for $2.50 you would just break even after hundreds of trades. Obviously, in the real world, you get one shot at any particular option assuming all other variables constant. But we still must look at long-run averages to determine the fair price, or fair value, of an option.

We just stepped through an intuitive way of finding the fair value by picking call prices out of the air and seeing how our profit would perform in the long run. We can take a short cut and figure the fair value out mathematically by simply multiplying each probability by the payout and then adding them all together. In this example, half the time the option is worth $5 and half the time it is worth zero so:

$$(0.50 * \$5) + (0.50 * 0) = + \$2.50$$

In mathematical terms, this is called the *expected value* and shows what the call option is expected to be worth in the long run. If we are expected to make a profit of $2.50 per trade in the long run then it also means this should be the price where it should be trading in the open market.

Here's why the market will end up pricing it at $2.50. Let's say you bid $1 for it. You would make $1.50 profit per trade in the long run (if the option is worth $2.50 and you pay $1, you'd expect to make the difference as a profit). We can show this another way. Half the time the option is worth $5 at expiration, which nets a $4 profit since you paid $1. Half the time the option is worthless and you'd lose your dollar. Mathematically, your expected outcome in the long run is:

$$(0.50 * \$4) + (0.50 * -1) = + \$1.50$$

So one dollar is too low of a bid since it results in a positive expected value of $1.50 for the option. Sure, you could lose on this option no matter how low of a price you pay. However, if there is a positive *expected value* then the markets will bid the price higher.

Let's assume another investor bids $2. We would expect him to make a long-run profit of 50 cents per trade, which again is the difference between the $2.50 expected value and the $2 price. Mathematically, we can show that the expected value is:

$$(0.50 * \$3) + (0.50 * -2) = + \$0.50$$

Once again, there is free money being left on the table over the long run so other traders will compete for this call option in the open market. This action continues until we reach a price of $2.50. If the price is $2.50 then the expected value is:

$$(0.50 * \$2.50) + (0.50 * -2.50) = \$0$$

At a price of $2.50, the call has a long-run expected value of zero; in other words, it is expected to just break even. So if the price is below $2.50, traders will bid the price up. If the price gets above $2.50, traders will sell the option thus putting downward pressure on its price. The net effect is that the option will be trading for $2.50 in the open market.

We've just shown that if a stock is $50 and can only rise to $55 or fall to $45 then a $50 call is worth $2.50 (assuming zero interest rates). Remember that we're trying to show that higher volatility equates to higher option prices. In this example, the $50 stock could either move up or down $5, which is a 10% move in either direction. Now let's change the size of the jumps to 20%, or plus or minus $10 and see what happens to the option's price:

$$(0.50 * \$10) + (0.50 * 0) = + \$5.00$$

If the $50 stock can now move to $40 or $60 at expiration then the $50 call is worth $5 for the same reasons we just covered. If traders bid less than $5, there will be a positive expected value. If they bid higher, a negative expected value occurs. Only when the option's price is $5 do we get a long-run break even price on the option. The most important point to understand is that even though you could certainly lose on either option, *the one with the 20% price jumps has more value than the one with 10% jumps. That is, higher volatility leads to higher option prices.* Fair value and the concept of the "long run" are very important concepts for options traders so let's go into it in a little more detail.

Fair Value - How Much is a Bet Worth?

Let's say we are offered the chance to play the following game indefinitely: A coin is flipped and we win $1 if it lands "heads" but lose our bet amount if it lands "tails." How much should we be willing to wager on this game? The value of any bet is determined by two things: 1) The reward and 2) The probability of winning that reward. As the reward or probability of winning increases, so does the value of the bet. In this problem, we know that the reward is one dollar so all we need to determine is the probability of winning. This is a critical step in understanding option pricing so it is worth repeating: *The first step in determining what we should pay for any bet is to determine the probability of winning.*

We can figure this out in a similar way that we did for our simple two-step option pricing model. We know there is a 50% chance of winning $1 and a 50% chance of losing X-dollars. We also know that the expected value should be zero:

(0.50) * +$1.00
+ (0.50) * -$X
Expected value = $0

We can solve this for X and find that it equals $1. If we substitute $1 for X, the calculation is saying there is a 50% chance of winning $1.00, which means that has a value to us of 0.50 * +$1.00 = 50 cents. But we also have a 50% chance of losing $1.00, which has a value of 0.50 * -$1.00, which equals -50 cents. The positive and negative 50 cents cancel out and we're expected to walk away with nothing after hundreds of flips.

The reason we have to solve for X when we didn't do that for the two-step call option is because options must always be paid for. When we bet, as with the coin example, no money changes hands prior to the bet and that changes the way we must calculate things. However, the principle of the expected value is exactly the same.

We can even run a computer simulation to see if we're right. Figure 6-2 shows a computer model with the number of tosses on the horizontal axis and our total profit or loss on the vertical axis:

Figure 6-2: Computer Simulation of Fair Value (Paying $1 to Win $1)

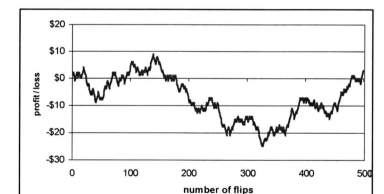

You can see that after 500 tosses, we're about back at break even. However, prior to that, we can certainly end up winning or losing due to chance. But in the long run, we'd expect to just break even. The "zero" horizontal mark in Figure 6-2 acts like a magnet for a fairly valued bet in that the profit and loss line doesn't get too far from it. The profit or loss line can stray from zero but it cannot just move away from it indefinitely. The profit and loss line just tends to oscillate around zero.

Let's use this same formula to see what it says about paying $1.50 for the $1 reward:

(0.50) * +$1.00
+ (0.50) * -$1.50
Expected value = -25 cents

The formula shows that we are expected to lose 25 cents per flip. Paying $1.50 for this bet is therefore too high of a price as we would expect to end up with certain losses over time. Figure 6-3 shows that a computer simulation agrees with the formula:

Figure 6-3: Computer Simulation Above Fair Value (Paying $1.50 to Win $1)

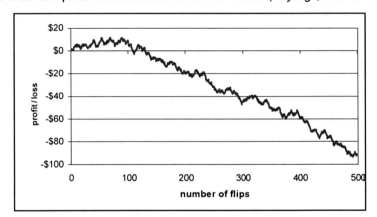

In fact, mathematically, after 500 tosses we would expect to end up at 500 tosses * -.25 cents = -$100 and that's roughly where the computer simulation ended. Curiously enough, notice that even though we're paying above fair value it's still possible for us to end up on the winning side in the short run. Figure 6-3 shows that we ended up on the winning side even after 100 flips. But that is just due to some short-term good luck on our side. We had significant winnings to cover our losses after 100 flips. But if we stay in the game long enough, the profit and loss line does not tend to get pulled toward zero. Instead, it moves into a definite downward path and never returns. Once again, this shows that $1.50 is too high of a price to bet on this coin flipping game.

Let's see what the formula has to say about wagering 50 cents for the $1 reward:

(0.50) * +$1.00
+ (0.50) * -$0.50
Expected value = +25 cents

Wagering only 50 cents to win $1.00 at the flip of a coin is a good deal for us as we now expect to win about 25 cents per flip. Figure 6-4 shows a computer simulation of this arrangement:

Figure 6-4: Computer Simulation Below Fair Value (Paying 50 cents to Win $1)

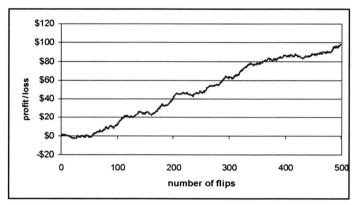

Again, we would expect to have 500 tosses * +25 cents = $100 profit after 500 flips and that's about where this computer simulation ends. Notice too, however, the chart shows we actually lost money after 75 flips even though the odds were on our side. That's because the profit and loss line dips below zero up until the 75th flip mark. At that point, we head into uninterrupted profits. This profit and loss line is not pulled toward zero in the long run. Although we could certainly lose in the short run, we will end up on the winning side after numerous flips, which is confirmed in Figure 6-4.

Only when the price of the bet is $1.00 can we say that it is "fair" for both parties. As a reminder, just because the bet is fair does not mean you cannot end up on the winning or losing side. The fair price for both just means that, *over the long run*, neither side is expected to end up on the winning or losing side.

Fair Value Depends on Perspective

In the coin toss example, we calculated that $1.00 was the fair value of the bet. However, that result is due to our assumption that the chance of winning (and losing) is 50%. Obviously, if we used different probabilities, we would get different results. This means the fair value of any bet depends on our perspective; it depends on our views of the probability of winning.

For example, let's assume that somebody offers to wager $1.50 for this bet. There are two ways we could look at it. First, we could assume there is a 50% chance of winning and losing and assume that is too high of a price since it results in an expected loss of 25 cents per flip:

(0.50) * +$1.00
+ (0.50) * -$1.50
Expected value = -25 cents

However, we could also look at this bet another way. We could assume that it's priced fairly since nobody should intentionally pay more than what they think is fair. If someone offers to pay $1.50, we could say that the gambler must think it is a fair price to pay. In order for that to be true, the gambler would have to think his chances of winning are 60% since that results in a fairly valued bet:

(0.60) * +$1.00
+ (0.40) *-$1.50
Expected value = 0

If a gambler were willing to pay $1.50 for this bet, we would say he is *implying* that his chances of winning are 60%. In other words, just by the fact he is willing to pay $1.50 for such a bet we can back into it mathematically and assume he believes his chances of winning are 60% otherwise he would not bid so high.

This shows there are two ways of looking at any bet. First, if we believe there is only a 50% chance of winning then paying $1.50 is too high of a price. Second, we can assume the $1.50 is a fair price and adjust the probabilities to make the expected value equal to zero. We can back into this figure algebraically and, in this case, we'd say the gambler willing to pay $1.50 for this bet is implying that there is a 60% chance of winning the $1.00 prize and a 40% chance of losing the $1.50 wager.

Now, as gamblers, it's up to us to decide which viewpoint is more realistic. Should we assume the chances of winning are 50% and be willing to pay only $1.00? Or is 60% a better assessment? Notice that if we assume 50% is the better guess we will be outbid by another gambler if he feels 60% is the more realistic probability. We would only be willing to bid up to $1 for the bet while he would be willing to pay up to $1.50. It is critical that we are confident in our assessments. If 60% sounds like too high of a probability, we're probably better off forgoing the bet and letting someone else make it. It's better to miss out on some reward rather than lose our money.

Whether we should use 50%, 60% (or something else) to value this coin flip is an important question. However, it's even more important when valuing options. However, few option traders ever check to see how the price of an option compares to their assessment of value. Failure to do so is the leading reason that option traders lose with options. In order to make that assessment, option traders need to use the Black-Scholes Model.

The Black-Scholes Option Pricing Model

We briefly mentioned the Black-Scholes Model in Chapter Five. There are many mathematical pricing models that can tell us what the price of an option "should be." Naturally, there will be minor variations in the answers depending on the assumptions in the model. The most famous is the *Black-Scholes Option Pricing Model* named after Fischer Black and Myron Scholes. Its development was no small feat as the model relies on complex mathematics and arbitrage pricing relationships to determine what the price of an option should be and is considered to be one of the biggest breakthroughs in the modern financial era. In fact, the 1997 Nobel Prize in Economics was awarded to Myron Scholes for its development (unfortunately, Fischer Black died in 1995 and the Nobel prize is not awarded posthumously).

According to the Black-Scholes Model, there are six factors needed to determine the price of a call and put option:

• Stock Price

• Exercise Price

- Risk-Free Interest Rate

- Time to Expiration

- Dividends

- **Volatility**

Notice the last factor, volatility. Of these six inputs, volatility is the most important for the fact that it's the only true *unknown* factor. For example, assume the risk-free interest rate is 5% and hundreds of traders are trying to value a 30-day, $100 call option on a stock trading for $95. We'll also assume the stock pays no dividends over the life of the option. Notice all of the factors are automatically determined except volatility:

- Stock Price = $95

- Exercise Price = $100

- Risk-Free Interest Rate = 5%

- Time to Expiration = 30 days

- Dividends = 0

- **Volatility = ?**

The only variable we're not sure of is volatility and that's why it's the most important variable in the model. If it's an unknown variable, then how did we look up volatility numbers for Google and McDonald's earlier? When we looked those numbers up they were historic numbers; they had already occurred in the past. When the Black-Scholes Model asks for volatility, it really needs to know the *future volatility* of the stock and not the historic volatility.

To understand why, go back to our two-price stock model where the stock could move up or down $5. If this is how the stock has behaved *in the past* then we would value the $50 call at $2.50. However, suppose we have reason to believe the stock will now move up or down $10 *in the future*. Now the $50 call is worth $5 and not $2.50. It's the future volatility of the stock that determines the price of an option and, unfortunately, that is something we will not know until expiration.

In order to truly know the value of an option we must know the future volatility of the underlying stock. And that is something that can never be known for sure until expiration.

Using the Black-Scholes Model

Let's take a look at how to use a Black-Scholes Model. There are many available on the web but one of the best can be found at the CBOEs website www.cboe.com:

Figure 6-5: The Black-Scholes Option Pricing Model (Calculator)

	Call	Put
Symbol:	N/A	N/A
Option Value	3.9947	3.0008
Delta:	0.5801	-0.4199
Gamma:	0.0444	0.0444
Theta:	-0.0061	-0.0034
Vega:	0.1954	0.1954
Rho:	0.2501	-0.2400

Style: European
Price: 50
Strike: 50
Expiration Date: FLEX
Days to Expiration: 365
Volatility %: 17.62
Interest Rate%: 2
Dividends Date (mm/dd/yy):
Dividends Amount:
Dividends Frequency: Monthly

Calculate

Implied Volatility
Option Price   Vola %
Put

Calculate

Let's assume we are looking at a stock trading for $50. We'd simply type "50" in the "Price" field on the left side of the calculator. If we wish to evaluate a $50 strike, we'd type 50 into the "Strike" field. We'll also assume that there are 365 days to expiration and that interest rates are 2%, which we type into their respective fields. Last, we're going to assume that the future volatility of the stock will be 17.62% over the course of the year (you'll find out why this specific number was chosen shortly). What is the $50 call worth under these assumptions? All you have to do is click the "calculate" button in the middle of the screen and the call and put prices show up on the right by the "Option Value" field (circled).

It's telling us the call should be $3.99 and the put should be worth $3. The reason 17.62% was chosen as the volatility is because that's the volatility that makes the put worth exactly $3, which fits an example we worked by hand in Chapter Five. If you recall in that chapter, we were trying to figure out what a market maker should charge for a one-year, $50 call with the stock at $50. We also assumed he paid $3 for the put and interest rates were 2%. From put-call parity, we calculated that the market maker should charge $3.98 for the call and the Black-Scholes Model in Figure 6-2 is coming up with $3.99. So we're off by a penny but that is due to differences in the interest compounding assumptions and number of days assumed in a year.

Although the Black-Scholes Model makes use of some very complex mathematics, the essence behind the calculations is similar to what we stepped through when trying to figure out how much the market maker should charge for a call option.

Why do you suppose the call in Figure 6-5 is roughly $1 higher than the put? Hopefully you remember from put-call parity that it's due to the cost of carry on the stock. If interest rates are 2%, it will cost $50 * .02 = $1 in lost interest to buy and hold the stock for one year. In other words, if you pay $50 for stock and hold it for a year, you could have had $51 at the end of the year if you had left the money in a risk-free account instead. So there is a $1 cost of carry on a $50 stock over a year if interest rates are 2%. That's why the call is priced $1 higher than the put. The Black-Scholes Model is a complex form of put-call parity with volatility as the key ingredient.

Why You Need to Understand Volatility

This chapter is by no means meant to be a full discussion on volatility. However, most beginning option books do not even mention it and that's a huge inequity to new traders and investors. If you don't understand the role of volatility, you can end up with unpleasant surprises as we will now demonstrate.

Many option traders believe option trading is a relatively easy task and that you buy calls when you think the stock is going up and buy puts when you think it's going to fall. After all, that's all that's needed to trade stocks. When most traders make the switch to options, they apply this same directional procedure to the options market. However, this approach ignores the time value of calls and puts in terms of volatility and unexpected, almost paradoxical, losses can occur as the following real-life example shows.

On September 16, 2004, Atherogenix (AGIX) was trading for $18.81 as shown by the quotes in Figure 6-6. At the time, there was tremendous bullish news on the stock regarding a new heart medication and most option traders who were bullish might be tempted to buy the $20 call since it's the next highest strike from the current stock price. Figure 6-6 shows the $20 call (circled) would cost $4.80, or $480 per contract.

Figure 6-6: AGIX Option Quotes

| AGIX (Nasdaq) | | | | | | | | | | | 18.81 | -0.08 |
| Sep 16,2004 @ 10:10 ET (Data 15 Minutes Delayed) | | | | | | Bid 18.80 Ask 18.81 Size 14x6 Vol 29728 | | | | | | |

Calls	Last Sale	Net	Bid	Ask	Vol	Open Int	Puts	Last Sale	Net	Bid	Ask	Vol	Open Int
04 Oct 15 (AUB JC-E)	6.70	pc	6.20	6.70	0	1103	04 Oct 15 (AUB VC-E)	2.50	pc	2.50	2.90	0	1158
04 Oct 17.50 (AUB JW-E)	5.10	pc	5.10	5.60	0	1972	04 Oct 17.50 (AUB VW-E)	3.90	pc	3.90	4.30	0	1150
04 Oct 20.00 (AUB JD-E)	4.80	-.10	4.40	4.80	25	3833	04 Oct 20.00 (AUB VD-E)	5.40	pc	5.50	6.00	0	1507

On September 22, just six days later, the stock had risen significantly from $18.81 to $21.18, which is a 12.5% gain in a short time. It certainly sounds like it should leave the trader with a nice profit on the leveraged $20 call but Figure 6-7 shows that is not what happened. The $20 call was bidding only $4.70 thus leaving the trader with a 10-cent loss for being correct on the direction of the stock!

Figure 6-7: AGIX Option Quotes (Six Days Later)

| AGIX (Nasdaq) | | | | | | | | | | | 21.18 | +0.46 |
| Sep 22,2004 @ 10:37 ET (Data 15 Minutes Delayed) | | | | | | Bid 21.17 Ask 21.19 Size 5x1 Vol 240954 | | | | | | |

Calls	Last Sale	Net	Bid	Ask	Vol	Open Int	Puts	Last Sale	Net	Bid	Ask	Vol	Open Int
04 Oct 15 (AUB JC-E)	7.50	pc	7.30	7.80	0	2280	04 Oct 15 (AUB VC-E)	1.50	-.10	1.30	1.55	5	1505
04 Oct 17.50 (AUB JW-E)	6.10	-.10	5.80	6.30	13	6106	04 Oct 17.50 (AUB VW-E)	2.45	-.10	2.20	2.60	4	4594
04 Oct 20.00 (AUB JD-E)	4.80	-.20	4.70	5.10	7	510	04 Oct 20.00 (AUB VD-E)	3.90	pc	3.50	3.90	0	1563

Direction versus Speed

What happened? How did this call option lose money even though the stock's price went up? Loosely speaking, the reason is because options are two-dimensional assets. That is, option traders must not only guess the *direction* of the stock correctly but they must also guess how quickly the stock's price will get there – the *speed*.

Stock traders, on the other hand, only need to correctly guess the direction; they are dealing with a one-dimensional asset. It doesn't matter how long it takes for the stock to move, just as long as it moves in the right direction.

As an analogy, you car moves in one dimension – horizontally. An airplane, on the other hand, can move in two-dimensions – horizontally and vertically. It is this second dimension that makes flying an airplane so much more difficult than driving a car. Just because you may have driven a car accident-free for 20 years does not mean you should just jump into an airplane and start flying. There is a second dimension you're not used to dealing with. Likewise, just because you may have been trading stocks successfully for 20 years does not mean you should just jump into the options market and start trading options based on direction. That's an equally bad idea.

In this example, the $20 call option trader got the stock direction right but not the speed; it took too long for the stock to get there. If the stock had moved to $21.18 in a shorter time, say a day or two (rather than six), the $20 call would certainly have made money. It is this second dimension of speed that makes options trading so much more difficult than stock trading. Notice that a stock trader would have made money by purchasing the stock for $18.81 and selling at $21.18. The speed at which the stock rises doesn't matter. So while both traders guessed the stock direction correctly, only the stock trader made money.

This example shows that call options are not necessarily a direct substitute for stock. If you think a stock is moving higher, you cannot just buy a call in place of the stock and expect to make money if you are correct. Yet most option traders mistakenly apply this one-dimensional stock trading technique to options and, consequently, end up losing money. What is responsible for this speed component? It's the time premium of the option. If the time premium is relatively high then the break even price is pushed too high and the option may lose money even though the underlying stock moves favorably. In order to prevent that from happening, option traders must learn to separate the price of an option from the value.

Price and Value

In order to understand the difference between price and value, let's take a look at a real-world example. In Figure 6-8, you'll see an eBay auction for one million Iraqi Dinars:

Figure 6-8

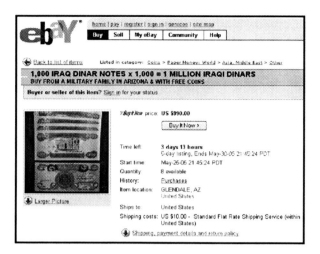

At the time of this auction, there were many similar auctions for this currency because of the radical changes taking place in Iraq. The country was getting lots of U.S. support to help its new government get underway. They also have the second largest oil reserves in the world so there is tremendous potential for their currency to rise against the dollar. If you buy a large block of their currency, you'd only need a small movement in the currency against the dollar and you could make a lot of money; at least, that's the investment story the sellers of Iraqi currency are touting on eBay. Figure 6-8 shows this opportunity could have been yours for the low, low price of only $990.

We know the price is $990 but that really tells us nothing. Any asset can be priced too high no matter how good the story is that comes with it. The rarest works of art and most precious gems can be a horrible investment if too much is paid for them. As investors, we cannot just look at the $990 price tag on this eBay auction and think it is a good deal because of a good story. We need to somehow compare the price to the value.

That's easy to figure out since there is an open market for currency. All we need to do is look at the exchange rate for Iraqi Dinars and convert them to U.S. Dollars. At the time of this auction (May 27, 2005), the exchange rate for U.S. Dollars per Iraqi Dinar was .00068, which means that one million Iraqi Dinars were worth 1,000,000 * .00068 = $680. Now we have a benchmark for value since we know what the crowd is willing to pay. However, this auction dealer wants

$990 for something that is worth $680 in the open market. Not only is this not a good deal but there's a more insidious side to the trade than just being overpriced. If you pay $990 for the block of money and its value rises, you could still lose. For example, if the block of money rises from $680 to $900, it certainly went up substantially in value but you still lost money since you paid $990. This is exactly what happened with our AGIX $20 call. The price of the underlying stock rose but our option was overpriced. The moral of the story is that if the price you pay is greater than the value, you can end up with a loss even if your directional outlook is correct. The legendary investor Warren Buffett said it beautifully: "Price is what you pay. Value is what you get."

 The price of an option is in no way related to its value.

Option Prices and Point Spreads

One of the best ways to understand option trading is to realize they can be viewed as a directional bet on the underlying stock. (This is not to say we are using options to bet on stocks. Instead, it's a framework to help us understand what went wrong with the AGIX $20 call.) As with any bet, you put up some money in hopes of making a particular reward. There is some probability of winning along with a probability of losing. The amount you're willing to wager on a bet can be thought of as the price of the bet. But, as we will show shortly, some prices reflect a good deal while others do not.

In order to better understand how some prices can be too high, imagine that it is 2004 and you are betting on the Super Bowl between the New England Patriots and Philadelphia Eagles. You do your homework and find that all of the analysts are predicting that New England will win. To the unwary, it sounds like betting is too easy; all you have to do is bet big on New England and you'll make money. Unfortunately, you find that *everybody* wants to bet on New England and you cannot find anybody to take the other side of the bet. How can you entice someone to take the other side? There are several ways but one of the easiest is to offer a point spread. While nobody may be willing to bet on the Eagles in actual points (or "even up"), people will take the bet if you create a point spread. For instance, if you offer a 7-point spread on New England then anybody betting on that team must subtract 7 points from the Patriots' score before comparing it to the Eagles' score in order to determine who wins the bet. If the Patriots win 21-14, there is exactly a 7-point spread and no money is won or lost. A bigger spread results is a win for the person betting on the Patriots while a smaller spread results in a win for the one betting on the Eagles.

If nobody accepts the bet with a 7-point spread, you can always increase it until you find a "buyer." At some point, people will think the bet is fair and take the other side. Figure 6-9 shows the spreads at the Stardust and Mirage Casinos and you can see they were offering a 7-point spread, which is designated by the -7 under each of their names:

Figure 6-9

NFL Odds

NFL Odds | NBA Odds | NCAA FB Odds | MLB Odds

Date	Teams	Expert Odds		Stardust	Mirage	Score
		Open	Current			
02/06	New England	-6.5	-7.0 -250	-7.0	-7.0	24 FINAL
18:25 ET	Phila.	46.5	47 +210	47	47.5	21

The spread acts as a way to even up the bet. It's the way in which markets are created; otherwise everybody would bet on the favored team and there would be nobody left to take the other side of the bet. The spread is increased until we find an equal number of buyers and sellers. If the spread is too big, bettors will realize that they are better off betting against their team even though they think they will win. It's only when the spread is just right that we end up with an equal amount of buyers and sellers of the bet.

Figure 6-9 shows the final score was 24-21 in favor of New England. *This means anybody betting on New England was correct that they would win but still lost the bet.* In other words, New England won but not by a big enough margin to win the bet.

Now let's see how this football analogy relates to the options market. At the time the AGIX quotes were taken there were numerous articles about upcoming experiments for one of their drugs to reduce the amount of fatty plaque that causes clogged arteries. If the experiment is positive, the stock's price could jump significantly.

Now think about this. If everybody believes that AGIX will rise, then everybody would want to buy call options (just as if everybody thinks the Patriots will win then everybody wants to bet on them). And if everybody wants to buy calls then there is a problem. Who is going to sell those calls? The answer is that nobody will. That is, nobody will sell them unless you offer a point spread on the "bet." And that's exactly what has happened with the AGIX $20 call.

Figure 6-6 showed that the $20 call was asking $4.80. In essence, anybody buying this call is really betting that the stock's price will be above $20 + $4.80 = $24.80 by expiration since that's the breakeven point on the option. The $4.80 time premium of the option acts in the same way a point spread does for a football bet. It's only because of this $4.80 point spread that a market between buyers and sellers could be created. If the time premium was higher than $4.80, then the "point spread" would be too big and we'd have too many people wanting to sell the bet and the price would fall. If the premium is less than $4.80, then the point spread is too small and traders would believe the $20 call is a good deal. We'd end up with too many people wanting to buy the call and the price will rise. A price of exactly $4.80 is what is required to balance the number of buyers and sellers at that point in time.

Notice that, at expiration, if the stock rises from $18.81 to $24.80 or less, any trader who paid $4.80 for the $20 call loses the bet – even though the stock's price rose. This is exactly what happened to those who bet on the Patriots with a 7-point spread. Even though they were betting on the correct team, they still lost the bet since they did not win by a big enough spread. And this is exactly what happened to the traders who bought the $20 call on September 16 and tried to sell it six days later. Although traders buying the call were correct on the direction, they accepted too big of a point spread on the bet. In short, the price of the call was much higher than the value.

When we value a football bet, there is no way to say for certain it is properly valued. It's a question of the perceptions of the bettors. The casinos simply find out how many people wish to bet on each team and then create the necessary point spread to balance the number of buyers.

Prior to 1973, this is exactly how the options market worked. Traders had to throw out bids and offers based on what they felt the trade was worth. Of course, this type of valuation means that traders tend to bid low and offer high, which creates very large bid-ask spreads. This makes the market very inefficient and never quite gets off the ground. Fortunately, that all changed in 1973 when Fisher Black and Myron Scholes created the Black-Scholes Option Pricing Model, which allows us to get a more scientific idea of what an option bet should be worth. It's no surprise that this was the very year the Chicago Board Options Exchange (CBOE) was created since there was now an objective way to readily determine the fair price of a "bet" with an option.

As you get more advanced with your option trading, it is imperative that you use some type of option pricing model. Option pricing models allow traders to judge whether the price of an option reflects a good value. As we will show later, had we used the Black-Scholes Model, there was a big red flag flying above the $4.80 price of the $20 call option.

Let's see how the Black-Scholes Model could have prevented us from taking this loss. We'll rewind back to the beginning when we were looking at the AGIX $20 call for $4.80. Before we make this trade, we need to get a benchmark for value very much like we did for the eBay Iraqi currency. As traders or investors, we cannot just pay the asking price as if it's the price of a lottery ticket. Lottery tickets have no point spread to them. You either win or you lose (mostly lose). You cannot be correct on the numbers for a lottery game and still lose the bet. With options though, it's different because the price we pay has a point spread built into it and we need to understand what that spread is. In order to value this $20 call, we need to estimate the *future volatility* of the stock.

Volatility Moves Sideways

Before we show you how to estimate the future volatility, we need to take a short detour here and explain a very important characteristic about volatility. That is, *volatility tends to move sideways over time.* For example, Figure 6-10 shows an 18-year history of the Volatility Index, or VIX, which measures the volatility of the S&P 500 Index. Although the index has risen substantially over this time period, notice that the volatility chart just moves sideways.

Figure 6-10: Volatility Index (VIX)

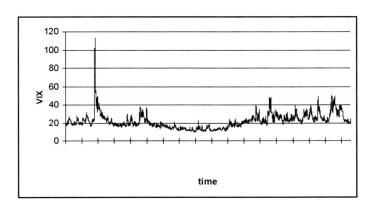

This sideways characteristic of volatility is about the only constant in options trading and that's why it's so important to understand. When volatility rises, there's a tendency for it to fall and vice versa. This shows that there is some long-term average that the volatility oscillates around. The tendency for volatility to fall toward the long-term average is called *mean reversion*. That is, volatility tends to revert to the mean (average). Mean reversion is nothing new and occurs in many types of events, not just options trading. In order to understand the mechanics of mean reversion let's take a look at a well-known, and rather intriguing mystery known as the Sports Illustrated Jinx.

The Sports Illustrated Jinx is a marvel well-known to professional athletes. The jinx states that if a professional athlete makes the cover of *Sports Illustrated*, they have just been jinxed and their performance is headed for a slump. There has been a very long (and quite convincing) history of this ever since *Sports Illustrated* was first published. The jinx became so commonly believed that in January 2002, *Sports Illustrated* wanted to publish a feature story about the jinx and asked St. Louis Rams quarterback Kurt Warner to pose on the front cover holding a black cat. But Warner refused so they shot the cover with the black cat by itself with the intriguing caption: "The Cover that No One Would Pose for. Is the SI Jinx for Real?"

Figure 6-11

It certainly sounds like it's no tribute to be an athlete featured on the cover of *Sports Illustrated*. But let's look at this phenomenon in another light. Figure 6-12 shows baseball superstar Mark McGwire made the October 1998 cover by hitting his 70th homerun of the season:

Figure 6-12

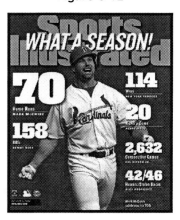

This was a feat that had never been done before in history. It was so remarkable, in fact, that it landed him on the cover of *Sports Illustrated*. So how many homeruns should we expect from him next season, 71? And then 72 the following season? Of course not. This was an all-time record high – that's why he made the cover of the magazine (you don't make the cover of *Sports Illustrated* by having an average season.) Upon some thought you'll realize that we should not expect him to outperform that record next season but, instead, fall back toward his long-run average. And he did, in fact, hit 65, 32, and 29 homeruns in the following three years – right in line with his long-term average of 35 homeruns per season.

Mathematician and author John Allen Paulos came up with a brilliant way to show that the Sports Illustrated Jinx is nothing but mean reversion at work and not an apparent slump as it appears. He suggests that they take the player with the *worst* record of the season and place his picture…on the *back* cover. He's quite certain that you will see an increase in their performance the following season. So whether you're the best player on the front cover or the worst player on the back, we should expect both players' averages to move toward the center. The bottom line is this: Anytime an extreme event happens, whether good or bad, chances are that following events will be less extreme, not more.

Figure 6-10 shows that the VIX tends to bounce back and forth between 20% and 40% most of the time. When it moves significantly outside of this range, we should expect it to revert back to the average rather than to continue to rise or fall. That's why the overall volatility trend moves sideways. We should not expect to see volatility rise month after month anymore than we should expect Mark McGwire to continually outperform his record each season. Instead, we should expect extreme events to be followed by less extreme events.

Using Volatility

Now that you understand volatility, let's see if there is a way we can use this sideways characteristic to gauge the value of an option. Let's go back to the AGIX trade we discussed at the beginning of the chapter. Figure 6-6 showed us that the $20 call was priced at $4.80. But we also said that there can be significant differences between an option's price and its value. How do we check the value? We must compare the current price with past volatilities. *Before we buy this (or any) option, we need to check the past volatility of the underlying stock.*

Most option brokers supply this information if you have an account with them. However, if they do not, there is a way to find some basic information free of charge. You can go to www.ivolatility.com and Figure 6-13 shows what you will see on the front page:

Figure 6-13

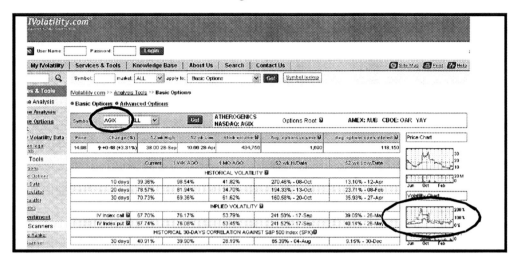

If you type the option symbol in the box shown by the upper circle and then click on the chart in the lower circle, it will take you to the moving average of the volatility of that stock. As a general rule, you'll want to match (at least closely) the volatility moving average to the expiration of the option. In this example, the AGIX $20 call had 29 days until expiration so we'd want to use a 30-day moving average, which is one of the standard time frames available from this website. Figure 6-14 shows the 30-day volatility moving average for AGIX over the previous year (9/16/2004 to 9/16/2004):

Figure 6-14: 30-day Volatility for AGIX

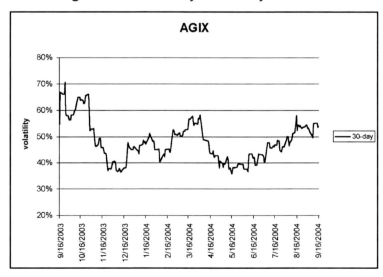

It's important to understand how to interpret this chart. Remember, this is not a price chart on AGIX; it's a chart of the volatility. To create this chart, the computer takes the first 30 days, calculates the volatility number, and then plots that number as a single point on the chart. Next, it takes days 2 through 31, finds the volatility number, and then plots that number as a single point on the chart. This process continues for all 30-day groups in the data. When it's done, all the dots are connected and you're left with a fluctuating line as shown in Figure 6-14.

You can see the highest 30-day group had a volatility of about 70% and the lowest around 35%. The current level is about 55%. The million dollar question now is which volatility should we expect over the next thirty days? In other words, which volatility should we use to determine the value of the AGIX $20 call?

Figure 6-14 shows us a yearly *historic* range but we need an estimate for the future – the *next* 30 days. Many traders use the *current* volatility level based on a simple theory the next thirty days should be about like the last thirty days. To understand this theory a little better, think of the weather. Our temperatures range from lows in the winter to highs in the summer. However, these temperatures are not random. We do not expect it to be 90 degrees and hot one day and then have snow on the ground the next. Instead, we observe that tomorrow's weather is about the same as today's. Weather changes slowly over time but any given small block of time has very similar temperatures. Under this theory, we should expect the next thirty days to have a volatility about like the last thirty days.

As Figure 6-14 shows, the current level is 55% and we may wish to use that as a future volatility estimate for the Black-Scholes Model. Although 55% is one estimate, it is not the only one we could use. Remember, volatility is the only true unknown in the Black-Scholes Model and now you see why – volatility does not stay constant. However, most option traders would agree the estimate you choose should be fairly representative of the average moves we observe in the chart.

Let's assume we decide to use 55% for our volatility estimate and see what the Black-Scholes Model says about this $20 call option. We know the current stock price is $18.81, we're interested in buying is the $20 strike, there are 29 days until expiration, and we're using 55% as a future estimate of volatility. One of the nice features about the CBOEs Black-Scholes Model is that it will find the current risk-free interest rate based on T-bills with the same maturity as the option so this is not even a number you need to look up. At this time, the risk-free rate was 2.42%. Figure 6-15 shows the fair value of this call option is just over 70 cents:

Figure 6-15: Fair Value of the AGIX $20 Call Option Assuming 55% Volatility

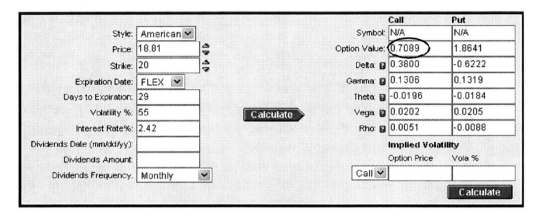

As a reminder, this means if we were able to take this exact trade over and over hundreds of times, we would just break even by paying 70 cents – assuming our volatility assumption in the model is correct.

Despite the fact that we do not know what the future volatility will be, we do have reason to believe our estimate of 55% should be reasonably close to the truth. So now we have a benchmark for value just as we did with the Iraqi currency. The open market told us the currency was worth $680 while the asking price on eBay was $990 so we knew that was a price to avoid. In a similar way, we have good reason to believe that 70 cents is a reasonable price to pay for the $20 call but the market asking price is $4.80.

Clearly, there is a discrepancy between what we think the call is worth when compared to the market price. In other words, the price of the option appears to be far greater than the value to us. What is causing this discrepancy? There's only one factor that we can change and that is volatility. Because the market must be using the same stock price, exercise price, time to expiration, dividends, and risk-free rate (at least reasonably close) this only means that the market's volatility estimate is different from ours.

This is where an option pricing model, such as the Black-Scholes, can really help with trading. Our volatility estimate is different from the market's estimate but how far off? If we had used 56% instead of 55% would we be closer in price?

Or would we have to drastically increase it to, say 800%, in order to match the market's estimate? This question is difficult to answer until you get a feel for how sensitive an option's price is to changes in volatility. And that's difficult to do since that depends on the time to expiration and strike price. That's where a pricing model such as the Black-Scholes really helps.

We can find the volatility estimate the market is using in one of two ways. First, we could gradually increase the volatility number in Figure 6-15 from 55% until the call's price equals $4.80 (we know to increase volatility since higher volatilities equate to higher option prices). Whatever volatility makes the price equal, $4.80 must be the one that the market is using to price the option.

Fortunately, there is an easier way. We can find out which volatility estimate the market is using by simply entering the $4.80 asking price into the "implied volatility" section in the lower right hand corner of the calculator, which is circled in Figure 6-16. (Make sure you also select the correct type of option from the drop down menu. In this case, we need to select "call"). After we hit the calculate bar below, the calculator shows the market is using a whopping volatility estimate of 251%!

Figure 6-16: Implied Volatility of the AGIX $20 Call

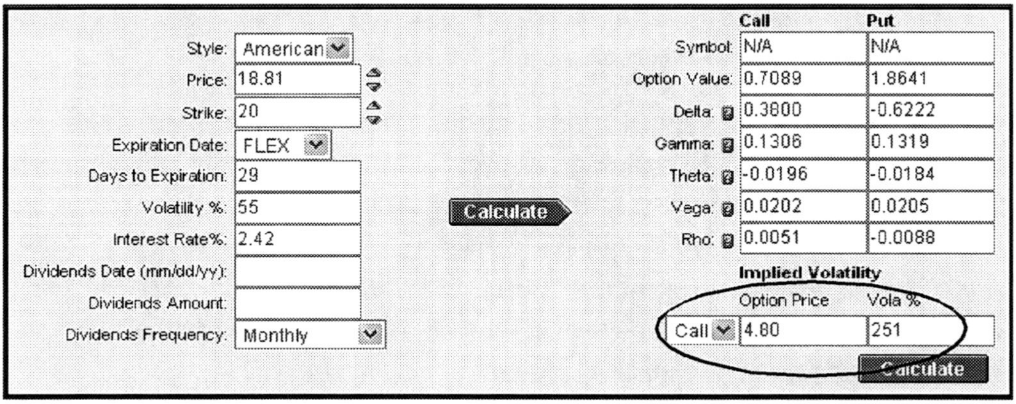

Because the market is willing to pay $4.80, we mathematically backed into the volatility and found they are using 251% to value the option. As a check, you could type 251% into the "Volatility %" field on the left side of the calculator (where we previously typed 55%) and the call's value would jump from 70 cents to $4.80. In other words, a volatility of 251% is required to make the option's price equal to $4.80. It's consequently called the *implied volatility* of the option since that is the volatility implied by the market just by the fact they are willing to pay $4.80 for the option.

Now, as option traders, we need to make a decision: Does this seem to be a reasonable estimate of volatility? After checking the volatility over the past year (or longer) we find it doesn't seem to be in line with any of the volatilities we've seen in the past. Further, we know volatility reverts to the mean. This does not mean that it's impossible to make money with this option but rather that the odds are stacked very much against us. It's like paying $1.50 to make $1 at the flip of a coin. It is a trade we're better off avoiding.

If you pay $4.80 for this option, you are probably overpaying for the option. Sure, there's a chance that the stock takes off like a rocket and you make money. After all, there is a tremendous amount of bullish news on the stock at this time. However, if you pay $4.80, you are facing an enormous point spread that is unlike any point spread we've ever seen in the stock. In our Super Bowl example, it would be like betting on the Patriots with a 30-point spread. Even if the volatility in the stock did rise to 251%, you can be reasonably certain that it will fall back to its average. If the volatility hits 251%, that's like Mark McGwire hitting his 70th homerun and we should not expect it to maintain that level much less rise above it. Instead, we should expect it to fall. And if it falls, it will drag down the option's price thus causing you to lose even if the stock's price rises.

That's exactly what happened with the AGIX trade. Figure 6-17 shows the stock did rise from $18.81 to a high of over $37, which certainly had a positive impact on the option's price. However, during that same time, the volatility fell from a level of about 260% right back down to the long-run average of 55%, which is what we used to value the option. This fall in volatility had a negative impact on the option's price. We ended up with a tug-of-war contest between the stock's price rising and the volatility falling.

Figure 6-17: Volatility was Falling as the Stock Price was Rising

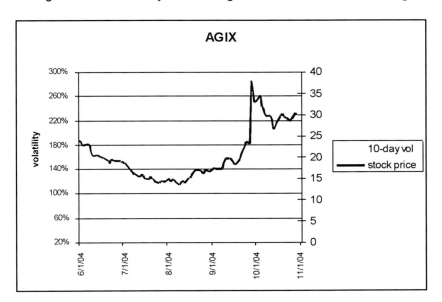

The falling volatility is what caused the loss on the AGIX $20 call even though the stock's price went up. Remember, option prices (calls and puts) get cheaper as volatility falls.

It's interesting to note the 30-day volatility did, in fact, rise to about 260% so the market was pretty good, in this instance, at guessing the future volatility. While they correctly guessed the volatility, they were not able to prevent the drastic mean reversion you see in Figure 6-17. (In Figure 6-17, we are using a 10-day moving average so you can see how quickly it fell since shorter-term volatilities are more sensitive to changes.)

The net result between these two forces was an overall loss at the time the quotes in Figure 6-7 were taken. Now, this does not mean the $20 call never became profitable. In this case, it did become profitable days later once the stock reached the higher price levels. The point we're trying to make is that at the time the quotes in Figure 6-7 were taken, the stock price had risen but the option's price had fallen. It's the timing of the movements between stock price and volatility that determine whether or not the trade will be profitable. Unfortunately, that's something we will never know until it's time to exit the trade.

In this example, it's also possible that AGIX may never have moved much higher than the $21.18 price in Figure 6-7 thus leaving the $20 call as an everlasting losing option. If AGIX never reached much higher than $21.18, the buyer of the $20 call would have paid $4.80 and never had a chance to sell it for a higher price. The decision to hold the option becomes a big dilemma for option traders. If you had purchased the $20 call for $4.80 and saw it trading for $4.70 with the stock significantly higher, would you continue to hold it? If so, everyday you hold it with no movement in the stock leads to bigger losses due to time decay. Further, everyday that volatility drops the losses are compounded. If the stock's price doesn't move, option traders have two potential forces that could drag down the price of their option – time decay and volatility. The decision to hold the option in hopes for profitability can become very costly.

Time Decay?

Many traders believe the AGIX $20 call lost money simply because of time decay. In fact, most traders believe that anytime you find an option whose value is less today than it was previously must be due to time decay (assuming the stock's price is about the same). You must remember that there are two forces acting on the option's price at all times – stock price and volatility. (Actually, there are other forces as shown in the Black-Scholes Model but they are relatively insignificant compared to these two.)

Find it hard to believe? Take a look at Figures 6-18, which shows the same set of eBay quotes taken seven days apart:

Figure 6-18

EBAY   **39.15**   **-0.27**

Oct 13, 2005 @ 14:13 ET (Data 15 Minutes Delayed)   **Bid** 39.15   **Ask** 39.16   **Size** 48x25   **Vol** 8295084

Calls	Last Sale	Net	Bid	Ask	Vol	Open Int	Puts	Last Sale	Net	Bid	Ask	Vol	Open Int
05 Oct 32.50 (XBA JZ-E)	8.40	pc	6.7	6.80	0	1458	05 Oct 32.50 (XBA VZ-E)	0.05	pc	0	0.10	0	7509
05 Oct 35.00 (XBA JG-E)	4.50	-0.40	4.30	4.50	4	6211	05 Oct 35.00 (XBA VG-E)	0.20	+0.05	0.20	0.25	15	17973
05 Oct 37.50 (XBA JU-E)	2.35	-0.35	2.35	2.45	60	20011	05 Oct 37.50 (XBA VU-E)	0.75	+0.20	0.65	0.75	61	19029
05 Oct 40.00 (XBA JH-E)	1.05	-0.20	1.00	1.05	105	50611	05 Oct 40.00 (XBA VH-E)	2.00	+0.35	1.80	1.90	45	17680
05 Nov 32.50 (XBA KZ-E)	7.40	-1.00	7.00	7.20	75	96	05 Nov 32.50 (XBA WZ-E)	0.20	pc	0.25	0.35	0	1263
05 Nov 35.00 (XBA KG-E)	5.20	pc	4.90	5.00	0	668	05 Nov 35.00 (XBA WG-E)	0.55	pc	0.60	0.70	0	1637
05 Nov 37.50 (XBA KU-E)	3.60	pc	3.10	3.20	0	7508	05 Nov 37.50 (XBA WU-E)	1.45	+0.30	1.30	1.40	4	4520
05 Nov 40.00 (XBA KH-E)	1.80	-0.25	1.80	1.90	564	14956	05 Nov 40.00 (XBA WH-E)	2.30	-0.05	2.50	2.60	52	5850

EBAY   **39.15**   **-2.86**

Oct 20, 2005 @ 16:18 ET (Data 15 Minutes Delayed)   **Bid** 39.55   **Ask** 39.08   **Size** 5x4   **Vol** 42056876

Calls	Last Sale	Net	Bid	Ask	Vol	Open Int	Puts	Last Sale	Net	Bid	Ask	Vol	Open Int
05 Oct 32.50 (XBA JZ-E)	7.40	+0.20	6.7	6.90	50	1444	05 Oct 32.50 (XBA VZ-E)	0.05	pc	0	0.05	0	7667
05 Oct 35.00 (XBA JG-E)	4.80	-2.20	4.20	4.40	80	5732	05 Oct 35.00 (XBA VG-E)	0.05	-0.05	0	0.05	20	18849
05 Oct 37.50 (XBA JU-E)	1.60	-3.00	1.75	1.90	275	18849	05 Oct 37.50 (XBA VU-E)	0.05	-0.10	0	0.10	247	26829
05 Oct 40.00 (XBA JH-E)	0.10	-2.30	0.05	0.20	4139	49640	05 Oct 40.00 (XBA VH-E)	1.00	+0.40	0.75	0.90	7824	27316
05 Nov 32.50 (XBA KZ-E)	9.40	pc	6.80	7.10	0	214	05 Nov 32.50 (XBA WZ-E)	0.10	-0.05	0.10	0.20	150	1369
05 Nov 35.00 (XBA KG-E)	4.70	-2.10	4.60	4.80	41	748	05 Nov 35.00 (XBA WG-E)	0.30	+0.10	0.25	0.40	1577	2376
05 Nov 37.50 (XBA KU-E)	2.85	-2.15	2.60	2.80	276	7661	05 Nov 37.50 (XBA WU-E)	0.80	+0.25	0.80	0.90	175	8245
05 Nov 40.00 (XBA KH-E)	1.30	-1.90	1.20	1.40	820	17350	05 Nov 40.00 (XBA WH-E)	2.00	+0.80	2.00	2.00	680	10371

Notice the stock price is identical for both days. However, the asking price for the October $32.50 is higher on October 20 than on October 13! How can that happen? Even though seven days have passed, the perceived volatility of the future stock prices has increased. (You can see the stock was down $2.86 on the second day, which showed higher price changes than in recent history.) The amount of that volatility increase was more than enough to offset the loss from time decay. Remember, an option's price can change for reasons other than time and stock price movements. But if you don't understand the role of volatility, it's easy to think that something is wrong with the quotes.

Let's go back to our AGIX $20 call and see if time decay was the culprit in creating the loss. First, let's define what we mean by time decay. Time decay means that time has been subtracted from the life of the option and therefore the option must be worth less money, *assuming all other factors are the same.* We can use the Black-Scholes Model to see if time decay was the culprit. Figure 6-19 shows that if we use 251% volatility then the price of the call is $4.80, which was the market price at the time we considered buying the $20 call:

Figure 6-19: $20 Call is Worth $4.80 at 251% Volatility

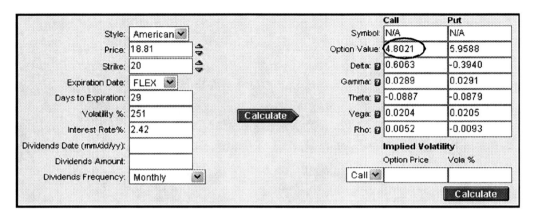

If we just change the "Days to Expiration" from 29 to 23 you will see the effect of time decay:

Figure 6-20: The Value of the $20 Call Six Days Later
(Assuming all other Factors Constant)

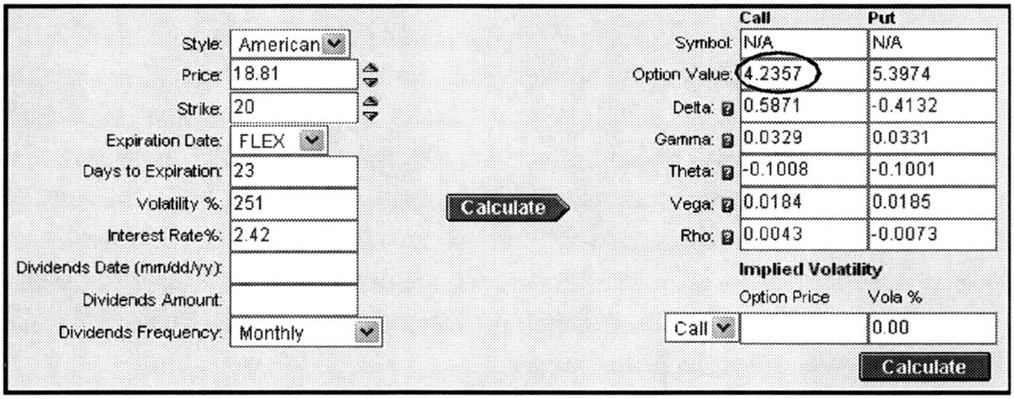

You can see that the $20 call price would have dropped from $4.80 to $4.23. That's the effect on the option by the passage of six days' time. You would only have lost 57 cents if all other factors remained the same. However, during that time, all else did not stay constant because the stock's price rose from $18.81 to $21.18. Figure 6-21 shows what the $20 call would be worth if we increase the stock price to $21.18 while leaving 23 days remaining until expiration:

Figure 6-21: Value of $20 Call Six Days Later
(Assuming all other Factors Constant)

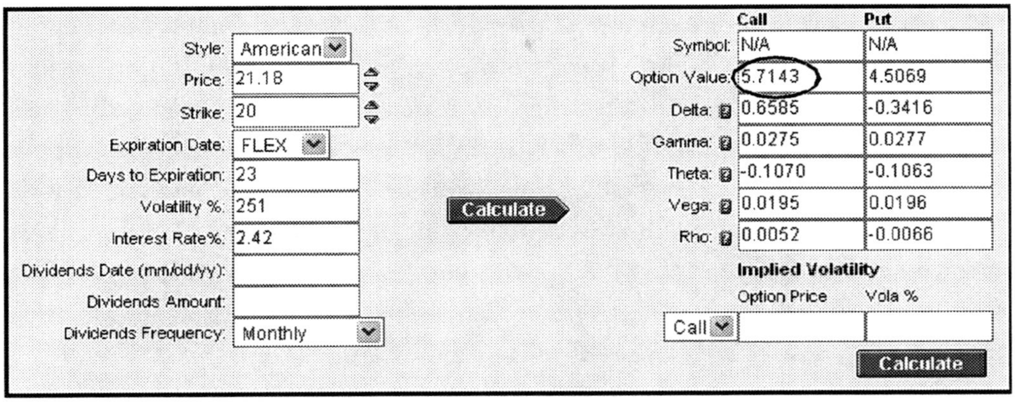

The $20 call would not be in for a loss because the model shows us it would have been worth $5.71 and we paid $4.80. So the fact that time decayed by six days was not the culprit of the loss on the AGIX $20 call. You cannot just look at an option whose price is lower in the future and necessarily claim it's due to time decay.

So if the $20 call should be worth $5.71, why was it bidding only $4.70? The only variable that we could possibly change is volatility. What is the volatility necessary to create a $4.70 bid price? Figure 6-22 shows that an implied volatility of about 200% (199.45%) creates a $4.70 call price. This shows the reason the $20 call lost money was not because of time decay but rather that the implied volatility fell from 251% to 200% in six days.

Figure 6-22: Falling Volatility was the Reason for the
Loss on the $20 Call

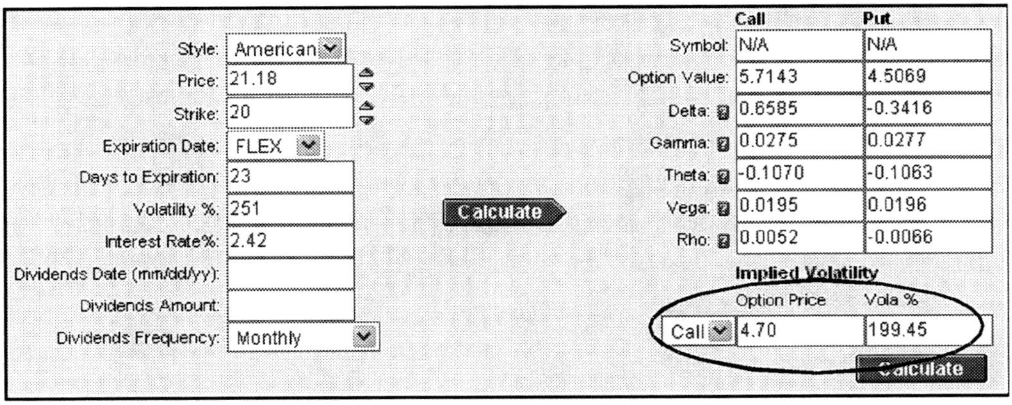

The Black-Scholes Model allowed us to see the volatilities the market was using to price the $20 call. Had we not used the model, all we'd see is the $4.80 call price and have to make our decision on which option to buy based on our belief about the *direction* of the stock. But as we've seen, there's more to profiting on options than correctly guessing on the direction. We must also guess how quickly the stock will move. Had AGIX moved from $18.81 to $21.18 the next day, there's no doubt the call would have been profitable. But it took six days to get there and that's a different story. Although that may sound like a negligible amount of time, it's a lot once you understand that the $4.80 price was extraordinarily high to begin with. And extraordinarily high priced options have a lot of premium to decay. Their prices can fall rapidly with decreases in time and volatility.

Creating a Winning Trade

We've just demonstrated with a real-life example that option trading requires more than a directional belief about the underlying stock. In other words, just because you may be bullish does not mean buying calls is the right strategy to capitalize on that outlook. The reason is, as we previously learned, long option positions have a "point spread" built into them in the form of a time premium. If that time premium is too high, we can lose on the option even though the stock price may rise.

In order to trade options successfully, you have to remember they are two-dimensional assets. If your only opinion is that you are bullish on the stock, you may be better off just buying the stock since it is a one-dimensional asset. But if you want to use options, having an opinion on the direction of the stock is certainly part of the puzzle but we also need to have an opinion on the volatility level. Using our football example, just because we may think the Patriots will win does not necessarily mean we should bet on them. We need to know what the point spread is before we take the bet. If we feel the point spread is too big, we would be better off betting against the Patriots even though we think they'll win. In the same way, we cannot just believe that AGIX is moving higher and buy the call options until we understand the point spread facing us. That is, we must have an opinion on the volatility.

In this example, we were bullish on AGIX and, as we have discovered, it appears that volatility is too high. We believe volatility will be 55% over the next 30 days but the market is pricing the $20 call at 251%. In addition, volatility has never been remotely close to 251% in the past. Because we believe volatility is too high, the price must be too high (and the point spread is too big). That is, although we think the stock will rise, we're not so sure it will rise past $18.81 + $4.80 = $23.61 at expiration. Remember, this is the "at expiration" break even point. You could certainly make money on this option even if the stock never reaches $23.61 – but the stock has got to move quickly.

Now, if the point spread is too high, do we want to be the buyer or seller of the bet? Obviously, we want to be the seller. In order to use options to make a bullish play on AGIX, in this example, we'll need to be the seller of the option.

On the surface, many traders erroneously think that if the time premium is too high then we should simply sell options, whether calls or puts, but that's not necessarily true. The options appear to be priced at astronomical volatility levels but it is possible there is good reason. Remember, there is some potentially powerful news circulating on the stock at this time. If we sell the call and the stock's price jumps much higher, we could end up with devastating losses. So we don't necessarily want to sell calls "just because" volatility is high. Also remember that selling calls is contrary to our directional outlook. In this example, we are bullish on AGIX but selling calls is a bearish strategy.

In order to make a successful trade, we must pick a strategy that properly aligns both beliefs – direction and volatility. Always remember that options are two-dimensional assets and we must be right on both counts. We must take into account our beliefs on the direction of the stock *and* the volatility of the options. In this case, our beliefs are:

- **Direction** = Bullish on the stock

- **Volatility** = Option volatility is too high (need to be the seller)

How can we create a bullish trade by selling an option? We need to *sell puts*. A long put is bearish since it makes money if the stock falls. A short put, being on the opposite side of the trade of a long put, is bullish. Most traders who are bullish are tempted to immediately reach for the long calls. It just seems to makes sense because of the unlimited gains afforded by long calls. If we were to buy calls, we could make unlimited gains but would be facing an unrealistically large point spread.

A short put also makes money if the stock rises. But more importantly, short puts will also make money if the stock stands still. And there's the big difference between long calls and short puts. *A long call option needs the stock to move.* But by selling puts, we can only make a limited gain; however, *we do not need the stock to move.* We don't need to have the stock rise for us to make money; we just can't have it fall. We have eliminated the speed component of the option.

So by selling a put, we are taking a bullish position and are not exposed to the large point spread. We have aligned both directional and volatility outlooks correctly. How would we have done if we had sold puts? Figure 6-23 is a reprint of the before and after quotes on AGIX (Figures 6-6 and 6-7) and you can see that we could have sold the $20 puts for $5.50 and bought them back for $3.90, which is a winning trade:

Figure 6-23

AGIX (Nasdaq)   18.81   -0.08
Sep 16,2004 @ 10:10 ET (Data 15 Minutes Delayed)   Bid 18.80 Ask 18.81 Size 14x6 Vol 29728

Calls	Last Sale	Net	Bid	Ask	Vol	Open Int	Puts	Last Sale	Net	Bid	Ask	Vol	Open Int
04 Oct 15 (AUB JC-E)	6.70	pc	6.20	6.70	0	1103	04 Oct 15 (AUB VC-E)	2.50	pc	2.50	2.90	0	1158
04 Oct 17.50 (AUB JW-E)	5.10	pc	5.10	5.60	0	1972	04 Oct 17.50 (AUB VW-E)	3.90	pc	3.90	4.30	0	1150
04 Oct 20.00 (AUB JD-E)	4.80	-.10	4.40	4.80	25	3833	04 Oct 20.00 (AUB VD-E)	5.40	pc	5.50	6.00	0	1507

AGIX (Nasdaq)   21.18   +0.46
Sep 22,2004 @ 10:37 ET (Data 15 Minutes Delayed)   Bid 21.17 Ask 21.19 Size 5x1 Vol 240954

Calls	Last Sale	Net	Bid	Ask	Vol	Open Int	Puts	Last Sale	Net	Bid	Ask	Vol	Open Int
04 Oct 15 (AUB JC-E)	7.50	pc	7.30	7.80	0	2280	04 Oct 15 (AUB VC-E)	1.50	-.10	1.30	1.55	5	1505
04 Oct 17.50 (AUB JW-E)	6.10	-.10	5.80	6.30	13	6106	04 Oct 17.50 (AUB VW-E)	2.45	-.10	2.20	2.60	4	4594
04 Oct 20.00 (AUB JD-E)	4.80	-.20	4.70	5.10	7	510	04 Oct 20.00 (AUB VD-E)	3.90	pc	3.50	3.90	0	1583

Notice that just because volatility was high, we cannot just arbitrarily sell calls or puts and necessarily make money. For example, if we had sold the $20 calls, Figure 6-23 shows we would have sold them for $4.40 and bought them back for $5.10 for a loss. Traders who sold these calls were correct for selling options because volatility was so high. However, they were wrong about the direction of the stock – the stock went up. And again, just because we believe the stock will rise, that doesn't mean we can immediately jump to conclusions and buy calls. As we showed before, the traders that bought the $20 calls paid $4.80 and sold for $4.70. They were correct on the direction but wrong about the volatility. It is only the traders who were correct on direction *and* volatility that made the winning trade; it was the traders who sold puts.

Is the sale of the $20 puts the only winning trade in the Figure 6-23 matrix? No, the trader who bought the $15 calls could have paid $6.70 and sold them for $7.30. We could also have purchased the $17.50 calls for $5.60 and sold for $5.80. Why were the $15 and $17.50 calls profitable while the $20 call was not? Hopefully, you are starting to understand why. The $15 and $17.50 calls have less time premium in them because they are in-the-money. This means they have a smaller point spread (break even point) and are not subjected to the "speed" component of the option like the at-the-money or out-of-the-money options. If you remember from Chapter Two, in-the-money options are less risky and now you clearly see why. They are not subjected to the volatility component in quite the same way as their riskier at-the-money or out-of-the-money counterparts and can make money even if volatility falls.

Regardless, please note the trade that produced the *biggest* profit was the one that made best use of direction and volatility – it was the sale of the $20 puts. The sale of any of the puts made money but not as much as the $20 puts since they had the highest time premium. Table 6-24 shows all of the long call and short put trades and their profits or losses:

Table 6-24

Trade	Bought	Sold	Profit/Loss
Long $15 call	$6.70	$7.30	+60 cents
Long $17.50 call	$5.60	$5.80	+20 cents
Long $20 call	$4.80	$4.70	-10 cents
Short $15 put	$2.50	$1.55	+95 cents
Short $17.50 put	$3.90	$2.60	+1.30
Short $20 put	**$5.50**	**$3.90**	**+$1.60**

Volatility is Relative

One of the most important concepts to learn as an option trader is that volatility is relative. If volatility is relative then so are option prices. This simply means you cannot look at an option that is priced low, say $5, and conclude that it must be a good value. In fact, we just found an example of one priced at $4.80 that was a horrible value – even though the price may appear to be relatively cheap. Conversely, we might find an option that is priced high, say $12, that turns out to be a steal. However, you will find countless people, including "professionals" who confuse these issues. For example, here is a sample of an email ad we received for an option training DVD:

Option Advertisement

There is one critical secret to buying options. It's quite simple really... value investing.

When you buy stocks, you look for an undervalued company. The rules are the same for options investors: Buy only undervalued options and sell them only when they're overvalued.

Before you buy any option you need to carefully assess its value to make sure that you're adhering to this easy principle. In my free DVD seminar, I'll tell you how ...

You can see this professional got it wrong too. According to his "simple" rules, you only need to buy an option when it is undervalued and sell it when it is overvalued – just as you do for stocks. Let's assume you run the Black-Scholes Model and find an option priced at $3 that is undervalued so you buy it. Later, it is trading for $1 but, according to the model, is overvalued so you sell it. You can see that paying $3 and selling for $1 is no way to make money even though you bought undervalued options and sold overvalued options. Undervalued and overvalued options are *relative* to your perceptions of future volatility. Value has nothing to do with cheap and expensive in absolute terms.

Which Strike Should I Buy?

Table 6-24 shows that the in-the-money calls ($15 and $17.50 strikes) made profits while the $20 call did not. Once again, this is due to the fact the stock did not rise fast enough for the $20 call to make a profit. In other words, the time value on the $20 call was too high and therefore had more to decay with time. The in-the-money calls, however, had a much smaller time premium so were able to show a profit.

Even though in-the-money calls are less risky that does not mean you shouldn't buy the lowest strike call (or highest strike put) available. The reason is there may be many strikes with high deltas and we only need one that has a sufficiently high delta but not more. The goal is to find a good balance between intrinsic and time values.

As a general rule, if you are buying short-term options, say three months or less, you should look for options with deltas around the 0.80 to 0.85 level. In fact, this delta level is a good rule to always follow regardless of the time frame if you are using options as a stock substitute. However, if you are considering longer-term options, say up to a year, you may be able to get away with using slightly lower deltas. And if you are using options with more than a year's time, you might decide to use an at-the-money option or even slightly out-of-the-money. The reason we mention these different levels is because investors invariably avoid in-the-money calls when they see the prices get expensive in terms of absolute dollars. It's difficult for most traders to buy an option with a price of $20, $30, or higher even though it may be the right thing to do mathematically. So we're not saying to never buy an at-the-money or out-of-the-money option. However, most traders stick with shorter-term options (usually because they're cheaper) and buying deltas below 0.80 is often a huge mistake. For example, Table 6-25 shows option quotes for Dell Computer:

Table 6-25

DELL INC(DELL)						35.62 ● +0.24				

Symbol	Last	Time	Net	Bid	Ask	Reference price	Div freq	Div amt	Historical Volatility
DELL	35.62	14:09:21	+0.24	35.6200	35.6300	35.62			13.900%

Calls						Sep 2005	Puts						
Ticker	Last	T-Val	Delta	Gamma	Theta	Implied Volatility	Strike	Ticker	Last	T-Val	Delta	Gamma	Theta	Implied Volatility
DLQIY	7.9	8.18	1.00	0.000	-0.003	0.00%	27.5	DLQUY	0	-0.00	-0.00	0.000	-0.000	0.50%
DLQIF	6.4	5.68	1.00	0.000	-0.004	84.65%	30.0	DLQUF	0.05	0.00	-0.00	0.000	-0.001	41.03%
DLQIZ	3.4	3.19	1.00	0.000	-0.006	36.40%	32.5	DLQUZ	0.05	0.00	-0.00	0.000	-0.003	24.82%
DLQIG	1.1	0.89	0.73	0.248	-0.011	20.78%	35.0	DLQUG	0.4	0.20	-0.27	0.248	-0.007	20.47%
DLQIT	0.15	0.04	0.07	0.699	-0.024	20.59%	37.5	DLQUT	1.9	1.84	-0.93	0.699	-0.020	17.81%
DLQIH	0.01	0.00	0.00	0.000	-0.062	21.74%	40.0	DLQUH	4.6	4.30	-1.00	0.000	-0.058	44.81%
DLQIS	0.05	0.00	0.00	0.000	-0.153	39.91%	42.5	DLQUS	6.4	6.79	-1.00	0.000	-0.149	0.00%
DLQII	0.05	0.00	0.00	0.000	-0.361	50.22%	45.0	DLQUI	8.3	9.29	-1.00	0.000	-0.357	0.00%

If we were bullish on Dell and wanted to buy a call option, we should look for one with a delta of around 0.80. This delta provides a nice balance between performance and price. For instance, we could buy the $27.50 call, which has a delta of 1.0, which is obviously equivalent to owning the stock (remember, long stock has a delta of one since it rises dollar-for-dollar with itself). However, that $27.50 comes with a price of $7.90 as shown by the last trade. We could therefore do better by purchasing the $30 strike because it also has a delta of 1.0 but only costs $6.40. If both calls provide a delta of 1.0, why pay the extra $1.50 for the $27.50 call? Remember, the key to finding the right strike is to find a good balance between delta and the cost so let's keep looking at higher strikes.

The $32.50 call also has a delta of 1.0 and only costs $3.40. But the $35 call has a delta of 0.73 and costs $1.10; that's the strike we want to trade. It has a sufficiently high delta (near the 0.80 mark we're looking for) without paying the higher prices that come with the lower strikes. It will behave about like a long stock position yet cost a lot less and provide tremendous downside protection.

If your broker does not provide delta values there is a little trick you can use for times when you cannot look up the values on the other sites we mentioned. In Chapter Five, we said that the time value of the call (above the cost of carry) must equal the price of the put. If that's true, then we can look at the put prices for one that is bidding a small amount, say 30 or 40 cents *above the cost of carry* and that should correspond to a sufficiently high delta for the corresponding call. If you are trading relatively short time periods, say 3 months or less, the cost of carry component will not be too great and you can just look for a put with a total value of 30 or 40 cents. In Figure 6-25, you can see that the $35 put was worth 40 cents and that is the same strike as the call we determined to buy by looking at deltas.

How Option Prices are Affected by the Model Factors

The Black-Scholes Model assumes we can fully determine the fair value of an option just by knowing the six factors that go into the model. Up to this point, we have touched on the way option prices behave based on changes in some of these factors. Despite the overlap, Table 6-26 lists all six Black-Scholes Model variables and shows how call and put prices respond to changes in these variables:

Table 6-26

	If this factor is **Increased**:	**Call Price**	**Put Price**
1	Stock Price	▲	▽
2	Exercise Price	▽	▲
3	Risk-Free Rates	▲	▽
4	Volatility	▲	▲
5	Time To Expiration	▲	▲
6	Dividends	▽	▲

The most important thing you can learn from Table 6-26 is that option prices can move for reasons other than changes in the stock's price. Let's run through each of them just to be sure you have the concepts down.

Stock Price

Table 6-26 shows as the stock price increases, the price of a call will increase and the price of the put will decrease with all other factors constant. But after reading this chapter, you should know this is a theoretical statement and you should not be alarmed if your call option is not up even if the underlying stock is trading higher. The reason is that the other factors rarely stay constant. Even though the stock price rises, you could have a decrease in volatility. And if that decrease is big enough, the price of the call option will be down even though the stock is up.

Exercise (or Strike) Price

The exercise price is closely related to the stock price. In fact, they are really just two ways of looking at the same thing. When we were considering movements in the stock price above, we assumed the strike price (as well as all other factors) remained constant. Now, if we hold the stock price constant but change the strike price, we are effectively changing the relative value of the option. That is, we are making it more in-the-money or out-of-the-money. This is just another view of Pricing Principle #1 from Chapter Two. That principle stated that lower strike calls and higher strike puts must be more valuable with all other factors the same.

For example, if we lower the strike price of a call, effectively we are raising the stock price. We are moving the call option more in-the-money. Therefore, rising stock prices (or falling exercise prices) are beneficial for call option holders. Falling stock prices (or rising exercise prices) are good for put holders. Movements in the strike price are no different from movements in the stock's price.

Interest Rates

How interest rates affect calls and puts are a little more difficult to understand. In Chapter Five, we showed that call options are a form of borrowing money by the following rearrangement of put-call parity:

$$C = S - Pv\ (E) + put$$

Once you look at this variation of put-call parity, it should be clear why call options increase with increases in the interest rate. Notice in the above equation the call price equals the stock price minus the present value of the exercise price. As interest rates rise, the present value of the exercise price falls and the right hand side of the equation gets bigger. That is, the price of call options increases. Although this is fairly easy to show mathematically, it is easier to remember if you understand it conceptually so let's look at another line of reasoning.

Say interest rates are very high, perhaps 20%. You have $100,000 in the money-market that you would like to invest in stocks. You can either buy the stocks today or, for a fee, buy a call option which gives you control of the stock but allows you to defer payment. The choice should be easy; buy the call option so you can hang on to your money and continue to earn interest. Investors in the market follow this same line of reasoning and bid the calls higher as interest rates rise.

What about the puts? Puts give you the right to sell your stock, which represents a cash flow into the account, which is nice to have if interest rates are really high. So do you elect to buy puts to defer the sale? No, in fact, you may even *sell* the puts to generate cash into the account so it can earn the high rate of interest. The lack of put buyers (or the increase of put sellers) causes the price of puts to fall.

As with all the other factors, we must remember that these relationships assume that the other factors remain constant, which is rarely the case in the real world. So if interest rates rise suddenly, do not be surprised if your call options decrease in price rather than increase as we have said so far. This is due to the fact that stock prices fall when interest rates rise and falling stock prices correspond with falling call prices. But it should be evident that all factors did not stay the same in this case since we assumed interest rates rose *and* stock prices fell. However, if all factors remain constant and the only thing that changes is an interest rate hike then we will see call prices rise and put prices fall.

Volatility

We have shown that increases in volatility cause increases in call and put prices. The reason had to do with the asymmetrical payoff structures of options. Because increased volatility can only help option prices then the market bids them higher.

Remember this is backward from our normal view of risk. Riskier assets usually have their prices bid down, which is what we discovered in the Pricing Game in Chapter Two. But options are an exception to this principle since they have an asymmetrical payoff structure.

Time to Expiration

This factor is fairly straightforward. Pricing Principle #2 in Chapter Two stated the more time to expiration, the higher the prices of calls and puts. We said earlier an option could be viewed as a bet that the stock will be above the strike price (for calls) or below the strike price (for puts) by expiration. In other words, you are in effect betting the option will have intrinsic value. Because of this, the more time available, the more likely the stock will have intrinsic value.

Dividends

Lastly, we will consider the effect of dividends on calls and puts, which is fairly straightforward too. If a stock pays a dividend, the price of the stock is reduced by the amount of the dividend for the next trading session. The reason the price is reduced is because the company has paid out cash – one of its assets – so the company is now worth less than before it paid the dividend. If the stock price is down and all other factors stay the same, what will happen to the options? Call prices fall and put prices rise with all other factors the same.

Option prices can change for any of the six factors listed in the model and this is what makes option trading more difficult to understand than stock trading. It is for this reason that you should be well aware of these six factors and how they affect option prices.

Some Final Thoughts

This chapter is not meant to teach you how to trade volatility as that is an advanced subject upon which entire books could be written. This is an introduction designed to give you the basic concepts. It's unfair to turn new traders loose into the options arena without letting them know about the volatility component of an option and how that component can adversely affect an option's price.

I remember working for an active trader option team and one day answered the phone only to hear, "Give me the number to the SEC." The client was noticeably upset so I asked what the problem was. The client proceeded to show me a call option he was ready to close out that would result in a loss even though the stock had risen in a short time. He concluded his dispute by saying, "I placed my bet, I was correct, and I demand to be compensated. This is fraud."

I then had a very lengthy conversation with the client about the volatility component of options and, as you can tell from this chapter, is not an easy thing to talk out over the phone. But the client managed to understand the basic concept and said he wished he had been told that when he started trading options. So that's why we've included this chapter. It is meant to alert you to what can happen if you are not aware of volatility or do not take it into account when buying or selling options.

When call option prices fall while stock prices are rising (or when put prices fall while the stock is falling), it is called a *volatility trap*. In trader's lingo, we would say that anybody buying the AGIX $20 call for $4.80 and then wishing to sell it six days later when the stock was trading higher was caught in a volatility trap since they'd only receive $4.70 at that time.

How can you avoid volatility traps when starting out? You should buy in-the-money options. Chapter Two showed that in-the-money options are less risky. Remember that options are two-dimensional assets; you must correctly guess the direction and speed of the underlying stock. Shares of stock, on the other hand, are one-dimensional asset since you only need to determine if it is going to rise or fall. When stock traders become option traders they often buy at-the-money call options (since they are cheaper) as a substitute for the stock. Doing so subjects them to a two-dimensional asset when they are used to trading a one-dimensional asset and that's where the problems begin. When you are starting out, buy in-the-money calls with deltas in the 0.80 to 0.85 range and you will have an asset that behaves about like the stock you're used to trading. They will be more expensive but they are actually less risky. That's a difficult concept to explain to new traders but hopefully this chapter has convinced you that it's true. You cannot beat the laws of probability when trading options but you can use those laws to put the odds on your side by selecting the right strategy and strike price. Understanding volatility is the key.

 Key Concepts

1) Volatility can be thought of as a measure of how far a stock price typically drifts from its average..

2) Volatility is the key component to an option's price.

3) Volatility is the only unknown variable for determining an option's price.

4) The fair value of an option is the price at which you would break even over the long run if you were allowed to buy (sell) it many, many times at that price.

5) The price of an option is in no way related to its value. Very "cheap" options can be grossly overpriced and very "expensive" options can be a steal. It all depends on the volatility.

6) Volatility moves sideways over time.

7) To trade options successfully, you must take direction and volatility into account. If you wish to trade on option based on a directional outlook then use 0.80 to 0.85 deltas.

|||||||||||||||||||||||||||||||||||||||||||||||||||||||||||||||||||||||||||||||||||||||||||||||||||||||

Chapter Six Questions

1) **If a bet is fairly valued then that means that you are expected to:**
   a) Break even over the short run
   b) Lose over the long run
   c) Win over the long run
   d) Break even over the long run

2) **If you pay more than fair value then you are expected to:**
   a) Break even over the short run
   b) Lose over the long run
   c) Win over the long run
   d) Break even over the long run

3) **You run a Black-Scholes calculation and find that the theoretical price of the call option is $3.50. What does this mean?**
   a) If you pay $3.50 for similar calls hundreds of times you'd just break even
   b) If you pay $3.50 or less you will definitely make money
   c) If you pay $3.50 or less you will definitely lose money
   d) If you sell for $3.50 you will definitely make money

An Introduction to Volatility

4) **In order to successfully trade options you must be correct about the underlying stock's direction and:**
    a) Earnings
    b) Speed
    c) Forward P/E ratios
    d) Price to Sales ratios

5) **Over time, volatility tends to move:**
    a) Sideways
    b) Up
    c) Down
    d) There is no discernable pattern

6) **To find the true value of an option with the Black-Scholes Model, we need to know the:**
    a) Forecast volatility
    b) Implied volatility
    c) Future volatility
    d) Historic volatility

7) **If you are bullish and wish to trade options you should:**
    a) Buy calls
    b) Sell puts
    c) Sell calls
    d) Either a or b depending on how quickly you think the stock will move

8) **To reduce the "speed" component of an option, it is advisable to buy options:**
    a) With a delta around 0.80 to 0.85
    b) With a delta near 0.50
    c) With a delta near 0.25
    d) With the lowest delta possible

9) **Whether you feel an option is fairly valued or not depends on your:**
    a) Strike price
    b) Time to expiration

c)   Perception of the future volatility

d)   Broker

10) **If your call (put) option loses money even though the stock is rising (falling) quickly that is most likely due to:**
   a)   Discrepancies in fair value
   b)   Arbitrageurs
   c)   Price manipulation
   d)   Falling volatility

11) **If you buy a put and the stock falls, you:**
   a)   Will at least break even
   b)   Will definitely lose money
   c)   May or may not make money
   d)   Will definitely make money

12) **The fact that volatility measurements tend to move toward the long term average is known as:**
   a)   Mean reversion
   b)   Reverse conversion
   c)   Conversion
   d)   Put-call parity

13) **The time premium on an option can be thought of as the:**
   a)   Point-spread on a bet
   b)   Bid-ask spread
   c)   Fair value
   d)   Delta

14) **A low priced option:**
   a)   Is low risk since there's little to lose
   b)   Is better to buy than a high priced one
   c)   Puts the odds in your favor of making money
   d)   Is not necessarily a good value

15) **How many factors are needed in the Black-Scholes Model to determine the fair value of an option (including dividends)?**
   a)   6
   b)   5

c)   4

d)   3

16) **What happens to the price of a call if interest rates rise assuming all other factors stay the same? Call prices will:**

a)   Rise

b)   Fall

c)   Stay the same

d)   Cannot be determined

17) **What happens to the price of a put if dividends rise assuming all other factors stay the same? Put prices will:**

a)   Rise

b)   Fall

c)   Stay the same

d)   Cannot be determined

18) **What happens to the price of calls and puts if volatility increases?**

a)   Call and put prices rise

b)   Call and put prices fall

c)   Call prices rise; put prices fall

d)   Put prices rise; call prices fall

19) **Increasing the time to expiration has what effect on call and put prices?**

a)   Prices Increase

b)   Prices Decrease

c)   Prices stay the same

d)   Cannot be determined

20) **One of the key differences between long and short options is that:**

a)   Long options need stock price movement to make money; short options do not

b)   Long options do not need stock price movement to make money; short options do

c)   There is no difference between the outlooks for long or short positions

d)   Short calls need stock price movement but short puts do not

Chapter Six - Answers

1)   If a bet is fairly valued then that means that you are expected to:

    d)   Break even over the long run

The fair value of any bet is the price where you are expected to break even over the long run. That is, after hundreds and hundreds of similar bets, you'd walk away no richer or no poorer.

2)   If you pay more than fair value then you are expected to:

    b)   Lose over the long run

If you pay more than the fair value for a bet, you are expected to lose over the long run (after hundreds and hundreds of attempts). If a bet is priced above fair value, you can certainly win it over the short run but not over the long run.

3)   You run a Black-Scholes calculation and find that the theoretical price of the call option is $3.50. What does this mean?

    a)   If you pay $3.50 for similar calls hundreds of times you'd just break even

The theoretical price of any investment (or any bet) is the same thing as the fair value. A call option that has a theoretical value of $3.50 means that if you were to pay $3.50 for hundreds or thousands of similar calls that you'd just break even over the long run. Bear in mind that the theoretical price of an option depends on your perspective of the future volatility. So while the theoretical value of an option does carry a distinct definition, it is impossible to really say what that value is in practice.

4)   In order to successfully trade options you must be correct about the underlying stock's direction and:

    b)   Speed

When trading options, you must not only get the direction of the underlying stock correctly but you must also determine how quickly it will move. It's this second dimension of "speed" or "pace" that separates options from stocks. If you buy a stock, you will make money if it rises today, tomorrow, or next week. This is not true for an option. Long options generally need fast, aggressive moves in the underlying stock to be profitable.

5)   Over time, volatility tends to move:

    a)   Sideways

Volatility tends to move sideways over time due to mean reversion. There is a long run average for volatility so when it rises above this average it tends to fall and vice versa.

6) **To find the true value of an option with the Black-Scholes Model, we need to know the:**

    c)   Future volatility

In order to really know the true value of an option, we need to know the future volatility of the stock. That is, we need to know what the volatility will be over the life of the option. In practice, we substitute a forecasted volatility in for the future volatility. This forecast is usually some type of moving average of the past volatility.

7) **If you are bullish and wish to trade options you should:**

    d)   Either a or b depending on how quickly you think the stock will move

Long calls and short puts both make money as the stock rises so they are therefore bullish instruments. If you think the stock will rise sharply, you may wish to buy the call as that gives you unlimited upside potential but it comes at the expense of time decay. On the other hand, if you sell a put, the stock doesn't need to rise for you to make money; it just cannot fall. The tradeoff is that the gain is limited to the amount of the premium received.

8) **To reduce the "speed" component of an option, it is advisable to buy options:**

    a)   With a delta of around 0.80 to 0.85

The higher the delta, the less time premium is present in the option. And it's the time premium that creates the speed component. If you buy options with relatively high deltas, say 0.80 or higher, then you will not need the stock to move as aggressively for the simple reason that there is relatively little time value on the option. It's advisable for new traders to buy options with deltas of 0.80 or higher for the fact they will behave more like the stock, which is what most people new to options are familiar trading.

9) Whether you feel an option is fairly valued or not depends on your:

c) Perception of the future volatility

As stated in Question 3, your perception of volatility is not a fact so there's no way to say for sure if an option is fairly valued or not. To say that an option is fairly valued means you must make a judgment call as to the volatility used in calculating that fair value. If that volatility seems reasonable then you may feel the option is fairly valued. The fair value of an option depends on your perception of the future volatility.

10) If your call (put) option loses money even though the stock is rising (falling) quickly that is most likely due to:

d) Falling volatility

If the stock is moving quickly and the option is losing money then this is likely due to falling volatility. If the stock were moving slowly, then the option may be losing to time decay. But the question states the stock is rising quickly so we can assume that volatility must be falling.

11) If you buy a put and the stock falls, you:

c) May or may not make money

Whether you make money or not depends on how quickly the stock's price falls. If it falls sharply there is a good chance you'll make money. But if it slowly and steadily falls then there's a chance you won't make money since the option will be gaining intrinsic value but losing value due to time decay. For long options, the speed at which the underlying stock moves is critical.

12) The fact that volatility measurements tend to move toward the long term average is known as:

a) Mean reversion

Mean reversion just states that the data rise and fall toward their long term average.

13) The time premium on an option can be thought of as the:

a) Point-spread on a bet

It's the time premium on the option that creates the speed component. The reason is that you must recoup this time premium by expiration in order to be profitable. In a sense, the time premium acts as a point-spread on a bet since you must beat the spread before making money on the bet.

14) A low priced option:

   d)   Is not necessarily a good value

Just because an option is fairly inexpensive does not mean it's a good value. To the contrary, it could be greatly overpriced. Whether an option is a good deal or not depends on the volatility assumption that went into pricing it. If that volatility assumption appears to be way out of line to the high side then the option is considered to be overpriced even though it is relatively cheap. When option traders speak of "cheap" or "expensive" they are referring to volatility and not the absolute price.

15) How many factors are needed in the Black-Scholes Model to determine the fair value of an option (including dividends)?

   a)   6

The six factors are the stock price, exercise price, risk-free interest rate, time to expiration, dividends, and volatility.

16) What happens to the price of a call if interest rates rise assuming all other factors stay the same? Call prices will:

   a)   Rise

Rising interest rates will increase call option prices assuming all other factors stay the same. Remember though, this may not be what you experience in the real world. When interest rates rise, stock prices generally fall, which will also drag down options prices. But assuming all factors remain the same (of which stock prices would be included) then rising interest rates will increase call option prices.

17) What happens to the price of a put if dividends rise assuming all other factors stay the same? Put prices will:

   a)   Rise

As dividends rise, the price of the underlying stock will fall and that means put option prices will fall as well. As with Question 16, we must remember this assumes all other factors remain the same. In the real world, rising dividends will generally increase stock prices, which would decrease put prices.

18) What happens to the price of calls and puts if volatility increases?

   a)   Call and put prices rise

Rising volatility creates higher call and put prices. The reason is that higher volatility creates the potential for higher (or lower) stock prices and that means call and put options have a greater chance of being profitable so the market bids their prices higher. Remember that higher volatility would normally bring asset prices down but because options have asymmetrical payoffs their prices will rise with increased volatility.

19) Increasing the time to expiration has what effect on call and put prices?

 a) Prices Increase

More time to expiration means that the stock has more time to either rise or fall, which is good for calls and puts. This means call and put prices will rise as the time to expiration increases.

20) One of the key differences between long and short options is that:

 a) Long options need stock price movement to make money; short options do not

Option buyers must pay a time premium and this time premium must be recouped before a profit can be made. Long options therefore need the stock to move before a profit can be made. Short positions collect a premium up front, which is also the maximum profit they can make on the trade. Short positions do not need for the stock to move but, instead, just cannot have it move adversely.

Chapter Seven

Covered Calls

Up to this point, we have covered many topics on options and are now ready to put those concepts to use so you can understand and appreciate some basic option strategies. Before we get started though, it's imperative to reiterate that all strategies are about tradeoffs. Chapter Three showed us by looking at a profit and loss diagrams, we can find the tradeoffs between any two strategies. Strategies are tools used to take advantage of particular opportunities much like hammers, saws, and screwdrivers for a carpenter. No option trader should tell you one strategy is superior to another any more than a carpenter should tell you that one tool is better than another. It depends on what you're trying to accomplish. Each strategy presents a unique set of risks and rewards and it is up to you to decide which is best for the opportunity you have uncovered.

There are several basic strategies and it's difficult to say which is the easiest to start with. Many books start with long calls and long puts since they represent rights. However, we are going to start with a strategy called the *covered call* since it represents a good starting point for most option traders. The reason is that it is one of many "stock friendly" strategies, which means this strategy requires you to own stock. Further, covered calls are initiated by purchasing stock and often exited by selling stock, which also makes it easy for investors to understand. Since you probably already own stocks, the covered call represents an easy way to explore options.

However, covered calls can contain an unforeseen risk depending on subtle changes in the way the strategy is carried out. Covered calls can be a wonderful strategy if used properly so it is critical that you understand the principles and risks described in this book before attempting to make use of this popular strategy and find if it's right for you.

Covered Call Strategy

When you enter into a covered call, you buy the stock and then sell (or write) a call option against those shares. The shares of stock can be purchased at the same time the call is written or the shares may have been sitting in your account for some time. As long as you own shares, you can write calls against them.

The investor writes calls in a 1:1 ratio against the stock. For example, if you own 100 shares, you'd write one contract, 200 shares and you'd write two contracts, 300 shares and you'd write three contracts and so on. For every 100 shares of stock, you write one call option. Be careful that you are not writing an option that controls more than 100 shares. One of the biggest mistakes that investors make is to find option premiums that look relatively high and then sell them against 100 shares of their stock. Many times they find out the reason the option's price looked so enticing is because it controlled 150 shares. (Naturally, if you owned 150 shares then you could certainly write such an option against them.) Just be sure that you own the same number of shares as the amount you are giving someone the right to buy.

We'll find out later there may be times where you'd want to write fewer calls against your shares but you will never write more. For example, if you own 400 shares of stock, you may decide to write only three contracts (rather than four) but you would never write more for reasons we'll talk about shortly.

For every call option you sell, you have the *potential obligation* to sell 100 shares of stock for the strike price. It is a potential obligation because it is up to the long call holder to decide if he wishes to exercise those calls and buy your shares. Just because you write a call does not in any way guarantee you will sell your shares; it just locks you into the obligation to sell your shares if the long position decides to buy. Of course, in exchange for accepting that obligation, you are paid a fee that is yours to keep regardless of what happens.

Why is it called a "covered" call? If you sell a call option without owning the shares of stock that is called a "naked" call since you do not have the shares in your account to deliver. If you are assigned on a naked call and forced to sell 100 shares of stock, you must go into the open market and buy those shares and there is no telling what that price might be! Because of this, naked call writing is considered to be among the riskiest of all option strategies since there is no limit as to how high a stock's price can rise. This is why you never write contracts that represent a greater number of shares than what you own (such as writing 5 contracts against 400 shares). By doing so, you are never exposed to this potentially devastating upside risk.

However, by selling call options in proportion to the number of shares you own the upside risk is eliminated since you already own the shares. In other words, the upside risk of naked call writing is "covered" because you will always be able to deliver the shares at a known cost. You have already paid for those shares and that cost will never change.

The important point to understand now is that *selling calls creates the potential obligation to sell your shares for the strike price*. For example, if you buy 100 shares of ABC stock for $50 and then write a $55 call against them, you have the potential obligation to sell those shares for $55 no matter how high that stock may be trading. At some point though, every investor's goal is to sell the shares so this potential obligation is not a risk in the strategy. While it's true that you may end up selling your shares far below the current market value it is NOT a risk of the strategy since it still represents a profit. Selling below current market value at a profit is simply a lost opportunity and risk is never defined as missing out on some reward.

As long as you remain in the covered call position, you have limited upside potential since the most you will ever receive for your shares is the strike price. As with any option, you can get out of the contract by simply buying it back at some time but for now just remember that a covered call limits your upside potential.

The fact that you are capping your upside potential profit means the covered call strategy is designed for those investors who have a *neutral* to *slightly bullish* outlook on the stock. You should not write calls on stocks you feel will make explosive upward moves nor should you write calls on shares you think will fall in price. You should be reasonably confident that the stock price will fluctuate sideways through the life of the option (neutral outlook) or you should feel it may climb somewhat higher (slightly bullish).

Philosophy

The goal of the covered call writer is to collect many option premiums over a long period of time. Every time you write a call option against your shares you are effectively lowering your cost basis on those shares. This reduces your risk since you are reducing the amount of cash you have in the position. Covered call writers are not attempting to profit from rising stock prices; remember that the position is neutral to slightly bullish. It's okay if the stock price rises (since higher stock prices will not generate a loss) but that is not the main goal of the strategy. If you are bullish on the stock you should just buy the stock (or long calls as we'll find out in the next chapter) and just hang on. Covered call writers, on the other hand, have limited upside potential because they are obligated to sell their shares for a fixed price so the strategy is not designed to make money from rising stock prices. The goal is to generate your profits by writing calls over and over – collecting premiums – against those shares.

Covered Call Basics

Let's start with the basics of covered calls by looking at an example using the AGIX quotes we have used earlier, which have been reproduced as Table 7-1:

Table 7-1

AGIX (Nasdaq)												18.81	-0.08
Sep 16,2004 @ 10:10 ET (Data 15 Minutes Delayed)										Bid 18.80 Ask 18.81 Size 14x6 Vol 29728			

Calls	Last Sale	Net	Bid	Ask	Vol	Open Int	Puts	Last Sale	Net	Bid	Ask	Vol	Open Int
04 Oct 15 (AUB JC-E)	6.70	pc	6.20	6.70	0	1103	04 Oct 15 (AUB VC-E)	2.50	pc	2.50	2.90	0	1158
04 Oct 17.50 (AUB JW-E)	5.10	pc	5.10	5.60	0	1972	04 Oct 17.50 (AUB VW-E)	3.90	pc	3.90	4.30	0	1150
04 Oct 20.00 (AUB JD-E)	4.80	-.10	4.40	4.80	25	3833	04 Oct 20.00 (AUB VD-E)	5.40	pc	5.50	6.00	0	1507

Assume you buy 100 shares of AGIX for $18.81 and then sell the October $20 call for the current $4.40 bid. By selling the call, you will immediately receive $4.40 *100 = $440 cash in exchange for the potential obligation to sell your shares for the $20 strike price through expiration Friday in October (29 days later). That $440 is yours for assuming the potential obligation to sell your shares of stock for the strike price if the long call holder decides to exercise the call.

The above transactions show up in your account as a long position of 100 shares of AGIX valued at $1,881 and short $20 call valued at *minus* $480. New traders often wonder why they see a -$4.80 next to the short $20 call. After all, if they received cash, shouldn't it be a positive number? The answer is that long positions show up as positive values while short positions show up as negative values. If your account shows that you are long 100 shares valued at $1,881 then that is how much you will receive if you sell those shares (100 shares at $18.81). On the other hand, the short $20 call is valued at -$480 because that is how much you will have to spend right now to buy it back (the current asking price). So where did the $440 cash go? If you look closer at your account, you will find that your money market has been credited with $440 cash. In this example, your account value will not immediately increase by $440. Instead, it will show a slight loss of $40 since you received $440 cash but must pay $480 if you wanted to close out the call right now. As the value of that call drops toward zero, your account will slowly increase by $440 assuming all other factors constant.

Because you collect cash, the cost basis (net cost) of your stock is immediately reduced. In this example, you paid $18.81 for the stock and then immediately received $4.40 cash, which means you effectively paid $18.81 - $4.40 = $14.41 for the stock. We will often make reference to the cost basis of the stock when talking about covered calls since it is an important characteristic of the strategy. Please understand the reason we can subtract the full $4.40 from the $18.81 stock price is because we have assumed you wrote one call against 100 shares of stock; that is, the calls were written in equal proportion to the shares of stock. As we said earlier, it is possible you might decide to write fewer contracts and we'll find out the reason for that later. If you do write fewer contracts though, you cannot just subtract the option price from the stock price to find your cost basis. For example, if you bought 200 shares of AGIX for $18.81 and then wrote one call for $4.40, your cost basis is *not* $14.41. In these cases, we must find the weighted average by subtracting the $440 cash from the 200 * $18.81 = $3,762 total cost of the stock, which is $3,322. If we divide $3,322 by the 200 shares, we get $16.61 for the cost basis.

Let's go back to our example of buying 100 shares of AGIX and selling one $20 call. By selling the $20 call, you are potentially obligated to sell 100 shares of stock for the $20 strike price no matter how high that stock's price may be at expiration. This means the most you will receive from the sale of your stock over the next 29 days is the $20 strike * 100 shares = $2,000 (the *exercise value* of the contract).

From a profit and loss standpoint, this AGIX covered call looks like Figure 7-2:

Figure 7-2

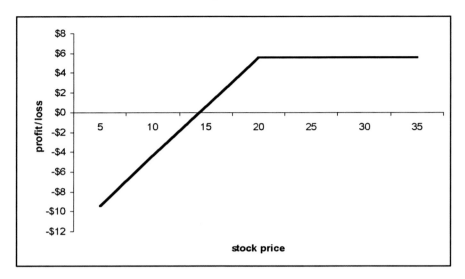

The profit and loss diagram shows that the covered call provides for a limited upside gain. Notice that the "bend" in the profit and loss diagram occurs at the $20 strike. This shows that no matter how high the stock's price may be at expiration, the most the covered call writer will ever receive is the $20 strike price at expiration. No matter how high the stock's price may rise, the covered call writer can only gain a limited amount.

The profit and loss diagram also shows that the covered call writer is vulnerable to all of the downside risk in the stock and that is something you cannot forget when writing covered calls. We'll talk more about this risk later but just realize that the covered call writer has limited upside potential and unlimited downside risk.

If the strategy has limited rewards and unlimited downside risk then why would anybody use it? Remember that all strategies are tradeoffs in risk and reward. The strategy is less risky that the outright ownership of stock yet can yield some impressive returns. In this example, you have the potential obligation to sell your shares for a fixed price of $20, which is not a bad deal when you consider your cost basis is only $14.41. How good of a deal is it? For this, we need to turn to several performance numbers that will help you determine if a particular covered call will accomplish your goals.

Return if Exercised

One calculation you'll want to make is called the "return if exercised." To calculate it, you simply find the percentage increase between the cost basis and the strike price. In this example, you'd have a gain of $20 - $14.41 = $5.59 if assigned on the call. Because you made this $5.59 gain from a principal value of $14.41 then this represents a $5.59/$14.41 = 0.39, or 39% return in only 29 days.

Another method for finding the return is to simply divide the ending value by the beginning value and subtract one. Here, the answer would be $20/$14.41 = 1.39. After subtracting one, we're left with the same answer of 0.39, or 39%. Use whichever method is easiest for you to remember.

In we want to annualize the figure, we just need to find out how many "29-day" groups there are in a year, which is found by 365/29 = 12.6. This tells us that if we were able to replicate this same trade throughout the year, we'd have 12.6 trades so our annualized percentage return at the end of the year would be 12.6 * 39% = 491%. Of course, being able to replicate this trade for about 12 times during the year is an unrealistic assumption but it still allows us to make comparisons with other investments since rates of return are always posted on an annualized basis.

Notice that this rate of return is abnormally high, which should give you a clue to the risk in the position. Remember high rewards come with high risk. Why do you suppose these rates of return are so high? Because the last chapter just showed us the volatility on AGIX was very high and, in order to execute the strategy, you must be willing to *own the stock*. That stock was very volatile at the time, which means it could rise – or fall – substantially. We'll look more at the risk in a covered call later but just understand you shouldn't think this is a "conservative" strategy when you find rates of returns like this. There is a reason the market is willing to pay such high rates of return. That reason is risk.

Static Return

There is another calculation we can do to find out if a particular covered call strategy is appealing. That calculation is called the "static return," which calculates the return if the stock's price is unchanged or "static" at expiration. In the "return if exercised" calculation, we allowed for the stock's price to rise from the current level of $18.81 to the $20 strike in order to calculate the return. For this calculation, we want to see how the strategy would perform if the stock closed at the current price of $18.81 at expiration. We know the cost basis is $14.41 so the static return is $18.81/$14.41 = 1.3053, or 30.5%.

The static return doesn't assume the stock's price will remain unchanged throughout the life of the option. Instead, it assumes that it will finish at the same price. Whether this is a realistic assumption or not, it is just meant to give us an idea about the rate of return from the option time premium alone and not considering movements in the stock's price. This clearly shows that covered call writers can make money on stocks without any movement in the stock's price. That is definitely something that cannot be done with stock alone.

Break-even Return

Another calculation we'd like to check is the break-even return. This just tells us how far the stock can fall before we'd break even. In this example, the stock could fall by the amount of premium received from selling the call, which is $4.40. The $4.40 cash collected acts as a downside hedge in the event the stock falls. If the stock falls $4.40, that represents a drop of $4.40/$18.81 = 0.23, or 23%. Or if you prefer the second method of calculating the return, the ending price would be $18.81 - $4.40 = $14.41. If we divide the ending value by the beginning value and then subtract one we get $14.41/$18.81 = 0.7661. After subtracting one, we find the answer is -0.23, which is a 23% drop.

In other words, if the stock is $14.41 at expiration we will just break even on the trade since we effectively paid $14.41 for the stock. Remember, with the stock at $14.41, the $20 call will be worthless so there is no cost for us to get out of the contract. Any stock price below $14.41 at expiration will lead to a loss in the position. This calculation shows that we can afford for the stock's price to fall 23% before the position heads into losing territory. Figure 7-2 compares a long stock position in AGIX at $18.81 (shaded line) to the covered call (bold line). The arrow shows that the break even point is reduced by 23%:

Figure 7-3

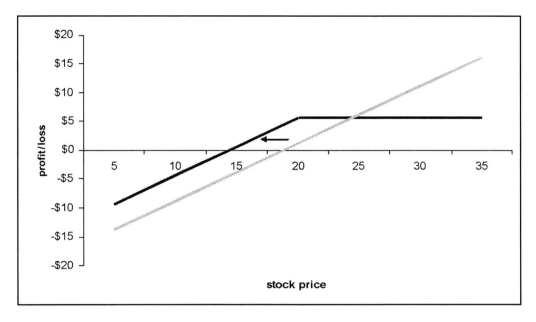

The breakeven calculation gives us an idea about the size of the downside hedge in the strategy. When we say the position is "hedged" that just means you are not losing money for some *adverse* moves in the stock's price. If the stock price falls, that loss will be offset by the increase in the short call. The size of the hedge depends on the premium you received from the sale of the call options.

Max Gain, Max Loss

The maximum you can ever make from a covered call position is the amount of premium received from the sale of the call plus any potential capital gains that may be available as shown by the "return if exercised" calculation. Another way of looking at the maximum gain is that it is the difference between the cost basis of the stock and the exercise price. The maximum loss is the amount of the cost basis.

Do I Need to Stay in the Contract Until Expiration?

There is nothing that says you must remain in the covered call position over the next 29 days; you can always get out of the contract at any time by buying back the call option. Once you buy back the contract, the shares of stock are yours, free and clear, with no obligations attached. Of course, there is nothing that says you will be able to buy that call back at a favorable price. Whether you buy back the call at a lower or higher price depends on what has happened to the stock's price and volatility of the stock during the intervening time. But you can always get out of the contract.

There are many scenarios we can create with buying back the call option since the option's price can rise or fall all by itself (with no movement in the stock) due to changes in volatility. And if the stock's price moves then it will definitely have an impact on the option's price. Regardless of the scenario you choose, the calculation for finding your return is always the same. You simply take the cost basis of the stock and add back the purchase price of the call. Then you compare that figure to the current stock price and see what your return is.

For example, let's assume the stock's price stays the same at $18.81 but the value of the call is dropping due to time decay. At a later date, you may, for example, be able to buy back the call for $2, which is a favorable price since you sold the call for $4.40. In this case, your return is the $14.41 cost basis + $2 to buy back the call for a new cost basis of $16.41 on the shares of stock. You are now out of the contract and could sell the stock for the current price of $18.81, which represents a return of $18.81/$16.41 = 1.146, or 14.6%. Again, this shows that investors can make money on a stock whose price is not moving (or fluctuating sideways) over time by using covered calls.

If the stock's price stays the same or relatively flat then time decay will erode the call's price and the investor can buy the call back at a cheaper price. The reason this example worked out to be a gain is because the time premium was $4.40 when the call was sold but only $2 when it was purchased back. However, it is possible to profit from a covered call even if you buy the call back at a higher price. As you go through the following examples, notice it's the net *time premiums* that determine whether or not the covered call is profitable or not. In other words, if you receive more time premium than you spend you will be profitable; otherwise, you have losses.

Example

Let's look at an example assuming the stock's price has moved higher. Assume the stock quickly rises to $20 and the option's price rises from $4.40 to $6. If you wish to get out of the contract, you could buy back the $20 call for the current $6 market price. By purchasing the call option, you no longer have the potential obligation to sell your shares. Your cost basis is now $14.41 + $6 = $20.41 and you could sell the stock for $20, which represents a slight loss. The reason this scenario ended up with a loss is because of the relationship between the time premium and stock price. The stock's price rose from $18.81 to $20, which is a $1.19 gain and that certainly helps the long stock position. However, the time premium on the option rose from $4.40 to $6, which represents a loss on the call option since you must pay $1.60 more to buy back the call. The net difference is $1.19 gain - $1.60 loss = 41 cents loss. This 41 cents loss is exactly the difference between our $20.41 cost basis and the current market price of $20.

However, just because the stock's price rises does not necessarily mean you will be left with an overall loss. Assume the value of the call is still $6 as in the previous example but this time it is mostly represented by intrinsic value. For instance, consider what would happen if the stock rose to $25 and the $20 call was $6. Now the $20 call has $5 of intrinsic value and only $1 of time premium. If you buy back the call, your cost basis is $14.41 + $6 = $20.21 and you could sell the stock for $25, which is a 23.7% gain. In this example, you still took a loss on the call since you sold it for $4.40 and bought it back for $6. However, the stock's price rose substantially so the intrinsic value came back to you when you sold the stock. In other words, the $5 intrinsic value that you paid to buy the option was returned to you since you could now sell the stock for the current price of $25 rather than the $20 strike. You paid $5 to increase your sales price by $5, which is not a loss. It is therefore not enough to only consider whether the call was purchased back for a gain or a loss to determine profitability. The covered call strategy involves two assets – stock plus a short call – and it is the relative performance between the two assets that determines the performance.

To really drive the point, let's consider a very high call price. Let's still assume your cost basis is $14.41 and the stock is trading for $40 and the $20 call is trading at parity, or $20. Is it a bad idea to buy back the call at a loss? Surprisingly, the answer is that it doesn't matter from a financial standpoint. Many investors are inclined to believe so and just let their shares go rather than take this "loss." But if you step through the math, you'll find there isn't a financial difference. First, if you choose to do nothing, you will be assigned on the call and receive the $20 strike price, which represents a gain of $5.59.

Now let's take a look at your second choice, which is to close out the call the $20 intrinsic value. If you sold the call for $4.40 and bought it back for $20 then that is a huge loss *for the call*. Your cost basis on the stock rises to $14.41 + $20 = $34.41 but you can now sell the stock for $40, which still represents a gain of $5.59, or a return of $40/$34.41 = 1.1625, or 16.25%. Once again, the $20 cost of the option is returned to you since you can now sell the stock for $40 rather than $20. In other words, you spent $20 cash to free up $20 worth of intrinsic value. With this second choice, you are giving up $20 cash for certain in exchange for a $20 *unrealized gain* in the stock (it's an unrealized gain until you sell the shares). Either choice nets you a $5.59 gain at that moment in time. The first choice creates a $5.59 gain for sure while the second choice results in an unrealized $5.59 gain. It's a different set of risks and rewards too since you are still holding onto the shares with the second choice. But, financially speaking, there really is no difference between the two choices at that moment in time *provided that you are still comfortable in holding the stock.*

The bottom line is that any intrinsic value in the call option will not hurt your performance if you buy back the call. The reason is that the call option's price will reflect all intrinsic value (Pricing Principle #3 from Chapter Two) and that value is also reflected in the stock's price. It's only when you pay more *time value* to buy back the call that the amount of time value you received at the time of the sale will hurt the covered call's performance.

We can show this easily by considering that an in-the-money call option's value prior to expiration equals the intrinsic value plus some time value, which we can write as $(S - E + T)$. Next, if you buy stock, S, and sell the call then you receive cash and your account has a value of stock + cash $(S + C)$. Your account is therefore long $(S + C)$ and short $(S - E + T)$ since you wrote the in-the-money call. The value of the position today is then:

$$(S + C) - (S - E + T)$$
$$= S + C - S + E - T$$
$$= (E + C) - T$$

This shows the value of that covered call position (assuming the call is in-the-money) is simply the exercise price plus the cash you received from the sale of the call *less any time premium* you must pay to close out that call. Of course, if you wait until expiration and the call stays in-the-money then the time premium will be zero and the position is worth the exercise price plus the cash. This shows that only increases in the time premium will hurt your position since that is the only negative in the equation. No matter which scenario you construct with the call being at-the-money or in-the-money, we can immediately tell if it is a losing or winning situation by simply looking at the time premium you received versus the time premium you must pay to close out the call. If the scenario you create involves a falling stock price then all we need to be concerned with is that the stock's current market price remains above the cost basis.

As a recap, there are only two situations that a covered call can be in. Either the call is in-the-money or it is not in-the-money (which includes at-the-money). If the call is in-the-money we will have a loss if we close out the call by paying more time premium than we received. If the call is out-of-the-money, we will have a loss if our proceeds selling the stock and buying back the call are less than the cost basis.

Which Strike Should I Write?

One of the first questions new traders have is which strike they should write. There really is no correct answer although, upon reflection, some strikes will certainly sound better to you than others. If you remember the covered call is a premium collection strategy it makes sense to sell an option that is rich in time premium; hopefully you remember that is the at-the-money strike. It would also make sense to sell a relatively short term option, say 30 days to expiration or so since these options are hit hardest by time decay. By selling a short-term, at-the-money option, you have a mathematical advantage by bringing in a relatively large premium that will quickly lose its value, which is good for you as the covered call writer.

However, different investors have different objectives and every strategy comes with a unique set of risks and rewards so we can't really say that selling the at-the-money option is "the best." It's just that it has a lot of nice characteristics but there are always tradeoffs.

Which strike to write boils down to different philosophies of why you're writing the calls in the first place. Because options are classified as out-of-the-money, at-the-money, and in-the-money then those are the different scenarios we can create with covered calls. Each comes with its own philosophy and sets of risks and rewards so let's look at each in detail.

Writing Out-of-the-Money Calls

One of the most common approaches is to write calls against your long stock position but with the intent of never losing the shares. These investors usually write short-term, out-of-the-money (higher strike) calls. Investors who write out-of-the-money calls are really hoping the stock will rise to the strike price (or very close) but still leave the call out-of-the-money at expiration. In the AGIX example presented earlier, we assumed the investor wrote the $20 call for $4.40. This investor would ideally want the stock to rise to $20. If the stock's price does not exceed $20 at expiration, there is no reason for the long call holder to exercise the call since they could just pay $20 in the open market. The $20 call expires worthless but the covered call writer enjoys the price appreciation of the shares *plus* the premium received from the sale of the call yet is never forced to sell the shares. Avid covered call writers with this philosophy hope this situation happens time after time so they can write new calls when the current call expires while continuing to hang on to the shares. The sale of many call options can greatly enhance the returns that you may otherwise receive from holding onto the shares alone. In fact, if you successfully write calls month after month, you may even write your shares into a negative cost basis.

For example, assume an investor buys the stock at $18.81 and writes the $20 call for $4.40. Let's assume the stock rises during this time very close to $20 at expiration. Because the stock price doesn't exceed $20, the call will expire worthless and the investor keeps his shares and can write another call the following month. With the stock near $20, perhaps the investor will write a one-month, $22.50 call. The price received obviously depends on the price the market is placing on that call at the time. But let's say it is trading for $4. If the investor writes this call, the cost basis for the stock falls by another $4 to $14.41 - $4 = $10.41. The investor then hopes the stock will rise but close near $22.50 at expiration. At that time, the investor may write a $25 strike for $4 thus making his cost basis $6.41 and so on. Of course, hoping a stock will behave this well for sustained periods is an unrealistic expectation but the covered call strategy will still work even under less favorable assumptions. We're just saying this is the ideal situation for those investors who choose to write out-of-the-money calls.

The covered call strategy would also work with the stock price remaining the same. In the previous example, we had written the cost basis down to $6.41 with the stock price near $22.50 at expiration. Obviously, there's nothing wrong with this cost basis if the stock's price had remained at $18.81.

Investors who never want to lose their shares tend to write out-of-the-money call options. They are willing to take a small chance for the stock's price to exceed the strike in exchange for collecting monthly premiums.

The problem with the philosophy of writing covered calls with the intent of never losing the stock is that you are really acting like a "naked" call writer even though you also happen to own the underlying stock. A naked call writer, as we said earlier, is one who writes calls but does not own the underlying shares. This is a high risk strategy since there is no limit as to how high the shares may be trading if you are forced to deliver them. Naked call writers definitely do not want the stock to rise. If you are writing call options against your stock but do not want to lose the shares then you are acting like a naked call writer. Because of this, you will tend to write short-term, out-of-the-money calls to reduce the chance you'll lose your shares. But when you write short-term, out-of-the-money calls, you will usually not bring in much premium either (since higher strike calls are cheaper) but still have the potential obligation to sell your stock.

Because there's not much time premium involved, you will not have a lot of downside protection either. Writing out-of-the-money calls can yield very high returns but most of those returns are due to stock price movement and not from the sale of the option. So for many investors, writing out-of-the-money calls doesn't make a lot of sense no matter how small the chance of getting assigned ("called out") may seem.

Writing At-the-Money Calls

If there were such a thing as a textbook definition of a covered call, it would probably be defined as one where the investor writes the front month, at-the-money call. Remember, the idea behind the covered call is to collect a relatively large premium from an option that will quickly decay in value. The strike that carries the most time value and sharpest decay is the at-the-money strike. Investors who write at-the-money calls collect the highest amount of time premium and also create a lower cost basis on the stock thus providing a little bigger downside hedge.

Investors who write at-the-money calls will not have the room for capital appreciation like out-of-the-money call writers. However, at-the-money calls provide a little more downside protection so they are less risky.

Risk of Covered Calls

As Figure 6-2 showed, the covered call writer is exposed to all of the downside risk of the stock (less the premium received from the option). The one thing you don't want to have happen as a covered call writer is for the stock's price to fall below the cost basis. This also corresponds to why we said that covered call writers should have a neutral to slightly bullish outlook. You do not want to write a call if you think the stock is going to crash. However, many new investors believe that you write calls against stocks that you think are about to fall. You must remember when combining assets in a portfolio (such as shares of stock plus short calls) that it is the overall behavior of all assets that counts. When new investors learn about options, they learn that selling a call is bearish so they immediately infer that the covered call strategy is bearish since they are selling a call. But this ignores the fact that the covered call writer is also long the stock. In Chapter Two, Pricing Principle #5 showed us that the maximum price for a call option is the price of the stock. This shows that the call option will always be worth less than the stock. So if you own the shares and write the calls, you are holding an asset (stock) that is far more valuable than the calls. The last thing you want is for the price of that asset to drop significantly even if that action may be beneficial for the lesser valued option.

Obvious as this may seem, there are many "professional" brokers of financial planners who will emphatically tell you that the risk of the covered call is that you give up potential price appreciation. In fact, here are three samples found on three different financial sites on the Internet:

- Since the short call is covered by the portfolio, *this strategy has no downside risk. The only upside risk is that you give up the price appreciation above the strike price of the call;* however, the call premium paid at the outset may compensate for this risk.

- *While the covered-call writer has no risk of losing huge amounts of money, there is an attendant risk of missing out on large gains.* This is pretty simple: if a stock has a large run-up in price, and calls are nearing expiration with a strike price that is even slightly in the money, those calls will be exercised before they expire, i.e., the covered call writer will be forced to deliver shares (known as having the shares "called away").

- Writing covered calls (i.e., call options over stock that you own) is *perhaps the safest of all options strategies and possesses minimal risk.* The aim is to generate income through premiums with the potential to collect capital gains as well, should the share price remain below the exercise price.

You can see that the suggestion or tone of many "professionals" is that covered calls are essentially risk-free. In fact, the first and second examples state that the risk is that you miss out on large gains. As we said before, the risk of any financial asset is *never* defined as missing out on some reward and you must question the judgment of anyone who tells you that it is. If that were true, then the risk of buying Microsoft at $30 is that you might sell it later for $35 only to see it trading higher. Missing out on potential gains is always a regrettable possibility with any asset – but it is not the risk. To combat the downside risk of the covered call, many investors write in-the-money calls and there are many benefits to considering this often overlooked variation.

 The risk of the covered call is that the stock price falls. The risk is not getting assigned on the short call and selling below market price. That is a missed opportunity and risk is never defined as missing out on some reward.

Writing In-the-Money Calls

New investors often wonder how it is possible to profit by purchasing a stock for one price and giving someone else the right to buy it for less money. The answer is that there is a time premium associated for that right that more than makes up for this loss. We know this from Pricing Principle #4 in Chapter Two which showed us that all call options must be worth their intrinsic value plus some time premium. If you sell an in-the-money call, you receive more money than the intrinsic value you're sacrificing.

For example, using Table 7-1, you could buy AGIX for $18.81 and sell the $15 call for $6.20. Notice that you are taking a loss on $18.81 - $15 = $3.31 worth of intrinsic value but are paid $6.20, which more than covers the loss.

Pricing Principle #1 showed us that lower strike calls are more expensive. Therefore, writing in-the-money calls against your shares provides a bigger cushion if the stock price should fall. Even though in-the-money calls are more expensive overall, they carry a smaller time premium and it's the time premium that reduces the cost basis of the stock. This is why writing in-the-money calls increases the downside hedge (they are more expensive) but provides lower returns (there is not as much time premium as an at-the-money call). In other words, investor's who write in-the-money calls are taking less risk and will therefore get lower returns.

Buying the stock for $18.81 and selling the call for $6.20 gives you a cost basis of $18.81 - $6.20 = $12.61 and gives you the potential obligation to sell your shares for $15 call, which represents a 12.6% return.

Figure 7-4 compares the profit and loss diagrams for selling the $20 call (bold line) verses the $15 call (shaded line). You can see that the $20 call provides for a higher return but the $15 call provides better downside protection. Selling the $20 call carries more risk and more reward than sale of the $15 call:

Figure 7-4

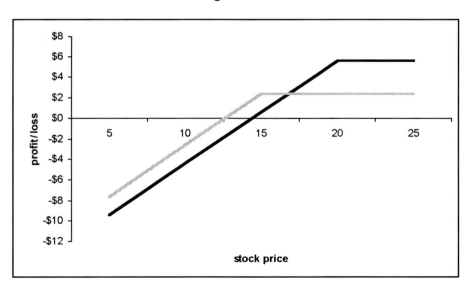

If there were lower strikes available for AGIX, we would find that the returns would eventually converge on the risk-free rate. Notice this is consistent with our observations about time premium in Chapter One where we said that lower strike calls will have very relatively small amounts of time premium in them and it's the time premium that creates the returns for the covered call strategy. Now that you understand the covered call strategy, you have another way of understanding why time premiums shrink as you move deeper in-the-money. If you write calls that are so far in-the-money then the shares will be *nearly* guaranteed to be called away and, as with any guaranteed investment, you will only receive the risk-free rate of return.

For example, assume a stock is trading for $100 and that a one-year $20 strike exists. Interest rates are 5%. How much should the $20 call be trading for? In this case, if you buy the stock for $100 and write the $20 call, the market would probably view this as being a nearly guaranteed sale for $20 in one year. If you are "guaranteed" to receive $20 in one year, then it is worth $20/1.05 = $19.05 today, which means there is a cost of carry of $20 - $19.05 = 95 cents. We know the call must also be trading for the intrinsic value so it should be worth $80.95. You can verify this by using a Black-Scholes Model with a volatility of 50% or lower so that our assumption of "nearly guaranteed" is valid. You'll find the $20 call is worth $80.95. As a call writer, you'd only receive the cost of carry for this trade since you're not taking that much risk in the eyes of the market. If you increase the volatility to something higher than 50%, you'll find the time premium starts to increase showing these higher volatility levels are casting some doubt as to whether that option seller is guaranteed to receive $20 in one year.

Which Expiration Should I Write?

As with strike prices, there will be several expiration months from which to choose. All things being equal, you're better off writing the shorter-term contracts for a couple of reasons. First, shorter-term contracts are exposed to a much more rapid pace of time decay. This means their value diminishes quickly, which is what you want to happen as the writer. A second reason is that short-term options are more expensive per unit of time, which we learned from Pricing Principle #5 in Chapter Two.

But this does not mean there's no benefit in writing longer-term options. Longer-term options do provide more money and therefore provide a larger hedge if the stock should move against you. As we have shown, the risk of a covered call is that the stock falls and, by bringing in higher premiums, longer-term options help to hedge against this risk. Also, what if it takes a while for a fallen stock's price to recover? During the recovery time, you may not be able to write the strike prices you had hoped and may end up not able to write any calls until the stock recovers (if at all). By writing longer-term options, this risk is mitigated.

Every option strategy in the world is a unique tradeoff between risk and reward so it's not correct to say you should only write short-term options. We're just saying all things being equal you're better off writing shorter term calls. And having the stock price remain the same month after month is one of the assumptions in the phrase "all things being equal." If the stock price is very volatile, you may consider writing a longer term option against it to further hedge the downside risk. When people tell you to only write the short term options, they are implicitly assuming the stock price will remain fairly constant and they will be able to write calls month after month. If that turns out to be false, then writing a longer term option may end up being the better strategy. So when deciding which month or strike to write, just be sure to take all risks and rewards into account and make sure they are in line with your outlook on the stock.

Regardless of which month or strike you choose to write, most covered call writers wait for the time value to get near zero, which will be close to expiration and then write another call at that time. The idea is to continually collect premiums over time. The covered call strategy is usually not used as a "one time" strategy although it certainly could be used in that way or for shorter-term applications. But for the most part, the strategy is designed to be a long-term, systematic way to continually collect premiums and reduce the cost basis of your shares and enhance returns.

Covered Call Rationale

Now that you understand the profit and loss profile of the covered call, we can answer one of the most frequently asked questions about the strategy. Many investors wonder why anybody would write a covered call since it limits your upside potential. They reason that it doesn't make much sense to take in a couple of bucks up front in exchange for limited upside gains and therefore must be a bad strategy.

But let's take a little different view by considering the fact that for any stock price, there is a range of possible stock prices that fall into a bell curve pattern. So while "unlimited" upside gains are a possibility, they do not come with equal probability. Each successive higher stock price is less likely than the previous price. Figure 7-5 compares a long stock position in AGIX (shaded straight line) to the long stock + short $20 call position (bold line). We have also overlaid a bell curve at the current stock price of $18.81 to simulate the possible range of stock prices at expiration:

Figure 7-5

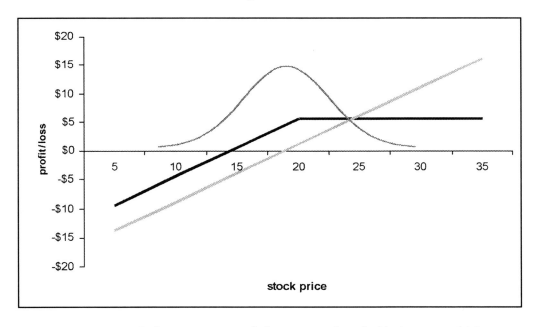

Now we see a different picture. If the range of *probable* (not possible) prices falls under the bell curve, notice that the covered call beats the long stock position for the majority of the ranges under the curve. In other words, the bold line lies above the shaded line for nearly all stock prices under the curve. This means that over time, the covered call will provide more stable returns and will provide higher returns most of the time. However, this does not mean that the covered call strategy produces higher returns for less risk. The covered call writer attempts to keep a steady increase in the returns while allowing the compounding of those returns to work to his advantage.

While it may be the winning strategy for some stocks (or for some periods of time) it cannot always be the higher return strategy for the market overall. The reason is that you will miss out on occasional homeruns by continuously staying in the covered call. Notice though, that these "homeruns" occur well outside of the bell curve, which means these homeruns are more like lottery tickets and that you shouldn't invest with the expectation of those returns. Covered call writers are looking for steady gains month after month. And when it comes to investing, slow and steady can produce remarkable returns especially when you consider the compounding effects over time. It is often the strategy that wins the race and is one of the strongest motivations for using covered calls.

Covered Call Trap

At the beginning of this chapter, we said that covered calls can contain an unforeseen risk and we're now ready to show how investors unknowingly can take step right into a trap if they believe that all covered call positions are conservative.

Because most investors do not realize the downside risk inherent with covered calls, they unknowingly choose their covered call trades based on the volatility of the underlying stock. An investor new to the covered call strategy may hear that covered calls are conservative and, when searching for investment ideas, will end up choosing the call options that have the highest premiums. After all, if all covered calls are conservative, they feel they might as well choose the call option that brings in the highest premium. However, if you choose the call options with the highest premiums, you have automatically chosen the riskiest stocks since it is the higher volatility (risky) stocks that command higher option premiums. The investor ends up holding onto a highly volatile stock that he otherwise would not be comfortable holding. These call writers are often called "premium seekers" since they seek out the options with the highest premiums and then they buy the stock for the sole reason of writing the calls. This is a high-risk way to use covered calls and can lead to disastrous results.

For example, assume that you are comfortable holding stocks in your IRA (Individual Retirement Account) such as Conservative Consolidated Company but not comfortable with highly volatile stocks such as Gargantuan Growth

Company. If you are new to options and decide to write calls, you would find that the premiums for Conservative Consolidated are not nearly as large as they are for Gargantuan Growth. The reason is simply that Gargantuan Growth is far more volatile. And when stocks are more volatile, option traders are willing to pay more for the options so that they *don't* have to hold the stock. When you decide on which stock to buy in order to write calls, you may see a one-month, at-the-money call on Conservative Consolidated trading for 50 cents while an at-the-money call on Gargantuan Growth may be $5.

When faced with these prices, you may think that it doesn't make sense to buy 100 shares of Conservative Consolidated and only receive $50 from the sale of the call when you can buy 100 shares of Gargantuan Growth and receive $500. So you decide to buy 100 of Gargantuan Growth and write the call to gain the $500. But look what just happened. You ended up with the stock that you weren't comfortable holding. It was the high option premiums that lured you into buying the stock. That's what happens when you let option premiums dictate which stocks to buy. Investors who base their covered call decisions on option prices end up taking far more risk than they intend and end up holding a risky asset that could fall substantially.

Example:

Around 1998, I remember one investor who bought 7,000 shares of Egghead Software (EGGS) at $53 during the "dot-com" craze. (To make matters worse, he bought the shares on margin or borrowed funds.) He thought he was laughing all the way to the bank when he discovered that a three-week option was bidding $8 for a $55 stock. "Wow, that is over 15-fold on your money" he exclaimed. "At that rate, it would take less than two and a half years to turn $1,000 into $1,000,000."

The trader bought the shares and wrote the calls waiting patiently for his windfall to arrive. At option expiration, the stock was trading at $4. Yes, he did get to keep the entire $8 premium for the calls. I will let you decide if it was worth it.

This trader was correct in realizing that the $8 premium was tremendously high. But there was a reason the markets were bidding up the call options so high.

They wanted someone else to hold the risky stock. The risk of a covered call is that the stock falls.

Notice how it's possible for two investors to be using covered calls and yet may be on nearly opposite ends of the risk spectrum. Options are risky only if used improperly. Don't be misled into thinking that all covered call positions are conservative no matter how convincing the argument may sound. If any broker tells you that the risk of a covered call is that you miss out on upside gains then ask him why the strategy is called "covered." He will immediately tell that it's because you're *not* at risk if the stock rises since you already own the stock. That's the correct answer but it presents a dilemma since he also believes that you're at risk if it does rise. The reason that people make this mistake is because they are confusing "risk" with "missed opportunity." Once again, risk is never defined as missing out on some reward (missed opportunity). People who forget the simple risk and reward relationship are easily led to believe that the risk of a covered call is that they miss out on the upside gains and are inevitably led to writing calls on the riskiest stocks they can find. If the "risk" is that you may miss out on some upside gains, you might as well collect the biggest premium you can! These investors usually learn the hard way that there is a big difference between risk and missed opportunity.

The very best tip we can give you for writing calls in a conservative way is to be sure you're buying stock that you wouldn't mind holding anyway *even if options were not available.* That way, it shows you're willing to assume the downside risk and the sale of the call does not change the risk. It simply provides a downside hedge. Don't let the tail wag the dog by purchasing stocks based on the prices of the options. Of course, it doesn't mean that it's wrong to write covered calls because of the high premiums; it just means that it changes the nature of the strategy from conservative to speculative. The point to remember is that all covered calls are not equal. Just because you've written a covered call does not make it a conservative strategy. It is your reason for doing it that dictates the risk in the strategy.

Synthetic Positions

We can use put-call parity to show us added insights into any strategy so let's see what it has to say about the covered call strategy. Let's start with the basic equation found in Chapter Five (Formula 5-15):

$$S + P - C = 0$$

Now let's solve it for a covered call. We know that a covered call is the combination of long stock plus a short call so we need to get those two assets on one side of the equation. We can see that they are already on the left side so let's just move the long put to the right side and change its sign in the process:

$$S - C = -P$$

This equation tells us that the combination of long stock and a short call (left side) is equal to a short put (right side). Any broker will tell you that short puts are one of the riskiest strategies available. Brokerage firms will require your account to have the highest option approval rating along with significant equity before they will allow you to write naked puts. At the same time, they will tell you that the covered call is conservative in nature. Both statements cannot be correct. It depends on how they are used. If you want to use them in conservative ways, make sure you are buying stock you don't mind holding.

Another way to verify if a particular covered call is suitable for you, ask yourself if you would be comfortable selling naked puts at that time. If the answer is no then you should not be using a covered call because it is exactly the same thing packaged a little differently.

Hedging with Covered Calls

Many investors are attracted to covered calls because of the immediate cash that can be generated into the account. Because of this, they tend to write the "full amount" of contracts against their shares. For example, if they own 500 shares, they will write 5 contracts. While this does maximize the amount of cash generated for any given strike (and create the largest downside hedge), it does have its drawbacks. That is, if the stock makes a sudden move upwards, then your gains are capped and the covered call writer often has regrets about having written the calls in the first place. One way to combat this potential regret is to not write the full amount of contracts against your shares. For example, if you own 500 shares, you may consider writing something less than five contracts – anything from one to four contracts. While you will not bring in as much money, you will keep some of the upside open in the event the stock does spike up. By writing less than five contracts, you are hedging your bet between writing no calls and writing the full amount. It's just something to consider, especially in cases where you believe there is potential for the stock to break out of a range and continue higher. It's very tempting to want to write calls but it may come with large regrets later. Hedging the position by writing fewer calls can be a simple solution. How does this affect the position? Take a look at Figure 7-6. The shaded line is the profit and loss curve for an investor who buys 300 shares of AGIX and writes three of the $20 calls for $4.40. The bold line is the curve for the investor who buys 300 shares but only writes *two* of the $20 calls for $4.40:

Figure 7-6: Long 300 Shares AGIX Plus Two Short $20 Calls (Bold Line)

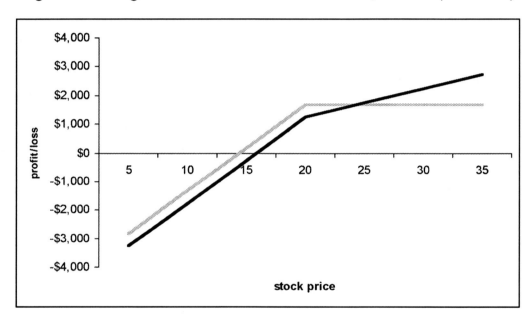

Notice that the profit and loss diagram for the bold line does not flatten out after the $20 stock price. The reason is that this investor purchased 300 shares but only wrote two calls so is only obligated to sell 200 of those shares. This investor will always have 100 shares free and clear to participate in upside gains above $20.

The tradeoff between writing two calls instead of three is that you don't get as much of a downside hedge since you receive less money. Figure 7-6 shows that the bold line doesn't have as much downside protection. It is therefore riskier and that's why it comes with a bigger reward.

This is a good example showing once again that all option strategies are about tradeoffs. Anytime you buy or sell an option to create some type of advantage there must be a negative aspect somewhere. *Do not enter into any strategy until you clearly understand what the benefits and drawbacks are.* It is impossible to find a strategy that only offers benefits. It is also impossible to find a strategy that beats all other strategy for all stock prices. It is up to the investor to decide which benefits are worth having in exchange for the drawbacks.

Will I get Assigned Early?

If you write a covered call, don't expect to get assigned or "called out" early even if the stock's price is well above the strike price. In Chapter Four, we showed that it is never optimal to exercise a call option early with the exception of collecting a dividend. With a covered call, you have a short call position; another trader somewhere has the long side of that trade. If it is not in his best interest to exercise that call early then you shouldn't expect to get assigned early.

Now that you have a better understanding of covered calls, we can revisit that topic and gain a new appreciation why it is not in the best interest of the long call holder to exercise early. Assume that you buy stock for $100 and write a one-year, $100 call for $10. That means that the most you could make from this trade is $10 if the stock's price is above $100 in one year, which would net you a 10% gain (actually, your gain would be higher than 10% since you're collecting the $10 up front but we're just trying to make the example simple to follow). But if you hold the position for less than a year, your gains are magnified. For example, if you are assigned after six months, then your annualized rate of return jumps to 20%. If you are assigned after three months, your annualized return is 40% and so on. This shows that the shorter time frame you hold the covered call, the better off you are since you were paid $10 to hold the stock for a full year but end up holding it for less time. *The better off you are then the worse off is the long call holder.* Since the long call holder controls the right to buy stock (he controls the exercise instructions), he will not exercise early. This shows that you should not enter into a covered call with the intent of being called out early. Also remember that it is not your decision as to when to end the contract; that's up to the long call holder.

As an example, I remember a client who once wrote covered calls with nearly a year until expiration. He collected a healthy premium but the stock quickly rose above the strike price, which means his account wasn't reflecting any of the daily gains in the stock. He called in one day and said, "I think I'd like to be called out on this stock now." After I explained that it was only the long position that could submit exercise instructions, he then realized the tradeoff of writing longer term calls. While he did get a much higher premium for writing a longer term contract, his money will be tied up in the stock for the next year. The investor could buy the calls back but then that cuts into the anticipated gains. So if you are writing longer term contracts, you should not expect to get assigned until expiration. Also, you should not expect to get assigned even if a dividend is about to be paid. The reason is that upon exercising a call, the long position sacrifices the call (he cannot sell it) so loses all of the time value in the call. If you are writing longer-term calls, the value of the time premium is probably far greater than the dividend.

However, anything is possible in the markets. We have seen people get assigned (called out) early on covered call positions. If this happens it is only an advantage to the call writer. Remember, if you get assigned early you are just receiving your money earlier rather than later. It's a huge advantage to you. But again, this is why you shouldn't expect it to happen.

How will I Know if I'm Assigned (Called Out of a stock)?

If you are ever assigned on a call, you will be notified by your broker the following business day.

But be careful at expiration and do not assume that you will not be assigned just because the stock closed below the strike price on Friday. The reason is that many brokers allow you to exercise the call after the closing bell. It is possible that after-hours news could propel the stock to new higher prices and you could get the assignment notice on Monday.

Using our AGIX example, assume you have purchased 100 shares and sold one $20 call. It is now expiration day and the stock is trading below the $20 strike, say $19. Because its price is below the strike, you decide to not pay the commission to close the call and just let it expire worthless. However, after the close, a news story hits stating that the company will be bought out at $30 per share. Upon hearing this news, the long call holders who thought their $20 calls expired worthless could potentially make $10 just by exercising the call. All they have to do is call their broker and exercise the call option.

They will pay $20 but receive stock worth $30, which they can immediately sell for a $10 gain rather than the 100% loss they took by letting the option expire. Even if the call owners are afraid the stock might fall on Monday, they could short shares in the after-hours market for $30 per share and then cover it for $20 by exercising the option. That's the risk-free route. The point is that there will be big demands to exercise the call and you get bet that assignment notices are likely to follow on Monday. If you do not have an assignment notice on Monday morning following expiration (assuming that's not a holiday), you can be sure that you were not assigned on the call.

Buy-Writes

There is a special order that allows traders to enter into a covered call as a "package deal" to the market maker, which is called a *buy-write*. With a buy-write, you can send an order to "buy" the stock and simultaneously "write" (sell) the call, which can be executed "at market" or as a "limit order." Regardless of how the order is placed, any executed order results in a net debit (because the stock must always be more valuable than the call). Since you're giving the market maker two trades rather than one, you will generally get a little better price for the package deal and every little bit helps.

Are Net Debits Confusing?

Sometimes new traders have trouble with the concept of net debits but it's very similar in concept as when you negotiate with a car dealer to trade in a used car for a new one. If the dealer is asking $30,000 for a new car and you would like to receive $10,000 for your used car then there is a $20,000 difference between the two prices. You may, for example, try to make a deal by telling the dealer that you want to buy the new car by trading in your used car plus $18,000 cash. In other words, you're telling the dealer you want to buy one asset and sell another for a net payment or "net debit" of $18,000. It's should be of no concern to you if the dealer says he cannot sell the new car below $30,000 but is willing to give you $12,000 for your trade-in since that is still a net payment of $18,000 to you. Car dealers often work with the *differences* between the two cars.

This is exactly the idea behind the net debit with buy-writes. When you enter a buy-write, you're telling the market maker that you don't care what price they charge you for the stock or what price you receive for your calls as long as it is executed for a price less than or equal to your net debit limit.

The simultaneous execution of both positions eliminates *execution risk*, which is the result of adverse price movements. For example, assume the stock is $50 and you wish to buy the stock and then sell a $50 call, which is trading for $3. Notice that this means you are expecting to end up with a net debit of $47 for the two trades. However, if you place an order to buy the stock at market, you may get filled at a little higher price than $50, say $50.25. Then you immediately place the order to sell the $50 call and the stock's price suddenly drops making the call price $2.90. Because of the adverse price fluctuations, you paid more for the stock and received less for the call and end up with a net debit of -$50.25 + $2.90 = 47.35 instead of the expected $47. If you enter the two trades as a buy-write, you will not face this adverse movement. If the stock's price suddenly jumps higher while the order is being executed, you'll pay more for the stock but will also get more for the call. If the stock price drops lower during execution, you'll get less for the call but also pay less for the stock. The result is that the net debit should stay pretty close to the same and not leave you with any unwanted surprise fills.

Incidentally, there is a mirror-image trade that allows the investor to simultaneously get out of a covered call, which is called an *unwind*. If you unwind a covered call, you will sell your stock and simultaneously buy back the call option. As before, the reason for doing both transactions simultaneously is to prevent execution risk. Most brokerage firms that offer buy-write screens also have unwind screens available online. If you are an avid covered call writer, you should strongly consider using the buy-write and unwind transaction screens if you are buying the shares at the same time you are writing the calls.

At the beginning of this chapter, we said that investors can write calls against shares they have been holding in the account. This is usually called *overwriting* and generally leads to a conservative use of covered calls since the investor was obviously willing to assume the downside risk. The buy-write, however, is typically used as a one-time strategy for the sole purpose of writing the call, which is a speculative use of covered calls. The buy-writer's philosophy is usually (not always) to find a high option premium and then buy the stock and simultaneously write the call. After all, why would they need to buy the stock at that same moment? The answer is that they have usually wish to capture a premium-rich option and must buy the stock to cover the upside risk. Entering the orders together as a buy-write gives these investors a little added edge.

While buy-writes are generally speculative, they do not have to be. Some investors, as we discussed previously, may be perfectly comfortable holding a certain stock but wish to write in-the-money calls to provide for a bigger downside hedge. These investors often do end up getting assigned and losing the shares. Buy-writes can be a cost-efficient way to continually enter into new trades.

Regardless of whether you are comfortable in assuming the downside risk or not, the buy-write can add a little edge for those times when you wish to buy the stock and write the call in the same transaction. You may wish to check with your broker to see if they offer a "buy-write" screen and get in the habit of using it whenever you wish to enter the two trades simultaneously. If you are entering buy-writes, just be certain that you have properly identified your reason for buying the stock. If it is purely for the ability to write the call then understand that it is a speculative investment and adjust the size of your trade accordingly.

Roll-Outs

We learned earlier that it doesn't really matter if the stock price rises above the strike of the short call at expiration since this is the maximum gain portion of the profit and loss curve. While it may not be the ideal situation, it is not a losing situation by any means. When this happens, most investors feel they only have two choices. First, they can let their shares get called away. Second, they can buy back the call and end up with an unrealized gain in the stock. However, there is a third and often overlooked strategy available, which is called a *roll-out*.

Assume that AGIX is $21 at expiration and the October $20 call that you sold is trading for the $1 intrinsic value and November $20 call is trading for $3. You could buy back the October $20 call and simultaneously sell the November $20 call for a net credit of $2. In other words, you have *rolled out* to the following month. Effectively you sold another $20 call for $2, which again lowers the cost basis of your stock by the same amount.

Of course, you could choose to sell other strikes as well. If, instead, you sold the November $25 call you would be *rolling out and up* (rolling out in time and up in strikes). This strategy is used when the stock makes a significant upward move. For example, assume AGIX is trading for $25 at October expiration and the $20 call you sold is trading for the $5 intrinsic value. Further assume that the November $25 call is trading for $3. You could buy back the October $20 call and sell the November $25 call for a net debit of $2. Effectively, you have paid $2 for the chance to make an additional $3 (the difference in strikes less the $2 paid) if AGIX is above $25 at expiration.

In our example, you had a cost basis of $14.41 on the stock. If you buy back the $20 call and sell the $25 call then your cost basis increases by $2 to $16.41 and you could make a maximum of $25 for a net gain of $8.59, which is $3 more than your previous gain. Rolling out or rolling up trades are collectively known as *rolling trades* and they allow investors to make another investment based on the same shares that are already in the account. If you don't want to let go of your shares, you can always execute a rolling trade. *The important point is that you make your decision based on sound objectives rather than rolling up just because you don't want to see your stock taken away.*

Roll-Downs

A roll-down is the reverse of a roll-up. With roll-downs, the investor buys back the existing strike but sells a *lower strike* call against the shares. Investors are often forced to do this when the stock price falls since the higher strike price may be trading for too low of a price to make it worthwhile. For example, assume AGIX is trading for $15 at expiration. The October $20 call you sold is close to worthless but you may find that the November $20 isn't commanding much of a premium either. You could execute a simultaneous order to buy back the October $20 call and sell the November $15 call.

The problem with writing the $15 call is that it reduces the potential sales price of the stock. By selling the $15 calls, you have the potential obligation to sell your shares for $15, which means the potential sales price is reduced by five dollars. You will always reduce your potential selling price when you roll down. For example, assume you can buy back the October $20 call and sell the November $15 call for a net credit of $2. Your cost basis on the stock is reduced from $14.41 to $12.41

but now you have the potential obligation to sell you shares for $15. In this case, the roll-down worked out okay but, depending on the cost basis of the stock you could lock yourself into a potential loss if assigned. For instance, if you cost basis on the stock was $18 and you rolled down for a net credit of $2 then your cost basis is $16 but you may have to sell the shares for $15.

Remember that the covered call strategy is a neutral to slightly bullish strategy. If the stock price is falling then you may be in the wrong trade and it's usually not the best idea to try to "write" your way out of the loss by selling lower strike calls. In most cases, you just end up digging a deeper hole. But depending on your cost basis, it can be a viable trade so is worth understanding.

In the Long Run, Covered Calls are Less Risky

There are some studies that have shown where covered calls have produced superior returns to the market while reducing downside risk, which seems to go against the premise of the risk-reward tradeoff. But these studies are considering shorter time periods when the markets are relatively flat and, in these times, covered calls will outperform the market. But it's a myth that they will always outperform the market while reducing your risk, which is what these studies lead many to believe. They are not taking into account the "homeruns" that stocks sometimes hit during good markets and covered call writers will not participate in these to the same degree as long stock holders. In the long run, covered call writing is a more conservative than owning stocks. As stated before, this doesn't mean that there won't be situations where the covered call writer outperforms the long stock holder. We're just saying that you cannot consistently reduce your risk and increase your returns over time.

Despite this fact, covered call writing can be a very lucrative and rewarding strategy. In fact, in 2002, the CBOE created a buy-write index (BXM), which shows how a portfolio of covered calls would have performed over a given time period by writing slightly out-of-the-money calls against the S&P 500 Index. At certain times, the BXM can boast some pretty impressive results. Covered calls are also a good strategy that can be combined with other strategies; they do not need to be used as an independent strategy.

For example, rather than buying shares of stock, you could start by selling naked puts as a way to acquire the stock. Remember, if you sell a put, you create the potential obligation to buy stock. Selling naked puts is not a strategy that we will cover but we're just trying to make the point of how option strategies can be used in conjunction with one another. Continuing, once the stock is acquired, you could then write calls as a way to sell the stock. By adding the additional step of selling puts, the investor acquires at least two option premiums – one to buy the stock and one to sell the stock. He may acquire more if he's able to write additional puts to acquire the stock and additional calls to sell the stock.

So while covered calls may be presented as a basic strategy, don't think that experienced investors do not use them. They can be very powerful when combined in the right ways for specific situations. As with any strategy, there are many ways to fine-tune them to suit your needs. The important thing is that you understand the basics. Once you do, you'll find that covered calls may not be so basic after all.

||||||||||||||||||||||||||||||||||||||||||||||||||||||||||||||||||||||||||||||||||||||||||||||||

 Key Concepts

1) Covered calls are created by selling calls in a 1:1 ratio against your long stock.

2) The covered call strategy is a neutral to slightly bullish outlook.

3) The risk of a covered call is that the stock price falls.

4) Covered calls are synthetically equivalent to naked puts. If you would not write a naked put on a particular stock then you should not use a covered call either.

5) Do not expect to get assigned (called out) of a covered call early. If you do, it only helps the position since you receive the maximum reward early.

6) You can buy stock and sell calls simultaneously with a buy-write.

7)   In the long run, covered calls must be more conservative than long stock.

||||||||||||||||||||||||||||||||||||||||||||||||||||||||||||||||||||||||||||||||||||||||||||||||

Chapter Seven Questions

1) **You own 300 shares of ABC stock, trading for $60, and have written 3 $65 calls. You have the:**
    a)   Right to buy 300 shares of ABC for $65
    b)   Obligation to buy 300 shares of ABC for $65
    c)   Right to sell 300 shares of ABC for $65
    d)   Obligation to sell 300 shares of ABC for $65

2) **You purchased 200 shares of stock at $40 and have written 2 $40 calls for $1. Your cost basis on the stock is effectively:**
    a) $39
    b) $41
    c) $38
    d)   Cannot be determined

3) **You have written 4 $50 call options against your stock. How much money will you receive if you are assigned?**
    a) $200
    b) $5,000
    c) $2,000
    d) $20,000

4) **The risk of a covered call is that:**
    a)   You might have to give up your stock at a very unfavorable price
    b)   The stock price falls
    c)   The premium of the short call falls
    d)   The stock price stays the same

5) **Covered call writers should:**
    a)   Only write short-term calls since they are exposed to the sharpest time decay
    b)   Write the month that brings in an adequate premium relative to the risk.
    c)   Never write out-of-the-money calls
    d)   Never write in-the-money calls

6) **Assuming you are not looking for highly speculative investments, one of the most important standards for selecting stocks to write calls against is for you to:**
   a) Write calls that have large premiums
   b) Write calls against stock that you are comfortable holding
   c) Write calls on highly volatile stocks
   d) Write calls only on long-term options

7) **If you write a covered call and the stock's price rises above the strike price prior to expiration, you should:**
   a) Expect to get assigned on the ex-date
   b) Expect to get assigned the following day
   c) Expect to get assigned that day
   d) Only expect to get assigned at expiration if the stock's price is still above the strike

8) **You have written a $50 call against your stock, which is trading for $57 with 20 days remaining until expiration. If you decide to buy back the $50 call and simultaneously sell the $55 call (same expiration), what is this called and will is produce a net credit or debit?**
   a) Roll-up, net credit
   b) Roll-up, net debit
   c) Roll-down, net credit
   d) Roll-down, net debit

9) **You bought 200 shares of ABC stock for $30 and have written two calls against it for $1 each. The calls have expired worthless and you wish to write calls again for the following month. However, the stock has now dropped to $25 so you decide to write two $25 calls for $2 each. What is your new cost basis and what is your profit or loss if you are assigned?**
   a) $30 cost basis, $5 loss
   b) $27 cost basis $2 loss
   c) $24 cost basis, $1 loss
   d) $24 cost basis, $1 profit

10) **You bought 1,000 shares of XYZ stock for $20 and wrote 10 $20 calls for $2. At expiration, the stock is trading for $15. What is your unrealized profit or loss at this point?**
   a) $2 gain
   b) $2 loss
   c) $3 gain
   d) $3 loss

11) **You bought 100 shares of ABC stock for $50 and wrote the $50 call for $1. At expiration, the stock trading for $55 and the call is trading at parity (worth the $5 intrinsic value). If you buy the call to close:**
   a)   You will be left with a loss since you sold the call for $1 and bought it back for $5.
   b)   You will have a $1 gain
   c)   You will have a $5 loss
   d)   You will just break even

12) **If you write a covered call, you:**
   a)   Can always exit it by purchasing the call back
   b)   Must remain in the covered call until expiration
   c)   Can exit the position by exercising the call
   d)   Can exit the position by selling a put

13) **You bought 100 shares of ABC for $30 and wrote the $30 call for $2. What is your static return?**
   a)   8.4%
   b)   6.7%
   c)   7.1%
   d)   5.8%

14) **You bought 100 shares of ABC for $30 and wrote the $30 call for $2. What is your breakeven return?**
   a)   8.4%
   b)   6.7%
   c)   7.1%
   d)   4.8%

15) You bought 100 shares of ABC for $70 and wrote the $70 call for $3. What is your return if exercised?

    a)   5.9%
    b)   3.2%
    c)   6.2%
    d)   4.5%

16) If you write an in-the-money call against your shares, you:

    a)   Can only make the risk-free rate as a maximum return
    b)   Are guaranteed to make money on the position
    c)   Cannot make money on this position
    d)   Can make money as long as a time premium is present

17) In the long run, covered calls must be:

    a)   More risky due to the added risk of the short call
    b)   More risky due to the downside risk of the stock
    c)   More conservative and therefore have lower returns
    d)   More conservative and therefore have higher returns

18) Buy-writes are orders that are used primarily to:

    a)   Increase execution risk
    b)   Eliminate execution risk
    c)   Increase your cost basis
    d)   Increase the break even point

19) You purchased 100 shares of XYZ for $50 and sold a one-month $50 call for $2. The stock is $53 at expiration and you are assigned on the call. What is your ANNUALIZED rate of return?

    a)   30%
    b)   40%
    c)   50%
    d)   60%

20) What is the rationale for the covered call strategy?

    a)   To make lower returns by increasing risk
    b)   To make higher returns by lowering risk
    c)   To make higher returns by increasing risk
    d)   To make more consistent returns and allow compounding to work for you

Chapter Seven - Answers

1) You own 300 shares of ABC stock, trading for $60, and have written 3 $65 calls. You have the:

d) Obligation to sell 300 shares of ABC for $65

Writing calls creates the potential obligation to sell your shares for the strike price. It is a potential obligation because you're only required to if the short call exercises. You can also get out of the obligation by buying the $65 call to close.

2) You purchased 200 shares of stock at $40 and have written 2 $40 calls for $1. Your cost basis on the stock is effectively:

a) $39

Because you wrote a contract equivalent number of calls against your shares, the premium can just be subtracted from the cost in order to find the cost basis. In this example, you paid $40 for the stock and received $1 from selling the call, which means your cost basis is $39. We can show this another way too. You paid 200 shares * $40 = $8,000 for the stock and received 2 contracts * $1 = $200 for the options, which makes your total cash outlay $7,800. Because you own 200 shares, your average cost is $7,800/200 = $39 per share.

3) You have written 4 $50 call options against your stock. How much money will you receive if you are assigned?

d) $20,000

If assigned, you will sell 400 shares for the $50 strike, which makes the total you will receive equal to $20,000.

4) The risk of a covered call is that:

b) The stock price falls

The risk of a covered call is that the stock falls. Giving up your stock at an unfavorable price is a missed opportunity but certainly not a risk of principal.

5) Covered call writers should:

b) Write the month that brings in an adequate premium relative to the risk.

All else constant, short-term calls are good to write for many reasons. But you must remember that all strategies are tradeoffs between risk and reward. Short-term options do decay faster but they do not bring in as much premium as longer-term options. It is up to the investor to find the right mix of premium and time so that you feel you are fairly compensated for the risk.

6) **Assuming you are not looking for highly speculative investments, one of the most important standards for selecting stocks to write calls against is for you to:**

    b)   Write calls against stock that you are comfortable holding

If you are willing to hold the stock regardless of whether options are traded or not, then you are willing to assume the downside risk. Writing calls with this mindset means that the calls are generating income and reducing your downside exposure, which makes it a less risky position.

7) **If you write a covered call and the stock's price rises above the strike price prior to expiration, you should:**

    d)   Only expect to get assigned at expiration if the stock's price is still above the strike

No matter where the stock price may be, it is not in the long call holder's best interest to exercise early. While it can happen, you shouldn't expect to get assigned early.

8) **You have written a $50 call against your stock, which is trading for $57 with 20 days remaining until expiration. If you decide to buy back the $50 call and simultaneously sell the $55 call (same expiration), what is this called and will is produce a net credit or debit?**

    b)   Roll-up, net debit

You are rolling up from the $50 strike to a $55 so this is a roll-up. Because you're buying back the *lower* strike price (more valuable strike) that means you will spend more money than you are receiving, which makes the trade a net debit. This trade will increase the cost basis of your long stock position but will also increase your potential selling price from $50 to $55.

9) **You bought 200 shares of ABC stock for $30 and have written two calls against it for $1 each. The calls have expired worthless and you wish to write calls again for the following month. However, the stock has now dropped to $25 so you decide to write two $25 calls for $2 each. What is your new cost basis and what is your profit or loss if you are assigned?**

    b) $27 cost basis $2 loss

Your original cost basis is $30 - $1 = $29. If you roll down to the $25 strike, you will receive $2 for it, which makes your new cost basis $27. However, by rolling down the strikes, you're also getting less money from the sale of the stock if you should get assigned. Your cost basis is $27 but you'd only receive $25 if assigned, which potentially locks you into a $2 loss. It's not a loss at this point as you could roll up to a higher strike at a later date. But if you were assigned at this point, you'd have a $2 loss.

10) You bought 1,000 shares of XYZ stock for $20 and wrote 10 $20 calls for $2. At expiration, the stock is trading for $15. What is your unrealized profit or loss at this point?

d) $3 loss

Your cost basis is $18 (paid $20 and received $2 for the calls) and the calls are worthless so you have no obligation to sell your stock. However, with the stock at $15, you are currently in a $3 loss if you should sell the stock for the current $18 stock price. This example shows that the risk of a covered call is that the stock falls.

11) You bought 100 shares of ABC stock for $50 and wrote the $50 call for $1. At expiration, the stock trading for $55 and the call is trading at parity (worth the $5 intrinsic value). If you buy the call to close:

d) $3 loss

When you purchased the shares for $20 and wrote the calls for $2, your cost basis was $18 and you had the potential obligation to sell your shares for $20 at expiration. With the stock at $15 at expiration, you have a $3 unrealized loss at that point. In other words, because you effectively paid $18, if you sold those shares for the current market value of $15, you'd have a $3 loss.

12) If you write a covered call, you:

a)   Can always exit it by purchasing the call back

You can always escape your obligations of a covered call (or of any option position for that matter) by entering a reversing trade. For the covered call, this means you would have to buy back the call since you originally sold it.

13) You bought 100 shares of ABC for $30 and wrote the $30 call for $2. What is your static return?

c)   7.1%

If you pay $30 for the stock and write the $30 call for $2, your cost basis is $28. The static return is measured assuming the stock is the same price at expiration, which is the current value of $30. So if you were to sell the stock at that moment, you'd have a gain of $2/$28 = 7.1%.

14) You bought 100 shares of ABC for $30 and wrote the $30 call for $2. What is your breakeven return?

b)   6.7%

You purchased shares for $30 and wrote the $30 call for $2, which makes your cost basis $28. This means the stock can fall from its current price of $30 down to your cost basis of $28, or 6.7%, and you'd just break even on the trade.

15) You bought 100 shares of ABC for $70 and wrote the $70 call for $3. What is your return if exercised?

d)   4.5%

You bought shares for $70 and wrote the $70 call for $3 so your cost basis is $67. If the long position exercises, you will sell your shares for the strike price of $70, which means your return is $3/$67 = 4.5%.

16) If you write an in-the-money call against your shares, you:

d)   Can make money as long as a time premium is present

If you write an in-the-money call against your long stock position, you can still make money on the trade as long as the call has some time premium. For example, if you buy shares at $50 and write a $45 call for $6, then there is $1 time value on the call and that is the amount you could make by selling this call. Your cost basis would be $44 and you'd have the potential obligation to sell your shares for $45. The only time you cannot make money by selling an in-the-money call is if the option is trading at parity (exactly for the intrinsic amount). In this example, if the $45 call was trading for $5, then selling this call makes your cost basis $45 and you'd have the potential obligation to sell your shares for $45.

17) In the long run, covered calls must be:

c)   More conservative and therefore have lower returns

Covered calls have less risk than a long stock position for the fact that you are reducing your downside risk by selling the call. If you have less risk, you must have lower returns. Again, this does not mean that a covered call writer cannot beat the long stock position in certain markets. But overall it is a less risky position and will have lower returns for the market as a whole.

18) **Buy-writes are orders that are used primarily to:**

    b)   Eliminate execution risk

Buy writes allow you to simultaneously buy the stock and sell the call. This prevents adverse price movement between the trades. The buy write therefore eliminates execution risk.

19) **You purchased 100 shares of XYZ for $50 and sold a one-month $50 call for $2. The stock is $53 at expiration and you are assigned on the call. What is your ANNUALIZED rate of return?**

    c)   50%

By purchasing the stock for $50 and selling the one-month $50 call for $2, your cost basis is $48. If you are assigned, you will receive $50 per share, which means your simple return is $2/$48 = 4.17%. To annualize this figure, we must realize there are 12 one-month periods in a year so we'd multiply 4.2% * 12 = 0.50, or 50% annualized return. This is just telling us that if we were able to continue this performance for one year that we'd have a 50% return (not counting the compounding of returns).

20) **What is the rationale for the covered call strategy?**

    d)   To make more consistent returns and allow compounding to work for you

Covered call writers are trying to capture the more probable returns more often. This allows for more consistent returns and thus allows compounding to take effect.

Chapter Eight

Long Calls & Long Puts

In the last chapter, we found out that the covered call strategy relies on the purchase of stock and the sale of a call. We also found that the strategy has a potentially large downside risk since you must buy the stock and the sale of the call may only provide a relatively small downside hedge. Holding stock creates one of the biggest risks for investors – whether using covered calls or not.

Short stock positions create an equally big risk for short-sellers wishing to capitalize on a fall in the stock's price. Investors and speculators can get the nearly the same benefits of long and short stock positions but with far less risk by understanding the strategies of the *long call* and *long put*.

As we learned earlier in the book, puts work in exactly the same way as calls but in the opposite direction. So for this chapter, we have combined the strategies of long calls and long puts rather than presenting them separately. If you understand the motivation and techniques for buying and rolling call options, you will also understand how to apply those techniques for puts. So to make better use of our time, we're going to look at the long call strategy in detail and just close with a quick example using puts.

One way that investors can greatly reduce the downside risk of stock ownership is to simply buy calls rather than stocks. But downside protection is not the only benefit that investors get by purchasing call options. They also gain tremendous leverage and the ability to better diversify their investments. So there are three main reasons why investors and traders buy calls rather than stock:

* Protection
* Leverage
* Diversification

Which reason is most important depends on what type of investor you are and what you're trying to accomplish. While any one of these benefits may appear to be the best to you now, it's equally important to understand the other two so let's take a look at each in turn.

Protection

Let's assume you are bullish on IBM and believe it will rise sharply over then next six months and wish to buy 200 shares. Table 8-1 lists the current stock price along with some April IBM option quotes with 230 days until expiration:

Table 8-1: IBM Option Quotes

IBM												79.46	-0.08
Sep 04, 2005 @ 10:50 ET (Data 20 Minutes Delayed)							Bid N/A	Ask N/A	Size N/AxN/A		Vol 3680800		

Calls	Last Sale	Net	Bid	Ask	Vol	Open Int	Puts	Last Sale	Net	Bid	Ask	Vol	Open Int
06 Apr 50.00 (IBZ DJ-E)	0	pc	30.20	30.50	0	0	06 Apr 50.00 (IBZ PJ-E)	0	pc	0.05	0.15	0	0
06 Apr 55.00 (IBM DK-E)	0	pc	25.40	25.70	0	0	06 Apr 55.00 (IBM PK-E)	0	pc	0.15	0.25	0	0
06 Apr 60.00 (IBM DL-E)	0	pc	20.70	21.00	0	0	06 Apr 60.00 (IBM PL-E)	0	pc	0.30	0.40	0	220
06 Apr 65.00 (IBM DM-E)	0	pc	16.20	16.50	0	0	06 Apr 65.00 (IBM PM-E)	0	pc	0.60	0.75	0	24
06 Apr 70.00 (IBM DN-E)	13.00	pc	11.90	12.20	0	32	06 Apr 70.00 (IBM PN-E)	0	pc	1.20	1.35	0	51
06 Apr 75.00 (IBM DO-E)	0	pc	8.10	8.30	0	30	06 Apr 75.00 (IBM PO-E)	2.05	pc	2.30	2.45	0	1164
06 Apr 80.00 (IBM DP-E)	5.50	pc	5.00	5.20	0	871	06 Apr 80.00 (IBM PP-E)	4.00	pc	4.20	4.40	0	1187

If you buy 200 shares of stock it will cost about $16,000, which also represents the maximum amount you could lose on the investment. Although it would be hard to imagine that IBM becomes worthless, you'd certainly have to agree that a loss of, say 30% or $4,800 is not out of the question. Let's see if we can construct a more favorable risk-reward profile for less money by purchasing call options.

In this example, we're assuming that you're bullish on IBM, which is a *directional* outlook. In other words, you are buying the call option as a near *substitute* for a stock and you are not attempting to trade the volatility component of this option. The only decision you've made is that you think the stock's price will rise. With this one-dimensional outlook in mind, make sure you buy an option that has a high *directional* or stock component to it. Chapter Six showed us that if you wish to buy a call as a stock substitute that you should look for one with a delta in the 0.80 to 0.85 range.

As stated in the Chapter Two, your brokerage firm should certainly supply the delta values. However, if the firm does not, you can find them at a number of online resources, free of charge, such as at the Options Industry Council's (OIC) site at www.888options.com, from PCQuote at www.pcquote.com, or from the Philadelphia Stock Exchange at www.phlx.com.

If not, that same chapter showed that we can find a sufficiently high delta by looking for a put option with about 30 to 40 cents above the *cost of carry*. The corresponding call (same strike) will have the delta we're looking for. So which strike is this? At the time these quotes were taken, the risk-free interest rate was about 3% so the cost of carry for a $79.46 stock for 283 days is $79.46 * .03 * 283/360 = $1.87. If we tack on 40 cents to this price, we get $2.27 and the closest put to that value is the $75 strike.

We can also find a close approximation for the delta in a roundabout way by using a little theory we learned in Chapter Two. There we learned from Pricing Principle #6 that the difference between any two call (or put) prices cannot exceed the difference in their strikes. We can use this principle to give us a reasonable estimate of the delta. For example, look at the asking prices for the $50 and $55 calls, which are $30.50 and $25.70, respectively. The difference in these prices is $30.50 - $25.70 = $4.80. The maximum that difference could ever be is the difference in strikes, or $5. So the average delta between these two strikes is $4.80/$5.00 =0.96. This tells us that the delta of the $50 call (lower strike) is somewhat higher than 0.96 while the delta for the higher $55 strike is somewhat less. Regardless, the delta of the $50 call is too high.

As we check the other combinations, we'd find that the $70 and $75 calls are $12.20 and $8.30, respectively. The difference in their prices is $12.20 - $8.30 = $3.90. If we divide that by the $5 difference in strikes, we'd find that the average delta is $3.90/$5 = 0.78. This means that the $70 strike has a somewhat higher delta and the $75 strike has a somewhat lower delta so the $75 strike looks like the one we'd want to trade. In fact, at the time these quotes were taken, the delta on the $75 strike was 0.73.

If you buy a strike lower than $75, you are paying for additional intrinsic value unnecessarily. If you buy a higher strike, there is too much time premium in the option and it may not respond to smaller changes in the stock's price. (And that means you could lose on the option even if the stock price rises.)

It's very important to understand why we choose a strike with a delta of roughly 0.80. The reason is that a call option with a delta of 1.0 is no longer an option; it is now a perfect stock substitute. There is no time premium in a call option with a delta of 1.0 and it will rise and fall dollar-for-dollar with the underlying stock. Keep in mind that this is only true as long as the delta remains at 1.0. It could decrease if the underlying stock price falls sufficiently. However, a call with a delta of 1.0 contains a lot of intrinsic value that we would rather not pay for. So you do not need to find a delta of 1.0 but should get close and the 0.80 to 0.85 range will suit your needs as a means for stock replacement.

On the other hand, an option with a much lower delta, say 0.50, has a lot of time premium and therefore behaves more like an option rather than stock. When we say "behaves like an option," we really mean that it doesn't respond too systematically with the stock. Its price can also be greatly affected by time decay as well as volatility. The important point is that you want to initially purchase an option that behaves much more like the stock.

 If you are buying call options as a means of stock replacement then buy relatively high deltas in the 0.80 to 0.85 range.

Now that we've located the proper strike ($75), we simply place the following order:

Buy to open, two April $75 calls, symbol IBMDO, at market (or limit)

Of course, you could place a "limit order" rather than a "market" order to assure the price but then you cannot guarantee that the order will fill. By placing a market order, we are allowing some price fluctuations while the order is being routed but are also guaranteed to get the order filled.

Once the order is filled, we are effectively controlling 200 shares of stock for up to the next 230 days. We do not need to remain in the contract for the full term as we can certainly exit the contract at any time by selling it.

Assume that the order is filled for the $8.30 asking price. Your account will be debited 200 * $8.30 = $1,660 plus commissions. Notice that it was going to cost you nearly $16,000 to buy 200 shares of stock but you can effectively control those same shares for only $1,660. And it is this difference in prices that represents the protection you get from call options since the most you can lose with the call is $1,660. Figure 8-2 shows the profit and loss curve for our two IBM April $75 calls:

Figure 8-2

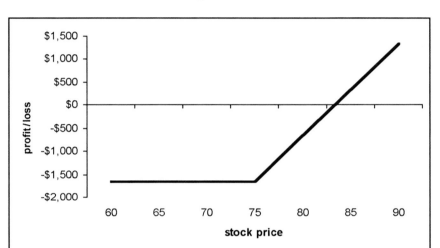

Notice the flat part of the profit and loss curve to the left of the $75 strike. This shows that our maximum loss is defined and that is the absolute most we can lose. In other words, the call option provides protection. For example, assume that IBM has a bad earnings report and the stock plummets down over 30% to $55, down $24.46. The stock trader is down 200 shares * 24.46 = $4,892. The option trader is down only $1,660. If the stock price continues to fall, the stock trader continues to lose money while the option trader's losses are capped at $1,660. The option trader's maximum loss is 100% defined the second the trade is placed.

There may be those investors who believe this is an unrealistic comparison because they would never allow this type of loss to happen to them because they use stop orders. But as our discussion in Chapter Four showed, stop orders do not prevent losses. In most cases, stop orders can work reasonably well but the point is that they are not guaranteed to limit you to a fixed sized loss. Call options will. In this example, the call trader is 100% certain that the maximum loss is $1,660 while the stock trader cannot make any such claim.

Another reason that options provide better protection than stop orders is that stop orders are "path dependent" while options are "time dependent." This simply means that the performance of a stop order depends on the "path" the stock takes. While it is possible for a stop to protect you, it is equally likely that it may force you to sell too early. For instance, assume you have the above 200 shares of IBM and place an order to sell your shares at a stop price of $78. The stock might take the path of falling to $78 – thus forcing you to sell your shares – and then immediately turn around and climb much higher. In this instance, the stop order did prevent you from losing but it also forced you to miss future gains *because of the particular path* the stock took. Had you been holding the $75 call however, you never would be "triggered" out of the position just because of the path of the stock. Instead, by holding the call, you are locked into the $75 buy price over a period of time. Only if the stock's price rises after the call option expires will you miss out on future gains. In other words, you are constrained by time, which is why we say that options offer protection that is *time dependent* while stop orders offer protection that is *path dependent*. Unfortunately, most of the major losses in stocks come after the close and there is nothing you can do with a stop order but wait for the opening price. Stop orders are not an equal substitute for options.

In order to be fair with our comparisons, isn't it possible that our call option could expire worthless at expiration but *then* the stock could rise thus making the stock trader better off? That's true, but in many cases the call buyer has the ability to buy the stock at the lower market price. For example, let's go back to the beginning when we were deciding on whether or not to buy the stock. At that time IBM was trading for $79.46 and the April $75 call was trading for $8.30. If you have $79.46 available per share to buy the stock but decide to only spend $8.30 to buy the call then you have $79.46 - $8.30 = $71.16 in cash that can earn interest. Now let's assume that the stock price falls to $70 thus making your call option expire worthless at expiration. It appears that the stock owner is better off because at least he has shares that might rise in the future while you have lost 100% of your investment with the $75 call. However, if you are still bullish on the stock at that time, you can buy the shares at $70 market price out of the $71.16 that you have sitting in cash.

The $71.16 price is the crossover point between the two strategies of buying 200 shares of stock versus buying two April $75 calls as shown in Figure 8-3:

Figure 8-3: Comparison between Long Stock and Long $75 Calls

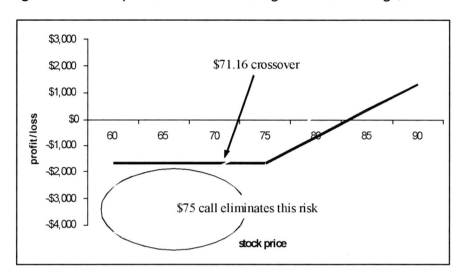

If the stock's price is below $71.16 at expiration then you will have enough money sitting in cash to buy the shares of stock if you wish. However, if the stock's price is above $71.16 then you will not have enough money to buy the shares unless you contribute more money. We could increase this $71.16 number a bit if we wanted to include the interest you could have earned on the cash but that will probably be negligible. The point is that the stock trader is not necessarily better off just because the call option trader lost on the option. The option trader can always elect to buy the shares in the open market at the lower market price.

If the stock's price is above $71.16 at expiration, the option trader will under perform the stock trader as shown in Figure 8-3; that's why the stock line lies above the call option line. The reason is that the call buyer must pay a time premium for the $75 call and that money is gone for good at expiration. The time premium is the cost of losing less money for all stock prices below $71.16. In this example, the $75 call has $3.84 worth of time premium and that can never be recovered. It is the true cost of being able to always buy shares for $75.

For example, assume the stock is $85 at expiration. The stock trader makes a profit of $85 - $79.46 = $5.54. With the stock at $85, the $75 call is worth exactly $10, which means the option trader makes a profit of $10 - $8.30 = $1.70. Notice that the difference in their profits is $5.54 - $1.70 = $3.84, which is exactly the amount of the time premium in the $75 call. Pick any expiration stock price above the $75 strike and you'll find that the stock trader's profits are exactly $3.84 larger than the option traders. This can be seen by plotting the $75 call option's profit and loss diagram against that of the long stock position as shown in Figure 8-4:

Figure 8-4

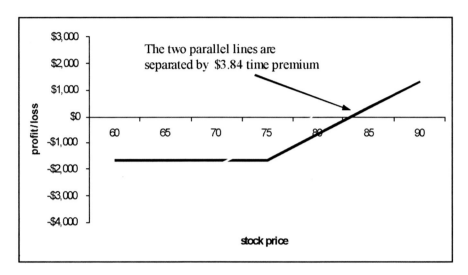

In Chapter Five, the put-call parity formula showed us that if you were absolutely certain that a stock was going to rise that you should either buy the shares with borrowed funds or buy the call and sell the put. Figure 8-4 shows why. The reason is that the long call buyer will always under perform the long stock buyer by the amount of the time premium for all regions above the strike price. Notice that above the $75 stock price, the two profit and loss curves run parallel to each other. Those two lines will never meet at any higher stock price and that's a way of showing that the long call buyer will never get the time premium back. However, since we don't know for sure whether a stock will rise, the call option provides a lot of protection by removing all of the downside risk that we showed in Figure 8-3. The time premium is the cost of that protection.

If the call buyer performs worse than the stock buyer by the amount of time premium then why would anybody buy the call option? Because it's that same $3.84 time premium that provides the downside protection. Option traders give up a little bit of upside profit potential in exchange for greatly reducing the downside risk.

If you look to the left of the crossover point in Figure 8-4 you'll see that if the stock falls below $75, the call owner will lose less than the long stock owner. With the stock below $75 at expiration, the call owner loses all intrinsic value in the option but also loses the $3.84 time premium, which means the total loss would be $75 - $3.84 = $71.16 and is exactly the crossover point that we previously calculated.

So protection is one of the big benefits of buying options. Call options provide protection from the downside risk of the stock. In this example, you can spend $79.46 per share today for the 200 shares of IBM and take a very big chance that the stock's price will fall by more than the $8.30 cost of the $75 call option. Or you can spend $8.30 today for the call option and fully benefit if the shares rise or even if they fall below $71.16 at expiration.

How does the call option protect us from the large downside risk of a stock? Our put-call parity formula showed us that it comes from the fact that call options are really leveraged long stock plus a put option in disguise:

$$C = S - Pv\ (E) + put$$

If you own a call option, you are effectively borrowing money to buy stock, S – Pv (E), and then buying a put option to protect your downside. Long stock owners do not have the put option, which is why they have a much bigger downside risk.

Let's see if the put-call parity formula holds true. At this time, the risk-free rate is roughly 3%, which means the effective interest rate for 230 days is .03 * (230/360) = .0192. Therefore, the present value of the exercise price is $75/1.0192 = $73.59. Using the quotes in Table 8-1 we see the $75 put is worth $2.45. Using our put-call parity formula, the value of the call must be S – Pv (E) + P, or $79.46 - $73.59 + $2.45 = $8.32, which is very close to the $8.30 quoted call price. This shows that when you pay the $8.30 price for the $75 call that the $75 put is included in that purchase.

This clearly demonstrates our first motivating factor for buying calls – protection from large losses. It also shows that call options with high deltas and long terms to expiration can be viewed as less risky than long stock purchases. Your maximum risk is much smaller and known up front and that is something we cannot say for stock owners.

Leverage

Leverage is our second motivating factor for buying call options. Leverage is a term borrowed from physics, which is simply defined as a mechanical advantage that allows the user to magnify a force. For example, if you need to change a car tire, you can lift a car off the ground with very little effort with a jack. The jack provides a tremendous mechanical advantage to the user making a seemingly impossible task easy enough to do with one hand.

In a similar way, options provide tremendous financial leverage to the user. For any given stock price movement, you can create a bigger "force" and get a bigger return from a fixed amount of money. For example, let's revisit a comparison we made between the two investors in the last section. The stock investor buys shares of IBM at $79.46 while the option buyer pays $8.30. Now let's assume that IBM closes at $85 at expiration. To the stock trader, that represents a return of $85/$79.46 = 1.069, which is approximately 7%. With the stock at $85 at expiration, the $75 call is worth the $10 intrinsic value. The return to the call trader is then $10/$8.30 = 1.205 = 20.5%, or roughly 21%. In other words, a 7% increase in the stock's price led to a 21% return on the option. Just as with mechanical leverage, the option was able to take a tiny "force" of 7% and magnify it nearly three-fold.

Leverage is an elusive concept though. To many investors, it sounds as if the option trader performed better simply because of the higher returns. After all, it appears obvious that you would make more money with a 21% return on your money rather than only 7%. That would be true if we were investing the same dollar amounts. But if you work through the numbers, you'll find that the dollar amounts are vastly different. In this example, we assumed the stock rose from $79.46 to $85, which is an increase of $5.54. The stock trader therefore makes a profit of 200 shares * $5.54 = $1,108. At expiration, the $75 calls are worth 200 * $10 = $2,000 and cost $1,660, which means the profit to the call buyer is only $340. If the option trade performs better in terms of percentages, why doesn't it perform as well as the stock in terms of *total dollar* profit?

Again, this is a direct result of the $3.84 time premium in the option; that amount is never returned to you. If the option trader had this time premium returned when the option was sold then there would be an additional profit of 200 * $3.84 = $768. Notice that if we add this amount back to the $340 profit we get $768 + $340 = $1,108, which is exactly the same profit of the stock trader. We can look at this relationship another way. Assume there was no time premium in the option when it was purchased, which means it would have been trading for only the intrinsic value of $4.46 rather than $8.30. When it was sold for $10 at expiration, the net gain to the option trader would be $10 - $4.46 = $5.54, which is exactly the same dollar profit as the stock trader. This clearly shows that all intrinsic value is returned to you at expiration, which is why it is less risky to "pay" for intrinsic value. As long as the underlying stock does not move adversely then all intrinsic value remains with the option. The time value, however, is never returned to you under any circumstance.

In order to truly understand the leverage of an option, we must compare "dollar equivalent" exposure. For example, let's assume the $75 call trading for $8.30 has a delta of 0.60. For the next one-dollar move, this option's price will rise by the delta, or 60 cents, from $8.30 to $8.90. This 60-cent move is equivalent to $60 per contract. Now let's see what a stock investor must spend to get this same $60 gain from a one-dollar move in the stock. A stock buyer must buy the delta equivalent number of shares, which is 60 shares of stock and would cost 60 * $79.46 = $4,767.60. So if an option trader buys the $75 call and a stock trader buys 60 shares of stock then both will capture a $60 profit on the next one-dollar move in the stock. Now we just need to compare the costs of these dollar equivalent exposures. The stock trader spends $4,767.60 while the option trader spends $830, which means there is $4,767.60/$830 = 5.7 times as much leverage in the option as compared to the stock. (But keep in mind that this number will change as the delta of the option changes. We're just saying this is how you'd need to calculate the leverage in the option at this point in time.)

Other Views of Leverage

Although the above calculation is probably best for comparing the true leverage of an option there are other views we could take.

For example, say a stock is trading for $100 and a $100 call is trading for $5. One way to view the leverage is to realize that the option trader, in this example, has leveraged the returns by a factor of twenty. That is, for every 100 shares the stock investor buys ($10,000 worth), the option buyer can buy 20 contracts ($10,000/$500 per option = 20).

Let's assume that the stock now rises from $100 to $115. If the stock trader buys 100 shares then the total value would be 100 * $115 = $11,500, which leaves a profit of $1,500. With the stock at $115, the $100 call would be worth $15, or $15 * 2,000 = $30,000 for the 20 contracts.

If we multiply the $1,500 *profit* of the stock trader by 20 we end up with $30,000, which is the value of the option trader's *total position*. In this example, the option trader's total value will always be worth 20 times the stock trader's profit, assuming the $100 call option has intrinsic value. This is a somewhat awkward view of leverage since we're comparing the profit of the stock trader to the total value of the option trader. Still, it is a very common use that you will run across.

It's important to understand that this method only works in such a straightforward way if we compare at-the-money options. Using our IBM example, the stock is $79.46 and the $75 call is trading for $8.30, which means the option trader has leveraged the returns by a factor of $79.46/$8.30 = 9.5 times. Once again, this means that for every 100 shares the stock investor buys ($7,946 worth of stock) the option buyer can control 950 shares since $7,946/$830 = 9.5 contracts, or 950 shares. (You cannot buy fractional contracts but we must assume this to make the comparisons.) Now we should expect that for any given gain in the stock's price, the option's *total value* would by 9.5 times as great as the stock trader's *profits*.

Let's see if it works. Assume the stock rises from $79.46 to $85 by expiration. The stock trader invested $7,946 and can sell for $8,500 for a total *profit* of $554. With the stock at $85, the $75 call would be worth $10, or a total value of 950 shares * $10 = $9,500. However, we see that $9,500/$554 = 17 times. Why does it not equal 9.5 times? The reason is that this option is not at-the-money. The stock is $79.46, which means this $75 call has $4.46 worth of intrinsic value that we must back out. The value that must be subtracted from the $9,500 total option value is then 950 shares * $4.46 = $4,237, which leaves us $5,263. If we take $5,263/$554 we get leverage of 9.5!

Gearing

The leverage described above is known as *gearing* and is actually just an old British term that means leverage. It is not uniquely defined but the two most common definitions are (1) The *stock* price divided by the option price or (2) The *strike* price divided by the option price.

Using definition 1, the way to find gearing is to simply divide the stock price by the option price:

Gearing = Stock price / option price

In our first example, the stock was $100 and the option was $5 so $100/$5 = 20.

This is just another way of saying the stock trader required twenty times the amount of capital to control the same amount of shares.

Using the second definition, gearing would be:

Gearing = Strike price / option price

This gives the same answer of 20. But if the strike was $110 then the gearing is $110/$5 = 22. In this way, the option trader may pay $110 for the stock but is controlling it for $5, so is leveraged by a factor of 22. Many of the trading software you will encounter will have a column labeled "gearing" and it simply shows one of these definitions of leverage.

Omega

There is another term you may see that describes leverage and is called *omega*. Omega measures the relative percentage changes between the stock and the option, which is called an *elasticity* measure. For instance, assume the call in the above example has a delta of 0.50. With the stock at $100 and the call at $5, if the stock were to move $1 (a 1% move) the call will move roughly one half of a point from $5 to $5.50 for a 10% increase. Because the option moved 10 times faster relative to the stock (10% compared to 1%), the elasticity (omega) is 10.

$$\text{Omega} = \frac{\text{Delta / option price}}{1 \text{ / stock price}}$$

This numerator of this formula simply compares the "share equivalent" terms of the option to its price (delta / option price). The denominator just compares one share of stock to its price (1 / stock price). Omega simply finds the ratio of these two values.

Omega can also be written as (stock price / option price) * delta. Using the earlier example, we have a $100 stock price divided by a $5 call option with delta of 0.50 so $100/$5 * 0.50 = 10. Regardless of which measure you use, don't forget the most the most important concept: The higher the leverage the more speculative the position.

The option's leverage comes from the fact that the strike price is simply a partition of the stock price. In this example, if you buy shares of IBM at $79.46, you get all of the upside gains but are also exposed to all of the downside losses. That's because a long stock position contains value for all stock prices above zero. In fact, Pricing Principle #5 from Chapter Two showed us that an option with a zero strike price and infinite time to expiration would be trading for the same price as the stock. A long stock position can therefore be thought of as an option with a zero strike price and no expiration date.

However, if you are holding the $75 call at expiration, it will not have value for all stock prices above zero. Instead, it will only have value for all stock prices above $75. The $75 strike simply splits the stock into two parts: All prices below $75 and all prices above $75. When you buy the $75 call, you're only participating in the gains if the stock rises above $75 but not if it falls below, which is why long call options have an asymmetrical payoff to their profit and loss diagrams.

So option returns appear much higher because we're partitioning the stock's price. In this example, the stock buyer must pay $79.46 but the option trader only pays $8.30 to participate in the gains for all stock prices above $75. It is this difference in bases – $79.46 compared to $8.30 – that creates the leverage. A one-dollar gain to the stock trader produces a much smaller percentage gain than a one-dollar gain to the option trader. However, the total dollar gain to the stock trader will be larger than the total dollar gain to the option trader since the option trader loses out on the time premium.

Many investors get attracted to options because they hear about the high leverage and think they will make more money by trading options rather than stocks. It would be easy to think you would have done much better with options since you would have earned 21% on your money rather than 7% in our example. However, this is really a misperception and comes from the fact that option traders have a much smaller dollar amount of money invested if they are trading an equivalent number of shares in the options. True, their percent returns are higher but the investments are smaller, and the total dollars earned might actually be less than those investing in stocks. In this example, the stock buyer earned 7% on a $16,000 investment while the call buyer earned 21% on a $1,660 investment. The important point to understand is that if you trade the contract equivalent number of shares with options that you will have higher percentage returns but lower total dollar returns (assuming that both the stock and options are profitable).

Couldn't we get a 21% return on our investment if we had purchased $16,000 worth of options? The answer is yes; however, that is a very dangerous (although quite common!) way to use leverage.

There are actually two definitions of leverage that you need to understand:

- Control more shares with the same amount of money (risky use)
- Control the same amount of shares with less money (conservative use)

The great mathematician, Archimedes, once said, "Give me but one firm spot on which to stand, and I will move the earth." He was, of course, talking about the enormous power of the lever. Investors who do not understand the difference between the above two definitions of leverage may end up paying a lot of money to find out just how powerful a force it really is.

Risky Uses of Leverage

Let's take look at the consequences for someone who tries to control more shares with the same amount of money. In our example, the option trader could have invested the full stock amount of nearly $16,000 into the options in which case he would definitely come out ahead of the stock trader in terms of total dollar profits. In that case, he'd truly be earning 21% his stock investment instead of only 7%. However, if you are willing to put $16,000 into stock then you should in no way be willing to place that same amount into an option. Leverage is an incredibly powerful tool but it is a double-edged sword because it magnifies the losses with equal force.

For example, assume you put $16,000 of your allotted IBM stock funds into the April $75 calls. With the stock at $79.46, it would only need to fall to $75 or lower at expiration, or only 5.6%, and you'd lose 100% of your investment. If you had purchased the stock, you'd only be down 5.6%. If mechanical leverage is capable of moving the Earth, financial leverage must also be capable of destroying your account – if you are willing to give it a firm place to stand. If you place the total dollar amount that you're willing to spend on a stock into an option then you're providing a rock-solid foundation inside your account for leverage to stand.

Another reason for not investing the same dollar amount into options as you would for stocks is that you end up controlling a much larger number of shares than you're comfortable holding. If you had placed your stock funds into the April $75 calls, you'd end up controlling $16,000/$830 = 19 contracts, or 1,900 shares. One tiny drop in the stock's price and you're greatly magnifying the dollar swings in your account; there is simply too much leverage working against you if you are only willing to hold 200 shares.

In the previous example, we saw that option traders could spend the same dollar amount on the options that they're willing to spend on stock. This fits the first definition of leverage and is the one you want to avoid. However, by using options, we can also use the second definition of leverage and control the same amount of shares with less money. That's the better way to use options as a risk management tool.

Conservative Uses of Leverage

As stated previously, one conservative use of leverage is to control the same number of shares with fewer dollars at risk. If you are willing to buy 200 shares of IBM and wish to buy calls then stick with two contracts since that controls 200 shares. The leverage you're getting is based on the fact that you're controlling the same amount of shares for less money. You may not make as much in terms of total dollars as a stock trader but you won't lose as much either.

There is another way you may wish to consider using leverage. This method allows us to buy more shares but without jeopardizing great losses. Let's assume you are willing to buy 200 shares of IBM for about $16,000. At the same time, let's also pick a level that you're willing to lose, say 20%. From our previous discussions, we know that stop or stop limit orders cannot guarantee a limited loss. However, you can guarantee a limited loss by using options. In this case, let's take the 20% that you're willing to lose, which is 0.20 * $16,000 = $3,200 and use that money to buy the options. In this example, you would buy $3,200/$830 = 3.8 contracts, which we must round down to three contracts since you cannot buy fractional contracts. You'd end up investing 300 *$8.30 = $2,490 and that is *definitely* the most you could ever lose. You could never define a loss this precisely for the traders buying 200 shares of IBM no matter how closely they may be placing their stop orders. Further, you gained some added leverage because you are now controlling 300 shares rather than 200. This is a nice method for those investors looking to increase their leverage a little while still managing the downside risk. The idea is that you buy options with the amount of money you are willing to lose with the stock. At the beginning of this book, we said that the risk in options depends on how they are used. Hopefully you're starting to find out why. This section showed that we can definitely use them in risky ways, which are often the same ways that create sensational stories for the financial press when things go wrong. However, with a little understanding we can certainly use them in conservative ways.

Diversification

Our third reason for buying options is diversification. Diversification just means that you don't put all your eggs into one basket. The idea is to spread your investment dollars through many different investments. Diversification is the sole reason for the creating of index funds. For instance, if you put $10,000 in an S&P 500 mutual fund and one of the stocks goes belly-up, your investment will not be affected too greatly since there are 499 other stocks to back you up. However, if you had unluckily placed all of your funds into that one stock then you've lost everything. By spreading your investment dollars across many stocks you get the benefits of diversification. Spreading the risk keeps you from having to guess which stocks will perform the best.

Many investors, especially when they are starting out, cannot adequately diversify simply because they do not have enough money to do so. For example, assume you have just $10,000 in your account and wish to buy stocks. If you buy 100 shares of IBM based on the quotes in Figure 8-1, you'd spend over $7,900 on that one investment, which doesn't leave much money left over for anything else. However, because of the reduced cost of options and availability of longer terms to maturity, investors can spread their risk by purchasing call options thereby controlling numerous stocks with relatively little money.

A Brief Detour on Diversification

Many investors buy a fixed number, say 100 shares, thinking this limits the risk. On one hand that's true as you are limited to $100 loss per $1 downward move in the stock. On the other hand, it's deceptively false. Here's why: Say you purchase the following portfolio of six stocks shown with their performances after one year:

Shares	Purchase Price	After 1 year:
100	20	Up 22%
100	18	Up 24%
100	190	Down 18%
100	45	Up 30%
100	15	Up 27%
100	22	Up 34%

On the surface, it certainly looks like an impressive year. There are five gainers and only one loser. Further, all of the gainers are up by a higher percentage than the one loser. But would you be surprised to find out that the overall portfolio is down? That's right. The investor would have less money after one year than he initially invested.

The reason the investor lost money is because the *total dollars* invested in each position are not equal. The maximum amount of money placed among all the gainers was $4,500 (100 shares at $45) while the one position that lost had $19,000 invested (100 shares at $190). So even though there are more winners that are all up by higher *percentages* than the one loser, the overall result is a loss.

The moral of the story is that constant share amounts do not diversify your risk. If stocks are presumed to move in a random fashion, some will be winners and some will be losers. However, if you are placing a much higher investment one particular stock, you are, in effect, pressing your bet on that one stock, which is not optimal in a random market. Think about it this way: If you walked into a casino to bet $10,000 on 10 spins of a roulette wheel, would you feel inclined to bet various amounts on each spin? Do you think your chances are better to win on, say the third spin rather than the eighth? If not, it should make sense to you to bet $1,000 on each spin so that you have constant risk across all spins. The same analogy can be applied to your investments. If you treat each investment as the "spin" of a roulette wheel, you should not bet more money on some spins versus the others.

You will do much better with your investments over time if you pick a dollar amount, not share amount, which you are comfortable investing on each trade. Use that dollar amount for all investments and *let the number of shares (or contracts) fall where they may.* Let's use the same portfolio we used earlier but, instead, use constant dollar amounts and see what happens.

The portfolio at the beginning had $31,000 invested in 6 positions. That's an average of about $5,165 for each position. So let's build the portfolio with a constant dollar amount of $5,165 per position:

Shares	Purchase Price	After 1 year:
258	20	Up 22%
286	18	Up 24%
27	190	Down 18%
115	45	Up 30%
344	15	Up 27%
234	22	Up 34%

Notice how the number of shares is allowed to fluctuate. We buy more shares when the stock is cheap and fewer shares when it's expensive. We will buy 258 shares of the first stock ($5,165/$20), but only 27 shares of the third ($5,165/$190). What is the result with constant dollars? Now the portfolio is up a healthy 20% instead of the slight loss using constant share amounts.

The constant dollar method can be used for options as well. If you find that you seem to be correct in your outlooks but find that your option trades are netting losses there's a good chance the problem is having unequal "bets" throughout your trading. If you always buy a fixed number of contracts, say 5 contracts, it's certainly a different dollar amount if you pay $3 for an equity option versus $80 for a Nasdaq 100 index option. *Instead, pick a dollar amount you're willing to risk with each trade and put that amount into each option trade; let the number of contracts fall where they may.* You will likely see a big difference in your performance when you're not trying to guess which trade will be the bigger winner. Let the averages work for you by using constant dollars.

Because options allow investors to control the same number of shares for less money (our conservative definition of leverage), you have a better way to diversify your portfolio.

At any time, you can choose to get out of the contract by selling it in the open market. If the option is in-the-money then it is worth the intrinsic value at expiration. If it is prior to expiration, it is worth the intrinsic value plus some time value. If it is not in-the-money when you sell it then it is worth the time value and it is up to the market to decide what that is worth. Regardless of price, you would enter the following order to exit the contract:

Sell to close, two April $75 calls, symbol IBMDO, at market (or limit)

We've just stepped through a simple buy and sell order for a call option as well as our motivations for doing so. Now that you understand the motivations for buying calls – protection, leverage, and diversification – let's run through another example but this time we'll show you an even more fascinating side of options trading – how to *hedge* the contract.

 Options provide protection, leverage, and diversification.

Rolling with Call Options

Options create tremendous possibilities for investors – far more than what is already apparent from the preceding chapters. The real power of options comes from our ability to alter risk-reward profiles as prices change and that is something you cannot do with stock alone. To demonstrate, let's go through another long call example but this time we'll show you the roll-up strategy. In the last chapter, we talked about the roll-up for covered calls in the last chapter but let's see what it can do for those holding long calls.

You are a long-term investor who is bullish on Google (GOOG) and wish to buy 100 shares on August 8, 2005. Table 8-5 shows the stock was trading for about $293, which means it would cost $29,300 for the 100-share lot:

Table 8-5

Calls	Last Sale	Net	Bid	Ask	Vol	Open Int	Puts	Last Sale	Net	Bid	Ask	Vol	Open Int
GOOG										293.07	+0.72		
Aug 08, 2005 @ 15:04 ET (Data 15 Minutes Delayed)						Bid 293.04 Ask 293.11 Size 7x1 Vol 3482811							
07 Jan 250.0 (OUW AJ-E)	88.60	pc	79.30	80.40	0	1682	07 Jan 250.0 (OUW MJ-E)	23.10	pc	22.30	22.80	0	3996
07 Jan 260.0 (OUW AL-E)	74.10	-1.90	73.20	74.30	5	2009	07 Jan 260.0 (OUW ML-E)	27.40	pc	25.80	26.60	0	1080
07 Jan 270.0 (OUW AN-E)	69.70	pc	67.50	68.50	0	993	07 Jan 270.0 (OUW MN-E)	30.00	pc	29.70	30.30	0	1298
07 Jan 280.0 (OQD AP-E)	61.70	pc	62.00	63.00	0	1263	07 Jan 280.0 (OQD MP-E)	32.60	pc	34.00	34.50	0	903
07 Jan 290.0 (OQD AR-E)	60.30	pc	56.90	58.00	0	1134	07 Jan 290.0 (OQD MR-E)	38.40	pc	38.50	39.40	0	767
07 Jan 300.0 (OQD AT-E)	54.60	pc	52.20	53.30	0	5841	07 Jan 300.0 (OQD MT-E)	43.80	pc	43.50	44.00	0	2218

Rather than put that much money into one stock, you could, instead, just buy one call option. However, notice that the prices are expensive in terms of total dollars as the cheapest one (Jan. $300) is $53.30! This is due to the high volatility of Google along with the fact that there are nearly 1.5 years until expiration. This is one of those times that you may wish to buy a strike closer to at-the-money. Let's assume we decide to buy the $290 call for $58, or $5,800 per contract to control 100 shares over the next 1.5 years. All you have to do is place the following order:

Buy to open, one contract, Google Jan. '07 $290 call (OQDAR), at market (limit)

Once the order is filled, you are now long one contract and have the right to purchase Google at any time for $290 per share. Of course, your goal as an option trader is to simply trade the contract and never actually buy the shares of stock. For example, on September 12, just 35 days later, the stock had moved up sharply to $308.25 and the $290 call was bidding $64.20:

Table 8-6

Calls	Last Sale	Net	Bid	Ask	Vol	Open Int	Puts	Last Sale	Net	Bid	Ask	Vol	Open Int
GOOG										317.00	+7.38		
Sep 30, 2005 @ 14:35 ET (Data 15 Minutes Delayed)						Bid 316.96 Ask 317.00 Size 1x2 Vol 5696732							
07 Jan 260.0 (OUW AL-E)	85.00	+13.00	86.80	87.50	1	2027	07 Jan 260.0 (OUW ML-E)	18.30	pc	16.20	16.60	0	1096
07 Jan 270.0 (OUW AN-E)	75.60	pc	80.10	80.90	0	1040	07 Jan 270.0 (OUW MN-E)	21.20	pc	19.10	19.60	0	1351
07 Jan 280.0 (OQD AP-E)	71.90	pc	73.70	74.60	0	1352	07 Jan 280.0 (OQD MP-E)	25.90	pc	22.30	22.80	0	1019
07 Jan 290.0 (OQD AR-E)	60.90	pc	67.70	68.60	0	1256	07 Jan 290.0 (OQD MR-E)	27.50	pc	25.90	26.40	0	832
07 Jan 300.0 (OQD AT-E)	57.20	pc	62.10	62.90	0	6084	07 Jan 300.0 (OQD MT-E)	30.60	pc	29.80	30.40	0	3737
07 Jan 310.0 (OQD AB-E)	50.40	pc	56.70	57.40	0	1361	07 Jan 310.0 (OQD MB-E)	34.00	pc	34.10	34.70	0	584

You could sell the contract to close and take your profits. If you choose to do this, you would place the following order:

Sell to close, one contract, Google Jan. '07 $290 call (OQDAR), at market (limit)

You bought the contract for $58 and sold for $64.20, which is a profit of $6.20 ($620 per contract), or $64.20/$58 = 1.107 = 10.7%. Had you purchased the stock, you would have paid $293.07 and sold for $308.25, which is a profit of $15.18, or 5.2%. Once again, this clearly shows that the stock trader's total profits are greater but represent a lower rate of return.

However, selling the option at the first sign of profit is usually a mistake. We're not saying to never take profits but the fact is that *trends generally last much longer than we expect.* If you sell at the first opportunity for a profit, you will usually regret the sale at a later date no matter how many times people tell you, "You can't go broke taking a profit." The truth is that you *can* go broke taking profits if you tend to take them too early. A lot of tiny profits can easily be overcome by one single loss. Option losses will always occur so it is up to you to allow your profits to run if you want to survive over the long run. This presents a dilemma though. After all, you are staring a sizable profit in the face. Does it really make sense to do *nothing?* The answer is that you can do a little of both; you can take some profits and stay in the position by doing a simple hedging technique called a *roll-up.* If you are long a call option, you execute a roll-up by selling your current option and simultaneously buying a higher strike option.

For example, you can place an order to sell the $290 call and simultaneously buy the next higher strike, which is $300. To place this roll-up, you would simply enter the following pair of orders to be executed simultaneously:

Sell to close, one contract, Google Jan. '07 $290 call (OQDAR) and simultaneously

Buy to open, one contract, Google Jan. '07 $300 call (OQDAT) at market (limit)

One of the nice features of roll-ups is that they always produces a credit to the account since lower strike calls are always more expensive than higher strike calls (Pricing Principle #1 from Chapter Two). Because you are selling the lower strike (more valuable) and using some of that money to buy a higher strike option (cheaper), you will always get a net credit to the account. Table 8-6 shows the $300 strike was trading for $59.50 so in this case, you'd get a credit of $4.70:

Sell $290 call	=	+$64.20
Buy $300 call	=	-$59.50
Net credit	=	$4.70

If you were filled at the above prices, you would be long one $300 call *plus* have $4.70 * 100 = $470 sitting safely in cash. You have effectively "taken some money off the table" but still control 100 shares. You have now spent a total of $53.50 as shown by the total transactions:

Buy $290 strike	=	- $58
Sell $290 strike	=	+$64.20
Buy $300 strike	=	-$59.50
Net debit	=	$53.30

In other words, you are still controlling 100 shares of Google but now have reduced the amount you have invested from $58 to $53.30. Granted, you own a higher strike which is less valuable than your original $290 strike but you have done something more important in that you've reduced the risk. Every time you roll up, you slowly chip away at the cost basis of the option thus removing some risk *while staying in the position.*

When Should You Roll Up?

The stock price at which you roll up depends on what you're trying to accomplish. If you wish to keep your option at-the-money then you should roll up to the $300 strike when the stock is trading for $300. However, maybe you're trying to hold a higher delta and only roll it to the next higher strike when it is $10 in-the-money. If so, you would want to roll up to the $300 strike once the stock price hits $310 and then roll up to the $310 call once the stock hits $320 and so forth. This way the option will stay ten points in-the-money thus providing a nice delta all while sweeping profits into the account. The choices are endless and that's what makes options so powerful.

The desire to use the roll-up is the reason we elected to use slightly in-the-money options to start with. If we had used a far out-of-the-money option such as the $320 strike, we may not have been able to roll up at this time at a significant credit. Buying far out-of-the-money options means that the stock must make a far bigger move before you can roll the position up. Once again, the out-of-the-money options do not provide the same benefits as in-the-money options. Out-of-the-money options are riskier and the inability to roll up in strikes is another way of showing why.

Let's assume we want to increase our delta position and roll up to the $300 strike when the stock reaches $310 as we have done in Table 8-6. With the stock at $308, you can see that we rolled up a little early. However, if you look at the net change, you'll see the stock was up over nine points at that time, which is a healthy move even for a volatile stock like Google. This is where you must make some pragmatic decisions. Check the net credit you're going to receive from the roll-up relative to your current cost basis and the commissions and see if it seems like a good business decision. If so, then it's time to roll up. This means we may roll up for a $2 credit if we paid $5 for the option since $2 is 40% of the cost basis. At the same time, we would not roll for a $2 credit on a $58 option. You must balance the costs with the effects.

By holding the $300 call, you are still controlling 100 shares of Google but for even less money than you originally invested. The net credit you received ($470) can be used immediately to withdraw, invest, or simply left in cash to be used at a later time.

As long as the stock moves in your favor, you should continue to roll it. Table 8-7 shows that Google was up over seven points and trading for $317 so let's roll it up again:

Table 8-7

| GOOG | | | | | | | | | | | | 317.00 +7.38 | |
| Sep 30, 2005 @ 14.35 ET (Data 15 Minutes Delayed) | | | | | | Bid 316.96   Ask 317.00   Size 1x2   Vol 5696732 | | | | | | | |
Calls	Last Sale	Net	Bid	Ask	Vol	Open Int	Puts	Last Sale	Net	Bid	Ask	Vol	Open Int
07 Jan 260.0 (OUW AL-E)	85.00	+13.00	86.80	87.50	1	2027	07 Jan 260.0 (OUW ML-E)	18.30	pc	16.20	16.60	0	1096
07 Jan 270.0 (OUW AH-E)	75.60	pc	80.10	80.90	0	1040	07 Jan 270.0 (OUW MH-E)	21.20	pc	19.10	19.60	0	1351
07 Jan 280.0 (OQD AP-E)	71.90	pc	73.70	74.60	0	1352	07 Jan 280.0 (OQD MP-E)	25.90	pc	22.30	22.80	0	1019
07 Jan 290.0 (OQD AR-E)	60.90	pc	67.70	68.60	0	1256	07 Jan 290.0 (OQD MR-E)	27.50	pc	25.90	26.40	0	832
07 Jan 300.0 (OQD AT-E)	57.20	pc	62.10	62.90	0	6084	07 Jan 300.0 (OQD MT-E)	30.60	pc	29.80	30.40	0	3737
07 Jan 310.0 (OQD AB-E)	50.40	pc	56.70	57.40	0	1361	07 Jan 310.0 (OQD MB-E)	34.00	pc	34.10	34.70	0	584

As before, we just need to enter an order to exchange the two options simultaneously:

Sell to close, one contract, Google Jan. '07 $300 call (OQDAT) and simultaneously

Buy to open, one contract, Google Jan. '07 $310 call (OQDAB) at market (limit)

Sell $300 strike = +$62.10
Buy $310 strike = -$57.40
Net credit = $4.70

Again, the net credit reduces our original cost basis. The cost basis prior to this point was $53.30 and is now reduced by another $4.70 to $48.60. The roll-up allows the investor to maintain the position for longer periods of time because it reduces the risk of investing – it reduces the fear of holding the position.

There are many times when you can execute roll-ups. You may decide to always roll up to the at-the-money option thus bringing in more cash (a bigger net credit) at the expense of needing bigger moves in the stock before rolling up again. It all depends on your goals and risk tolerances. Some investors will roll up sooner while some take a little more risk and roll up less frequently in the search for higher profits due to fewer bid-ask spreads and commissions.

For example, at the time of this writing, Google had released very positive earnings and was starting to move aggressively upward. In light of this news, you might decide to hold the option for longer periods of time to reduce the commissions you must pay to execute each roll-up. Let's assume you decide to hang on for a while before rolling up again. Table 8-8 shows that one month later Google was trading for over $380!

Table 8-8

GOOG									**380.44**	**+1.06**		
Nov 02, 2005 @ 10:24 ET (Data 15 Minutes Delayed)						Bid 380.41	Ask 380.61	Size 1x3	Vol 3225455			
Calls	Last Sale	Net	Bid	Ask	Vol	Open Int	Puts	Last Sale	Net	Bid	Ask	Vol	Open Int
07 Jan 290.0 (OQD AR-E)	120.10	pc	122.70	123.70	0	1159	07 Jan 290.0 (OQD MR-E)	18.00	pc	16.50	16.90	0	814
07 Jan 300.0 (OQD AT-E)	117.40	+2.00	115.80	116.70	1	5974	07 Jan 300.0 (OQD MT-E)	19.10	-0.60	19.20	19.60	5	3500
07 Jan 310.0 (OQD AB-E)	86.10	pc	109.20	110.40	0	1384	07 Jan 310.0 (OQD MB-E)	22.40	pc	22.00	22.60	0	808
07 Jan 320.0 (OQD AD-E)	70.50	pc	102.90	104.00	0	1195	07 Jan 320.0 (OQD MD-E)	26.60	pc	25.30	25.90	0	851
07 Jan 330.0 (OQD AF-E)	97.79	pc	96.80	97.70	0	4406	07 Jan 330.0 (OQD MF-E)	31.20	pc	28.90	29.40	0	871
07 Jan 340.0 (OQD AH-E)	88.90	pc	91.00	92.00	0	1054	07 Jan 340.0 (OQD MH-E)	34.20	pc	32.70	33.30	0	538
07 Jan 350.0 (OQD AJ-E)	85.50	+3.10	85.50	86.70	1	1424	07 Jan 350.0 (OQD MJ-E)	39.60	pc	36.80	37.50	0	270
07 Jan 360.0 (OQD AL-E)	80.10	pc	80.20	81.20	0	1515	07 Jan 360.0 (OQD ML-E)	41.80	pc	41.30	41.90	0	119
07 Jan 370.0 (OQD AN-E)	77.00	pc	75.20	76.10	0	1605	07 Jan 370.0 (OQD MN-E)	55.90	pc	46.00	46.70	0	308
07 Jan 380.0 (OQD AU-E)	71.30	+15.60	70.50	71.40	8	289	07 Jan 380.0 (OQD MU-E)	49.80	-42.00	51.10	51.70	1	132
07 Jan 390.0 (OQD AV-E)	67.20	pc	66.00	66.90	0	208	07 Jan 390.0 (OQD MV-E)	57.60	pc	56.30	57.00	0	121

If you rolled up at this time, you'd want to roll up to a strike that is closer to the current price of the stock rather than rolling to the $320 strike, which is the next strike higher than the $310 strike we're currently holding. The reason is that the $320 strike is very deep in-the-money and we'd like to hold an option that is only one strike in-the-money or possibly at-the-money, which allows us to sweep more money out of the position. Let's assume we decide to roll up to the at-the-money strike, which is the $380 strike. All you have to do is place the following order:

Sell to close, one contract, Google Jan. '07 $310 call (OQDAB) and simultaneously

Buy to open, one contract, Google Jan. '07 $380 call (OQDAU) at market (limit)

The net credit produced would be $37.80 as follows:

Sell $310 call	=	+ $109.20
Buy $380 call	=	-$71.40
Net credit	=	$37.80

Prior to this trade, our cost basis was $48.60. After receiving the $37.80 credit, the cost basis is reduced to $11. Notice that we could choose to roll up to an out-of-the-money strike such as the $390 call. If we do, we'll end up with a bigger credit from the roll since we are spending less money to buy the $390 call thus providing for a bigger credit. The tradeoff is that the stock must now move higher before we're able to execute the next roll-up.

Regardless of which choice you make, you're still controlling 100 shares of Google but have taken a tremendous amount of cash out of the position. It is doubtful that the "conservative" stock owner would have held out for this much profit because there's too much to lose as the stock price climbs to seemingly inexplicable levels. However, with options, we can sweep money out of the position and still control 100 shares by using options. As we've tried to point out, options can be used in conservative ways.

This example highlights the importance of rolling up at more frequent intervals. When we started this exercise, we purchased the Google $290 call for $58. After the last roll-up, we figured that the cost basis is now $11 which means we have taken $58 - $11 = $47 out of the position through several roll-ups. Using Table 8-8, notice that if we had never rolled up until now that we could have sold the $290 call for $122.70 and purchased the $380 call for $71.40 thus bringing in one giant credit of $51.30, which is not too far from the $47 we've pulled out so far. Why the difference? The reason is the bid-ask spread. Every time we buy or sell, we must pay the asking price and receive the bid price. These actions create a small leak in the total credits we'll receive. Commissions will obviously reduce the total credits even further. In this case, if we had waited until now to execute the roll-up, we would have received and additional $4.30 ($51.30 - $47 = $4.30). However, we must ask if that amount of additional profit is worth the risk of holding the $290 call while the stock climbed all the way to $380. Our first goal as option traders should be good money management and we need to do all we can to avoid the downside risk. Even though this example worked in our favor, there's nothing that says it should. This stock could easily have moved against us at some point thus leaving us with a $58 loss if had never rolled up. That's why good option traders roll up frequently. If there were no bid-ask spreads or commissions there would be no difference between rolling up frequently or infrequently. But if we wish to protect profits and reduce the risk of holding the stock, most option investors feel that the small losses from the bid-ask spreads and commissions are worth the reduction in risk that frequent roll-ups provide.

Long Puts

We've covered the basics of call options in detail. Once you understand the reasons for buying calls, you'll automatically understand the reasons for buying puts. All of the benefits that apply to calls apply to puts – just in the opposite direction. But just to make sure you've got the concepts, let's run through an example with puts.

Assume that your outlook on Google has turned from bullish to bearish. In fact, at the time that's exactly what was happening. The stock was trading at $340 and on a quick, downward spiral from the recent high of about $390 (with all-time high up over $475). This was due to negative outlooks issued by the company as well as analyst downgrades.

Let's assume you are speculating on a short-term fall. If you wish to capitalize on the bearish outlook by shorting 300 shares of stock, you have unlimited upside risk. In addition, you're going to have a large margin requirement (roughly $25,000) to short 300 shares. And if the stock rises past the price where you shorted it, you'll end up with maintenance calls, which means you'll have to send more money to your broker in order to keep the short position open.

Rather than shorting such a volatile stock, you can buy a put option. Because long puts give you the right to sell shares of stock they become more valuable if the underlying stock falls sufficiently. When you buy a put option, you are long the asset, which means you can only lose the amount you put into the trade. The put call-parity equation showed us that a long put is identical to short stock position plus a long call ($P = -S + C$) and it is the implicit long call in a put option that protects the put buyer from unlimited upside risk.

Table 8-9 shows the March and April quotes at the time:

Table 8-9

Calls	Last Sale	Net	Bid	Ask	Vol	Open Int	Puts	Last Sale	Net	Bid	Ask	Vol	Open Int
06 Mar 320.0 (GGD CD-E)	23.40	-1.70	22.90	23.50	238	2089	06 Mar 320.0 (GGD OD-E)	2.80	+0.10	3.00	3.20	735	11665
06 Mar 330.0 (GGD CF-E)	16.00	-1.60	15.40	15.80	364	1807	06 Mar 330.0 (GGD OF-E)	5.00	+0.20	5.20	5.50	1056	12214
06 Mar 340.0 (GGD CH-E)	10.20	-1.60	9.50	9.70	901	4855	06 Mar 340.0 (GGD OH-E)	9.10	+0.90	9.20	9.40	4304	14781
06 Mar 350.0 (GGD CJ-E)	5.60	-1.40	5.20	5.40	1026	11213	06 Mar 350.0 (GGD OJ-E)	14.20	+0.80	14.90	15.40	805	12452
06 Apr 320.0 (GGD DD-E)	35.80	-1.90	35.20	36.00	27	238	06 Apr 320.0 (GGD PD-E)	14.10	+1.60	14.00	14.30	53	2395
06 Apr 330.0 (GGD DF-E)	27.50	-3.40	29.30	29.80	13	292	06 Apr 330.0 (GGD PF-E)	18.00	+1.00	17.70	18.10	64	1478
06 Apr 340.0 (GGD DH-E)	24.40	-2.30	23.60	24.20	291	422	06 Apr 340.0 (GGD PH-E)	22.30	+0.80	22.20	22.90	195	3546
06 Apr 350.0 (GGD DJ-E)	21.00	--	19.00	19.40	88	2087	06 Apr 350.0 (GGD PJ-E)	27.00	+0.50	27.30	27.70	52	4482

GOOG — 339.69 -3.31 — Mar 10, 2006 @ 11:43 ET (Data 15 Minutes Delayed) — Bid 339.70 Ask 339.83 Size 3x1 Vol 8959224

You can see that Google was trading for about $340. Just as with call options, there is a question you must answer before deciding which strike to buy. That is, are you expecting a slow fall or a fast, aggressive one? If the answer is slow, you should buy intrinsic value and find a relatively high strike (preferably an 0.80 to 0.85 delta). However, if you expect that it will be a fast, aggressive fall then you may opt for the at-the-money. Because stock prices tend to fall much faster than they rise, the decision to buy an at-the-money put may be warranted in more cases than the at-the-money call. In addition, because volatility tends to rise quickly when prices are falling the at-the-money put will get a boost from that as well.

Let's assume that you decide to buy the three April $340 puts (42 days until expiration) by placing the following order:

Buy to open, three contracts, Google April '06 $340 puts (GGDPH) at market (limit)

If your order is filled at the $22.90 asking price, it will cost 300 * $22.90 = $6,870 and that is the most you could ever lose on the position.

During that same day, you can see that Google fell over eight points to $334.92 thus making the $340 put worth $24.40 as shown in Table 8-10:

Table 8-10

Calls	Last Sale	Net	Bid	Ask	Vol	Open Int	Puts	Last Sale	Net	Bid	Ask	Vol	Open Int
GOOG											334.82	-8.18	
Mar 10, 2006 @ 14:56 ET (Data 15 Minutes Delayed)						**Bid** 334.80 **Ask** 334.97 **Size** 3x2 **Vol** 15934964							
06 Mar 320.0 (GGD CD-E)	20.20	-4.90	19.00	19.70	388	2089	06 Mar 320.0 (GGD OD-E)	4.00	+1.30	4.00	4.20	2033	11665
06 Mar 330.0 (GGD CF-E)	12.50	-5.10	12.20	12.50	1384	1807	06 Mar 330.0 (GGD OF-E)	7.30	+2.50	6.90	7.30	4110	12214
06 Mar 340.0 (GGD CH-E)	7.50	-4.30	7.00	7.30	2744	4855	06 Mar 340.0 (GGD OH-E)	12.20	+4.00	11.90	12.20	5786	14781
06 Mar 350.0 (GGD CJ-E)	4.00	-3.00	3.80	4.10	2368	11213	06 Mar 350.0 (GGD OJ-E)	17.80	+4.40	18.30	19.00	1469	12452
06 Apr 320.0 (GGD DD-E)	32.20	-5.50	32.00	32.30	63	238	06 Apr 320.0 (GGD PD-E)	15.20	+2.70	15.40	15.70	110	2395
06 Apr 330.0 (GGD DF-E)	26.60	-4.30	26.00	26.40	37	292	06 Apr 330.0 (GGD PF-E)	19.80	+2.80	19.40	19.90	263	1478
06 Apr 340.0 (GGD DH-E)	21.20	-5.50	21.00	21.30	562	422	06 Apr 340.0 (GGD PH-E)	24.40	+2.90	24.40	24.70	274	3546
06 Apr 350.0 (GGD DJ-E)	16.60	-4.40	16.50	16.70	154	2087	06 Apr 350.0 (GGD PJ-E)	30.20	+3.70	29.70	30.30	93	4482

If you decided to close the three contracts at this time, you would enter the following order:

Sell to close, three contracts, Google April '06 $340 puts (GGDPH) at market (limit)

If the order is filled at the $24.40 bid then you purchased for $22.90 and sold for $24.40 thus profiting by $1.50 * 300 = $450.

The roll-up strategy we used for calls can also be applied to long puts as a *roll-down*. With a roll-down, you will sell your long put and simultaneously buy a *lower strike* put thus collecting a credit (since the higher strike put that you are selling must be more valuable). All of the principles and advantages we discussed for calls can be applied to puts.

Options create different sets of risks and rewards for investors and traders. It is up to the investor to decide which is best for them at the time. In the previous example, we showed that you could have captured a $1.50 profit on the three puts; however, the short stock seller would have collected $339.69 - $334.82 = $4.87. Does this mean the short stock position is better? No, it means there is more risk. At the time, Google had large gap openings (the stock opens at prices much higher or lower than the previous day's close). If you were short 300 shares and the stock gapped up 10 points the next day you would have an unrealized loss of $3,000. The loss on the long puts would be no where near that since they would still maintain sometime premium even though they are out-of-the-money. If you're unsure that an out-of-the-money put on Google maintains significant time premium, check

Table 8-10 and you'll see the $320 put trading for $4.20 and it is nearly 15 points out-of-the-money. So even though $6,870 was spent for the three $340 puts, it's highly unlikely that you are going to lose anywhere near that much for a large, upward movement in the stock. Short stock sellers cannot make that assertion.

Options allow you to pick and choose which sets of risks you want to take. Before you put your money into long or short stock positions, be sure your account can handle significant adverse moves. No matter how small the probability may seem, large moves are more likely than you might suspect. On Friday, May 1, 1998 EntreMed (ENMD) closed a little over $12. Monday morning it opened at $83. If you are in doubt as to whether your account can withstand such adverse price swings then long calls and long puts will add a little certainty in a very uncertain world.

 ## Key Concepts

1) Long options (calls and puts) provide protection, leverage, and diversification.

2) Buy 0.80 to 0.85 deltas if using long calls or long puts as long stock or short stock substitutes.

3) If you are willing to buy $10,000 worth of stock you should not put that much money into the options. Instead, buy options representing the same number of shares you are willing to hold.

4) To better diversify your portfolio, try to put a similar dollar amount into each option position.

5) Roll up call options and roll down puts options when the proper opportunity arises.

Chapter Eight Questions

Use the following table of quotes for questions 1 – 9:

AGN													111.60 +0.22

Mar 06, 2006 @ 17:17 ET (Data 20 Minutes Delayed) — Bid N/A   Ask N/A   Size N/AxN/A   Vol 897600

Calls	Last Sale	Net	Bid	Ask	Vol	Open Int	Puts	Last Sale	Net	Bid	Ask	Vol	Open Int
06 Apr 105.0 (AGN DA-E)	6.90	pc	8.20	8.40	0	530	06 Apr 105.0 (AGN PA-E)	1.15	pc	0.85	1.00	0	275
06 Apr 110.0 (AGN DB-E)	5.80	+0.90	4.60	4.80	26	233	06 Apr 110.0 (AGN PB-E)	2.05	-0.85	2.20	2.35	25	468
06 Apr 115.0 (AGN DC-E)	2.50	pc	2.10	2.30	0	962	06 Apr 115.0 (AGN PC-E)	6.50	pc	4.70	5.00	0	97
06 Apr 120.0 (AGN DD-E)	0.95	-0.05	0.80	0.90	5	756	06 Apr 120.0 (AGN PD-E)	12.80	pc	8.50	8.70	0	39

1) Y ou wish to buy shares of AGN stock and would like to buy a call option instead. You believe the stock will rise slowly over the next month. Which strike should you buy?

   a) $105

   b) $110

   c) $115

   d) $120

2)   Assume you decide to buy THREE contracts of the April $105 calls "at market." Which of the following is the correct order?

   a)   Sell to close, three contracts, April $105 calls at market.

   b)   Buy to open, three contracts, April $105 calls at market.

   c)   Buy to close, three contracts, April $105 calls at market.

   d)   Buy to open, three contracts, April $105 calls at $8.00 or better.

3)   Assume you are filled at the asking price, how much will the trade in Question 2 cost not counting commissions?

   a) $270

   b) $3,360

   c) $690

   d) $2,520

4) What is the break-even point for the $105 call assuming you purchased it for the asking price?
   a) $113.40
   b) $116.40
   c) $112.20
   d) $105.00

5) What is the break-even point for the $120 call assuming you purchased it for the asking price?
   a) $122.40
   b) $120.90
   c) $119.10
   d) $120.00

6) Why is the break-even point higher for the $120 when compared to the $105 call?
   a) The $120 call is less risky
   b) The $120 call is riskier
   c) The $120 call is equally risky as the $105
   d) The $120 call has less time value so will have a higher break-even point

7) How much time value is in the $105 call?
   a) $6.60
   b) $8.40
   c) $2.20
   d) $1.80

8) What is the true risk of the $105 call compared to the stock?
   a) $1.80
   b) $8.40
   c) $6.60
   d) $2.20

9) Why is the risk of the $105 call NOT the full $8.40 value?
   a) There is $6.60 of intrinsic value that is also at risk if you owned the stock
   b) There is $1.80 of intrinsic value that is also at risk if you owned the stock
   c) The stock has time value and the option does not
   d) The option must expire with intrinsic value

Use the following table of quotes for questions 10 – 20:

AGN   **114.49 -0.14**

Mar 09, 2006 @ 11:43 ET (Data 20 Minutes Delayed)   **Bid** N/A   **Ask** N/A   **Size** N/AxN/A   **Vol** 529200

Calls	Last Sale	Net	Bid	Ask	Vol	Open Int	Puts	Last Sale	Net	Bid	Ask	Vol	Open Int
06 Apr 105.0 (AGN DA-E)	7.70	pc	10.70	10.90	0	532	06 Apr 105.0 (AGN PA-E)	1.15	pc	0.60	0.70	0	285
06 Apr 110.0 (AGN DB-E)	7.80	+1.10	6.60	6.80	31	245	06 Apr 110.0 (AGN PB-E)	1.25	-0.80	1.50	1.60	12	447
06 Apr 115.0 (AGN DC-E)	4.20	+0.80	3.50	3.70	28	1459	06 Apr 115.0 (AGN PC-E)	3.99	pc	3.30	3.50	0	97
06 Apr 120.0 (AGN DD-E)	1.90	+1.30	1.50	1.60	10	706	06 Apr 120.0 (AGN PD-E)	6.10	-6.70	6.30	6.60	11	42

10) **You own three $105 calls and wish to sell them "at market." Which of the following is the correct order?**
   a) Sell to close, three contracts, April $105 calls at market.
   b) Sell to open, three contracts, April $105 calls at market.
   c) Buy to close, three contracts, April $105 calls at market.
   d) Sell to close, three contracts, April $105 calls at $11.50 or better.

11) **Assume you purchased the $105 call for $8.40 and sold it for the $10.70 bid. What is the return on your investment?**
   a) 78%
   b) 27%
   c) 44%
   d) 21%

12) **What would your return be if you had purchased the stock for $111.60 and sold for $114.49?**
   a) 2.5%
   b) 4.2%
   c) 6.5%
   d) 7.8%

13) **If the $105 call expired right now, what would it be worth?**
   a) $9.49
   b) $10.70
   c) $10.90
   d) $7.70

14) **If the $120 call expired right now, what would it be worth?**
   a) $0
   b) $1.50
   c) $1.60
   d) $1.90

15) **If you purchased the $120 call for $0.90 and sold it for $1.50 your return would be 66%. Why is it so much higher than the return on the $105 call?**
   a)   The $105 call is riskier because it cost more money and will therefore have lower returns
   b)   The $120 call is less risky and therefore has higher returns
   c)   The $120 call is riskier and therefore has higher returns
   d)   The $105 call and $120 call are equally risky. The increased return on the $120 call is due to volatility.

16) **Assume you wanted to roll up from the $105 call to the $110 call "at market." Which of the following is the correct order?**
   a)   Sell to open the $105 call and simultaneously buy to open the $110 call
   b)   Sell to close the $110 call and simultaneously buy to open the $105 call
   c)   Sell to close the $105 call and simultaneously buy to open the $110 call
   d)   Buy to close $105 call and simultaneously buy to open the $110 call

17) **Assuming you rolled up from the $105 call to the $110 at the current bid and ask prices, the order would be fill for:**
   a)   A net debit of $3.90
   b)   A net credit of $3.90
   c)   A net debit of $4.30
   d)   A net credit of $4.30

18) **Assume you owned the $115 call and rolled up to the $120 call at the current bid and ask prices. The order would be filled for:**
   a)   A net debit of $1.90
   b)   A net credit of $1.90
   c)   A net debit of $2.20
   d)   A net credit of $2.20

19) Why is the net in Question 17 larger than that for Question 18?
a) The $105 and $110 strikes are out-of-the-money so they are more likely to expire with intrinsic value.
b) The $105 and $110 strikes are in-the-money so they are more likely to expire with intrinsic value.
c) The $105 and $110 strikes are out-of-the-money so they are more likely to expire worthless.
d) The $105 and $110 strikes are in-the-money so they are more likely to expire worthless.

20) Assume you originally thought AGN was going to fall and, instead, purchased THREE of the $115 puts from the first set of quotes. You later sold them for the bid price in the second set of quotes. What is your overall gain or loss not counting commissions?
a) $360 gain
b) $360 loss
c) $510 gain
d) $510 loss

Chapter Eight - Answers

1) You wish to buy shares of AGN stock and would like to buy a call option instead. You believe the stock will rise slowly over the next month. Which strike should you buy?
a) $105

Because you are uncertain about the speed at which the stock's price will rise, you will want to purchase a call that has a relatively high delta (relatively small time value). Because no delta values are shown, we can find a put that has about 30 or 40 cent in time value above the cost of carry. Because there are 43 days until expiration, we can ignore the cost of carry and find a put with roughly 30 to 40 cents in time value. There aren't any in that range but, for the quotes given, the strike closest to that is the $105 call.

2) **Assume you decide to buy THREE contracts of the April $105 calls "at market." Which of the following is the correct order?**

    b)   Buy to open, three contracts, April $105 calls at market.

You are buying the contract and you are "entering" or "increasing" your position so it is an "opening" transaction.

3) **Assume you are filled at the asking price, how much will the trade in Question 2 cost not counting commissions?**

    d) $2,520

The asking price on the $105 call is $8.40 so three contracts will cost 300 * $8.40 = $2,520 not counting commissions.

4) **What is the break-even point for the $105 call assuming you purchased it for the asking price?**

    a) $113.40

Because you paid $8.40 for the $105 call, the stock must be at $105 + $8.40 = $113.40 at expiration in order for you to break even on the trade. If the stock is $113.40 at expiration, the $105 call is worth the intrinsic value of $8.40 and you would just break even.

5) **What is the break-even point for the $120 call assuming you purchased it for the asking price?**

    b) $120.90

The $120 call will break even at $120 + 0.90 = $120.90 at expiration.

6) **Why is the break-even point higher for the $120 when compared to the $105 call?**

    b)   The $120 call is riskier

The $120 call costs only 90 cents which may make it appear less risky. However, once we check the break even point we find it is $120 + 0.90 = $120.90 and realize the stock price must move much higher at expiration before you would break even on the trade. The $120 call has a much better chance of expiring worthless so is riskier than the $105 call.

7) **How much time value is in the $105 call?**

    d) $1.80

With the stock at $111.60, the $105 call has $111.60 - $105 = $6.60 intrinsic value. Because it is trading for $8.40 the additional value of $8.40 - $6.60 = $1.80 must be due to time value.

8) What is the true risk of the $105 call compared to the stock?
   a) $1.80

The true risk of buying the $105 call rather than the stock is the $1.80 time value.

9) Why is the risk of the $105 call NOT the full $8.40 value?
   a)   There is $6.60 of intrinsic value that is also at risk if you owned the stock

Even though the option is trading for $8.40 and could end up worthless, the full $8.40 is not the total risk of the option. The reason is that if the stock price falls below $105 at expiration then the stock buyer and the $105 call buyer both lose $6.60 worth of intrinsic value. That intrinsic value is a risk that is common to both the option and the stock. The only risk over and above the stock is the $1.80 time premium.

10) You own three $105 calls and wish to sell them "at market." Which of the following is the correct order?
   a)   Sell to close, three contracts, April $105 calls at market.

You are "exiting" or "reducing" your position so it is a "closing" transaction.

11) Assume you purchased the $105 call for $8.40 and sold it for the $10.70 bid. What is the return on your investment?
   b)   27%

The return is found by taking the ending value and dividing it by the beginning value and subtracting one. In this case, $10.70/$8.40 = 1.27. After subtracting one, we find the return is 0.27, or 27%.

12) What would your return be if you had purchased the stock for $111.60 and sold for $114.49?
   a)   2.5%

Buying the stock will always produce a smaller percentage return. In this example, $114.49/$111.60 = 1.025, or 2.5%.

13) If the $105 call expired right now, what would it be worth?

    a) $9.49

With the stock at $114.49, the $105 call would be worth the intrinsic value of $114.49 - $105 = $9.49 if it expired this instant.

14) If the $120 call expired right now, what would it be worth?

    a) $0

    b) $1.50

    c) $1.60

    d) $1.90

15) If you purchased the $120 call for $0.90 and sold it for $1.50 your return would be 66%. Why is it so much higher than the return on the $105 call?

    c)   The $120 call is riskier and therefore has higher returns

Remember, as shown in Question 6, the break even point is higher so the $120 call has a much better chance of expiring worthless.

16) Assume you wanted to roll up from the $105 call to the $110 call "at market." Which of the following is the correct order?

    c)   Sell to close the $105 call and simultaneously buy to open the $110 call

When you are rolling up a call option, you are selling a lower strike call to close and simultaneously buying a higher strike (usually the next higher strike). After the order is filled, you are just left holding the higher strike call but bring in a credit for doing so.

17) Assuming you rolled up from the $105 call to the $110 at the current bid and ask prices, the order would be fill for:

    b)   A net credit of $3.90

You could sell your long $105 call for the current bid of $10.70 and use that money to buy the $110 call for the $6.80 asking price, which leaves you with a net credit of $10.70 - $6.80 = $3.90. This credit reduces your original cost basis and risk of your original principal.

18) Assume you owned the $115 call and rolled up to the $120 call at the current bid and ask prices. The order would be filled for:

    b)   A net credit of $1.90

You could sell the long $115 call for $3.50 and buy the $120 call for $1.60 thus receiving a net credit of $3.50 - $1.60 = $1.90.

19) Why is the net in Question 17 larger than that for Question 18?

    b) The $105 and $110 strikes are in-the-money so they are more likely to expire with intrinsic value.

Because the $105 and $110 strikes are in-the-money at this time, they are more likely to expire with intrinsic value when compared to the $115 and $120 strikes. Because of this, the market will bid up their prices higher. Remember that the maximum difference for $105/$110 roll is the $5 difference in their strikes. The very most you could even receive on this roll is therefore $5. The same is true for the $115/$120 roll. However, because the $115/$120 roll is less likely to have intrinsic value its net difference will be smaller.

20) Assume you originally thought AGN was going to fall and, instead, purchased THREE of the $115 puts from the first set of quotes. You later sold them for the bid price in the second set of quotes. What is your overall gain or loss not counting commissions?

    d) $510 loss

You would have purchased the $115 puts for the $5.00 asking price and sold them for the $3.30 bid price for a loss of $1.70 per contract or 300 * 1.70 = $510 for three contracts. Notice, however, that had you shorted the stock you would have sold $11.60 and purchased back for $114.49 for a loss of $2.89 or $867 for 300 shares. The puts reduced your losses for adverse movements due to the implicit call option they contain.

Chapter Nine
Vertical Spreads

Up to now, we have learned to use long or short options in conservative ways. Chapter Seven showed how to sell a call option against long stock to create a covered call. Chapter Eight showed how to purchase a call or put as a substitute for long stock or short stock positions. Both of these chapters, however, involved the use of a single option.

As you gain experience with options, you will find there are many strategies that involve the use of two or more options at the same time. While these are considered intermediate to advanced level strategies, we want to touch on a very popular one so you can gain an appreciation of the versatility of options. That strategy is called a *vertical spread*.

There are many "spread" strategies you can use with options. Regardless of the strategy, all spreads have one thing in common: They always involve the purchase of one option and the simultaneous sale of another of the same type (call or put). In other words, if you are using a spread strategy, you will be long and short the same type of option at the same time.

There are various names for these strategies depending on which option you are buying and which you are selling. These names can be confusing for new traders since there are no standardized names and you will see multiple names for the same strategy. However, there is a standard from which all names for spread strategies are derived. The strategy names came about from the way option quotes used to be printed at the exchanges prior to electronic quotation systems. Traders would create a grid by (usually on chalk boards along the walls of the trading floors) listing the various months across the top and the strikes along the side and then write the quotes in the appropriate boxes as shown in Table 9-1:

Table 9-1

	Jan	Feb	Mar
50	13.25	16.25	18.10
55	10.25	13.00	15.20
60	6.90	7.50	9.40
65	3.40	4.90	6.40
70	0.40	1.50	2.50

If you buy and sell different strikes within the same month then it is called a *vertical spread*. For example, using Table 9-1, if you buy the January $50 call for $13.25 and sell the January $55 call for $10.25 as shown by the vertical oval then it is called a *vertical spread* since the prices are listed vertically in the grid. A vertical spread is also known as a *price spread* since it is the prices on the vertical axis that are being spread (bought and sold).

On the other hand, if you buy the March $50 call for $18.10 and sell the February $50 call for $16.25 then it is called a *horizontal spread* since the prices are listed horizontally in the grid. Horizontal spreads are also called *calendar spreads* since it is the calendar months being spread or *time spreads* since the calendar months also measure time. So horizontal spreads, calendar spreads, and time spreads are three different names you will see that all represent the same strategy (calendar spread is probably the most commonly used).

Finally, if you buy and sell different strikes within different months then it is called a *diagonal spread*. If you buy the March $60 for $9.40 call and sell the February $65 call for $4.90 as shown by the diagonal oval then it is a diagonal spread.

While all of these are fascinating strategies, we are only going to focus on one of them since our goal is to introduce you to strategies where two options are used at the same time. Of these strategies, the simplest is probably the vertical spread so that's where we will focus the rest of the chapter.

Vertical Spreads

As stated earlier, all spreads are constructed by using all calls or all puts. In other words, if you buy a call you must sell a call. If you buy a put, you must sell a put. Spreads never involve the use of calls and puts at the same time.

The vertical spread is constructed by purchasing one call (or put) within a given month and selling a different strike call (or put) with the same expiration. For example, buying a January $50 call and selling a January $55 call or buying a March $70 put and selling a March $75 put are vertical spreads. The strike prices can be separated by any amount but, in practice, most traders use sequential strikes. Just understand that spreads are very flexible and you can buy and sell any strikes. Whichever strikes you choose, the options are always bought and sold in a 1:1 ratio which simply means that you are selling one option for every option you buy.

As a matter of notation, if you buy the $50 call and sell the $55 call it is called a $50/$55 vertical spread. Because you purchased the $50 call and sold the $55 call it is a "long" $50/$55 vertical spread. Why is it considered a long position? Because you bought the more valuable option (lower strike call) and that means that money must be spent to buy the spread. Anytime you spend money to acquire a position, it is considered a long position. Consequently, long vertical spreads are also called "debit" spreads. If you buy a $70 put and sell the $75 put it would be considered a "short" $70/$75 vertical spread. This is a short position since you sold the more valuable put (higher strike) so you collected money for entering the position. Anytime you receive money to enter the position, it is considered "short." Short vertical spreads are also called "credit" spreads.

Hopefully you're starting to see why it's so important to understand the Pricing Principles we discussed in Chapter Two. Investors who try to memorize these strategies (as well as more advanced ones) have a difficult time and are prone to making mistakes. By understanding the Pricing Principles we discussed in Chapter Two, you will always be able to determine with confidence if a particular vertical spread is long or short.

What does the profit and loss profile look like for a vertical spread? You know that long options have limited risk. You also know that selling an option (such as with the covered call) limits potential gains. Therefore, if you combine a long and short option within the same expiration month, you will get a profit and loss profile with *limited risk* and *limited reward*.

For instance, if you buy the January $50 call for $3 and sell the January $55 call for $1 then your profit and loss curve looks like Figure 9-2:

Figure 9-2: Profit and Loss Diagram for Long $50/$55 Vertical Call Spread

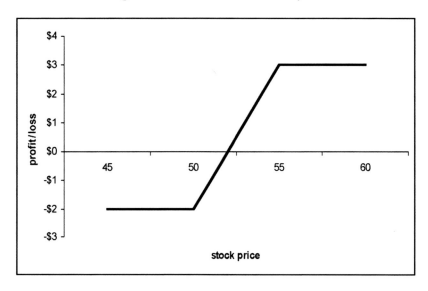

Notice that this is a "long" $50/$55 vertical call spread since you paid money to acquire it. We would say the trader is long the $50/$55 vertical call spread at a cost, or net debit, of $2. Again, the "net debit" just means it is the net amount spent on the trade. It doesn't matter if the trader spent $3 for the $50 call and sold the $55 call for $1 or if he paid $10 and sold for $8. The profit and loss diagram looks the same because the "net" amount spent in both cases was $2 and that is all that matters to the trader.

 Vertical spreads offer limited risk and limited rewards.

Max Gain, Max Loss, and Break Even

Figure 9-2 shows that the trader does, in fact, have limited downside risk and limited upside reward as we suspected. The maximum loss, as with any long option position, is the amount paid for the position, which is $2 for this example. What is the maximum gain? If you remember Pricing Principle #6, you should know that the maximum value between any two strikes within the same month is the difference in strikes. Therefore, if you are long the $50 call and short the $55 call then the most that spread could ever be worth is $5. Because you paid $2 for it, the most you could ever make is $3, which is exactly what Figure 9-2 shows.

We can arrive at the same answer by checking our rights and obligations. By purchasing the $50 call and selling the $55 call, the trader has the right to buy stock for $50 and the potential obligation to sell it for $55. If you purchase stock for $50 and sell it for $55 then that is a $5 profit. In order to acquire this right, it cost you a net debit of $2 so the most you could make is $3. If you add the maximum gain and maximum loss together you will always find they equal the difference in strikes.

The profit and loss profile for Figure 9-2 shows that the trader makes money if the underlying stock rises and it is therefore called a *bull spread*. Specifically, if the stock rises above the $55 strike then the trader makes the full $3 profit. The trader can make a smaller profit for expiration stock prices below $55 down to the break-even point. Where is the break-even point? The trader is effectively long the $50 call for a cost of $2 and that means the stock must be at $52 at expiration in order for the trader to break even. If the stock is $52, the $50 call is worth the $2 intrinsic value and the $55 call expires worthless thus making the trader break even. So the trader makes a profit at expiration for all stock prices above $52 and makes a maximum profit for all stock prices above $55. The trader takes a loss at expiration for all stock prices below $52 and has a maximum loss for all stock prices below $50. The maximum gains, losses, and break-points are fast and easy to calculate if you understand the Pricing Principles.

Vertical Spreads using Puts

Let's now take a look at how we can construct the same profit and loss diagram using puts. If you buy the $50 put for $1 and sell the $55 put for $4 then the profit and loss diagram looks like Figure 9-3:

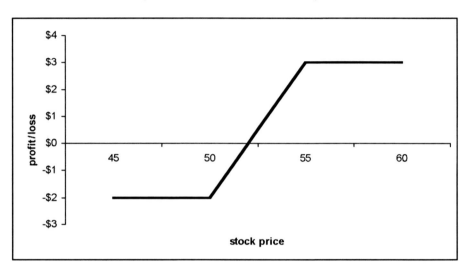

Figure 9-3: Profit and Loss Diagram for Long $50/$55 Vertical Put Spread

Notice that Figures 9-2 and 9-3 are identical. However, the way they arrive at the same shapes is a little different. If you buy a $50 put and sell a $55 put you will receive a *credit* for the trades since you are selling a higher strike (more valuable) put. Buying the $50 put and selling the $55 put is therefore a short $50/$55 vertical bull spread.

By selling the $55 put, you have the potential obligation to buy shares for $55. By purchasing the $50 put, you are assured that you can always sell shares for $50. If you buy shares for $55 and sell them for $50 then you have a $5 loss. However, since you were paid $3 for the spread position the most you could lose is $2.

Many traders make the incorrect assumption that credit spreads must be better than debit spreads based on the premise that it is better to receive money rather than spend it. The truth is that for any given strikes, debit and credit spreads are theoretically identical, which is confirmed by the profit and loss diagrams. In practice though, professional traders will choose one over the other due to slight favorable pricing variations that can occur for a number of reasons. For instance, using the call and put examples above, you may find that one has a maximum loss of $2 and a maximum gain of $3 while the other has a maximum loss of $1.90 and a maximum gain of $3.10, which is slightly better. But a professional trader would never choose the credit spread "just because" it produces a credit. You must always check the maximum gains and losses to determine which is better at that time.

We just showed that we can create a vertical bull spread by using calls or puts. Notice that there is a similarity between the two versions in that both are created by purchasing a lower strike option and selling a higher strike option. This is easy to remember if you look at the first letters of the phrase "<u>B</u>uy <u>L</u>ow, <u>S</u>ell <u>H</u>igh," or BLSH, which resembles the word "bullish." Any time you are buying a lower strike option and selling a higher strike option of the same type (call or put) then you have created a vertical bull spread.

Of course, if you do the reverse and buy a high strike and sell a lower strike, then that is a bearish position and you'd need the underlying to fall. Bear spreads work identically to bull spreads but in the opposite direction.

The important point to remember is that buying the vertical call spread is identical to selling the corresponding (same strikes) vertical put spread.

Vertical Bear Spreads

Let's now take a look at examples of how to create *vertical bear spreads*, which we found is created by purchasing an option and selling another at a lower strike. Using our previous example, you could create a vertical bear spread by purchasing the $55 call and sell the $50 call for a net credit of $2, which means it is a short position. How do we know this trade can be executed for a net credit of $2? It should make intuitive sense because it is just the opposite side of the trade. In the bull spread example, we assumed the trader bought the $50 call and sold the $55 call for a net debit of $2. Therefore, the trader on the other side must be selling the $50 call and buying the $55 call in exchange for the $2 that the long trader is paying. It is just two traders taking opposite views of the market and trading "packages" of options rather than a single call or put.

The profit and loss diagram for the short $50/$55 vertical call spread look like Figure 9-4:

Figure 9-4: Profit and Loss Diagram for Short $50/$55 Vertical Call Spread

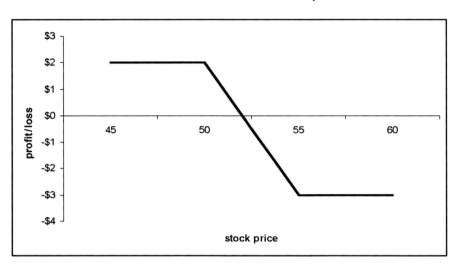

Figure 9-4 shows that the trader needs the stock price to fall in order to make money on the spread, which is why it is a bear spread. Specifically, the stock needs to fall below $50 at expiration in order to gain the maximum profit. With the stock below $50, both call options expire worthless and the trader keep the $2 credit. If the stock rises above $50 though, he will be facing an adverse stock price movement. Because of the $2 credit, the trader can afford to have the stock price rise $2 above the $50 strike, or $52, in order to break even at expiration, which is confirmed by Figure 9-4.

Let's step through the rights verses obligations to further understand what is happening. If you sell a $50 call, you have the obligation to sell shares at $50. If you buy the $55 call, you have the right to buy shares for $55. Therefore, if you buy for $55 and sell for $50 then you have a $5 loss. But because you were paid $2 to put the trade on then the maximum you can lose is $3. As with the bull spreads, notice that the maximum gains ($2) and maximum loss ($3) must add up to the difference in strikes ($5).

We can also accomplish the same profit and loss diagram by using puts, which is done in exactly the same way as the calls – buying one strike and selling lower strike. Using our previous put example, you could create a vertical bear spread by purchasing the $55 put for $4 and selling the $50 put for $1. Because this results in a net debit, it is a long vertical bear spread. If you buy the $55 put and sell the $50 put, the profit and loss diagram will be identical to that of Figure 9-4.

To understand why, let's check the rights and obligations of the trade. By purchasing the $55 put you have the right to sell stock for $55. Selling the $50 put gives you the potential obligation to buy stock at $50. If you buy for $55 and sell for $50 then you have a $5 gain but because you paid a net debit of $3 for the spread the most you can make is $2.

As with the call spread, both versions of the bear spreads should theoretically produce identical maximum gains and losses. Buying the vertical put spread is identical to selling the vertical call spread.

Buying the vertical call spread is identical to selling the corresponding vertical put spread.

Buying the vertical put spread is identical to selling the corresponding vertical call spread.

While the call and put versions of each spread are theoretically identical, small pricing discrepancies will cause one to be a little better than the other and that's the one the trader should choose. Again, do not choose the call version "just because" it produces a credit. Credits are not necessarily better than debits as the profit and loss diagrams show. It is the interaction between the right to buy and the obligation to sell that makes the strategy work.

We have shown that vertical bull spreads are created by purchasing the lower strike and selling the higher strike, or BLSH, which is bullish. On the flip side, vertical bear spreads are done by purchasing the high strike and selling the low strike. The problem with this mnemonic is that it relates to *strike* prices and not the option prices. If you buy the low *priced* option and sell the high priced option, you won't necessarily get the right answer (you'll be right for put spreads but not call spreads).

There is a second method (and probably more logical) for determining whether a vertical spread is bullish or bearish. This can be done as a two-step process. First, find out which option is most valuable and that is the one that *controls* the position. Second, find out whether that option is being bought or sold. Now just determine whether buying or selling that option *by itself* is bullish or bearish and you'll have the correct answer.

For example, using our $50/$55 vertical call spread, we know the $50 call is more valuable since it is a lower strike. Once we have identified the more valuable strike, we then need to find whether that option is being purchased or sold. If the $50 call is bought then you are really buying a call, which is bullish. Therefore, buying the $50 call and selling the $55 call must be a *bull* spread since the trader is buying the controlling call option. Buying a call is bullish.

On the other hand, if you sell the $50 call and buy the $55 call then it is a *bear* spread since the trader is selling the controlling $50 call. Selling a call is bearish.

Identifying the controlling option is an easy way to identify long and short vertical spreads once you start trading them. For instance, assume you find a quote for the $50/$55 vertical call spread. If you buy the vertical spread, you will be buying the $50 call and selling the $55 call. Again, buying the spread just means you are buying the more valuable option. On the other hand, if you sell the spread, you will be selling the $50 call and buying the $55 call. Selling the spread means you are selling the more valuable option. Notice that it is the more valuable $50 call that determines whether the spread is being purchased or sold.

Let's try it for the $50/$55 vertical put spread. The more valuable strike is the $55 strike. If you buy that strike then it is a *bear* spread since you are buying the controlling put. Buying a put is bearish. On the other hand, if you sell the $55 put then it is a *bull* spread since you are selling the controlling call. Selling a put is bullish.

While you are learning spreads, start by using the BLSH mnemonic to find if the strategy is bullish or bearish. But as you continue to work with spreads, gradually adopt the method of identifying which is the controlling strike and then identify whether you are buying or selling that strike and you will always be certain of your answer.

Rationale for Spreads

With this understanding, it is now easier to understand the rationale for vertical spreads. If you buy a vertical spread, you are buying the more valuable option. The sale of the other option is simply done to *reduce the cost* of the long option. Buying a vertical spread is a strategy, as we will found shortly, that allows investors and traders to enter into long option positions they may otherwise find to be too expensive. Long vertical spreads solve the expensive option problem.

On the other hand, if you sell a vertical spread, you are selling the more valuable option. Whenever you sell an option, you are accepting an obligation. By selling a call option, you have the obligation to deliver shares for a fixed price and there is no telling how high the price of that stock may be when it comes time to deliver the shares. Selling a put option gives you the obligation to buy shares at a fixed price and there's no telling how low the price of those shares may be at that time. In other words, selling an option by itself (naked) entails a lot of risk. However, the vertical spread requires that you purchase another option, which acts as a hedge and completely defines the maximum loss. In other words, when you sell a vertical spread, you are really interested in selling the more valuable option. The purchase of the other option is done to *reduce the risk* of the short option.

Cheap or Chicken

We have shown that the debit trader is really interested in purchasing the more valuable option. By entering the spread, the trader can reduce the premium paid for this long position. For the credit spread trader, the goal is to sell the more valuable strike and receive a premium; however, the trader is now exposed to potentially unlimited losses. By entering a vertical spread, the trader takes some of the premium from the sale of the short option and buys another option to hedge adverse stock price movement.

There is a somewhat humorous, although valuable way of understanding the philosophies between credit and debit spreads. We can say the debit trader is "cheap" since they do not want to pay a lot for the long call position by itself. Selling the less valuable option reduces the price.

For the credit spread, they are "chicken" as their goal is to sell the more valuable strike but they are fearful of the unlimited risk. Buying the less valuable option provides a hedge. So remember "cheap" or "chicken" to help identify the underlying philosophies.

Early Assignment

Traders new to vertical spreads often concerned that they may get assigned early on the short position. If so, does it pose a risk? Assume you buy one $50/$55 vertical call spread (bought the $50 call and sold the $55 call) for a net debit of $2. The very most this sprad could ever be worth is the $5 difference in strikes which would leave you with a $3 profit. Now assume that the stock rises above $55 prior to expiration and you are assigned on the short $55 call. If you are assigned on the $55 call, you are required to sell shares for $55 per share. However, if you do not have the shares then your broker will short shares in your account so that the stock can be delivered to the person exercising the $55 call. The end result is that you have a long $50 call plus a short stock position of 100 shares.

When you find out you have been assigned early, you can do one of two things. First, exercise your $50 call and cover the short stock position. This means you will have purchased shares for $50 and sold them for $55 thus locking in the guaranteed $5 maximum gain early, which is a very good thing. This shows that if the stock price is the same or higher the next day there is no risk to you. Simply exercise the long $50 call and collect the $5 maximum gain.

But what if the stock price is down? Put-call parity reveals that your combination of a long $50 call plus short stock is really a long $50 put in disguise. To verify, all we have to do is take the basic put-call parity equation $S + P - C = 0$ and rearrange it so that long call and short stock are on the same side of the equation and find that $P = C - S$. This means that you could do better than a $5 gain if the stock price falls since long puts will rise in value. For instance, assume the stock price falls from $55 to $49 the day you find out about the early assignment. In this case, don't exercise the $50 call. Instead, just buy the shares in the open market for $49 and deliver them against your short position at $55 and collect a $6 profit. The additional $1 gain is the effect of the synthetic $50 put against a $49 stock price. You would still be left with a free long call that may make even more money if the stock price should rise.

What if you had, instead, sold the $50/$55 call spread (sold the $50 call and bought the $55 call) for $2? Your maximum gain on this position is $2 and the maximum loss is $3.

Let's assume the stock is $53 and see what your choices are now. If you feel the stock will fall then you can hang onto the position and make a maximum of $2 if you are correct and the stock falls below $50 at expiration. However, if you feel the stock will rise then you could buy back the $50 call for more than $3 ($3 intrinsic value plus time value). So at this point, your two choices are to make a maximum of $2 or spend more than $3.

Now let's assume that you were assigned on the short $50 call and see how that would affect your alternatives. You will be short stock at $50 and long the $55 call, which is a synthetic long $55 put. If you believe the stock will fall from this point then hang on to the short stock and long $55 call combination and continue to profit in an unlimited fashion if the stock falls. If you were not assigned then you could only profit by $2.

However, if you believe the stock will rise then buy the short shares back in the open market for $53 using the $50 credit balance from the short sale, which results in a net loss of exactly $3 on that transaction. If you had not been assigned, it would cost you more than $3. You can verify a similar set of transactions for the vertical put spreads. Early assignment will therefore never hurt you in a vertical spread[3]. And it's all because you understand synthetic options!

Vertical Spread Examples

Let's go back to the Google quotes we used in the last chapter, which have been reproduced as Table 9-5 below:

---

3 The only exception is if you are trading *cash settled* options with American style exercise such as the OEX index. Early assignment on these products can hurt you since the value of cash does not change with levels of the index like it does for stock. But remember that our focus for this book is equity options so we are not going to cover those nuances here.

Table 9-5

| GOOG | | | | | | | | 293.07 +0.72 | | | | | |
| Aug 08, 2005 @ 15:04 ET (Data 15 Minutes Delayed) | | | | | | Bid 293.04 Ask 293.11 | | Size 7x1 Vol 3482611 | | | | | |
Calls	Last Sale	Net	Bid	Ask	Vol	Open Int	Puts	Last Sale	Net	Bid	Ask	Vol	Open Int
07 Jan 250.0 (OUW AJ-E)	88.60	pc	79.30	80.40	0	1682	07 Jan 250.0 (OUW MJ-E)	23.10	pc	22.30	22.80	0	3996
07 Jan 260.0 (OUW AL-E)	74.10	-1.90	73.20	74.30	5	2009	07 Jan 260.0 (OUW ML-E)	27.40	pc	25.80	26.60	0	1080
07 Jan 270.0 (OUW AN-E)	69.70	pc	67.50	68.50	0	993	07 Jan 270.0 (OUW MN-E)	30.00	pc	29.70	30.30	0	1298
07 Jan 280.0 (OQD AP-E)	61.70	pc	62.00	63.00	0	1263	07 Jan 280.0 (OQD MP-E)	32.60	pc	34.00	34.50	0	903
07 Jan 290.0 (OQD AR-E)	60.30	pc	56.90	58.00	0	1134	07 Jan 290.0 (OQD MR-E)	38.40	pc	38.50	39.40	0	767
07 Jan 300.0 (OQD AT-E)	54.60	pc	52.20	53.30	0	5841	07 Jan 300.0 (OQD MT-E)	43.80	pc	43.50	44.00	0	2218

Assume you are bullish on Google and wish to buy the $250 call but find that it is trading for $80.40 and decide that is too much to spend on the option. Rather than pass up the opportunity, you decide to use a vertical call spread to reduce the cost of the $250 call. This is the "cheap" version of the vertical call spread; you are selling another option to reduce the cost of the long position. If you buy the $250 call and sell the $260 call then you are long the $250/$260 vertical call spread.

Depending on your broker's trading platform, you would enter the order in one of two ways:

1) **Buy the Google Jan. $250/$260 vertical call spread at market (or net debit limit)**

2) **Buy the Google Jan. $250 call and simultaneously sell the Google Jan. $260 call at market (or net debit limit)**

If you place the order as a "market" order then you can currently buy the $250 call for the $80.40 asking price and simultaneously sell the $260 call for the $73.20 bid, which means a net cost to you (net debit) of $80.40 - $73.20 = $7.20. In most cases, the market order should fill at this $7.20 price. In some cases, you will pay slightly less since you are sending two orders to the exchange and may get a little better pricing. Of course, because it is a market order it is possible to be filled for a higher price than this as well. (Market orders guarantee the execution but not the price.)

On the other hand, you could decide to use a limit order and request to "Buy the $250/$260 vertical call spread at a net debit of $7.00" for example. This order will only execute if it can be filled for $7.00 or less. The risk is that it may not fill. (Limit orders guarantee the price but not the execution.)

Once the order is filled, you are long the $250 call and short the $260 call. You have the right to buy shares for $250 and the obligation to sell them for $260, which means the most you could make is $10 on the spread. But because you paid $2.80 for the spread, the maximum profit is $10 - $7.20 = $2.80. We also know the break-even point is the net debit added to the $250 strike, or $250 + 7.20 = $257.20. The profit and loss diagram in Figure 9-6 confirms the maximum gain, loss, and break even points we calculated based on our knowledge of option pricing principles:

Figure 9-6: Long $250/$260 Vertical Call Spread

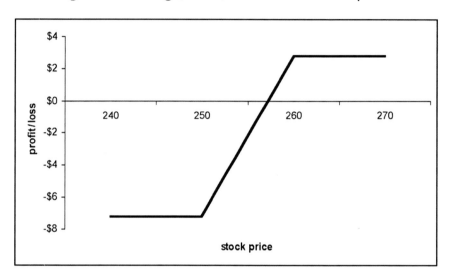

Now let's check the profit and loss profile for the corresponding put spread. Rather than buy the $250/$260 vertical call spread we know you could accomplish the same thing by selling the $250/$260 vertical put spread. Selling this spread means you will be selling the more valuable option, which is the $260 strike and that means you must buy the $250 strike.

According to the quotes, you can sell the $260 put for $25.80. However, this subjects you to unlimited downside loss, which is a frightening thought. To hedge this risk, you decide to use some of that premium to buy a lower strike put. This is the "chicken" version of the vertical spread. Your real goal is to sell the controlling $260 put but the purchase of the $250 put is done as a hedge. If you sell the $260 put and buy the $250 put then you are short the $250/$260 vertical put spread. The order to your broker would be placed in one of the following two ways:

1) **Sell the Google January $250/$260 vertical put spread at market (or net credit limit)**

2) **Sell to open, the Google Jan. $260 put and simultaneously buy to open the Google Jan. $250 put at market (or net credit limit)**

If you place the order as a "market" order then you can currently sell the $260 put for the $25.80 bid and simultaneously buy the $250 put for the $22.80 asking price, which means the net credit to you is $25.80 - $22.80 = $3.00. As with any market order, this is not guaranteed to fill for this exact price but it should be very close. If you want to ensure that you do not receive less than $3.00 you would need to use a limit order with a "net credit of $3.00."

Your broker will require a margin deposit for any credit spread equal to the amount of the maximum loss. In this example, if you sell one spread for $300, your broker will withhold $700 as a margin requirement (the $10 difference in strikes less the $3 credit). Again, this clearly shows that credit spreads are not better for the sole reason that it is better to receive money rather than spend it as so many traders adamantly believe. Credit spreads require a margin deposit exactly equal to the amount that debit spreads must pay to buy the spread. Whether it is called a debit or a margin requirement, both traders pay the same thing.

By selling the $260 put you have the obligation to buy shares for $260. Purchasing the $250 put gives you have the right to sell shares for $250. Therefore, it is possible you could end up buying for $260 and selling for $250, which creates a $10 loss on the spread but because you were paid $3 for the spread, your maximum loss is $7.00. Figure 9-7 shows the profit and loss diagram for the short $250/$260 vertical call spread:

Figure 9-7: Short $250/$260 Vertical Put Spread

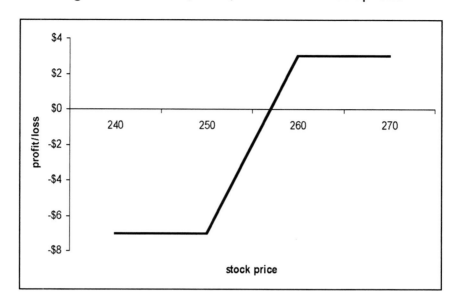

Notice that the shape of Figure 9-7 is identical to Figure 9-6, which confirms that selling the put spread is identical to buying the call spread. However, notice that the max gain for the put spread is $3 and is only $2.80 for the call spread while the max loss for the put spread is $7.00 but is $7.20 for the call spread. In other words, the short put spread offers a higher reward for less risk. This would be a time to choose the credit spread over the debit spread. The reasons why these slight pricing discrepancies occur are beyond our scope but a simple explanation is that the puts are out-of-the-money while the calls are in-the-money. Most investors fear the downside risk of the stock and are willing to "pay up" for out-of-the-money puts for insurance against their long stock positions. The out-of-the-money $260 puts are bid up a little higher than the corresponding in-the-money $260 call which makes the credit spread a little better in this instance. Remember, this will not always be the case and sometimes the debit spread will be the better choice. (For instance, using Table 9-5, buying the $290/$300 call spread provides a maximum reward of $4.20 while selling the corresponding put spread yields a maximum or $4.10. In this case, it is better to buy the call spread.)

Risk and Reward Revisited

Many traders who see spreads such as in this example believe that it is a "terrible" or "unfavorable" risk-reward ratio. They reason that it doesn't make a lot of sense to put $7.00 at risk in exchange for a $3.00 maximum profit. If you remember back to our discussion on risk and reward, you should realize that the reason the market has bid this spread to a relatively high level is because the stock price is $293 and is well above the short $260 strike. If the stock price rises, stays still, or even falls to $260 the trader will make the full $10 on the spread ($3.00 profit). When viewed in this light, you can see why the market is willing to pay what a relatively high price $7 price in exchange for a relatively low $3 reward. It is not an unfavorable risk-reward ratio but, instead, a reflection of the relatively low risk in the position.

You can verify this by considering a different vertical spread. Rather than selling the $250/$260 vertical spread, you could sell a set of strikes that are closer to the current stock price thereby taking more risk. For example, you may decide to sell the $280/$290 vertical put spread instead. You could sell the $290 put for the $38.50 bid and buy the $280 put for the $34.50 asking price for a net credit of $4.00. The profit and loss diagrams of the two vertical put spreads are compared in Figure 9-8:

Figure 9-8: Short $250/$260 Vertical Put Spread (Shaded Line) Compared to Short $280/$290 Vertical Put Spread (Bold Line)

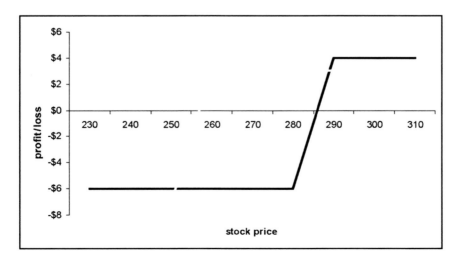

Figure 9-8 shows that selling the $280/$290 vertical put spread (bold line) does have more reward than the short $250/$260 vertical put spread ($4 vs. $3). Selling the $280/$290 vertical put spread also has less of a downside ($6 vs. $7). On the surface it seems like you get the best of both worlds – more reward, less risk. However, you must remember that we are not comparing the same strike prices. You are more likely to end up with losses with the $280/$290 spread because the short $290 strike is very close to the current stock price of $293. The $250/$260 spread will not fall into losing territory until the stock price hits $260, which is $30 less, which means it is less likely to happen. The $280/$290 vertical spread is riskier and that's why it has a higher reward.

Don't get trapped in believing that the spreads with the highest rewards and the lowest downside are superior. They are simply riskier and it is up to you to decide which sets of risks and rewards to take.

As a general rule, if the stock's price is exactly half way between two strikes, you will find that the maximum gain and loss will be equal to half the distance of the strikes. For instance, if Google was trading for $295, then it would fall exactly half way between the $290/$300 strikes. Because there is a $10 difference in strikes then half that amount, or $5, would be the maximum gain and maximum loss for the $290/$300 vertical spreads (calls or puts). In other words, if the stock's price is exactly half way between strikes then there is a 50-50 chance that it will make or lose money so the cost will be 50% of the distance in strikes.

If the stock's price is less than the half-way point, you will find that the maximum gain is greater than $5 (and the maximum loss is less than $5). Why does the maximum gain rise as the stock price falls further away from the strikes? If the stock price falls, the long call spread is becoming more out-of-the-money and therefore riskier so it will trade at a discount from $5. If you can buy the $10 call spread for less than $5 then you must end up with more reward. The long put spread, on the other hand, becomes more in-the-money as the stock price falls and trades at a premium to $5 since it is becoming less risky. Therefore, if you *sell* this spread, you will be receiving more than $5, which is your reward.

The opposite is true if the stock's price is above the half-way point of the strikes. If it is, the maximum gain becomes less than $5 (and the maximum loss is greater than $5). As the stock prices rises above the half-way point, the long call spread is becoming more in-the-money and therefore getting more expensive to buy (trades at a premium to $5). If you pay more for the spread, you must reduce your reward. The long put spread is becoming more out-of-the-money and is becoming cheaper to buy. Therefore, if you *sell* the put spread, you are receiving less money, which is your reward.

Figure 9-8 confirms these risk-reward relationships and shows the $250/$260 vertical spread has less reward than the $280/$290 vertical spread. Why? Because the stock price is so much further above the $250/$260 strikes thus making the call spreads trade at a premium (giving you less reward) and making the put spreads trade at a discount thus giving you less reward.

Let's run through one quick example to be sure you understand this principle applies to vertical spreads. Assume that ABC stock is trading for $50. What do you suppose the $45/$55 vertical call spread will cost? It should cost $2.50 and therefore have a reward of $2.50. If the stock is $49 the vertical call spread will cost less than $2.50 and offer a bigger reward. The reason is that it is getting riskier since the call strikes are more out-of-the-money. As the risk increases, the price goes down. If the stock is $51, the vertical call spread will cost more than $2.50 since the calls are a little more in-the-money and the spread is relatively less risky. As the risk decreases, price increases. Once you understand how these relationships apply to the long vertical call spread, the answers are identical (but for opposite reasons) for the short vertical put spreads.

Price Behavior of Vertical Spreads

Vertical spreads converge to a specific value as expiration nears. What is that value? Think back to the mechanics of long calls and puts. As expiration nears, all in-the-money options converge to intrinsic value while all out-of-the-money options converge toward zero. In the same way and for the same reasons, vertical spreads converge to either intrinsic value or zero.

For example, let's go back to our $250/$260 vertical call spread that was trading for $7.20. With the stock at $293, both of these calls are in-the-money, which means the spread must converge to the $10 difference in strikes as time goes by. If the stock price remains at $293, the long $250 call is worth the intrinsic value of $43 at expiration while the $260 call is worth the intrinsic value of $33. Since you are long the $250 call you will collect $43; because you are short the $260 call you will owe $33 and your net gain is $10. After subtracting the $7.20 cost, your profit is $2.80. As long as the stock price is above the short strike ($260) at expiration this spread will slowly start to increase to a maximum value of $10.

Why is the spread not worth $10 today? The answer is time value. The long call has time value of $37.40 ($80.40 premium - $43 intrinsic value). The short call has a time value of $40.20 ($73.20 premium - $33 intrinsic value), which is an amount you owe. Because you owe $40.20 of time value and own $37.40 worth of time value, the net amount you own is $40.20 - $37.40 = $2.80, which is exactly the amount of your maximum gain. Your maximum gain is simply earned by the passage of time. As the long and short time values fall toward zero, the amount you owe is reduced by a net of $2.80 and that's when the spread will converge to the full $10 difference in strikes.

What if the stock price is between $250 and $260 at expiration? In this case, the vertical spread will converge on the intrinsic value of the long call. For example, if the stock is $258 then the long $250 call is converging on the $8 intrinsic value while the short $260 is converging toward zero since it is out-of-the-money. You will collect $8 and owe nothing for a gain of $8. After subtracting the $7.20 cost, you are left with an 80-cent profit.

If the stock price is below $250 at expiration, both the long and short calls will converge toward zero since they are both out-of-the-money. As time passes, the value of the spread will therefore fall toward zero. The same reasoning exists for the vertical put spreads.

The important point to understand is that vertical spreads do not respond quickly to changes in the stock's price. The reason is that vertical spread consists of a long and short option. As the stock price moves in any direction, one option increases in value while the other loses value so the net change to the vertical spread is small. Further, the time value does not become zero until expiration so the full value of the spread cannot be realized until expiration. (It is also for these reasons why it is not a big risk to enter a "market" order.) As with any option position, you can certainly close it prior to expiration; however, do not expect it to be worth the maximum value. While vertical spreads do allow investors and traders to enter into option positions cheaply they do come with a drawback that you should not expect to exit with a profit unless a very favorable price change has occurred relative the time remaining on the option.

How Much Time?

When investors and traders learn about spreads one of the first questions asked is how much time to buy or sell. This is a very tough question to answer for spreads. As with any strategy, each set of strikes and time frames creates a unique set of risks and rewards. If both strikes are in-the-money then shorter time frames provide have a higher chance for the spread to expire with intrinsic value. In other words, if both strikes are in-the-money then shorter terms vertical spreads are less risky. As the risk-reward relationship shows though, these spreads may not provide too big of a reward. If you wish to increase the reward for any given set of strikes then you will need to increase the expiration date.

For instance, assume ABC stock is trading for $54 and the one-month $45/$50 vertical call spread is worth $4.50, which means the most you can make is 50 cents per spread. A longer-term contract will trade for *less* than $4.50 thereby providing a larger reward. Why is this? It is riskier to hold with more time remaining. If the $45/$50 vertical call spread were to expire right now then the spread would be worth the full $5 value. However, as you increase the time remaining on the spread then that just provides a chance for the spread to fall out-of-the-money so it becomes riskier.

On the other hand, if you are buying out-of-the-money strikes then buying longer time frames will give you a better chance for the strikes to expire in-the-money. Providing a better chance for intrinsic value is the same as saying it is less risky and that means the spread will not provide as much reward.

The trick is to balance the risk and reward to suit your tastes. In our Google example, most traders would never use a vertical spread with that much time remaining. However, by selling that much time, it allowed us to get strikes very deep-in-the-money and still provide a very nice return. If we would have considered a shorter time frame, we would find that the reward was less than $3. It's all about risk-reward tradeoffs and it is up to the investor to decide which to buy or sell.

When it is time to exit the spread, you simply enter the reverse set of transactions that got you into the trade in the first place. For example, 35 days later, Google was trading for roughly $308. If you wanted to close the spread, you would enter the closing transaction in one of two ways depending on your broker's platform:

1) **Buy the Google January $250/$260 vertical put spread at market (or net debit limit)**

2) **Buy to close, Google Jan. $260 put and simultaneously sell to close the Google Jan. $250 put at market (or net credit limit)**

Figure 9-9 shows that 35 days later the $260 put could be purchased for $20.90 and the $250 put could be sold for $17.40 for a net debit of $3.50:

Figure 9-9

Calls	Last Sale	Net	Bid	Ask	Vol	Open Int	Puts	Last Sale	Net	Bid	Ask	Vol	Open Int
07 Jan 250.0 (OUW AJ-E)	80.00	pc	88.40	89.30	0	1678	07 Jan 250.0 (OUW MJ-E)	19.50	-5.30	17.40	17.90	1	4011
07 Jan 260.0 (OUW AL-E)	72.00	pc	81.80	82.60	0	2009	07 Jan 260.0 (OUW ML-E)	23.90	pc	20.30	20.90	0	1060
07 Jan 270.0 (OUW AH-E)	63.70	pc	75.60	76.30	0	1019	07 Jan 270.0 (OUW MH-E)	27.40	pc	23.80	24.30	0	1335
07 Jan 280.0 (OQD AP-E)	55.60	pc	69.60	70.40	0	1349	07 Jan 280.0 (OQD MP-E)	31.50	pc	27.40	28.00	0	1024
07 Jan 290.0 (OQD AR-E)	58.50	pc	64.20	64.70	0	1222	07 Jan 290.0 (OQD MR-E)	31.70	-3.70	31.50	32.10	2	802
07 Jan 300.0 (OQD AT-E)	58.20	+5.60	58.80	59.50	11	6098	07 Jan 300.0 (OQD MT-E)	35.90	-4.70	35.80	36.50	2	2323

GOOG — 308.25 +9.16 — Sep 12, 2005 @ 11:10 ET (Data 15 Minutes Delayed) — Bid 308.25 Ask 308.26 Size 2x1 Vol 4190159

This clearly demonstrates that despite a positive move in the underlying stock from $293 to $308 that the spread would not be profitable. The spread was sold for $3.00 and purchased back for $3.50, a loss of 50-cents per spread. The reason this happened is because there are still 494 days remaining until expiration and a $15 move in a stock like Google is not significant relative to that amount of time remaining. If there were a shorter amount of time remaining, say three months, then the spread would definitely be profitable. But at this time, investors and traders were bidding up the value for the out-of-the-money $260 put for insurance and that is creating the 50-cent loss. In other words, on a net basis, the amount of time premium owed on the short $260 put increased, which is bad for you as the seller.

The main reason we showed this is to emphasize the fact that spreads need time to pass before becoming profitable. Many traders who are short-term in nature are disappointed to find that the stock has moved in their favor yet the spread is at a loss. So be aware that you will need to wait until very close to expiration before realizing the full value of the spread.

Vertical spreads allow you to profit on outlooks covering *specific ranges* of stock prices. They are also a perfect solution for time when you find options that you may too expensive or too risky. Option trading goes far beyond the purchase of a call or put to capitalize on a directional outlook. The main purpose of this chapter was to allow new investors and traders a glimpse into the world of options trading at a higher level. Options create opportunities that cannot be done with stock or any other asset. Once you master the concepts presented in this book a new door will open and you will find that vertical spreads are just one of many fascinating opportunities available to you.

 ## Key Concepts

1) Vertical spreads have limited risk and limited reward.

2) Vertical spreads have a bullish or bearish bias.

3) Vertical spreads allow investors to buy long options for less money (debit spreads). They also allow investors to sell options for less risk (credit spreads).

4) Buying the call spread is identical to selling the corresponding put spread and vice versa.

5) The higher the reward that a vertical spread offers the riskier the position.

6) Spread values tend to move slowly. If you wish to collect the full value of the spread (assuming it has moved in your favor) you must wait until very close to expiration. Otherwise, you will receive less than the maximum reward.

Chapter Nine Questions

1) **If you buy a $50 call and sell a $55 call it is a:**
   a) Long horizontal call spread
   b) Short horizontal call spread
   c) Long vertical call spread
   d) Short vertical call spread

2) **Spreads always involve:**
   a) Buying of a put and call
   b) Selling of a put and call
   c) Buying of a call and buying of a call in a different month
   d) Buying of one option and the selling of another of the same type

3) **A vertical spread is:**
   a) Buying of one option and selling of another within the same month
   b) Buying of one option and selling of another within a different month
   c) Selling of one option and selling of another month and strike
   d) Buying of one option and buying of another

4) **If you are short the $100/$105 put spread you are:**
   a) Short the $100 put, long the $105 put
   b) Short the $105 put, long the $100 put
   c) Long the $100 put, long the $105 put
   d) Short the $100 put, short the $105 put

5) **If you buy the $100/$105 call spread you are:**
   a) Short the $100 call, long the $105 call
   b) Short the $105 call, long the $100 call
   c) Long the $100 call, short the $105 call
   d) Short the $100 call, short the $105 call

6) **Vertical spreads have:**
   a) Unlimited risk, limited reward
   b) Limited risk, unlimited reward
   c) Unlimited risk, unlimited reward
   d) Limited risk, limited reward

7) **If you buy the $50/$55 vertical call spread for $3.50, the break-even point is:**
   a) $46.50
   b) $51.50
   c) $53.50
   d) $58.50

8) The maximum a vertical spread can be worth is the:
    a) The strike of the short less the time value
    b) The difference in strikes
    c) The sum of the strikes
    d) The strike of the long plus the time value

9) **If you buy a low strike option and sell a higher strike option of the same type and same expiration it is a:**
    a) Neutral spread
    b) Vertical bear spread
    c) Vertical bull spread
    d) Diagonal spread

10) **Long vertical spreads are always constructed by:**
    a) Buying the lesser valued option
    b) Buying the more valuable option
    c) Selling the more valuable option
    d) Selling the lower strike option

11) **Credit spreads should be used:**
    a) Always because they are better than debit spreads
    b) When the risk is greater than the corresponding debit spread
    c) When the reward is greater than the corresponding credit spread
    d) When there is a short time until expiration

12) **If you buy the $70/$75 vertical call spread you have the:**
    a) Right to buy shares for $70 and the right to sell for $75
    b) Right to buy shares for $75 and the obligation to sell for $70
    c) Right to buy shares for $70 and the obligation to sell for $75
    d) Right to sell shares for $70 and the obligation to sell for $75

13) **Buying the vertical call spread is identical to:**
    a) Selling the corresponding put spread
    b) Buying the corresponding put spread
    c)   Selling the corresponding diagonal spread
    d) Buying the corresponding horizontal spread

14) **Debit spreads are used to:**
   a)   Reduce the cost of the exercise
   b)   Reduce the cost of the long option
   c)   Increase the premium you receive
   d)   Decrease the risk of early exercise

15) **Credit spreads are used to:**
   a)   Reduce the risk of the short position
   b)   Reduce the cost of the long option
   c)   Increase the premium you receive
   d)   Decrease the risk of early exercise

16) **If you sell the \$30/\$35 put spread for \$2, the most you can lose is:**
   a)   \$2
   b)   \$3
   c)   \$4
   d)   \$5

17) **ABC stock is trading for \$74. What would you expect the value of the \$70/\$75 vertical call spread to be?**
   a)   \$2.50
   b)   More than \$2.50
   c)   Less than \$2.50
   d)   More than \$5.00

18) **If you sell the \$80/\$85 put spread for \$2, what is the break-even point?**
   a)   \$78
   b)   \$82
   c)   \$83
   d)   \$87

19) **If both strikes are in-the-money, what happens to the value of a vertical spread near expiration?**
   a)   Converge to the difference in strikes less the premium
   b)   Converge to the midpoint of the strikes
   c)   Converge toward zero
   d)   Converge to the difference in strikes

20) **The value of a vertical spread tends to change:**
   a)   In a steady, reliable way toward the difference in strikes
   b)   Quickly for longer term but not shorter term spreads
   c)   Quickly over time
   d)   Slowly over time

Chapter Nine - Answers

1)   **If you buy a $50 call and sell a $55 call it is a:**
   c)   Long vertical call spread

Whenever you buy a vertical spread, you are always buying the more valuable option. For call options, that will always be the lower strike, which is $50. So buying the $50 call and selling the $55 call is a long vertical call spread.

2)   **Spreads always involve:**
   d)   Buying of one option and the selling of another of the same type

There are many types of spreads but all of them involve the buying of one option and selling of another.

3)   **A vertical spread is:**
   a)   Buying of one option and selling of another within the same month

4)   **If you are short the $100/$105 put spread you are:**
   b)   Short the $105 put, long the $100 put

Short vertical spreads are always executed by selling the more valuable strike. For puts, that will always be the higher strike put. So if you are short the $100/$105 put spread you are short the $105 put and long the $100 put.

5)   **If you buy the $100/$105 call spread you are:**
   c)   Long the $100 call, short the $105 call

Whenever you buy a vertical spread, you are always buying the more valuable option. For call options, that will always be the lower strike, which is $10050. So buying the $50 call and selling the $55 call is a long vertical call spread.

6)   **Vertical spreads have:**
   d)   Limited risk, limited reward

7) **If you buy the $50/$55 vertical call spread for $3.50, the break-even point is:**

    c) $53.50

If you buy the $50/$55 call spread you are effectively buying the $50 call for $3.50. The sale of the $55 call just helps to reduce the cost of the more valuable $50 call. If you pay $3.50 for the $50 call then the break –even point is $50 + $3.50 = $3.50.

8) **The maximum a vertical spread can be worth is the:**

    b)   The difference in strikes

The very most any spread can be worth is the difference in strikes.

9) **If you buy a low strike option and sell a higher strike option of the same type and same expiration it is a:**

    c)   Vertical bull spread

A vertical bull spread is always constructed by purchasing the lower strike option and selling a higher strike option.

10) **Long vertical spreads are always constructed by:**

    b)   Buying the more valuable option

Whenever you buy the more valuable option you have a long vertical spread

11) **Credit spreads should be used:**

    b)   When the risk is greater than the corresponding debit spread

Credit spreads should be used when it provides a greater reward than the corresponding debit spread.

12) **If you buy the $70/$75 vertical call spread you have the:**

    c)   Right to buy shares for $70 and the obligation to sell for $75

If you buy the $70/$75 vertical call spread you are long the $70 call and short the $75 call. You have the right to buy shares for $70 and the obligation to sell shares for $75.

13) **Buying the vertical call spread is identical to:**

    a)   Selling the corresponding put spread

14) Debit spreads are used to:

    b)   Reduce the cost of the long option

One of the motivations for using debit vertical spreads is that they reduce the cost of the long option.

15) Credit spreads are used to:

    a)   Reduce the risk of the short position

Credit spreads are initiated by selling the more valuable option which subjects you to unlimited risk. Buying the lesser valued option reduces the risk of the short position.

16) If you sell the \$30/\$35 put spread for \$2, the most you can lose is:

    b)   \$3

If you sell the \$30/\$35 put spread you are short the \$35 put and long the \$30 put. You have the obligation to buy shares for \$35 and the right to sell shares for \$30, which leaves you with a \$5 loss. Because you were paid \$2 for the spread, the most you can lose is \$3.

17) ABC stock is trading for \$74. What would you expect the value of the \$70/\$75 vertical call spread to be?

    b)   More than \$2.50

If the stock were at the midpoint of the spread (\$72.50) you would expect the \$70/\$75 spread to be worth \$2.50. However, if the stock price were higher than \$72.50, you would expect the value of the spread to be worth more than \$2.50.

18) If you sell the \$80/\$85 put spread for \$2, what is the break-even point?

    c)   \$83

If you sell the \$80/\$85 put then you are short the \$85 put, which means the stock can fall by the \$2 premium to a price of \$83. If the stock is \$83 at expiration, the long \$80 put expires worthless and the short \$85 put is worth the intrinsic value of \$2. You could buy back the spread for \$2 thus breaking even.

19) If both strikes are in-the-money, what happens to the value of a vertical spread near expiration?

    d)   Converge to the difference in strikes

If both strikes are in-the-money then the value of the spread converges to the difference in strikes as the time premium slowly decays.

20) The value of a vertical spread tends to change:

d)   Slowly over time

The two options counteract each other as the stock price changes so the value of vertical spreads tends to change slowly over time.

Chapter Ten

Hedging with Options

The last chapter showed that option trading goes far beyond the purchase of calls and puts. We can mix and match calls and puts, longs and shorts, different expiration, different quantities and so on to create truly unique strategies and opportunities. But would you believe that is not the true power of options? The true power is realized once you understand how to hedge with options to shift your profit and loss curves in different directions as the underlying stock is moving.

This chapter is not intended to be a full course on hedging but rather a way to close our introductory journey into the world of options. Once you understand how options allow us to hedge, we believe that you will be in a better position to make your own decision as to whether options are risky or not.

Hedging

To get started, let's define what we mean by hedging. The word "hedge" is borrowed from early farmers who used to plant shrubs along the perimeter of their farm to create a protective barrier or fence. In the world of finance, a hedge is an investment that is taken out specifically to reduce or cancel out the risk of another investment. In other words, an investment that forms a protective barrier around your portfolio.

To fully appreciate what it means to hedge, let's ssume you must take the following ten-question matching exam and match the answers in the right hand column to the questions in the left hand column. You must get a 90% or higher to pass the class:

1) Call option _____   A. Exercise price

2) Put option _____   B. Right to sell

3) Strike price _____   C. Long stock + short call

4) Expiration date _____   D. $\partial\Delta/\partial s$

5) Long options _____   E. Long and short options

6) OCC _____   F. Right to buy

7) Covered call _____   G. $\partial c/\partial s$

8) Vertical spread _____   H. Third Friday

9) Formula for delta _____   I. Clearing firm

10) Formula for gamma _____   J. Convey rights

You start running through the questions: Number one, call option is F, the right to buy. Number two, put option is B, right to sell. Number three, strike price is A, exercise price and on down the list you go.

You easily move through the first eight questions apparently on your way to acing the test with a score of 100%. That is until you come to questions nine and ten: The formulas for delta and gamma? What is that?

You know they must correspond to answers D and G but have no idea which is correct. But now you have a little dilemma. Either question nine is D and question ten is G or vice versa. If you guess correctly, you will score 100 on the quiz and get an A. But if you guess incorrectly, you will score an 80 and fail the class and there is a 50-50 chance of either outcome. So now you're thinking how unfortunate it is that passing the class has come down to a guessing game – effectively the toss of a coin. Is there anything you can do to improve your outcome? What would you do?

The correct answer is to *hedge your bet* and guess "D" for both questions nine and ten (or "G" for both)[4]. Doing so assures you that you will receive the necessary 90% and passing grade. Notice what the hedge did for you. By sacrificing the 100%, you guaranteed the necessary 90%. If your goal is to pass the class then what difference is a 90% or a 100%? There is no difference. Yet many students

---

4 For those who are curious, the correct answers for 9 and 10 are G and D respectively.

lose sight of the true goal of passing the class and try to reach for the 100% grade. There is no benefit in getting a 100% but there are big negative consequences for not getting 90%. It only seems rational that you should hedge yourself and sacrifice the 100% in exchange for the guaranteed 90%. Rather than take the 50-50 chance of passing, you have effectively bet against yourself – a hedge – and created guaranteed success.

If you can understand that analogy then you understand what it means to hedge your financial portfolios. All of you have some type of goal whether it is to increase your account by so much per year, generate monthly income of a certain amount, or to have a certain amount at a future point in time, for examples. Whatever your goal happens to be, don't lose site of it. Those who lost site that the goal was to pass the class (90% grade) on the exam may have ended up in failure by guessing at the correct answer. Guessing is no way to pass an exam. Investors who lose site of their goals and do not hedge their bets may end up missing their goals or even in bankruptcy by trying to reach for maximum profits. Guessing what will happen in the market is no way to accomplish your financial goals.

Betting Against Yourself

Any hedge, whether with investing, betting, insurance – or taking exams – sticks to the same idea. Hedging means we give up some upside potential in exchange for less damage to the downside. For our exam, we gave up the chance of a 100% score in exchange for not getting 80% – we have hedged the score. With investing, hedging means we will give up some upside profits in exchange for removing some downside risk. In other words, a hedged portfolio means we bet against ourselves much like the exam. If we are bullish on the market, we may add a few bearish investments to hedge our bets.

Hedging is not a new concept for most fields but seems to be an elusive concept for many when it comes to finance. Here's another simple example of the power of hedging. Does your office have a football pool? You can even hedge to give yourself an edge there too. To make the example easy, assume there is only one game being played, which we'll say is between the Tampa Bay Buccaneers and the Atlanta Falcons. It costs $5 to play. You have a small office and the only person willing to play so far is Sam, who has bet $5 on Tampa Bay. The sign-up sheet has made it to your office and you have a decision to make. You can either bet on Tampa or

Atlanta. If you also bet on Tampa and they win then there will be $10 in the pot, which will be split between Sam and you leaving you each with $5. However, since you each put $5 in the pot, there's no way you'll make money from that bet. What happens if you bet on Atlanta? If Atlanta wins, you'll win the entire $10 as Sam's $5 will go to you. But if Tampa wins, your money will go to Sam and he'll take the $10 pot. So if you bet on Atlanta, you're faced with a 50-50 shot of winning (assuming the teams are equally matched). You'll either double your money or lose it all. If you take the opposite side of Sam's bet every week, you'll end up breaking even in the long run, which doesn't sound very appealing either. Most people would see these two alternatives (either betting on Tampa or Atlanta) as their only choice. But there is a third choice you can do. You can hedge your bet by betting against yourself. Although it doesn't sound like a way to make money, hedging is your best long-run alternative. Instead of betting on one team or the other, you simply put $10 in the pot and bet on both teams – you bet $5 on Tampa and $5 on Atlanta.

If Tampa wins, then you and Sam each hold a winning ticket and will split the $15 pot and each get $7.50 – you'll lose $2.50 overall. If Atlanta wins, you'll have the only winning ticket and keep the entire $15 pot thus making $5 overall. So half the time you'll lose $2.50 and half the time you'll win $5:

0.5 * (-$2.50)	=	-$1.25
0.5 * (+5.00)	=	+$2.50
Expected value	=	+$1.25

By hedging your bet, you've changed your long-run average from zero to +$1.25. This means that you will make, on average, $1.25 per game in the long run (assuming you and Sam are the only ones betting and that Sam doesn't catch on to your hedging scheme). Think about how powerful that is. If you bet on the same team as Sam, you'll end up with nothing. If you bet against Sam, you may win some money in the short run, but over the long haul, you'll end up with nothing. However, if you hedge your bet and bet against yourself, you can swing the odds in your favor. Strange, huh? Hedging is powerful because it works.

In this example, you put up 2/3 of the money pool in exchange for guaranteeing a winning ticket. You'll either lose 25% of your money or gain 50% on your money, thus giving you a long run average gain of 12.5%. The more elaborate the football pool and the more people who bet, the harder it becomes to hedge. For example, you may have to pick the winning team from among ten games that week. However, the idea is still the same. You'd just have to find the total number of combinations that *could be* made then find out which of those *have been* made. It's not too hard from there to determine which combinations will hedge your bet.

Hedging is the key to making consistent money in the markets. But in order to further understand the importance of hedging, we need to find out what kind of risk takers we are.

What Kind of Risk Takers Are We?

 Every day we're faced with making decisions about risk. You may not realize that you do, but subconscious calculations are always taking place on which risks to take and which to avoid. Walking across the street is, technically, risking your life to get to the other side. On one hand, you may think that sounds farfetched, but it is the *worst* thing that could happen from crossing the street. However, despite the risk, we walk across streets countless times because, intuitively, we know the probability of that worst-case scenario is very, very low. It's an acceptable risk, so we choose to take it. Depending on the situation, people tend to avoid risk, accept risk, and in some cases, even seek to take risk.

Psychologists have created three general categories to classify these risks:

1) Risk averse (those who avoid risk)

2) Risk neutral (those who accept reasonable risks)

3) Risk seeking (those who accept high-risk situations)

You are risk averse if you buy insurance and you are a risk seeker if you skydive. You are probably risk neutral about crossing the street. In most cases, people have different attitudes toward risk and it's not easy to say if they are risk averse, risk neutral, or risk seeking for a particular event. That is, until it comes to money. When it comes to money, people become very predictable and display a consistent view of risk. It is this view of risk that causes many mistakes in trading. Do you fall into the same category as most people? Here's how to find out: An eccentric millionaire asks you to choose between the following two choices. You only get to play the game once. Which would you choose?

A) $500 gain for sure

B) Flip a coin and get $1,000 if heads and nothing if tails

Both choices are similar in the sense they have the same long run average. In mathematical terms, they are said to have the same expected payoff, or *expected value*, which is nothing more than a mathematical long run average. If you were allowed to play this game thousands of times, you would *expect* to be up $500 per try regardless of which alternative you choose. Obviously, Choice A always yields $500 with each try. Choice B, on the other hand, yields $1,000 half the time and nothing half the time so, in the long run, you'd be up $500 per try.

A risk averse person will only take Choice A while risk seekers will choose Choice B. A risk neutral person would be indifferent between the two choices.

We Really Despise Risk

Dr. Robert Anthony said, "Most people would rather be certain they're miserable, than risk being happy." Sadly enough, most of the research in the field of behavioral finance shows this to be true. In fact, in 1979, two famous psychology researchers, Daniel Khaneman and Amos Tversky, published an influential paper in *The American Psychologist* showing our risk-averse natures – and with a remarkable twist. In that study, the researchers gave subjects a choice between the following two alternatives that we saw earlier:

A) $500 gain for sure

B) Flip a coin and get $1,000 if heads and nothing if tails

Most people picked Choice A without hesitation. This was no surprise to the researchers as they were aware of our risk averse tendencies. However, the researchers added an interesting twist and asked the following intriguing question:

C) Take a $500 loss for sure

D) Flip a coin and lose $1,000 if heads and nothing if tails

By similar reasoning with the first set of choices, the second set encompasses an *average* loss of $500 regardless of which you choose. The difference here is that Choice C results in a guaranteed loss. Choice D *may* be a $1,000 loss, but it could also result in no loss, both with equal probability. The two researchers expected that if subjects displayed a risk avoidance behavior as with the first set of questions, they should still avoid risk and accept a $500 loss for sure. But oddly enough, the researchers found that most subjects selected Choice D – they accepted the gamble to try and avoid the loss! *This means that investors' aversion to loss overcomes their aversion to risk.* The paradox is that we detest risk so much that we're willing to take risk to avoid it.

This is a fascinating observation about human nature and demonstrates why it's so important to hedge trades. If a trade is moving against us, it's our nature to try to gamble our way out. It goes against our makeup to take the for-sure loss. Likewise, when we have winning trades, it goes against our nature to hang on – we're too afraid of losing the gains we already have. *Hedging your positions prevents both of these behaviors and allows you to capture bigger profits.*

How many times have you heard "you can't beat the professionals" or "the market makers always win" or other similar phrases? The reason they are basically true is that professionals know how to hedge. Retail investors end up taking the risky side of the bet and are in trades too soon and out too early. They rely too much on timing and direction and end up losing. Add to this our risk aversion and willingness to gamble our way out of losing situations and you have the very reason so many investors and traders miss their goals with investing.

Hedging is a powerful tool and the key to financial success. Options were designed to hedge. It's now time to discover the option secrets used by professional traders.

Stock Swap

Of all the hedging techniques, this is the probably the simplest and most useful for most traders so is a great place to start. Unfortunately, it's also the least used. Anybody who trades stocks needs to understand this strategy.

Let's use eBay as an example. Between October and December 2002, eBay made a phenomenal run from around $50 to $70, which you can see in Figure 10-1:

Figure 10-1

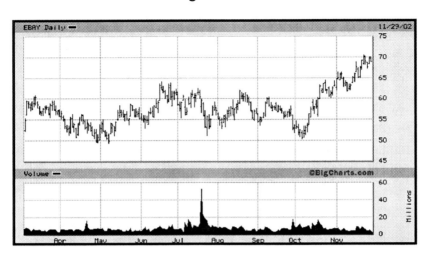

Assume you purchased this stock during the uptrend at $55; it would certainly be tempting to take the profit at $70. After all, eBay made a substantial move and it's sensible to think it will pull back. But if you accept the fact that you're probably not at the very top, the more prudent move is to stay in the trade but protect the existing unrealized profits. We can do that by utilizing a stock swap strategy. It's very simple and here's what you do: *Sell all your shares and buy an equivalent share amount of call options.* In effect, you are "swapping" your stock for calls.

Incidentally, these two trades, selling your stock and buying calls, can be executed *simultaneously* through most brokers. Let's assume you originally purchased 300 shares of eBay at $55 and it's now $70. That means you have an unrealized profit of $15, or $4,500. To execute the stock swap, you'd sell your 300 shares and simultaneously buy 3 calls. If our goal is to get a lot of cash off the table, we would probably consider buying the at-the-money $70 call. The actual quote for an eBay January $70 call at that time was $2.75.

Selling your shares will bring in $21,000 (300 * $70) cash and buying 3 $70 calls costs $825 (300 * $2.75), which means you get a net credit of $20,175 *cash* to your account. The shares originally cost $16,500 ($300 * $55) so you've now locked in a profit of $20,175 - $16,500 = $3,675, or 22%. But not only did you lock in a profit, *you are still effectively long 300 shares of stock.* Any increase in eBay only increases your profit, and there is no risk of losing your original principal;

it's sitting safely in the money market. Figure 10-2 shows graphically the effect of our hedge:

Figure 10-2

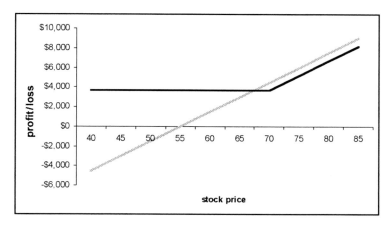

The straight shaded line represents the original long stock position at $55. The solid line is our new long $70 call including the net credit we received from selling the stock. Effectively then, we own 300 shares of stock at a cost better than free; we cannot lose and we may make more. Notice that the trade eliminates the downside risk at the expense of reducing the upside potential, which fits our definition of hedging. In other words, for all stock prices above the $67.25 crossover point we would be better off holding the stock as its profit and loss curve sits higher on the chart. But it's not the fear of lost opportunity that drives us to get out early; it's the fear of loss and the stock swap hedge removes all that fear. Now we've changed our perception of the trade and made it less risky. We can now stay in for much longer than we normally would and possibly catch a huge homerun trade.

Notice too that the hedge does not rely on timing. With the stock at $70, are we at the top of a peak? Statistically speaking, probably not. It's much more likely that we didn't sell at the *highest* point. However, our risk averse nature prods us to take the sure $15 profit and run. Rather than take the $4,500 gain, we hedged the position and captured a sure gain of $3,675. We now can gamble in hopes that we were not at a peak and try for some real money.

As the stock rises, we would continue to roll the calls up as discussed in Chapter Eight. Each roll up generates more cash and shifts the profit and loss curve higher. For example, assume that eBay moves from $70 to $75 and we roll the position up for a net credit of $3.50. While this is a hypothetical credit, we can use some option pricing theory to justify it. To roll the position up you would sell the $70 call to close and simultaneously buy the $75 call to open. Now, just look at that trade disregarding the "opening" or "closing" designations. The trade is selling the $70 call and buying the $75 call – a short $70/$75 vertical call spread.

What is this spread worth? To make it easier, imagine that you were long the $70/$75 spread with the stock at $75. We know it must be worth more than $2.50 (the half-way point) but less than the full $5 difference in strikes. So to buy this spread would cost somewhere between say $2.50 and $4.50 depending on how much time is remaining, which is why we assumed $3.50. Therefore, if you sell this spread, you will receive a credit in the same amount. If we were looking at actual quotes, you'd find that the roll up must be executed at a price very close to this. Again, this is why it is so important to understand the fundamentals presented in this book as the strategies will become second nature to you.

If you roll up for a net credit of $3.50 on 300 contracts, that will generate an additional 300 * $3.50 = $1,050 to your account. You had locked in $3,625 from the first roll to the $70 call and now locked in another $1,025 from the second roll to the $75 call for a total guaranteed profit of $3,625 + $1,025 = $4,650. However, because you are still effectively long 300 shares (long 3 $75 calls) you will continue to profit if the stock price should continue to climb. The profit and loss graph will shift from the shaded line to the bold line as shown in Figure 10-3:

Figure 10-3: Effect of Rolling from $70 Call to $75 Call

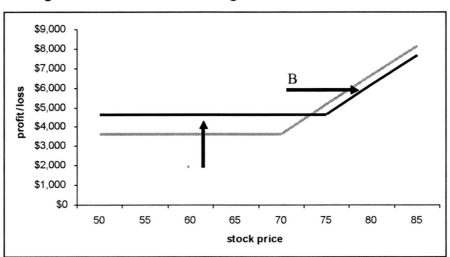

Notice that the new bold line has been shifted higher as shown by Arrow A representing the higher guaranteed return. No matter how low the stock's price may fall you are now guaranteed to receive $4,650. And if the stock price rises, you will benefit in an unlimited way. The tradeoff is that the bold line has been shifted to the right as shown by Arrow B. For all stock prices above the $73.42 crossover point, the previous profit and loss curve would have performed better. But notice the relatively small space lost by the shift at Arrow B compared to the relatively large space gained by Arrow A. It is a small sacrifice of upside potential in exchange for a much higher guaranteed return. You have hedged your investment and it was done without losing control of the 300 shares.

What if you were more concerned about protecting profits? We could use other hedging strategies as well. For instance, when you rolled up to the $75 call, you could also sell the $80 call thus creating the $75/$80 vertical call spread. Assume that you could sell the $80 for $1. Selling three of these calls would generate an additional 300 * $1 = $300 profit but it would also limit your upside potential. If you rolled up to three of the $75 calls and sold three of the $80 calls then the profit and loss curve in Figure 10-3 would look like the one in Figure 10-4:

Figure 10-4: Effect of Rolling Up to Three $75 Calls and Selling Three $80 calls

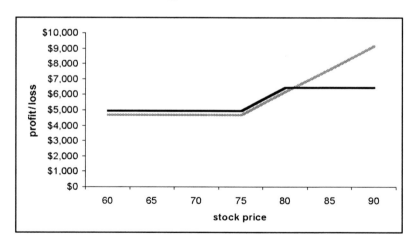

Figure 10-4 shows that you have increased your guaranteed return by another $300 at the expense of limiting your profits for all stock prices above $80. If you don't think the stock price will rise above $80, why not sell that part of the range to someone else in the market? Try doing that with stock.

If the idea of completely capping your upside potential is unappealing then you can hedge that bet too and roll up to three of the $75 calls but perhaps sell only two of the $80 calls. Your profit and loss curve would then look like Figure 10-5:

Figure 10-5: Effect of Rolling Up to Three $75 Calls and Selling Two $80 calls

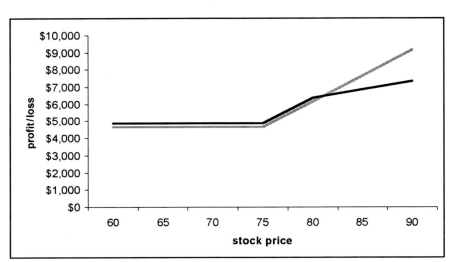

The bold line has shifted higher by $200 from the sale of the two $80 calls at $1 each. Because you control 300 shares and have sold off 200 shares, you are still net long 100 shares for all stock prices above $80 and that's why the profit and loss curve doesn't flatten out like it did in Figure 10-4. The possibilities are endless once you understand the fundamentals of options.

Figure 10-6 shows why hedging is usually the best choice. Trends usually last longer than most people expect and eBay was no exception. The arrow shows the point where we were considering selling the stock. But the stock swap and subsequent roll ups allowed us to capture a guaranteed profit and hold on through August to the price of $110 (eBay had a 2:1 split at this time so Figure 10-6 only shows a $55 price):

Figure 10-6

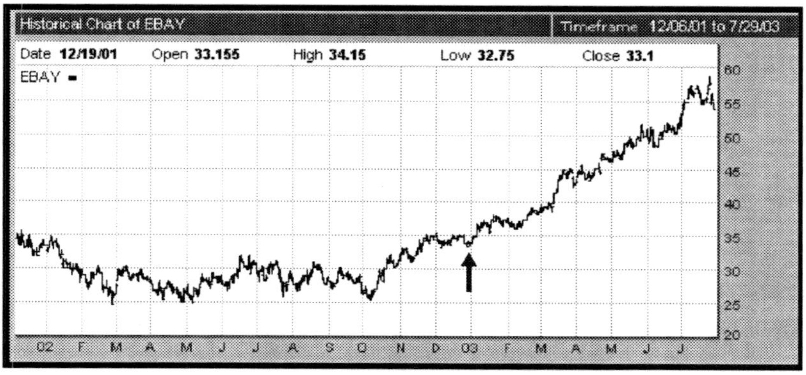

No matter where you may decide to completely exit this trade, you are *better off* than if you sold the stock at $70. The stock swap and roll up hedges allowed us to capture a profit of over $10,000 with no downside risk of principle. The cash from the stock swap and roll ups was always sitting safely in money market.

Laddering Hedging Strategy

Hedging is so versatile that we can even create hedges where we get our money back and actually increase the amount of reward. Using the above example, when you originally sold the 300 shares of stock, you could swap it for a higher number of contracts, such as four $70 calls instead of three. This still produces a guaranteed return to your account (although lower) but now adds some leverage if the stock should continue its bullish trend. When the stock hits $75, you could add more leverage and roll up from four $70 calls to say, 5 $75 calls. When you swap or roll up to a higher number of calls (or down for puts), that's called a *laddering* strategy, which implies that you're changing the risk at each rung or step of the rollup process. There is no set amount or percentage that needs to be applied. As long as you are rolling up to a higher quantity of long positions, it's a laddering strategy. Each choice presents a different set of risks and rewards and it's entirely up to you which is best.

Selling Spreads against Stock

Chapter Nine introduced you to vertical spreads. As with all option strategies, they can be applied in unimaginable ways and the vertical spread is a perfect example. How many people would think of selling spreads against a long stock position? And what do you suppose it would do to the shares of stock you own?

The following is a real case study that we used for a client in a private mentoring service. The client had 500 shares of WMT at $53 and it was now $56.50. He felt the stock was going to trend sideways for some time and may even fall substantially. He was obviously afraid of losses but didn't want to pay for the put. Is there an option strategy we can develop that will profit from a sideways stock price and protect the downside risk? Table 10-7 shows the actual option quotes at the time:

Table 10-7: Wal-Mart Option Quotes

	Calls		Puts	
	Bid	**Ask**	**Bid**	**Ask**
Aug $50	7.30	7.40	0.50	0.55
Aug $55	3.20	3.30	1.45	1.55
Aug $60	0.80	0.85	4.00	4.10

We purchased 5 puts to protect the downside risk he feared. In order to generate enough cash to pay for the put and provide a return in the event the stock price moved sideways we sold 10 – twice as many – $55/$60 vertical call spreads:

Buy 5 $50 puts at 0.55 = -$275
Sell 10 $55 calls at $3.20 = +$3,200
<u>Buy 10 $60 calls at 0.85 = - $850</u>
Net credit = +$2,075

Figure 10-8 shows the effect of the above three transactions against the long stock:

Figure 10-8

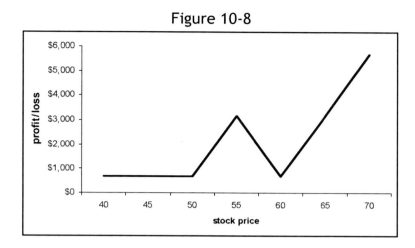

The long puts have completely protected the downside risk and the sale of the vertical call spreads generated enough of a credit to shift the entire profit and loss curve above zero and create substantial profits if the stock price stays still as projected. As a bonus, the investor still maintains all of the upside potential. We must remember that these benefits did not come for free. If we overlay the original stock position, we can see the tradeoffs clearly in Figure 10-9

Figure 10-9

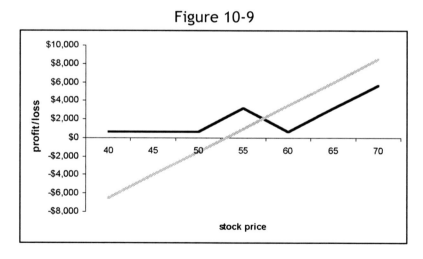

Figure 10-6 shows that the investor hedged all of the downside risk and will profit nicely if the stock price stays still, which is exactly in line with his outlook. He accomplished this at the expense of giving up some (not all) of the upside potential. He has sacrificed the very best profit potential in exchange for a guaranteed a return on his money and still has the opportunity to earn more money if the stock price rises. The best news is that similar vertical spreads can be sold month after month, which allows the investor to continually shift the profit and loss curve higher, protect his downside, and still have the potential for unlimited gains.

What would happen if the investor sold 20 spreads instead of 10? Figure 10-10 shows the effect of buying the five puts but selling 20 $55/$60 vertical call spreads:

Figure 10-10

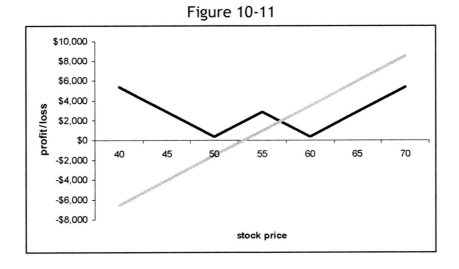

This type of a strategy can be used if the investor is far more bearish on the stock and willing to give up much more upside in exchange for more profit to the downside. What if the investor wanted to actually profit from a fall in the stock's price? He can do that too by purchasing 10 puts rather than five. Figure 10-11 shows the effect of buying 10 puts and selling 10 $55/$60 vertical call spreads:

Figure 10-11

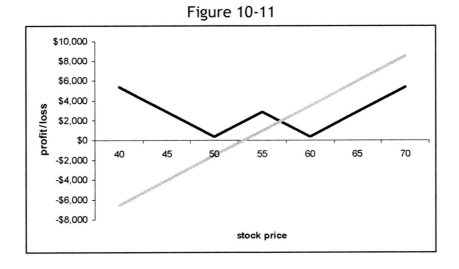

The purchase of 10 puts actually allows the investor to profit to the downside at the expense of profit at the center and to the upside. The possibilities are endless for those who take time to explore the world of options. As stated at the beginning, this chapter is not designed to be a full course on hedging techniques as an entire book could be written on that subject. Instead, we wanted to introduce you to advantages that options provide by allowing you to buy and sell risk. As you continue to learn about options, you will find that all other strategies will be self-evident if you understand the fundamental concepts presented in this book.

In order to succeed in the financial markets, you must invest relatively large dollar amounts and let the profits run. However, we also know that our risk averse natures won't allow that to happen. We feel much more comfortable placing small bets and being assured that it is the most we can lose – even if it means we will most likely lose it. By trying to avoid risk, most investors and traders actually place their money in maximum jeopardy.

All hope is not lost. In order to reach for bigger profits, you must remove the fear of loss. You must hedge your bets and bet against yourself. And the only way to do that is with options since they are the *only* asset that allows you to buy and sell risk. Once you've locked yourself into a guaranteed winning position, hang on. Remember that trends last longer than we expect. Keep the position alive but continue to take profits and cover risk by additional hedges. Options remove fear. Use them conservatively to make money.

Edgar Watson Howe, a famous American writer, once said, "A good scare is worth more to a man than good advice." If you learn to hedge your trades, you'll never have to go through a good scare, and that is the best advice that the Options University can give.

OptionsUniversity©

Get Your *FREE*
Introduction to Options CD
($49 Value) When You Purchase
Bill Johnson's Beginner Options
Trading Classes Video Archive
Series Below

The Options University Presents

Bill Johnson's Beginner Options Trading Classes are normally taught LIVE to our online class of hundreds, using our web conferencing technology. This class is normally $397, but today you can order the video CD archive of all four nights of classes for just $97 (and get the Introduction to Options CD above as a free bonus - a $49 value).

To take advantage of this opportunity, use the priority web link below (link is case sensitive):

http://www.optionsuniversity.com/introcd

Or fill out the form below and fax or mail it to us at the address below:

Yes! Send me the Beginner Options Trading CD Class
(And My Free Introduction to Options CD - $49 Value)

Name: _____

Address: _____

Email: _____ Telephone: _____

Credit Card Type: Mastercard   Visa   Amex   Discover

Credit Card # _____

Expiration Date: _____ Security Code _____

Mail This Coupon To:
Free Shipping Worldwide

Options University LLC
925 S Federal Hwy, Ste 510
Boca Raton, FL 33432
1-561-395-4844 (Fax)

Printed in the United States
75403LV00002B/151-198